ALIENATED AFFE

200

t

ALIENATED AFFECTIONS

THE SCOTTISH EXPERIENCE OF DIVORCE AND SEPARATION, 1684–1830

Leah Leneman

Edinburgh University Press

Edinburgh University Press
22 George Square, Edinburgh

Typeset in Ehrhardt
by Hewer Text Composition Services, Edinburgh, and
printed and bound in Great Britain by
the Cromwell Press, Trowbridge, Wiltshire

A CIP record for this book is available from the British Library

ISBN 0 7486 1031 6 (paperback)

CONTENTS

FIGURE AND TABLES

AUTHOR'S NOTE

Much of this book is in the original words of the participants. In all quotations original spelling and punctuation have been retained, except when they impede understanding. Abbreviated words, including 'ye' for 'the', are given in full, and ampersands have been replaced by 'and'. Double ffs have been replaced by capital Fs. Underlinings have been rendered as italic; double underlinings as italic plus underlining. Under Scottish law a wife retained her maiden name, though in ordinary circumstances she would be called 'Mrs' and her husband's name, so, to avoid confusion, in the text men are usually referred to by their surnames, and women by their first names.

ACKNOWLEDGEMENTS

I gratefully acknowledge the generous financial support of the Economic and Social Research Council for the research – initially just on divorce; subsequently on separation and annulment as well. And I am grateful to the Department of Economic and Social History, University of Edinburgh, for backing and resources.

Particular thanks are due to the late Peter Vasey of the Scottish Record Office for bringing this marvellous source material to my attention, and to the staff at West Register House for their unfailing helpfulness. W. D. H. Sellar read drafts of articles based on the research and provided help and encouragement on the legal side.

Words cannot convey my love for, and gratitude to, my partner and 'in-house' editor, Graham Sutton.

INTRODUCTION

Divorce in Scotland, as in England, is now so common that it is difficult to project the mind back to earlier eras when to break up a marriage, particularly by a formal legal process, was exceptional. Remarriage was no less usual than it is now, but that was only because childbirth, fevers, and other mortal illnesses created so many widows and widowers. Those who were unhappily married were exhorted to resign themselves to their fate and make the best of things.

However, there was an important difference between the two countries before the mid-nineteenth century, for England did not allow divorce (except for a minuscule number of the very well off, who could obtain one by a private act of parliament), whereas Scotland did. As we shall see in Chapter 1, the number of couples suing for divorce rose dramatically in the late eighteenth century, though compared with the present divorce statistics they were still very few. Lawrence Stone concluded from this that variations in the strictness of divorce laws were largely irrelevant, since in spite of the availability of divorce to either party in Scotland from the sixteenth century onwards, 'until the twentieth century the divorce rate remained almost negligible', while legal separation there 'was almost unheard of'.[1] So, why should anyone want to read – let alone research and write – a detailed account of divorce and separation in Scotland between 1684 and 1830?

The prime reason is that the divorce court records document the relationship between husbands and wives in earlier centuries in a way which no other source can rival. Naturally they had little to say about *happy* relationships. But because the court demanded such detailed evidence – ranging from the personal testimonies of friends, neighbours and servants, to letters between spouses and lovers – those records describe not only dysfunctional marriages, but also the views of witnesses about what was considered desirable and *normal* at different points in the century and a half being looked at here. Gender expectations and relations (including the abuse of wives), attitudes toward children, sexuality, alcoholism – those are just some of the aspects of life in eighteenth- and early nineteenth-century Scotland that are illuminated by the records of the Commissary Court.

For example, there was a fundamental difference in women's rights between Scottish and English law. To the English, 'Even a single act of adultery by a wife was an unpardonable breach of the law of property and the idea of hereditary descent', writes Stone; 'Adultery by the husband, on the other hand, was generally regarded as a regrettable but understandable foible, rather than a serious threat to marriage'. Not until 1923 did English law grant a wife a divorce on the same grounds of simple adultery as a husband.[2]

Contrast this with the sixteenth-century Scottish divorce law making simple adultery equal grounds for divorce for men and women; where in the late eighteenth and early nineteenth centuries nearly half the divorce petitions came from wives who certainly did not regard their husbands' extra-marital activities as 'a regrettable but understandable foible'; and where the commissaries (judges) felt no scruples about granting a divorce to such wives on those grounds. As at least one Scottish Enlightenment figure, Francis Hutcheson, argued, a wife's infidelity was 'the greatest wrong imaginable, as it robs men of what is dearest to them, and the end of all their worldly cares, a certain offspring,' but though a husband could not deceive a wife 'by imposing on her a spurious brood . . . in all other respects the moral turpitude is the same . . . The natural passions of the woman as much require a friendly society, and unity of interest in the joint education of the common offspring as those of the man.'[3]

This is not to argue that there was no double standard in eighteenth-century Scotland, for in the course of this book various manifestations of that double standard will emerge. But the distortion caused by an Anglocentric view of adultery and divorce can be rectified by a study of divorce in the part of the United Kingdom where it was permitted in earlier centuries. English law was as much out of step with the rest of the Protestant world as it was with the lives and needs of its citizens.

Those are some of the chief reasons for studying divorce and separation in Scotland during the eighteenth and early nineteenth century. Equally valid is the human interest angle, for divorce court records are fascinating in the way they reveal the lives, loves, and lusts of men and women of every social class during a period when frankness rather than reticence was the rule.

This introduction will begin by outlining the changing mental world of the period, particularly with regard to sexuality. It will then provide the background – both legislative and procedural – on divorce and on legal separation and nullity (annulment). After that we look at the overall picture of divorce and separation between 1684 and 1830. Two chapters follow on how adultery was proven. We then look at adulterers who unsuccessfully contested a divorce action, and then at cases where the charge of adultery was not proven. Then the focus switches to divorce within the different ranks of society, with a chapter on aristocratic divorces, one on gentry divorces, and two on 'common' divorces, interspersed with a chapter on both male and female adultery with a social inferior. A final chapter on divorce for adultery looks at English couples who came to Scotland with hopes of dissolving their marriages. Desertion – the other ground for divorce – is the theme of the next chapter, and nullity is the subject of the one after that. There follow three chapters on separation. Finally the overall picture of divorce and separation is assessed, and questions raised in the first chapter are dealt with in the last chapter.

CHANGES IN THINKING

In a divorce case of 1771 Jean Home, daughter of Henry Home of Kames, and wife of Patrick Heron of Heron, was guilty of adultery with a young ensign. A witness declared that after this had been discovered, when Mrs Heron was ill she often wished she were dead, 'and said that she hoped that God almighty would not punish her for the only crime she could charge herself with, which was the gratification of those passions which he himself had implanted in her nature'.[4] As so much of this book is concerned with adultery we need some understanding of a world where such a statement would cause no surprise.

In 1684 it certainly *would* have been cause for surprise. When the commissaries started keeping registers at the end of the seventeenth century Scotland was still dominated by the Church, which had by then imposed a hierarchy of courts throughout the land with, in each parish, a kirk session keeping a close watch on the morals of its parishioners. No one could enter a new parish without producing a 'testificat' of their behaviour in their last one. An unmarried woman (or a wife whose husband had long been absent), who became pregnant would immediately be cited before the session, and would subsequently have to stand before the congregation on three or more occasions and be publicly rebuked, before being absolved. However, it was not only the woman who had to undergo public penance, for the man she named as father of her child would be treated in the same manner. The Church's attempt – albeit not always successful – to treat both sexes in the same manner is striking. So is the fact that when the public penance had been completed the sin was deemed to have been 'purged', and the guilty parties as 'pure' as if they had never sinned, in contrast to the nineteenth-century branding of women who bore bastards as permanently 'fallen'.[5]

The system broke down in the cities in the mid-eighteenth century and by the 1780s had ceased to work in most rural parishes as well. But this phenomenon of remarkably effective morality courts covering the country over such a long period of time has no parallel in England. Another fundamental difference was that after 1753 the marriage customs of the two countries diverged widely. Scotland continued to adhere to medieval canon law whereby a woman (over the age of twelve) and man (over fourteen) who agreed between themselves to marry and followed this agreement with intercourse were thereby legally married, without consent of parents, calling of banns, minister, church, or witnesses.[6]

At the beginning of the eighteenth century Scotland was relatively backward amongst European states, but the explosion of activity from mid-century onwards transformed it utterly. In the areas of industrialisation, urbanisation, and agricultural improvement Scotland not only caught up but forged ahead. At the same time changes in the quality of transport facilities, and the use made of them, also had great impact. People moved from place to place, sometimes through necessity but often by choice, and their movements could no longer be controlled by the system of 'testificats'. Urban expansion, new centres of industry, the erection and successful management of turnpikes, all contributed to a flow of people to new places and new opportunities, which in turn led to a new scale of urban concentration.[7] And the extraordinary collection of brilliant minds who represented the Enlightenment in Scotland put the country at the forefront of Europe.

What were some of the ideas of the Enlightenment that affected behaviour in the late eighteenth century? 'Rejecting original sin and the Calvinist corruption of the flesh', writes Roy Porter, 'the enlightened argued that Nature was good, and that proper behaviour should seek to realise human nature, rather than to deny, fight and conquer it. Man's nature lay in his senses; its essence was a capacity to be happy.' This meant that 'erotic desire, far from being sinful, itself became desirable', and, 'amongst the most marked features of Georgian sexuality was its public stamp, its openness and visibility.'[8] Consider *Ranger's Impartial List of the Ladies of Pleasure in Edinburgh*, which appeared in 1775. 'No enthusiasm is so strong, so stimulous as that of copulation,' wrote the 'celebrated Wit' who contributed the preface; 'it brings its warrant from nature's closest cabinet, and bears even the seal of heaven, "increase and multiply;" all nature echoes to the general, the universal mandate.'[9] All this sheds light on Mrs Heron's comment quoted earlier.

An extraordinarily radical view was presented in Robert Wallace's essay, 'Of Venery, or of the commerce of the two sexes'. Marriage contracts, he suggested, should be made and renewed 'by the free consent of each of the parties, from time to time.' Couples should not be 'bound for life': 'Let them be att [sic] full liberty to separate when they please'. Wallace believed that the possibility of divorce would make couples 'kinder & more complaisant to one another.' He thought that people should marry young but not expect to remain together for life. Wallace's essay was not published in his lifetime, but he was a highly respected Church of Scotland clergyman who wrote philosophical works and engaged in debate with David Hume and Lord Kames, among others, so it is possible that such ideas were circulated in Enlightenment circles, though kept discreetly to themselves.[10]

However, there is another important strand of eighteenth-century thinking to be taken into account: the cult of 'sensibility'. The concepts of refinement, decency, delicacy, and the move away from vulgar, earthy, 'animal' passions to 'civilised' conduct informed the thinking of the 'polite' classes and spread downward, so that much 'robust' behaviour tolerated at the beginning of the eighteenth century became less and less acceptable by the end of it. 'Ranger' could even write about one of his 'ladies of pleasure': 'she pursues the strict regard imaginable to decency and decorum, which renders her a good many admirers.' (And of a bawdy house keeper that 'She keeps a very genteel house'.) This worked to the advantage of women in some ways, for they were seen as the 'refined' sex essential to the civilising process of men, and therefore it was important that they 'join with men in the public social spaces for the "pleasure and entertainment" created in cities.'[11] In divorce cases witnesses' explicit descriptions of the sexual act, quite usual in the early eighteenth century, were gradually replaced by standard, anodyne phrases.

The cult of sensibility played a crucial role in separation cases as well. In the late seventeenth century it was considered perfectly acceptable for a husband physically to chastise his wife, children and servants. Therefore, in order to bring an action for separation on the grounds of maltreatment, a woman normally had to prove attempted murder or, at the very least, severe physical injury. This changed over the century, and a hundred years later the rhetoric of the court makes clear that for a man to strike a woman, whether she be a wife or servant, no longer conformed to the concept of civilised behaviour adhered to by the lawyers and judges who ruled.

Where did the Scottish Church fit into this picture? For much of the eighteenth century a group of ministers known as the moderate party held sway.[12] Some of the leading Enlightenment figures, like Adam Ferguson and Alexander Carlyle, were themselves clergy, and theology therefore expanded from its narrow, post-Reformation, base to encompass ideas of rationality, politeness, and freedom. The Enlightenment was also able to encompass the views of David Hume, the protagonist of those sceptical, or even hostile, to theology and organised religion. Hume was one of the first to discuss the pros and cons of divorce, and though he came out against it his pro-divorce arguments are in fact the more convincing.[13] Adam Smith and Francis Hutcheson were two other Scottish Enlightenment figure who discussed the subject of divorce.[14]

While the moderate clergy dominated the Church, there was little conflict between religious and secular ideology, and when they ceased to dominate it, this too was in line with what was happening throughout Britain. For as the eighteenth century closed, so did the period in which 'there was something like the modern freedom in the relation between men and women'.[15] The new movement (which ultimately fused with the cult of sensibility) was evangelicalism, spearheaded in England by William Wilberforce and Hannah More. Evangelicalism perceived life as a moral trial, to which the idea of the pursuit of pleasure was anathema. This was the period when Bowdler's version of Shakespeare first appeared (1804); by 1818 there had already been six editions, and two years after that the *Edinburgh Review*, in spite of its progressiveness, expressed strong approval, commenting that Bowdler's ought to become the standard Shakespeare.[16] By this time the whole weight of the Scottish intellectual elite had shifted from the moderate party to the evangelical, following their own group of philosophers, the Common Sense school founded by Thomas Reid and later led by Dugald Stewart.[17]

The century and a half in which the Commissary Court kept its registers therefore witnessed major changes in thinking about sexuality and the relationship between men and women, many of which are echoed in the records of divorce and separation. Because the treatment of the subject is thematic rather than chronological, these changes may be harder to detect, but in every subject covered, whether a section or sub-section of a chapter, the examples have been given in chronological order, and it is hoped that a sense of different periods within the same legal framework will emerge.

DIVORCE

Before the Reformation in 1560, separation *a mensa et thoro* (from bed and board) was available for adultery or extreme cruelty, as was 'nullity' (annulment) for defect of consent, lack of capacity, or for being within the forbidden degrees of relationship, but full divorce (*a vinculo*), allowing remarriage, was not allowed. In that year the parliament of Scotland repudiated the authority of the pope, and the old church courts came to an end. In common with other European countries which adopted Protestantism, Scotland no longer held marriage to be a sacrament, and divorce was countenanced on the grounds of adultery. The right to divorce had to be the same for both sexes for, in Calvin's words, 'A man may hold the primacy in other things, but in bed he and his wife are equal'. The logic was that the Bible enjoined death for an adulterous wife, and 'in modern times (the sixteenth century) divorce was a substitute for that punishment'. Therefore when a divorce was granted the guilty party was pronounced legally dead in relation to his or her former spouse.[18]

There were three years of flux in Scotland after 1560, when kirk sessions (parish courts) followed the line of the European reformers and granted divorces to men and women whose spouses were guilty of adultery. After that local 'commissary courts', and a central court in Edinburgh – the only one which could pronounce on matters concerning marriage and divorce – were established. Although initially they were in a sense spiritual courts, they were gradually secularised, and from the very beginning the Court of Session, Scotland's supreme secular civil court, exercised a supervisory jurisdiction. Unlike purely spiritual courts, the Edinburgh Commissary Court made no attempt to reconcile husbands and wives who wished to divorce or separate. The commissaries saw their function as that of any secular court: to hear all the evidence and decide whether a valid legal case had been made for the conclusion called for.[19]

When it became clear that the State would not follow the Church's line and execute adulterers (though 'notour', or persistent, adultery was a capital offence), decades of debate ensued with regard to the right of the guilty party to remarry. An Act was finally passed in 1600 forbidding the marriage of the guilty party to the person he or she was guilty with, as named in the decreet.[20]

The history of divorce for desertion was different. In 1573 the Earl of Argyll wished to divorce his wife, who had left him, but found no mechanism for doing so as she had not committed adultery. He first brought an action of adherence against her before the commissaries, thereby proving that she had deserted him and refused to return. He then went to a civil court and had his wife declared a rebel and 'put to the horn'. Next he petitioned the bishop or superintendent of her place of residence and requested that she be publicly admonished and then excommunicated. After that he obtained a divorce. When parliament passed a statute allowing divorce for desertion after four years, they enshrined all those bizarre procedures as requisite. After presbyterianism abolished the offices of bishop or superintendent, the petition had to be presented to the presbytery, which was expected formally to refuse to have anything to do with it. Once all of those formalities had been observed, a divorce for desertion, or 'non-adherence', would be granted.[21]

In order to raise a divorce action for adultery the first step was to engage lawyers, a 'procurator' licensed to plead before the commissary court and an agent to carry out the investigations and do all the paperwork. The lawyers would draw up a libel,[22] with the facts supporting the pursuer's claim for divorce. The libel began by giving the date of the marriage, and went on:

> in consequence of their marriage they afterwards cohabited together as Husband and Wife owned and acknowledged each other as such and were holden and reputed married persons by all their friends neighbours and acquaintances for several years past. And although by the Laws of God, as well as by the mutual vows and faith plighted to each other upon their entering into the aforesaid marriage they were reciprocally bound to a strict adherence to each other, and to that constancy and chastity which ought to be inseparable from the marriage state; Yet true it is and of verity that the said —— ——, casting off the fear of God, and disregarding the matrimonial vows and engagements, whereby he/she stood bound to preserve the marriage bed inviolate, has, for a considerable time past . . . left the society of the Complainer, totally alienating his/her affections from her/him and given up him/herself at different times and places to adulterous practices, fellowship and correspondence with other women/men, one or more, known not to be the Complainer, and had carnal, adulterous conversation intercourse and dealing with such women/men.[23]

There was a good deal of standard verbiage about the defender being guilty with 'various lewd and wicked women' – or men – even if in fact he or she had had only one other partner, followed by 'In particular . . .', when the specific facts of the case were laid out. After the libel would come the summons. The messenger would deliver this to the defender's residence, calling for him or her to appear in court for the first hearing a fortnight later. If the defender's residence was not known and he or she was believed to be out of Scotland then the messenger would call out the summons at three locations – the market square of Edinburgh and pier and shore of Leith – with a longer time span before the first hearing. If the defender did not answer then the action continued in his or her absence.

The next step was the oath of calumny. The pursuer had to swear a solemn oath that he or she believed the spouse was guilty of adultery and that there was no collusion between them. The guilty party might agree to the divorce, but the action had to be raised because of the adultery, not the adultery committed in order to allow a divorce. Although the pursuer was supposed to appear in court to swear the oath, pursuers living abroad, or at some distance from Edinburgh, could petition for a commission to be granted to a local magistrate to administer it. After the oath of calumny the commissaries would allow the pursuer to proceed to proof, and in contested actions it was at this point that defences – discussed in Chapters 4 and 5 – had to be taken seriously.

After proof was concluded the commissaries would, if convinced, issue their interlocutor finding the adultery sufficiently inferred and grant the divorce. The effect was to declare the guilty party legally dead and the innocent party entitled to everything that would have come to him/her on the death of the spouse. For a woman this would normally be a third of his moveable estate and of the life-rent of his heritable estate if there were children, or one half of the estate and a third life rent if there were no children, as well as anything written into the marriage contract.[24] The innocent party was free to remarry anyone, while the guilty party could remarry but not the person named in the decreet. Successful women pursuers could also claim the expenses of the case on top of everything else they were awarded out of their husband's estate or effects.

What we cannot know, unfortunately, is how divorce and divorced people were regarded, and to what extent this changed over the period. A popular ballad – 'Rosie Anderson' – suggests that by the beginning of the nineteenth century divorce was part of the Scottish consciousness. The case referred to was that of Thomas Hay Marshall, merchant in Perth, against Rose Anderson. Hay Marshall's first divorce action, in which he cited Lord Elgin and a Dr Harrison, was unsuccessful, as he was unable to produce convincing proof. But even while that action was under way, Rose was sleeping with various officers, one of whom testified in court that he 'had enjoyment of her person', and the divorce was granted in November 1803.[25] In the ballad, Rose is considered to have been guilty with Lord Elgin, and 'Hay Marshall's on to fair London, with money in his purse,/And all for to get witnesses his Rose to divorce':

> Hay Marshall had twenty witnesses and Rosie had but two:
> 'Woe's me', cries Rosie Anderson, 'Alas, what shall I do?'
>
> 'If 'twere to do that's done', she says, 'If 'twere to do that's done',
> Hay Marshall's face I would adore, Lord Elgin I would shun'.
>
> 'But spring is coming on,' she says, 'Some regiment will be here,
> I'll maybe get some officer my broken heart to cheer'.
>
> Now Rosie's got an officer, and he has proven untrue;
> Now he has gone and left her, her folly for to rue.
>
> 'In Bedlam I maun lie my lane, in Bedlam I maun cry;
> In Bedlam I maun lie', she says, 'And in Bedlam I maun die'.
>
> Come all ye ladies far an' near, a warnin' take by me,
> To never leave your own husband for any that ye wid see.[26]

According to Gavin Greig, a collector at the beginning of the twentieth century, 'few traditional songs are so well and so widely known as 'Rosie Anderson'.[27] However, in the ballad Rose is condemned for betraying her husband, a traditional theme throughout history, not because her husband divorced her on that score, so this does not answer the question of how divorced women were regarded.

In 1783 a letter in the *Scots Magazine* compared the situation in that year with the situation twenty years earlier. In 1763, 'The breach of the seventh commandment was punished by fine and church censure – Any instance of conjugal infidelity in a woman would have banished her from society, and her company would have been rejected even by the men.' But in 1783, 'church-censure is disused, and separations, divorces, recriminations, collusions, separate maintenances, are becoming almost as frequent as marriages – Women who have been rendered infamous by public divorce, have been permitted to marry the Adulterer; – and the known Adulteress has been, by people of fashion, again received into society'.[28] Even if exaggerated, this view, which accords with the openness about sexuality in Georgian Britain, suggests a high degree of acceptance of divorced women.

But such an attitude cannot necessarily be projected forwards in time. Stone thought it likely that 'in the early nineteenth century, as the ideal of the companionate marriage and the cult of domesticity took hold, the attitude of high society towards divorced and remarried women became more severe than it had been in the more easy-going days of the eighteenth century.' Searching for further evidence, he found that 'some divorced and remarried aristocratic wives were successfully reintegrated and accepted by most of high society' but that others 'were forced to live lonely and isolated lives in the countryside or abroad'. He was unable to discover what became of divorced wives lower down the social scale.[29]

SEPARATION AND NULLITY

There was no radical break with the past in allowing a maltreated wife a legal separation from her husband. As we will see in later chapters, many couples separated without coming before the Commissary Court at all; if both were amenable then informal arrangements could be made. But a husband who was unwilling to allow his wife to live separately could bring an action of adherence against her and force her to return to him, and even if he was willing to let her go she might not be in a position to support herself. In such cases her only recourse was to bring an action for separation *a mensa et thoro* (from bed and board) before this court. If she succeeded, then her husband could not compel her to return to him, and the court would award her a yearly aliment for the remainder of her life, which would be as legally enforceable as any other debt. Neither party could remarry, for the existing marriage had not been dissolved, but at least the woman was free from fear. The libel for separation would begin with the date of the marriage and period of cohabitation and continue along the following lines:

Notwithstanding whereof, and by the laws of God and man, he the said defender, was bound to protect and cherish his said spouse, yet true it is, that the said defender, having shaken off all regard to his conjugal vows, instead of behaving himself towards the pursuer with tenderness and humanity, has conducted himself towards her as a tyrant and tormentor, and has maltreat and abused her by words and deeds in a variety of instances . . . so that her life, which was rendered a burden to her, would have been endangered if she had continued to live with him.

This would be followed by details.

No oath of calumny was required, since collusion was not anticipated, and the husband might agree that a separation was desirable, but otherwise the procedure was the same: summons, defences, answers, proof, appeals to the Court of Session, etc. Unlike divorce actions, where the financial implications would be worked out elsewhere, in separation cases the commissaries would determine the amount of the aliment, and even the dates at which it would be paid (usually bi-annually, but sometimes quarterly). The wife would have to produce a statement of her husband's financial circumstances; he, naturally, could dispute this, and cases where the separation was granted within a few months could then drag on for years longer with the dispute over the amount of the aliment.

'Nullity' was a different matter entirely, because it was meant to prove that a marriage had never existed at all. Before the Reformation it was apparently sometimes brought on the grounds of alleged closeness of relationship to allow monied couples the equivalent of a divorce, but in our period it was never brought on such grounds. A man or woman who discovered that their spouse had in fact married previously could bring an action of nullity on the grounds of bigamy, and would thereafter be free to marry someone else. In the early period nullity cases were also brought on the grounds of a husband's impotence, but though it remained legally valid, increasing 'sensibility' made such an action repugnant to the court and tended to close that option.

For a century and a quarter after 1560, the only evidence for actions of divorce, separation, and nullity were the process papers. Very few have survived, and there is no way of estimating how many divorces there actually were during that period. From 1684 a register of extracted decreets began to be kept. The 'decreet' was the final finding of the court, and there was no requirement to have it recorded anywhere but within the process papers; however, once a register was kept, it became possible to have the details of the case, and the final decreet, recorded in that register. This was known as 'extracting' a decreet. Although it cost more to do this, it was obviously worthwhile to have the decreet recorded where anyone could see it, and so the majority of litigants did extract their decreets. The court also began to retain process papers more systematically. All of the evidence, whether spoken by witnesses, or written in letters, was reproduced in full in those records.

In 1830 the functions of Edinburgh Commissary Court were transferred to the Court of Session, and thereafter divorce and separation cases were subsumed within all other cases before that court. But between the years 1684 and 1830 there is a unique record of all the matrimonial cases in Scotland, and that record forms the basis for this book.

Inevitably, there are problems in utilising court records. Lawyers, not litigants, drew up the documents and used phrases which the men and women they represented might not have thought of themselves. Facts could be distorted, even when litigants or witnesses believed they were telling the truth. A great deal of irrelevant material was dragged in, though it must be said that when that happened the historian is often the gainer. For example, the ages of the husband and wife were not stated in the record (though the ages of witnesses were), but where there was a great disparity in ages this often emerges in the course of a husband or wife's version of the events of the marriage. Whatever the caveats, the claim made by Lawrence Stone that consistory court records 'offer a deeper and more intimate insight into the psychology, behaviour, and even speech of actors in the past than can be obtained from any other source'[30] is borne out in the Edinburgh Commissary Court records.

NOTES

All cc references are in the Scottish Record Office.
1. Lawrence Stone, *Road to Divorce – England 1530–1987* (Oxford, 1992), 5, 357.
2. Ibid., 7; Keith Thomas used the difference in grounds for divorce as a linchpin for his argument on 'The Double Standard', *Journal of the History of Ideas*, 20 (1959), 199.
3. Francis Hutcheson, *A System of Moral Philosophy* (London, 1754), vol.2, 156–9.
4. cc8/5/13.
5. Rosalind Mitchison and Leah Leneman, *Sexuality and Social Control – Scotland 1660–1780* (Oxford, 1989), and the revised version, *Girls in Trouble – Sexuality and Social Control in Rural Scotland 1660–1780* (Edinburgh, forthcoming); Leah Leneman and Rosalind Mitchison, *Sin in the City – Sexuality and Social Control in Urban Scotland 1660–1780* (Edinburgh, forthcoming). This view contradicts that of writers who believe that the Scottish church was an instrument of women's oppression, e.g. Elspeth King, *The Hidden History of Glasgow's Women – The Thenew Factor* (Edinburgh and London, 1993), 26–33.
6. W. D. H. Sellar, 'Marriage, divorce and the forbidden degrees: Canon law and Scots law', in W. N. Osborough, ed., *Explorations in Law and History – Irish Legal History Society Discourses, 1988–1994* (Dublin 1995), 64–6; A. D. M. Forte, 'Some Aspects of the Law of Marriage in Scotland: 1500–1700' in Elizabeth Craik, ed., *Marriage and Property – Women and Marital Customs in History* (Aberdeen, 1984), 104–18. See also Leah Leneman and Rosalind Mitchison, 'Clandestine Marriage in the Scottish Cities 1660–1780', *Journal of Social History* (vol.26, no.4, 1993), 845–61, and relevant chapters in the two books cited above.
7. Ian D. Whyte, *Scotland before the Industrial Revolution* (London, 1995), chs 10, 11, shows that the urban sector in Scotland there grew more rapidly in the eighteenth century than in any other European country.
8. Roy Porter and Lesley Hall, *The Facts of Life – The Creation of Sexual Knowledge in Britain, 1650–1950* (New Haven and London, 1995), 18–20.

9. *Ranger's Impartial List of the Ladies of Pleasure in Edinburgh* (privately printed Edinburgh, 1775; reprinted Edinburgh, 1978). A 'ranger of stews' meant a man who frequented brothels.

10. Norah Smith, 'Sexual Mores in the Eighteenth Century: Robert Wallace's "Of Venery"', *Journal of the History of Ideas*, 39 (1978), 419–33.

11. Porter and Hall, *The Facts of Life*, 28; *Ranger's Impartial List*; G. J. Barker-Benfield, *The Culture of Sensibility: Sex and Society in Eighteenth-Century Britain* (Chicago, 1992), 135, 137.

12. Richard B. Sher, *Church and University in the Scottish Enlightenment* (Edinburgh, 1985).

13. David Hume, *Essays Moral, Political, and Literary* (Indianapolis, 1985 ed.), 187–9.

14. Adam Smith, *Lectures on Jurisprudence* (Glasgow edition, Indianapolis, 1892), 160, 445; Hutcheson, *System of Moral Philosophy*, vol.2, 156–9.

15. Marion Lochhead, *The Scots Household in the 18th Century* (Edinburgh, 1948), 51.

16. Barker-Benfield, *The Culture of Sensibility*, 394; Boyd Hilton, *The Age of Atonement; the Influence of Evangelicalism on Social and Economic Thought, 1750–1865* (Oxford, 1988), 90; Porter and Hall, *The Facts of Life*, 32; Muriel Jaeger, *Before Victoria* (London, 1956), 121.

17. Hilton, *The Age of Atonement* (quoting C. Duncan Rice, *The Scots Abolitionists 1833–1861*), 25–6.

18. Sellar, 'Marriage, divorce and the forbidden degrees', 62; Lord Salvesen's evidence to *Royal Commission on Divorce and Matrimonial Causes, 1912, (Parliamentary Papers, 1912–13)*, vol.18, 258; Patrick Fraser, *Treatise on the Law of Scotland as applicable to The Personal and Domestic Relations* (Edinburgh 1846), vol.i, 654; Roderick Phillips, *Putting Asunder: A History of Divorce in Western Society* (Cambridge 1988), 53.

19. Sellar, 'Marriage, divorce and the forbidden degrees', 63. An example of a court which attempted to reconcile couples is provided by S. S. Cohen, ' "To Parts Unknown": The Circumstances of Divorce in Connecticut, 1750–1797', *Canadian Review of American Studies*, 11 (1980), 284.

20. David Baird Smith, 'The Reformers and Divorce: A Study in Consistorial Jurisdiction', *Scottish Historical Review* 10 (1912), 16–19 and 29–34; J. R. Hardy, 'The Attitudes of Church and State in Scotland to Sex and Marriage, 1500–1707' (unpublished M.Phil. thesis, University of Edinburgh, 1978), 246–78; Sellar, 'Marriage, divorce and the forbidden degrees', 74–5.

21. Hardy, 'Attitudes', 285–6; Lord Salvesen's evidence to *Royal Commission*, 259.

22. Obviously the word came to have a very different meaning in English legal terminology, though both have their roots in canon law and the Latin *libellum*, or little book (i.e. written rather than oral evidence). I owe this point to W. D. H. Sellar.

23. The standard wording changed somewhat over time; this is a fairly late example. The description of the procedures comes from my reading of all the cases.

24. Lord Salvesen's evidence to *Royal Commission*, 258.

25. cc8/5/27. The process papers for the first action do not appear to have survived, but the result is summarised in the second.

26. *Folk Song Journal*, 1965, 76–7. I am grateful to Caroline Jackson-Houlston for bringing this ballad to my attention and tracking it down.

27. Gavin Greig, *Folk Songs of the North-East* (1909 edition reprinted Haltore, Pennsylvania, 1963).

28. *Scots Magazine* XLV (1783), 620. The writer of the anonymous letter was William Creech; an edited version appeared as an appendix to the entry for Edinburgh in the Old Statistical Account.

29. Stone, *Road to Divorce*, 342–4.

30. Lawrence Stone, *Uncertain Unions – Marriage in England 1660–1753* (Oxford 1992), 4–5.

CHAPTER 1

THE OVERALL PICTURE

SOME FACTS AND FIGURES[1]

There were 904 divorce actions (including counter-processes) in commissary court registers and process papers in the period 1684 to 1830. Of these, 757 were successful and 147 unsuccessful (either abandoned or dismissed); 803 were for adultery and 101 for desertion.[2] Although we know that the population of Scotland roughly doubled in our period,[3] bad record-keeping combined with the prevalence of irregular marriage in Scotland means there is no way of estimating the number of marriages and hence no way of calculating the percentage that ended in divorce. The tally of separation cases in the period is very much lower, totalling only 175. And whereas just 16 per cent of divorce processes raised were unsuccessful, for separation cases nearly half (83) were unsuccessful (14 dismissed, the rest abandoned). There were also 28 annulment cases, 18 of which were successful. Bigamy formed the grounds for 14, impotence for six, while the remainder were for mental incapacity, incest and fraud.

Between 1684 and 1690 there was only one divorce case. From 1691 to 1770 there were one or two cases a year and then – as shown by Figure 1 – there was a spectacular rise. In this book, for purpose of analysis, the period from 1684 to 1770, with 118 divorce suits, will be referred to as Period 1, and the period from 1771 to 1830, with 786 divorce suits, as Period 2.

As can also be seen in Figure 1, the upsurge in divorce actions after 1770 was not matched by a similar upsurge in actions for separation. The upswing there did not take place until the beginning of the nineteenth century, but the numbers were still very small and did not continue to rise in the decades that followed. Of course, it was not necessary to raise a legal action in order to separate. An action before this court was a last resort to force a husband to pay for his wife's support, or to protect her from his violence or persecution.

Considering the drastic effects of a divorce, and the bar on collusion, one might expect that most cases for adultery would be contested. In fact, 42 per cent of successful adultery cases were contested, and only 29 per cent in Period 2. Because of this, divorce actions could be very swift. Table 1 shows that a quarter of cases lasted for less than three months and over half for less than six months. The very lengthy cases were not only the bitterly contested ones (though one such action was dragged out for seven years). There might be long delays in cases raised by pursuers abroad, and others might run out of money and abandon a case for a long time, then raise it again. A case in which nothing happened for over a year was said to be asleep and required a summons of wakening.[4]

Figure 1. *Divorce and separation processes, 1691–1830*

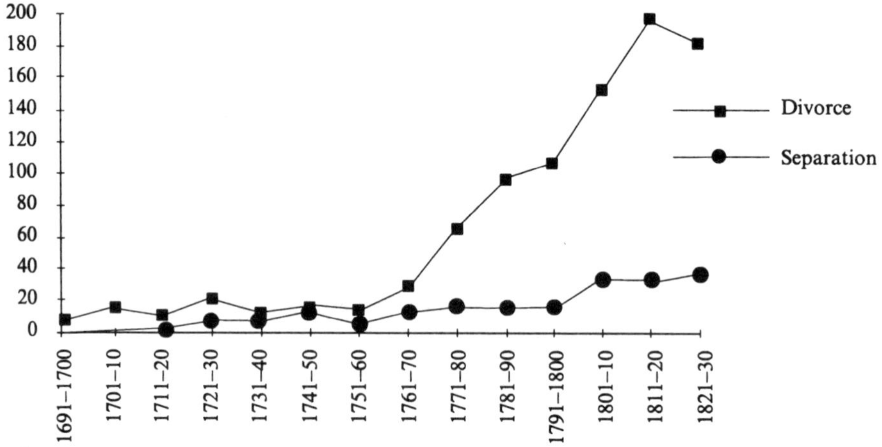

Table 1. *Length of divorce proceedings from summons to decreet*

		%
Total for which this information is known: (out of 657)	622	(100)
Under 3 months	156	(25.1)
3–under 6 months	201	(32.3)
6 months–1 year	146	(23.5)
Over 1–2 years	76	(12.2)
Over 2 years	43	(6.7)

Once again the separation picture is different. Of the 92 successful cases 64 (69 per cent) were contested. It must be recalled that whereas divorce allowed remarriage, a successful separation suit forced a man to pay his wife aliment (alimony) for the rest of his life without being able to marry another woman while she was alive. Nevertheless, a separation case in which many witnesses attested to the defender's violence against his wife could be concluded very quickly, so about a quarter of successful separation pursuers also received a decreet in under three months, and another quarter within a further three months, in line with divorce cases. However, months, and sometimes years, could go by between the decreet granting separation and the one setting out the financial settlement. In divorce cases the court merely pronounced the guilty party legally dead and the innocent one entitled to all that would come to them on their spouse's death, and let others decide what that was. But in separation cases it was this court which decided how much aliment was due to the wife, on the basis of statements by both parties on the husband's financial circumstances. The scope for presenting different versions of a man's financial affairs is all too obvious.

We can look at the cost of a divorce from expenses claimed by successful women pursuers, but the amounts varied enormously. One case lasting under three months in 1782 cost only £5 and one in 1788 only £4. Yet one in 1778 lasting under three months cost £41. 13s. 3d, because it was initiated by upper-class litigants.[5] Even in uncontested cases it might be necessary to pay for witnesses to come from distant parts, or there might be other expensive complications. In the early nineteenth century costs became higher – the lowest was £9. 16s. 8d, and more usual were sums between £15 and £30. How did this equate to income? One historian reckoned that the upper strata of Glasgow's working class were probably earning about 15 to 20 shillings a week in 1815, i.e. £45–£50 a year, and this is borne out for other parts of Scotland by information given in some separation cases. In cases of 1777 and 1823 wrights earned about £50 a year, while a tailor in 1825 earned a guinea a week (i.e. £54. 12s a year).[6] So a divorce was never a cheap option, though costs were much lower than in England, where an unopposed suit for judicial separation in the ecclesiastical court was likely to cost between £120 and £140 and a parliamentary divorce in the region of £700.[7]

And in Scotland it was possible to apply to be put on the poor's roll – the equivalent of legal aid – and have all expenses paid. In England litigants could sue as paupers only if they were worth less than £5, a useless benefit by the eighteenth century,[8] whereas Scots law did not specify an amount, leaving it up to the judges to determine whether genuine hardship existed. A certificate signed by the minister and elders of the parish affirming the poverty-stricken state of the petitioner was required, and the 'solicitors for the poor' had to be satisfied that he or she had a case. The commissaries rarely refused such applications, but only seven per cent of pursuers for divorce and eight per cent of pursuers for separation fell into this category. (As with legal aid today, it seems that those who did not earn either little enough to be rated a pauper, or sufficient to be able to afford legal costs, were in the most invidious position.)

At the other end of the spectrum, a contested divorce case that lasted over two years in the 1780s cost £150, while an aristocratic case lasting from 1811 till 1816 cost £628. 10s. But these costs were far below the English level, where after the two-year contested suit between the Countess and Earl of Portsmouth in 1828 the bill came to £3,820, and Lord Ellenborough's divorce suit in 1830 was reckoned to have cost him £5,000.[9]

On top of the other expenses of the case was the cost of 'extracting' the decreet. This too depended on the complexity of the case, for an extracted decreet, i.e. one written out and bound into the volume, could run to hundreds of pages. A man liable for expenses of a case costing £34. 8s. 5d in 1822 had to pay almost half again as much (£15. 7s. 7d) to extract the decreet, as did another in 1823 (£8. 2s. 1d on top of expenses of £17. 7s. 7½d). It was only from 1824 onwards, when the extracted decreet was just the final interlocutor granting the divorce, that this became standardised at 16 or 17 shillings. As extracting a decreet was not a legal requirement, it is not surprising that over a hundred litigants in divorce cases and 29 in separation cases did not do so.[10]

Looking at the sex ratio in divorce cases, Table 2 shows the sexes to be fairly evenly matched. In Period 1, about 65 per cent of cases were launched by men and in Period 2, about 53 per cent, which is surprising. However, for desertion the imbalance is greater, with three-quarters of cases having been brought by women.

Table 2.   *Gender breakdown of pursuers*

		%
Total divorce suits	904	(100)
Men:	493	(54.5)
Women:	411	(45.5)
Period 1 (1684–1770)	118	(100)
Men	76	(64.4)
Women	42	(35.6)
Period 2 (1771–1830)	786	(100)
Men	416	(52.9)
Women	370	(47.1)
Adultery total	803	(100)
Men	466	(58.1)
Women	337	(41.9)
Desertion total	101	(100)
Men	26	(26.3)
Women	74	(73.7)

To look at other countries that allowed divorce, in the principality of Neuchâtel between 1707 and 1806 women initiated 58 per cent of divorce suits, but divorce there was allowed not only for adultery but also for desertion, cruelty, and even incompatibility. For adultery alone it was men who initiated the majority of suits (59 per cent). In Massachusetts, women initiated 128 out of 229 suits (56 per cent), but this also includes annulment and separation suits, and as separation was normally granted for cruelty women were bound to predominate. Women initiators dominated most strikingly in France during the revolutionary period, where they accounted for 71 per cent of the total, but as the 1792 statute was entirely civil the grounds were incompatibility, cruelty, or desertion, not adultery. So a direct comparison is not possible.[11]

It is not feasible to classify Scottish litigants geographically, for there was simply too much physical mobility; it would be fair to say that small towns produced more litigants than totally rural areas, and the larger towns and cities more than anywhere else. Just about everyone seemed to pass through Edinburgh at one time or another, whether for pleasure, business, or in transit. The sharp rise in Glasgow's population toward the end of the eighteenth century is mirrored in the number of litigants appearing from that city in the later period. Thus, divorce in Scotland was largely urban, but then so, increasingly, was the population – Scotland was one of the most rapidly urbanising countries in the western world at the end of the eighteenth century.

Every man and woman in our period was acutely conscious of their rank and status in society. This emerges particularly clearly in separation cases, where the kinds of food and clothing suitable to the litigants might be a matter of contention. There were the 'higher' ranks and 'lower' ranks, and though it was possible for a woman to raise her rank by marriage, or a man to amass enough money to buy land and thereby raise himself into a higher rank, fundamentally the divide was between 'gently' born and the rest. The older son would have designation 'of' his estate after his name, while his brothers might become lawyers or officers in the armed forces, while continuing to move in the same social circles. At the top of the apex, with a lifestyle inconceivable to the lesser gentry, were the aristocracy. Breaking down the 'lower ranks' would be far more difficult, because of the difficulty of establishing criteria. Women were not categorised separately from their husbands since, as one writer put it, 'by convention a wife took her husband's rank and status'.[12] The classification may be crude, but later chapters flesh them out, and for now we can look at Table 3 for the breakdown for divorce cases.

Table 3.   *Social class of pursuers*

		%
Total	904	(100)
Aristocracy	30	(3.3)
Gentry	251	(27.8)
Common	623	(68.9)
Period 1	118	(100)
Aristocracy	4	(3.4)
Gentry	61	(51.7)
Common	53	(44.9)
Period 2	786	(100)
Aristocracy	26	(3.3)
Gentry	191	(24.3)
Common	569	(72.4)

The aristocratic/upper gentry level remained fairly constant at just over three per cent throughout this era. The number of gentry litigants actually quadrupled in Period 2, but as there were twelve times more 'common' litigants, gentry were a much lower proportion of the whole. To some extent this certainly reflects the rise of the middle class, but menial servants and labourers continued to be represented, and 56 of the 61 litigants who sued as paupers did so in Period 2. In separation cases there were only two aristocratic/upper gentry pursuers, both before the middle of the eighteenth century. Overall, gentry pursuers comprised only about a quarter of the total, and once again the shift toward lower-class pursuers in the later period is very marked.[13]

The situation contrasts strikingly with the picture of what happened with separation cases in England. At the Court of Arches, which heard matrimonial cases of all kinds, the poor vanished altogether by the 1780s, and there was 'a remorseless drift to greater and greater elitism in the ranks of the petitioners, as rising legal costs increasingly excluded first the poor, and then the lower middling sorts'. This was also true of the London Consistory Court, and though by 1830 the range of social classes was wider in parliamentary divorces, litigants had to be able to afford several hundred pounds.[14] Much closer to the Scottish situation was that of France during the Revolutionary years. A statute of 1792 established divorce on extremely libertarian grounds, including joint petitions on the grounds of incompatibility, and the financial obstacles were minimal. During the short period when the Act remained in force the social spectrum – like that of Scotland – ranged from noblewomen to the very poor. Nearly three-quarters of female instigators were working class, as were 69 per cent of men.[15]

MORE ON ADULTERY

What was the status of guilty parties vis-à-vis the 'paramour'? Looking first at upper-class male adulterers, out of 100 such cases, 13 were guilty with women of their own class and 87 with lower-class women. Distinguishing between the latter – i.e. trying to classify them as servants, whores or whatever – proved impossible, as the boundaries were so fluid. A woman who had had intercourse with the man in a bawdy house might when she later testified in court be respectably employed as a servant (or even be married), while a woman who had been employed as a servant could have ended up earning her living as a prostitute. Chapter 8 looks at examples of such liaisons.

Out of 92 upper-class women, 67 (73 per cent) were guilty with men of their own class, but a surprising 25 (27 per cent) had chosen lower-class men. According to Lawrence Stone, sexual intercourse between an upper-class woman and lower-class man was the great taboo,[16] so why does it manifest itself so strikingly in these records? In the first place, it is almost entirely a phenomenon of Period 1 when, for the most part, divorce was initiated only in cases of extremity. Perhaps some gentlemen would have jibbed at suing for divorce if their wives had strayed with a member of their own class but were utterly horrified by the discovery of adultery with a menial servant? In Period 2 wives who fell into this category were nearly all women whose status had been raised by marriage with a member of the gentry, i.e. the adultery was committed with a member of the class from which they had risen. This suggests that the taboo had become stronger, and the distance between 'ladies' and their servants greater as the eighteenth century progressed.

Not one of the lower-class male adulterers who was sued for divorce sinned with a woman of higher rank. Some 92 per cent of lower-class women were guilty with men of their own class, but eight per cent of lower-class women became the mistress of an upper-class man.

The information above has been extracted only when there was just one lover, or when all of those named were obviously of the same social class. Gentlemen who resorted to prostitutes but also had affairs with women of their own class, and wives who became prostitutes and had intercourse with men of different classes were excluded. Paying no attention to vague statements of guilt with 'one or more' lewd and wicked men/women, some 108 women seriously alleged that their spouse had committed adultery with more than one woman, which is about 37 per cent of the 290 successful female-instigated adultery cases. More surprisingly, 93 men, roughly a quarter of the 367 successful male-instigated adultery cases, alleged this of their wives. Forty-one of them provided convincing evidence that their wives had become common prostitutes, usually as a result of alcohol addiction.

Turning to a different aspect of divorce cases, the records allow us to see how long unsuccessful marriages lasted. About half of the couples had been married for over ten years, and proportions for both sexes were almost identical. In a handful of cases after years of stable marriage one partner suddenly developed a passion for someone else, but more typical were cases like that of Agnes Williamson, daughter of a tailor in Edinburgh, who brought a suit against Robert Preston under benefit of the poor's roll in November 1792. They were married in December 1776; in May 1777 she was 'under a necessity of leaving him at Greenock by reason of bad usage and treatment and to return to Edinburgh where she has continued ever since'. He went to America with his regiment and she had neither heard from him nor seen him till the previous September 'when she chanced to see him in Edinburgh when he informed her that he had just come home.' She had since 'found upon enquiry that the said Robert Preston had brought a woman with him and has for some time cohabited and still continues to cohabit with her in a state of adultery'. Or that of Robert Knox, a servant, divorced by Katherine Dillon, the daughter of a plasterer in Glasgow. They were married in April 1771, and the divorce suit was brought in 1792. In her oath of calumny Katherine swore that 'she had not seen the Defender for these fifteen years and had had no Correspondence with him by Letter or other ways during that period'. Or that of Jean Dinwoodie against William Black in 1810: married in May 1795, he left her the following year and 'They have lived separate ever since.'[17] Sybil Wolfram found a similar pattern in England, where 'in a fair number of cases the divorce suit was brought long after the separation'.[18]

One measure of marital stability is the length of time between the marriage and adultery, as stated in the libel. Again this reveals that many couples who were legally married for years had actually found different partners in the interim. Some 17 per cent of men and women had committed adultery within a year of marrying, and an additional 35 per cent had done so less than five years after the wedding. When Robina or Binnie Handyside brought a suit against her husband, Robert Wilkie, shawl manufacturer, in 1826, they had been married for five years, but he had deserted her a few days after the wedding to live with another woman. A witness deponed that that 'the Defender married the Pursuer in the belief that she was possessed of money to the amount of one hundred pounds whereas in fact she had only nine or ten pounds and after that was spent the Defender abandoned his wife saying it was of no use to live any longer with her.'[19]

A final question: how long after the adultery was first committed did the wronged party initiate divorce proceedings? There is some difference between the sexes here, as 24 per cent of men initiated an action within a year of the adultery whereas only 16 per cent of women did so. However, in both sexes over half initiated divorce proceedings between one and five years after the adultery had been committed, either because they had not been aware of it or, more usually, had been living apart.

In the nineteenth century the commissaries had misgivings about long gaps between the discovery of adultery and the divorce action. James Leslie, tinsmith in Edinburgh, had married Christian Brown in October 1802. After cohabiting for two or three days she 'insisted upon returning to her service where the Complainer understood she was to remain till the term of Martinmas thereafter but he very soon discovered in consequence of Letters from herself and otherwise that she had formed an adulterous connection with William Loch', son of her master. She became pregnant and bore Loch a daughter in November 1803, and had continued the relationship with him ever since. Leslie sued for divorce in February 1817, and the commissaries demanded justification for his waiting so long. 'The scanty stock which he had saved for his marriage was reduced almost to nothing by its unhappy result,' he declared, 'and his mind having been seriously affected by the domestic calamity which had befallen him, he had neither the means nor the capacity to apply to a Court of Law.' He delivered a tale of woe about fleeing from his house, vainly endeavouring to forget his plight, suffering mental illness, enlisting in the army, and borrowing money to buy himself out. Now that he was settled and had prospects 'he feels the more acutely the reproach of his situation. His wife being yet alive, he is married without knowing the solace of domestic happiness; he has a wife who instead of being her husband's ornament, is his disgrace. Nothing short of a dissolution of so degrading a tie can make his life, in his native place, endurable to him'. The commissaries granted him his divorce.[20]

A similar case was that of Janet Wardrope against John Hopkins, a labourer whom she married in 1802. She alleged that in 1809 another woman bore him a child in adultery, but she did not bring her divorce action until October 1827, and the commissaries insisted on knowing why she had waited so long. She replied that ever since her separation from her husband, 'which occurred a few months after the marriage' she 'had resided with a respectable family in Manchester as a principal Servant.' 'Not being molested' by her husband, 'and being desirous to avoid if possible the publicity of an action of Divorce, she delayed for these reasons bringing this Process until she was lately advised by her friends of the propriety and expediency of the measure.' She declared that she 'had neither seen nor had any communication' with John 'since the commencement of the adulterous intercourse condescended on'. Although the other woman was now dead, there were enough witnesses to confirm Janet's story, and she was granted her divorce.[21]

Up to now we have looked at successful divorce suits, but there are also things to be learned from unsuccessful ones. Out of 144 unsuccessful adultery cases, 45 were dismissed and the rest were seemingly abandoned. Four were dismissed because the marriage was not proven, and 19 because the adultery was not proven. Amongst the other reasons for dismissal, five were because the defender's domicile was not in Scotland. This includes two desertion cases at the end of the period; although earlier divorces were granted in similar circumstances, it was considered that those judgments were 'worthless as precedents' because 'jurisdiction can only be founded on domicile'.[22]

Most unextracted decreets consisted only of a scribbled note (the 'interlocutor') on one of the existing documents; by the end of the period this was almost always the witnesses' depositions. So, if the only document to survive was the libel, how can it be known if the case really was abandoned, or if the pursuer was granted a divorce? The answer is that it cannot, and that some of the cases labelled as abandoned may have succeeded. However, there are also cases where the reasons for abandoning it are stated, and these were nearly always financial. Chapter 5 looks at unsuccessful cases.

MORE ON DESERTION

As Lawrence Stone remarked, the simplest option for a man unhappy in his marriage was 'just to desert – to walk out of the house one day and never come back'. He does not entertain the same possibility for women but, as we shall see, an unhappy wife might return to her parental home, or be able to support herself. More than half the divorce suits in Connecticut between 1750 and 1797 were based solely on desertion, as they were in Neuchâtel between 1707 and 1806, and though we have seen that the proportion was very much smaller in Scotland, nevertheless the rise in suits based on adultery was matched by those for desertion.[23]

It is not possible to use the records of divorces for desertion in Scotland to examine the circumstances of the desertion because the bizarre requirements for such a suit meant that a preliminary case had to be brought for adherence, followed by various other procedures, so that the eventual divorce was really just a formality. However, adherence cases are instructive. A husband and wife were expected to cohabit, and if a wife left her husband she could be legally compelled to return to him unless she could prove good reason for her desertion. An adherence suit could also be brought against a deserting husband, and if he did not return he could be forced to pay the wife a yearly aliment. (Although such decreets are termed 'adherence and aliment' they are, in contrast to 'separation and aliment' decreets, actually either 'adherence *or* aliment'.)

This type of legal action was not meant to be initiated simply as a prelude to divorce, and even by the end of the period not all were raised for that purpose. Adherence often formed part of 'declarator of marriage' suits, in order to prove that the pursuer was legally married to the defender. As there are many such cases, often very complex, it has not been possible to examine them at this stage, but all the straightforward adherence cases, where the fact of the marriage was not contested, have been collected.[24] These amounted to 205 cases, of which 151 were successful and 54 unsuccessful (in ten of the latter the defender was absolved; the rest were abandoned). Two-thirds of the cases were initiated by women. Three cases were brought by the aristocracy/upper gentry, 46 by gentry/professional, and 156 by 'common' people; some six per cent were raised under benefit of the poor's roll. Of the 151 successful cases, 27 (18 per cent) were contested.

A graph of adherence cases would look entirely different from those for divorce or separation. Between 1684 and 1710, when there were only 23 divorce cases there were 25 adherence cases, yet later the numbers dropped to a mere four or five per decade and only rose again in the nineteenth century, so that 90 were brought after 1810. It is, of course, possible that many more mid-eighteenth century cases were also for declarator of marriage and therefore do not appear in this sample.

It might be supposed that in the early cases, when there were divorces for desertion, the pursuer really desired his or her spouse's return. In reality, most of the early suits brought by women were for aliment as well, sometimes with the aim of unlocking the assets of the missing husband. Christian Watson had been left an annuity and rents of a house in Burntisland by her first husband, all of which formed part of the *jus mariti* of her second husband, Robert Baird, whom she married in December 1740, and who deserted her three weeks later. In the adherence action she brought in January 1751, she asked for the right to the annuity and rents, 'and that the pursuer by herself alone can uplift and pursue for Discharge the same annuity and Rents without consent & concurrence of the said Robert Baird', and 'can possess the said House and Yard Inputt and outputt tennents and set Tacks of the same'. The commissaries agreed that she had sole entitlement to the money provided by her first husband, as long as her second one did not adhere.[25] After the first divorce for desertion in 1756 some two-thirds of extracted adherence decreets were followed by divorce decreets; in some of the remaining third aliment was granted, while others must either have changed their minds or died before suing for divorce (and there was a substantial block of adherence cases brought at the end of the period, most of which would have subsequently gone to the Court of Session for a divorce).

Table 4. *Interval between marriage and desertion*

Man instigator Total 40

		%
Under 1 year	21	(52.5)
1–5 years	12	(30.0)
6–10 years	5	(12.5)
Over 10 years	2	(5.0)

Woman instigator Total 96

		%
Under 1 year	38	(39.6)
1–5 years	36	(37.5)
6–10 years	15	(15.6)
Over 10 years	7	(7.3)

In 136 cases it is possible to tell how soon after the marriage the desertion took place. Table 4 reveals that, like Robert Baird above, some 40 per cent of husbands abandoned their wives within weeks or months of getting married – and that, surprisingly, an even higher proportion of wives (more than half) did the same. In the case of James Slimson against Maria or Mary Borthwick in 1824, a witness declared that within a month of their marriage in October 1808, 'the Pursuer became unwell, and the Defender left him and went home to her mother's house'. The witness did not know 'what her reason was, or whether she assigned any particular reason but she would not live with her husband any longer, and the Deponent understood that her relations had been against the marriage.' John Anderson, farmer in Nairn parish, married Barbara Marshall in December 1810. They cohabited for a few days in Edinburgh, after which Anderson 'returned home to a Farm which he then rented on the Estate of Brodie, and where his residence then was, and where the said Barbara Marshall promised to join him in a short time'. But she never did. For five years, hoping she would change her mind, he sent money for her support, and on two occasions when she promised to come he sent her money for the expenses of the journey. Seven years after the marriage she arrived at his house, 'where she cohabited only one day and one night with the Complainer, and then deserted from his house, and went to reside in the Town of Forres, where she remained in Lodgings for some weeks – That the Complainer and the said Barbara Marshall's friends and relations, entreated her to return home and to remain at home', but she refused and returned to Edinburgh.[26]

Anderson then waited another eleven years before his action for adherence. Some 17 per cent of men and 25 per cent of women waited over ten years before raising an action; only 10 per cent of men and 7 per cent of women raised an action of adherence within a year of the desertion. An action of divorce on the grounds of desertion could not be instigated until four years had elapsed, but in view of the various procedures that had to be followed before that final suit could be brought, some spouses brought their adherence case two or three years after being deserted. The bulk, however, lay in the four to ten year period.

The ostensible reason for bringing an action for adherence – to enforce the spouse's return – was shown up for the nonsense it usually was by the many cases where the spouse was beyond the reach of the Scottish courts, or whose whereabouts were unknown. (The Connecticut legal phrase was that the spouse had departed 'to parts of the world unknown'.[27]) This was true of 60 per cent of female-instigated cases and 25 per cent of male-instigated cases. In view of the situation described in the previous section, where the commissaries dismissed desertion cases on the grounds that the defender was not domiciled in Scotland, one might wonder what happened to such cases at the end of our period, and indeed the adherence case of Eliza Kerr against Alexander Henry Howell was dismissed in May 1829 because he was not domiciled in Scotland (she did not know where he was).[28]

When the pursuer was a man then usually the wife lived somewhere in the neighbourhood, and friends and neighbours attempted a reconciliation. For example, in the 1775 case of John Paterson, printer in Edinburgh, against Margaret Robertson, the couple had married in July 1771, but Margaret left him after the birth of a child in May 1773. Witnesses declared that she 'refused the pursuer admittance into her house and shut the door against other people and assigned as the reason it was in case the Pursuer should get access to the house and carry her off'. The local schoolmaster testified that Paterson had tried several times to gain admittance to his wife's house, but had been unsuccessful, and that he offered to 'take any room in Town for her But that she had refused the Offer and as the Deponent hears she still persists in deserting the Pursuers Fellowship and Company'.[29]

Did any husbands genuinely intend to force deserting wives to return? In the early period they occasionally did. In five successful separation cases it was either the husband's adherence action against the wife that caused her to bring a separation action against him, or else he brought an adherence action against her as a counter-suit to hers for separation – though in those cases there is no knowing if the husband really wanted his wife back, or if he simply wished to avoid paying her an aliment.

By the early nineteenth century it is difficult to imagine that a successful male pursuer would have compelled his wife to return. In the 1803 case of Alexander Allan, cutler and instrument maker in Edinburgh, against Helen Grant, a witness said that he accompanied Allan to Helen's house 'with a view to remonstrate with her, as to the impropriety of her conduct'. When Helen saw that her husband was with him, 'she appeared very angry and shut the door in their face, declaring that she did not wish to see her husband and expressing surprise at what brought him there'. The witness, 'having afterwards prevailed on her to speak to him she declared she never would in future live with her husband and did not even wish ever to see him again, and threatened in case he should have recourse to Law to compel her to live with him, she would do a mischief to one or other of them'. Another witness declared that 'she repeatedly expressed her hatred at the pursuer, and said in the most positive terms she never afterwards would live with him voluntarily declaring that if she was forced to live with him she would do every thing in her power to make him unhappy'. Fortunately, Allan had brought his adherence case in order to obtain a divorce rather than to get her back.[30]

The absurdity of bringing an action that demanded the return of an absent spouse when what was actually desired was a severance of all connection emerges particularly in cases like that of Robert Keill, day labourer in Dundee, against Helen White, in 1767. White declared that before deserting him she became addicted to drink and would sell his furniture and clothing to finance her addiction. Witnesses bore this out. One of them had heard that 'The reason of their separating was that the Defender disposed of her husbands Cloaths and furniture for drink and was catched lying with the soldiers near the church of Dundee by the pursuer who likeways told the deponent this last particular and added that after having catched her he in their return home gave her a drive with his hand and that she never came back to him after.' The witness added that Helen had returned several times to Dundee since then, and that on at least one occasion she had sent for her husband, 'who refused to go to her'. And this man obtained a decreet which stated that his wife must return and cohabit with him! Having got over those preliminaries, he obtained his divorce on the grounds of desertion.[31]

By the end of the period pretence had been dropped. In the 1819 case of Fanny Peacock against David Gibson, he was said to have used her 'with the greatest harshness frequently maltreating her in such a way as to force her from his house to seek refuge among her relations and friends in order to avoid her life being endangered'. She brought proof of this, including witnesses who saw the marks of violence on her. Powerful evidence, but hardly relevant to an adherence case. What it did establish was that 'his desertion was wilful and without any cause known to the pursuer', and subsequently she won a divorce.[32]

MORE ON SEPARATION

It was noted earlier in this chapter that about half the couples divorcing had been married for over ten years, and this is also true for successful separation cases (only six per cent being married for less than a year). As for the abuse that caused that separation, it is possible to date its onset in 59 out of the 92 successful cases: 31 were abused within a year of the marriage while 28 lived in relative harmony for some years before this happened. In the latter cases there was often a change of circumstances, such as moving from a rural area to the city. In virtually all cases of late-onset violence the abuse started when the husband became 'dissipated' and 'addicted to drink'. Nearly all the wives had left the marital home on more than one occasion, either fleeing to a neighbour for overnight refuge, or attempting a permanent break and being persuaded to return by a promise of better behaviour by the husband. Several entered into informal, or even formal, separation agreements, but these were not legally enforceable and the husbands reneged on them.

The Scottish legal system regarded judicial separation as 'belonging to the department of preventive police', which would never be granted 'except on the call of an imperative and overruling necessity.'[33] The questions which arise from this legal position are what degree of violence or abuse would convince the court, and whether their criteria changed in the course of the period.

In the first judicial separation case in the records, in 1714, which forms Study 14, there was no physical violence. Two other non-violent cases are discussed in Chapter 14, and one (which set a legal precedent) forms Study 15. By the end of our period Scottish legal opinion was moving in the same way as that of England, where Lawrence Stone noted that 'by the early nineteenth century, one or two physical confrontations, or even mere threats of violence, would suffice for a separation, and by the middle of the century the infliction of mental stress and a justified fear of physical cruelty were enough.'[34]

The most striking change toward the end of the period is in the wording of some of the commissaries' decreets. The final interlocutor was normally a very straightforward document, granting what the pursuer had asked for in the libel, and the wording of those for divorce or adherence did not change at all over time. Early separation decreets merely stated that the commissaries found 'maltreatments proven sufficient to Inferr the Separation Libelled against the husband'. Yet in the 1785 case of Mary Stuart against Andrew Taylor, the decreet stated that they 'Found it proven that the defender had maltreated the pursuer by beating and bruising her in a most cruel and barbarous manner as also by turning her out of doors and excluding her his house'. And in a particularly strongly worded decreet of 1818, in the case of Marion Frost against John Mather, they found that 'the Defender is proved on many occasions to have most brutally and disgracefully abused and beaten his wife the Pursuer altho her Conduct to him and her family was unexceptionable and exemplary and from no other Cause it appears but the unhappiness produced a short time before he drove her from his house by the undisguised and extreme profligacy of his own conduct as a husband and father'.[35]

Such decreets are expressions of the commissaries' personal disgust. One of them, James Fergusson, wrote in 1829 that 'in proportion to those of other descriptions, the cases of this class [separation on the grounds of cruelty] in which the husband has been successfully prosecuted, are disgracefully frequent'.[36] In quantitative terms this statement is quite untrue: between 1821 and 1830 there were 179 suits of divorce for adultery or desertion and only 34 for separation. But the impression those cases made on the minds of the commissaries was obviously deep.

A final point about separation on the grounds of cruelty is that under Scottish law it was available to men as well as women, and three husbands did in fact raise such actions. In the first instance, in 1809, the suit of a sergeant major of the Inverness-shire militia was uncontested, and the only unusual question asked of the witnesses was whether the wife possessed 'extraordinary strength'. They replied that she did not, 'but that her temper and disposition are very bad indeed', and that she was 'more wicked than strong.' The separation was granted. In the second case, in 1819, brought by a commander in the Royal Navy, there was no suggestion that his life was in danger, but his wife was an alcoholic who pawned or sold everything she could lay her hands on for liquor; it is a measure of the changing ethos of the court that he too was granted his separation. The third case, in 1826, involved counter-processes, each spouse alleging the cruelty of the other. The commissaries found it proved that 'the Parties have respectively been guilty of grossly maltreating and abusing each other' and granted the separation. The three husbands still had to pay aliment to their wives.[37]

The overall picture presented in this chapter raises some important questions. Why was there such a sharp rise in the number of divorce cases from the 1770s onward? Why was this not matched by separation cases? In view of the ease of obtaining a divorce in Scotland, after the figures began to rise, why did they not rise to something closer to modern figures? Anyone wishing a discussion of these points at this stage should turn next to Chapter 17; others may prefer first to enter more closely into the marriages, divorces, and separations of eighteenth and early nineteenth-century couples by reading the intervening fifteen chapters.

NOTES

All CC references are in the Scottish Record Office.
1. Some of the material in this chapter previously appeared in my article, ' "Forsaking the Matrimonial Vows" – Divorce in Eighteenth and Early Nineteenth-Century Scotland', *Journal of Social History*, vol.30, no.2 (Winter 1996), 465–82.
2. This figure does not include counter-processes mentioned in original processes (or vice-versa) where no papers have survived. Thus, the figure of 904 cannot be a complete tally of divorces in the period. Indeed, there are no surviving papers for some unsuccessful cases which are mentioned in other cases and in books as establishing important legal precedents; no doubt these were borrowed at some point by lawyers and never returned.
3. Michael Flinn, ed., *Scottish Population History* (Cambridge, 1977), 241, 271, 302.
4. Where there were two or more decreets, for example a subsequent one with the liablity for expenses, or where the judgment was appealed against and a later decreet affirmed the findings of the original one, the time intervals are to the first decreet awarding the divorce.
5. Sommerville vs Sommerville, CC8/5/16; Stewart vs Chapman, CC8/5/19; Maxwell vs Wallace Dunlop, CC8/5/15.
6. T. R. Gourvish, 'The cost of living in Glasgow in the early nineteenth century', *Economic History Review*, 2nd series, vol.25 (1972), 67n; Dick vs Ross, CC8/5/15; Baird vs Macarthur, CC8/6/135; Paul vs Stewart, CC8/6/144.
7. Colin S. Gibson, *Dissolving Wedlock* (London 1994), 15.
8. Ibid.
9. Davie vs Grant, CC8/5/17; Campbell vs Cunningham Fairlie CC8/5/35; Gibson, *Dissolving Wedlock*, 15; Lawrence Stone, *Road to Divorce – England 1530–1987* (Oxford 1992), 188;

Sybil Wolfram, 'Divorce in England 1700–1857', *Oxford Journal of Legal Studies* (vol.5, no.2), 166.

10. Woodcock vs Strachan, cc8/5/40; Easton vs Aitken, cc8/5/41. Amongst process papers unextracted decreets were most often just a scribbled and dated note – the interlocutor – on one of the other documents. Occasionally there is a 'scroll' decreet, a draft awaiting someone to fill in all the details of the libel, proof etc. In the most puzzling cases there is a final decreet, as complete as anything that appears in the registers; whether this was never paid for and hence never inserted into the relevant volume, or whether the clerk simply forgot to do so, I do not know.

11. Jeffrey R. Watt, 'Divorce in Early Modern Neuchâtel, 1547–1806', *Journal of Family History*, 14, (1989), 148; Nancy F. Cott, 'Divorce and the Changing Status of Women in Eighteenth-Century Massachusetts', *William and Mary Quarterly*, 33 (1976), 592; Roderick Phillips, *Putting Asunder: A History of Divorce in Western Society* (Cambridge 1988), 262.

12. Wolfram, 'Divorce in England 1700–1857', 162. Dr Wolfram also experienced difficulty in trying to place divorce petitioners into anything but the crudest categories.

13. In an American context, Merrill Smith found a wide range of social classes amongst divorce petitioners, with most of them in the 'middling range'; she did not note whether there were any changes over time. Merrill D. Smith, *Breaking the Bonds – Marital Discord in Pennsylvania 1730–1830* (New York and London 1991), 33.

14. Stone, *Road to Divorce*, 38–9, 186, 327. Between 1750 and 1857 about two-thirds of parliamentary divorces were initiated by the upper classes, but the aristrocracy dropped out almost completely by the early nineteenth century. Wolfram, 'Divorce in England 1700–1857', 163–5.

15. Phillips, *Putting Asunder*, 268–9.

16. Stone, *Broken Lives*, 243.

17. cc8/6/55; cc8/5/21; cc8/5/31.

18. Wolfram, 'Divorce in England 1700–1857', 176. According to Colin Gibson, in a divorce case of 1828 the Lords indicated their unwillingness to allow divorces where separation agreements had been entered into, 'holding that such agreements repudiated the very basis of the marriage contract', and if a couple had separated before the wife committed adultery, they considered that 'no injury was done to the husband who had voluntarily released his wife (his property) from consortium'. Gibson, *Dissolving Wedlock*, 31. This does not equate at all with Wolfram's findings.

19. cc8/6/150.

20. cc8/6/116.

21. cc8/6/155.

22. Maurice Lothian, *The Law, Practice and Style Peculiar to the Consistorial Actions Transferred to the Court of Session* (Edinburgh 1830), 133.

23. Stone, *Road to Divorce*, 142; Cohen, ' "To Parts of the World Unknown" ', 277; Watt, 'Divorce in Early Modern Neuchâtel', 149.

24. The element of proving a marriage was intrinsic to all suits for divorce, and, as has been noted, some were dismissed on the grounds that a marriage had not been proven. Nevertheless there was a difference between proving a marriage as a prelude to proving the grounds for divorce and proving a marriage the reality of which was contested. In the case of Lawson against Mortlock (cc8/5/15) the commissaries in December 1776 declared that 'in respect that there is no Conclusion for declaring the alledged marriage between the pursuer and Defender and that no decerniture for adherence could proceed without such Conclusion, Found that the proceedings in this process had been irregular and inept – and therefore assoilzied the Defender therefrom'. Lawson appealed to the Court of Session which ruled in his favour, and in April 1777 the commissaries granted him his decreet for adherence and subsequently a divorce (cc8/5/15). Needless to say, the commissaries never again demanded that any action for adherence also include a declarator of marriage.

25. cc8/5/9.
26. cc8/6/141; cc8/6/157.
27. Cohen, ' "To Parts of the World Unknown" ', 277.
28. cc8/6/164.
29. cc8/5/14.
30. cc8/5/27 & cc8/5/28.
31. cc8/5/11 & cc8/5/12.
32. cc8/5/37. That witness, their landlady, was asked 'what the pursuers Conduct was to her husband' and replied, 'I never saw any bad Conduct of hers to him – she always appeared crushed or broken hearted while she remained with us.' She was then asked if 'he intimated his intention of going away' and answered, 'He did not mention it to me He was of a very dour temper and I had very little conversation with him all the time he was in my house.' The divorce action is in cc8/6/124.
33. Patrick Fraser, *Treatise on the Law of Scotland as applicable to The Personal and Domestic Relations* (Edinburgh 1846), vol.1, 453.
34. cc8/6/105; Stone, *Road to Divorce*, 205.
35. cc8/5/18; cc8/5/36. Some of the material in this, and the following, paragraph, has appeared in ' "A Tyrant and Tormentor" – Violence Against Wives in Eighteenth and Early Nineteenth-Century Scotland', *Continuity and Change* 12(1) (1997), 31–54.
36. Fergusson, *Treatise*, 182.
37. Crawford vs Munro, cc8/5/30; Thomson vs Betty, cc8/5/37; McLeod vs Lyon et contra, cc8/6/149. In Pennsylvania one man, Alexander McArthur, raised a suit against his wife on the grounds of cruelty, but he was unsuccessful because the law there allowed that ground only to women. Smith, *Breaking the Bonds*, 28.

CHAPTER 2

PROVING ADULTERY – WITNESSES

'Proof of adultery is generally made up of minute and isolated facts, each of which would be insufficient to infer the conclusion by itself', wrote Patrick Fraser,[1] which is why two chapters are devoted to that subject here. He (and other legal commentators) noted that a great deal of evidence was necessary because the act was rarely seen. In fact, the records reveal that it was seen far more often than might have been expected, and some examples are given in the first section of this chapter. We then move on to other circumstances that led witnesses to conclude that adultery was being committed. But witnesses were not always passive bystanders; they sometimes actively intervened in the situation, an aspect which is shown in the third part. And, finally, we look at some instances where the lover was himself or herself a witness.

SEEN IN THE ACT

One day in 1717 Sir Alexander Dalmahoy of that Ilk must have been fairly desperate, for he had intercourse with his mistress in an Edinburgh back yard. A witness, Thomas Storie, said that Dalmahoy, with 'a young woman Iron coloured of a high stature [i.e. tall] in common habit', called at a neighbour's house and asked for a drink of ale and enquired 'if there was a yaird or any place for him and her to walk in', and that they went to the yaird in question where Storie saw him 'kissing and Imbraceing the said woman'. Subsequently John Sheills, baxter burgess of Edinburgh, saw 'a woman of high stature Lying on her back in the Yaird then possest by John Stewart gardner in Crossgates near the west kirk at the Inside of the hedge of the said yaird'. Sheills could see 'the said womans naked thighs her Clothes being up And . . . did also see the said Sir Alexander Dalmahoy defender Lying upon the said womans naked belly and his breeches down and see him make severall motiones upon the said woman her naked belly In such manner as man uses to converse with a woman in the act of Carnall copulation'. Sheills, and three other witnesses, found this highly objectionable and tried to seize the woman, but Dalmahoy persuaded them to leave her alone. Sheills added that 'the said woman was in Common habit and [he] knows she was not the pursuer whom the Deponent presently sees att the barr and that she appeared to the Deponent to be a young woman'. Dame Alice Paterson obtained her divorce from Dalmahoy in November 1720.[2]

In Alexander Macdougall's divorce action against Isobell Russell in August 1784, the particular incident that formed the grounds for the case occurred the previous month, when she was seen 'with a soldier in the avenue leading to Murrayfields house'. Thomas Greig, a carter at Coltbridge, saw a soldier and a woman kissing, and being curious he followed them and 'within the Gate the soldier laid the woman down and laid himself down above her'. Thomas immediately called David Greig to come along 'and he would show him some thing To which David Greig answered "what will you show me",' and Thomas 'said "I will show you a man playing with a woman"'. Greig came with him 'up the avenue to where the man and woman were and the deponent said to them "Good speed the work"', after which they arose, and others came along and identified the woman as Macdougall's wife. Similarly, in the 1805 case of William Armstrong against Mary Dalling, after riding away from a public house William Anderson heard his friend James Stewart calling him from within a dyke on the side of the road. He alighted and looked over the dyke to see Stewart lying beside Mary. He then 'got above her, and called to the Deponent "This is the way to do her off my lad", or words to that purpose'.[3]

In the 1819 case of Poor (meaning that he was admitted to the poor's roll for the divorce action) James Stevenson, baker at Gilmerton, against Janet Fairbairn, she was alleged to have committed adultery with William Borthwick, carter. William Dingwall, labourer in Gilmerton, aged twenty-one, deponed that at about eleven o'clock on a Friday night he was called from his bed by Mr Gordon, a schoolmaster, who asked him to follow Borthwick and Janet 'in order to see what they were to be about'. He did so in company with another labourer, named Rennie, and they saw Borthwick and Janet 'lying together at the Roadside and Borthwick lying above the Defender'. Dingwall and Rennie 'asked what they were doing and were answered by Borthwick "That it was a man at his prayers" to which Rennie replied that it was damned queer Prayers'. Dingwall was asked by the court 'In what situation the Clothes of the parties were when he saw them', and answered that 'he just saw them lying and her bare thighs up'. Asked if he believed they 'were engaged in a criminal connection', he said that he could not be sure but 'that such was certainly his impression on his mind at the time'.[4]

It was not only 'common' women who were seen in the act. Anastasia Gossen was married to Henry Martin Blake Esq. of Windfield in Galloway, Ireland, in 1814 and was guilty of adultery with Lieutenant Saunders in 1816, at which time Henry separated from her. She then had relationships with at least two other gentlemen, and in 1823 Henry brought a successful divorce action against her. Sally Mackie had been nurse to a child of theirs, and one day was out walking with Anastasia, the child, and Lieutenant Saunders, when Anastasia told her to sit down and wait. She and the lieutenant went into the trees and Sally saw him 'throw her down and get above her' and had no doubt about what they were doing. On another occasion Sally 'heard a noise in the parlour like rattling of the fireirons upon the fender I went towards the door betwixt the bedroom and the parlour and heard rustling and other noise within it as if persons together – I looked through the keyhole and saw my mistress and Lieutenant Saunders lying upon the floor of the parlour he was above her', and again there could be little doubt about what they were up to.[5]

Naturally, adulterers were far likelier to have been seen in the act through keyholes and other apertures than out in the open. 'Many discoveries have been made, and not a few trials for crim. con. ensued, in consequence of a peep through a key-hole', wrote Lawrence Stone with regard to England in this period. He also noted that 'keys were still very clumsy, and key-holes consequently large, which often provided the inquisitive with a good viewpoint'.[6]

It was amazing how much Janet Wilson managed to see 'by looking through a hole in the loft' in the 1729 case of Margaret Nimmo against Patrick Stone. He was clerk to the Regality of Torphichen, guilty of adultery from 1719 with Janet Mitchell, daughter to the regality officer of Torphichen. On one occasion Janet Wilson saw Patrick 'sitting upon a Chist or Chaise with the said Janet Mitchel upon his knee, the said Janet Mitchels Cloaths being up, and the defender handling her secret parts, and at the same time she observed the defender take up the said Janet Mitchell and put her betwixt him and the wall the defenders Cloaths being all opened upon him'. The witness admitted that she 'made use of a stool to stand upon to look up through the said Hole' – and sent for a neighbour to stand on the stool and look through the hole as well. At that time the neighbour, Margaret Wilson, heard Patrick 'desire Mitchel to Lay further up the Chist That he might see her secret parts Expressing them in the coarsest manner.'[7]

In the 1746 case of James Dun, tenant in Dunblane parish, against Isobell Bryce, Anne Sinclair, a servant, went to the back door of the barn 'and looking throw a hole towards the bottom of the Door which was made for letting out and in the catts, Observed and plainly saw the Defender Lying on the bed in the barn with her cloaths up, and the thighs and legs of the Defender naked, and James Bennet with his Breetches down Lying betwixt her Leggs and Making Motions'. A little later 'she saw them both sitt up right togither in the said Bed he Kissing and Caressing her as she was likeways doing him, And that in a little time he lay'd her back again and in the manner and way abovementioned she saw James Bennet making motions above the Defender'.[8]

In the 1778–9 case of John Tower, farmer and distiller at Dunmore Park, against Marion Burn, a servant (Jean Bruce, aged seventeen) saw the man visiting give her mistress 'a look', so Jean left the room and went into the pantry, where there was a hole where one could see into the other room. Through the hole Jean 'saw the defender standing by the drawers, but bending a little backwards and the man above mentioned standing by her – That the defenders petticoats were pulled up so that the deponent could see her bare thighs That the mans breeches were down and they seemed to the deponent to be then in the act of carnal copulation'.[9]

In a case of 1786–7 the commissaries went to verify the 'through a hole' testimony of a witness. Thomas Brockie, servant to Captain William Jardine of Applegirth, deponed that 'there were several holes made in the pannels of the Door of Mrs Jardines Bedchamber'. One evening he 'look'd through the hole of the door when Mrs Jardine and Mr Pleydel were in the room together and he then saw them lying Carnally together, Mr Pleydel was lying above Mrs Jardin And the deponent saw Mrs Jardines Naked knees and part of her thighs – That at this time they were lying upon Chairs, Mr Pleydel was making quick motions and Mrs Jardine's arms were round the small of Mr Pleydels back'. After the examination of this witness was concluded,

> The Judge Examinator went Immediately along with Mr McLaurin Counsel for the pursuer and Mr Dalziel Counsel for the defender and Viewed the Room in the pursuers house in George's Square where Thomas Brockie depones to seeing Mr Pleydel and Mrs Jardine lying Carnally together and likeways the holes made in the door of said Room for the purpose of seeing Mr Pleydel and Mrs Jardin when in said Room together, and Found the same to agree exactly with the descriptions given of them by said Thomas Brockie in his Deposition.[10]

Although actually witnessing the act of adultery was commoner than one might have expected, obviously it was not the norm, and many other circumstances could form part of witnesses' evidence.

SERVANTS

Servants were a key group of witnesses, and not only in gentry and aristocratic divorces, for even relatively humble families usually had at least one servant. Lawrence Stone commented on the high turnover of servants in eighteenth-century England, with most staying with the same employer on average only two to four years. In Scotland the situation may have been even more extreme, for thirty of the sixty servants employed by Lady Grisell Baillie between 1695 and 1704 left in less than a year, and only about a dozen stayed with her for more than two years.[11] Servants would be engaged for a term of six months at a time, and many who appeared as witnesses had stayed only one term. There could therefore be no expectation of any kind of loyalty from them; with such an uninvolved and peripatetic group it was curiosity that ruled.[12]

In 1730 Janet Haigie, wife of William Gilles, merchant in Kirkcaldy, tried to prevent their servant, Mary Bennett, from appearing as a witness against her, claiming that William had been guilty of adultery with her.[13] He responded that at the time this was supposed to have happened he had been 'Bedfast under heavy sickness and Indisposition of Body', and that Janet 'had good reason to be apprehensive that the said Mary Bennett from the occasion of being her menial servant had got too much into the secret of her Dark and whorish practises', so that the allegation 'was but an artfull invention to postpone the Testimony of that witness'. She did not get away with it, and Mary (aged twenty) provided damning testimony.

One evening when Gilles was away, she said, a man called Alexander Birnie came to the house, threw off his coat, and went into Janet's bed. 'After they were awhile in bed togither' Mary 'heard the bed shake', and also heard Birnie say to Janet that 'his wand then stood and would bide her another time or words to that purpose from which and the noise she heard she apprehended they were in the act of copulation'. One night several months later when Birnie was asleep in Janet's bed she asked Mary 'to bring a Light which she accordingly did', and Janet said to her that 'she belived Birnie was then poxed and she behooved to look into his body', and they both peered at the sleeping man. On another occasions Mary 'heard Birnie complaining he wanted money to pay the surgeon', and heard Janet say 'My Dear Sandy what would become of me if you Leaved the Country'. Mary also deponed that Janet had given some of her husband's shirts to Birnie, and that the last time she was ill she showed her (Mary) a ring and asked Mary to give it to Birnie if she died: 'there was loose hair wrapt about the ring' which Janet told her was Birnie's hair. Of course, Mary was not the only witness in this case. Thomas Grey deponed that he and Birnie

> were servants in the pursuers house and wroght att his Tobaccos betwixt Whitsunday and Martinmas 1728 During which time the deponent observed the said Birnie to have more money than he could earn by his Imployment and the deponent having questioned him how that he came by it he answered that he got it from the defender and that during the space forsaid the deponent had severall times observed Birnie wearing the pursuers shirts marked w.G. which he said to the deponent he got from the defender and deponed that he heard the said Birnie say that he belived if any body offered carnall dealing with the defender she would not refuse it.

Tobacco features in the next case too (in 1737), of Peter Rolland of Kinnaird, merchant and late baillie of Dunfermline, against Christian Dalgleish, for her lover was her husband's servant, James Beatie, described at the time of the divorce action as 'Tobacconist'. Jannet Richardson (aged sixteen), their servant, 'stood in the bedroom door . . . and saw the curtains moving and a little while after she heard the Defender say to Beaty you promised to tyre me but I think I have tyred you and the same night when Beaty rose from the defenders bed the deponent heared him complain that this was sore work upon which the Defender desired him to take a Dram out of a bottle of brandy that stood upon the head of the drawers and that would put strength in him'. One morning Jannet 'observed marks upon the bed cloaths' which she 'believed to be the effects of their lewd conversation together'. After Beatie left the service to take up his own shop, Christian sent him presents such as 'beef herrings kaill butter', and Jannet had also seen Christian slip money into his hand.[14]

Another merchant whose servant appeared as a witness was William Fergusson, in Kirkcudbright, who brought an action against his wife, Isabel Carson, in 1789. Mary Wylie had been nurse to their child and knew all about her mistress's affair with James Ireland, labourer. She said that when Ireland passed the house Isabel would wave to him if her husband was not at home and give a different signal if he was. On one occasion Isabel came into the house to find them sitting next to each other, and Ireland 'had one arm around the pursuer's wifes neck and the other arm he had thrust up below her Petticoats'. When he saw her he 'drew out his hand from below the said Isobell Carsons Petticoats and started up and walked out of the house'. Mary then 'challenged' her 'for such unseemly behaviour but she parried off the question by saying Ireland was only examining her apron'. Soon after that Mary was thirsty and her mistress told her to come to Ireland's house for a drink. When she got there 'upon entering the door she saw the said Isobell Carson sitting upon the said James Ireland's Knee with her back to him and her Petticoats up but the deponent was so shocked at an appearance so grossly indelicate that she started back and the pursuers wife got off his knee and Ireland rose up and handed to the deponent a draught of Bragwort'. That night her mistress returned home late and in the night Mary heard a man's voice from the garret where her mistress lay and out of curiosity went to the foot of the stairs; she recognised Ireland's voice and heard 'also such a fistling noise and movements as convinced her that Ireland and the said Isobel Carson . . . were in actual copulation'.[15]

Mary also deponed that during the period in question 'she was frequently offered and promised rewards to conceal from the pursuer and the neighbourhood her conduct with the said James Ireland', and when she 'threatened to reveal to her Master what she knew, her Mistress always complained to the pursuer that she invented lies upon her and which had the effect to produce a great deal of abuse and ill usage from the pursuer who would not credit any thing that was said but always used his wife with much civility and tenderness'.[16]

In a case of 1809, that of Edward Maccall, teacher in Edinburgh, against Elizabeth Hislop, the household had only one servant at any given time; none of them stayed very long, but all were in their time made use of by Elizabeth in her affair with their lodger, George Meek.[17] One of them, Catherine Auld (aged twenty), when asked by the court 'whether she had received or been promised any reward for being a witness in this cause', replied that that same morning Mrs Maccall said to her, 'You are going to the Court to day, Mr Meek will give you a reward if you will say' –, but that the witness 'interrupted her before she had mentioned particularly what she wished the deponent to say by saying that she would tell nothing but the truth.'

In fact, Elizabeth and her lover were fairly discreet, so that none of the succession of servants saw anything 'improper' between them, but the servant of the time was expected keep a look-out for Mr Maccall when his wife was alone with Meek, and after Meek no longer lodged there he would give the servant money not to reveal to her master that he had been there. One of them (Elizabeth Smith, aged seventeen) said her mistress once told her that 'Mr Meek had promised to marry her in the event of her husband's decease', and the witness had 'been often employed by the defender to dog the pursuer when he went out to see that he was fairly out of the way and that the deponent having done so used to return and inform her mistress'. After the divorce action was brought Meek came to the house of her new mistress asking to speak to her, 'and she having gone to the door to him he said "Betty it was a damned shame of you to inform Mr Maccall that I used to go to his house in his absence and if you were to go to the Court about it you must not mention my name." '[18]

None of the succession of servants evinced any dissatisfaction or unease over aiding a mistress's illicit love affair; no doubt it added excitement to a humdrum job. But in the 1829 case of John Ross Jr, merchant in Glasgow, against Anne McCailan, we find a more censorious attitude. Anne's lover was George Laing, surgeon or doctor of medicine. The servant, Mary McLellan, went into the dining room one evening when Ross was out, 'with some knives to put into a press, and upon opening the door of the Dining Room she heard a noise as of the Defender endeavouring to rise from the Sofa which was at the other end of the room'. She 'saw Dr Laing standing at the sofa, and . . . made haste without looking particularly, to put the Knives into the Press'. She then heard her mistress 'say to Dr Laing "did she see" and distinctly heard him in reply say "No" '. Mary 'felt very much agitated at what she had seen and heard' and 'took the opportunity of going to a Mrs Anderson who had recommended her to the place, and who lived in the same Court, Mentioned what she had seen, and asked her advice as to whether she should leave the pursuer's service'. Mrs Anderson 'advised her to remain' and 'to keep out of the way of seeing what was going on'. But however agitated Mary was it did not stop her peering through the keyhole of the bedroom and viewing more of the behaviour that disturbed her so much.[19]

NEIGHBOURS

As has already been made abundantly clear, unlike the situation in England where actions of crim. con. were chiefly brought by members of the upper strata of society, in Scotland divorce cases were brought by many in the humbler ranks. In view of the rapid urbanisation of the country, it should come as no surprise that neighbours were almost as important in providing evidence of adultery as servants.[20]

Witnessing an adulterous affair could be hazardous, as in the 1777 case of Malcom McDermit, changekeeper in Edinburgh, against Elizabeth Rhynd or Rhynie, whose lover was Alexander Paton, 'chairmaster'. The witness, Mary Mckercher (aged forty), was the wife of a soldier of the city guard, which was made up mainly of Highlanders, and she was examined in Gaelic and her testimony translated. She said that she had come into the house once and seen Elizabeth emerge from the bed: 'the curtains of the bed being opened' she saw a man in it and thought it must be Malcom, 'but upon speaking to him she discovered from his Voice tho' she did not see his face that it was another person and believed this person from his Voice to be Alexander Paton who threatned to butcher the deponent if ever she made the least Discovery of what she saw'. Mary added that both Elizabeth 'and the man in the bed spoke to the deponent in the Gallic Language'.[21]

In the case of James Robertson, surgeon on a ship trading from Liverpool to the coast of Africa, against Agnes Glendinning (1788–91), Sarah Skirrilaw, wife of a tide waiter in Dumfries, was a neighbour of Agnes's and as Agnes had two young children and was on her own Sarah would look in on her at night. One evening Agnes told her not to come, which made her curious, so she told Agnes she had lost her keys and was let in the house; while she was in the bedroom pretending to search for them she 'put her hand upon a Chair which stood close to the Bed side but her hand slipt from the Chair and lighted upon the knee of a man in the bed'. She 'than Exclaimed O! here is a man', and Agnes 'desired her to be silent for she would wake her Daughter Mary'. Next morning Sarah 'went to her house and asked her what John Roan was doing there so late'. Agnes 'answered that he had come with a pair of shoes that she had kept him a little for fear if the Neighbours would see and suspect him . . . That he was a dear sweet creature and meant nothing else than to feel her bare legs in Bed'. Sarah 'advised her to withdraw from Roans Company lest her husband should hear of it', but Agnes 'answered that she did not care for what the world said because her husband would never give ear to such a tale nor believe she was a bad woman'. (She subsequently eloped with Roan.)[22]

More unusual was the 1803–4 case of Peter Milne, baker in the Cowgate of Edinburgh, against Elspeth Clyne, who was known to be an alcoholic.[23] One night, after midnight, everyone in the tenement block was 'disturbed and alarmed with the noise of men cursing and swearing and a womans voice'. The noisy crowd were in the close below when it was discovered that they comprised Elspeth 'and three men that she had picked upon the street and brought along with her'. In the close she had intercourse with two of the men,

> and the third man would also have had carnal dealings with her, had not one of the family which stays immediately below the pursuer called out to him from a back window in their house, that some men were ravishing his wife, in his own closs, but the defender Elspeth Clyne who wished not to be discovered or disturbed, said to the man who was in contact with her at the time in a soft and low tone of voice 'Hush Hush thats Mrs Curries voice' upon which they all left her, but while the foresaid criminal intercourse was going on, and after the same was finished, the most indecent and obscene language passed between her and these men.

Naturally the neighbours were crucial witnesses here. Margaret Galloway, who lived across the street, could not see what was happening, but from what she heard 'she had every reason to suppose that one of the above mentioned men was in the act of having connection with the defender and immediately after she heard one of the men say to his comrade "Stand to you buggar, for that's a bitch has a lust for men" '. After the men left, Margaret saw Elspeth come out of the close 'and after reeling across the street, she fell down in the strand'. Mrs Isobel Currie, wife of a bookbinder, was awakened on the night in question and 'heard the voice of a man call out "stride your legs" upon which the deponent said "Is that you Mrs Milne" ' – which was when Elspeth said 'Hush that's Mrs Curries voice'.

However, while neighbours frequently appeared in divorce actions it was rarely because they had seen that kind of behaviour. For the most part they were simply witnesses to the fact that a man and woman were quietly cohabiting as man and wife; often they had had no idea that one of them was legally married to someone else. Many examples could be given, but one should suffice. John Mathie, shoemaker in Stirling, married Janet Sharp in 1811, but in 1812 she went off with Alexander Thomson, residing at Longstone near Slateford, and Mathie declared, when he brought his divorce action in 1819, that she had been cohabiting with him ever since. James Whyte, carter, deponed that Janet and Thomson had lived together 'for upwards of five years and that she and Thomson are considered by the Deponent and by all the neighbours as husband and wifes'. He added that 'they have had three Children two of which are now alive.'[24]

Not all witnesses remained passive; some actively intervened.

INTERVENTIONS

In a case of 1750 Grizell McAlpin had left her husband Ludovick Grant, writer (laywer) in Edinburgh, many years earlier, and lodged above John Shiriff, a 29-year-old slater.[25] One night Shiriff sent his apprentice upstairs for a candle that she had asked to be lighted, and the apprentice 'immediately came Running down stairs and said to him that there was a man in the house'. John went right upstairs 'with his own Candle and upon his coming in to the Room . . . observed one Paterson a sailor sitting in the Easy Chair with his Britches down and she sitting with her cloaths up behind, betwixt his thighs . . . in the act of copulation together'. Shiriff 'quarrelled Paterson for being there at that time of night and took him down stairs with him and showed him the way to the street', and 'Paterson said to him God damn you sir you have spoilt me a good fuck'. A few minutes later Shiriff heard Paterson going upstairs again, and sent up his apprentice again, 'who upon his return told him that Paterson was there again and that he was in bed with her', so Shiriff 'went up again where he saw the defender lying across the bed with her cloaths up above her knee, and the said Paterson hanging backwards from the Bed with his Breetches down'.

Up till then we might have thought that Shiriff was filled with righteous indignation, but at this point, when Shiriff advanced into the room, Grizell, far from being worried or affronted at being seen in that position, 'said to him Lord John I am very dry, get me a Bottle of ale' – which he did! And 'Paterson (who was standing with nothing on him but his Britches and a check shirt) gave him a penny for the ale', and when Shiriff left the room Grizell was in bed, and Paterson barred the door.

Lodging house keepers sometimes refused to allow adulterous couples to remain when they discovered their true relationship, but more direct action was taken by Thomas Aitkin, stabler in the Bowgate of Edinburgh, in the case of Archibald Nisbet of Carfinn against Emelia Proven in 1758. Emelia had brought a man to his house, and when the servant maid opened the door she 'saw lascivious behaviour betwixt them' and told her master. Aitkin went into the room, found them in bed together, 'took the man by the neck of the coat and pulled him off her into the Floor, where he saw his privities exposed with the marks of his having been in the Act of copulation'. He said to the man, 'What Sir, is this the use you make of my house you Scoundrel, Do you think that I keep a baudy house upon which he begg'd his pardon, and asked him the favour not to speak of what he had seen'.[26]

Another lodging house keeper intervened in a different way. In a 1766 case James Chalmers, a gentleman from Banffshire, had been so disillusioned with his wife, Margaret Marr, that he fled to Jamaica, though making financial provision for her before he went. Margaret took up lodgings with another man, William Flint in Edinburgh, and her landlady thought they were husband and wife until Margaret told her that 'she had been married to a Brother of Mr George Chalmers the Merchant who had gone abroad and that she had not heard from him for ten years and did not know whether he was dead or alive but owned she gott twenty shillings sterling every three weeks from his Brother Mr George Chalmers'. The landlady was so horrified that her lodger should be supported by her brother-in-law while living with another man, she promptly went and 'acquainted the said George Chalmers how much he was imposed upon'.[27]

The most usual style of intervention was simply for a neighbour to chide the guilty spouse for his or her behaviour. In the 1792 case of James Millar, servant, against Jean Douglas, Mary Lawrie, wife of the man who had let the room to Jean, said that Jean 'had sometimes one man and sometimes two in the Room with her all night'. Mary 'upon observing this behaviour of the defender sometimes scolded and sometimes flattered her in order to make her desist from those practices both because it would hurt the deponents house and that she was sorry for the Lad her husband'. Mary knew that Jean 'while she lived in that house was very much addicted to drink', and Mary was 'very much afraid that she would sometimes set the house on fire'. Mary's husband 'often proposed to burst open the door of the Defenders apartment and to take witnesses but the deponent would not consent because she rather wished her to fall in other hands.'[28] In other words, neighbours did not want to get *too* involved in others' affairs.

Servants also intervened at times. In the early case (1737–8) of William Montgomery, merchant in Edinburgh, against Elizabeth Eizatt, the 22-year-old servant,

Margaret Young, was a crucial witness.[29] On the night in question Elizabeth, 'having attired herself in the Gayest Manner' met Major George Welsh in a house in the Canongate 'wherein she had no Necessary lawfull Business', and in the evening took a coach to Leith. Margaret, as her maid, accompanied her. In the coach the major complimented Elizabeth 'upon her beauty and youth', while trying, unsuccessfully, to wrest the candle from the maid's hands. When they reached his lodging they went into the bedchamber and he kissed Elizabeth 'and said a great many pretty things to her about her beauty and his esteem for her'.

Margaret 'frequently pressed' her mistress to go home, who at first 'said she would go home in a little but afterwards she said she would stay there all night'. The major became annoyed and said 'do you pretend to direct your mistress, she knows what is proper for her to do, and at last he turned peevish and out of humour and desired the deponent to forbear, saying what is it to you if your mistress grant me a favour, you may stay all night and ly with my Man George he is a clean lusty fellow'. Margaret saw her mistress 'throw off her own gown and unlace her stays and then she put the deponent forcibly out of the Room from her and the Major shut the door behind her'. The maid had done her best.

Various servants and others attempted to intervene in the Highland case of Colin Mackenzie, factor to Lord Fortrose, against Katherine Mckenzie (daughter of Kenneth Mckenzie of Torridon) in 1744 (the depositions were all translated from Gaelic as few of the witnesses spoke English).[30] Katherine was guilty first with Roderick Mckenzie, her husband's servant, and another servant, Katherine McDonald (aged twenty) said that one night

> Roderick came from his Bed in the Brewhouse in his shirt and as he was going towards the defenders bedroom he fell over a Large Iron pott and cutt his shins, which pott the deponent put there Industriously suspecting he might have occasion to go that way that night, That upon his falling over the pott she and some others of the servants made ane alarm upon which the said Roderick thought proper to retire to his own bed again.

Colin learned of the affair and removed his wife to the Isle of Lewis, but she then took up with another man, 'one Donald McKenzie then a Merchant at Stornoway brother to Murdoch McKenzie of Achilly'. Murdoch McIver, a 45-year-old fisherman, was a friend of Donald's and 'took occasion to reprove him for his behaviour' with Katherine, 'which reproof was so much taken amiss that neither the said Defender nor Donald could afterwards abide the deponent'. One night Donald knocked at the door while Katherine was in bed, and Margaret McCulloch, a servant (aged twenty-five) said to her mistress 'who was then offering to rise Ly still Mistris and do not rise to let him in for we have had abundance of Mischief about him already and that it might occasion Murder or bloodshed'. Katherine, 'geting out of Bed and endeavouring to unlock the door', Margaret and another servant 'went after her struggled a little with her and endeavoured to keep the door fast', but Katherine 'some way or other unlocked the door'. There really was no way to stop a determined woman.

In the 1771–2 case of Patrick Heron of Heron against Mrs Jean Home various servants attempted to intervene in different ways.[31] The adultery was with Ensign Alexander Macnaught, and Jean used to leave the window open in the dressing room so that he could come in during the night (it was easily accessible from the outside whereas the bedroom window was not). Janet Grant (Jean's personal maid) told two other servants about this, and one night Janet closed the window, and the other two servants stayed up and watched until between midnight and one in the morning a gentleman tried to get into the dressing room, then returned with a stick and rapped on Jean's bedchamber window until she got up and opened the dressing room window again.

They told Janet Grant what they had seen, and Janet 'feigned a dream' and told her mistress of it, 'to this purpose, "That she (Mrs Grant) had seen a man coming in the dressing room by the window, and that the servants were so enraged that they threatened to shoot him"'. Jean called the cook maid, and 'asked if she had heard about the dream' and said that she would 'rather than any harm should happen to that man', she 'would see half of the servants damn'd . . . and supposing the servants would tell such things to Mr Heron when he came home he would not believe them'. William Brewer, the butler, was so upset at some of the familiarities he observed between his mistress and Macnaught that he told his master's brother about them, 'But Captain Heron desired the deponent to say nothing of it till he should observe something furder'. One night he was informed by one of the maids that Jean and Macnaught were alone in the dark together in the drawing room. The butler 'went up with an intention to disturb them, but did not do it, as he upon recollection was afraid of creating some dispeace in the family'.

A visitor to the house, Miss Molly Agnew, tried to intervene as well. She often said to Jean that 'it was very indecent in her to have Mr Macnaught so often about the house' while her husband was away, to which Jean asked her if she thought that 'any Body would take upon them to inform Mr Heron of it? That she was sure though they did Mr Heron would not believe it'. Molly 'once took the liberty' of telling Jean that 'if she persisted in such a life it would at last break out and end in the ruin of her self and character for ever, for at this time the defenders conduct and behaviour with Macnaught was become the common topic of Conversation in all the neighbourhood.' (It was an intercepted letter from Jean to her lover that finally provided conclusive proof for Heron to initiate the divorce action.)

Servants took decisive action in the 1778–80 case of John Fairlie, tenant in Renfrewshire, against Ann Corbett. They had become very suspicious of her conduct with Robert Birkmyre, and one night Helen Jarvie told John Macklean that Ann had gone to Birkmyre's bed. John, along with another servant, Thomas Reid, went into Birkmyre's room where they saw Ann in his bed. Reid actually pulled her out of the bed and onto the floor, but a few minutes later she was back in his bed.

So John, Thomas, Helen and another servant, George Knight, sat up in the kitchen all night, their purpose being 'to watch the defender and Birkmyre', and when Fairlie came home in the morning Reid went out to inform him. Fairlie went into the room, saw them in bed together and called the others as witnesses. Macklean deponed that when Ann arose, with 'nothing on her but her shift', Helen Jarvie said to her 'that she was a whore', to which Ann 'replied she owned she was a whore and a Damned whore'.[32]

Drastic action was also taken in the 1788 case of William Ker of Broadmeadows against Veronica Hay. There were 'scandalous reports' circulating in Berwickshire about Veronica and Mr Renton of Lamerton, and in fact her husband forbade him the house, but he continued visiting when Ker was not at home. One day when Ker 'was absent upon his rounds as Commissary of Musters Mr Renton rapped at the door of Meadowhouse and . . . the servants being unwilling to let him in, all ran out of the house', except Isabel Lawson, Veronica's maid, and Hannah Young, the chambermaid. When Isabel 'was going up the stair case leading to the Nursery she heard Effie Tait . . . cry out "there was Mr Renton at the door will no body let him in" ', to which Isabel 'answered he might rapp there seven years' before she would answer the door. One of those who ran out, Mary Swan, cook maid, 'heard the people going at the harrows on the other side of the water say, "the Comie (meaning the Commissary) must be from home as there is Mr Renton going up to his house" '. Veronica let him in herself.

Soon after that Veronica was absent all afternoon, and when she returned Hannah Young went to her 'and gave up her Service, as did all the other Servants'. One of them had seen their mistress with Renton, which they 'considered as confirming their former suspicions, and . . . did not think it decent or proper to continue in the service of a woman capable of such conduct'. They 'went in a Body to their Mistress to give up their Service and . . . Mary Swan the Cook maid told her Mistress before them all that the reports in the Country were no longer said things but seen things and for that reason they gave up their Service'. Veronica's response was that 'she would get other servants'. (However, after all was revealed – once again by an intercepted letter – she gave 'the Servants a good Character and exculpated them from any blame'.)[33]

The above cases have provided a glimpse into the complex relationships between neighbours or servants with adulterous couples, and has shown some of the reactions, attitudes and behaviour which followed on from their suspicions or sightings. Their depositions were obviously the crux of any divorce case, but over time an increasingly important witness was the lover, or 'paramour', of the guilty spouse.

PARAMOUR AS WITNESS

The first case in which an adulterous wife's lover was cited as a witness was that of Porterfield against Nicholson in 1771 – Case Study 10 – and her lawyers strenuously, but ultimately unsuccessfully, objected. The practice gradually became well established. As 'notour' (persistent) adultery was a criminal offence in Scotland such witnesses would be warned that they did not have to answer any questions that might incriminate them, but the crucial question was framed in such a way that they merely had to say that they knew the defender had been guilty with someone other than their husband/wife at a specified time and place. From the evidence of other witnesses it would be known who the paramour was, and the paramour's oblique testimony would be perfectly acceptable in civil cases of this kind, without making them liable for a criminal prosecution.

Some men still objected. In the 1791 case of John MacDonald of Clanranald against Catharine MacQueen, her lover, Captain William Payne, brought his advocate to court with him, who stated that 'he could not be obliged to give testimony as a witness and ought not to be put upon oath as such'. Clanranald's first question was to be whether Payne was acquainted with the pursuer and defender, the second whether he had visited the family at Ballencrieff at particular times when the pursuer was absent, and the third was: 'does it consist with your knowledge that any man different from the pursuer Mr Macdonald had carnal connection with Mrs Macdonald in the house of Ballencrieff or thereabout?'. Payne's advocate argued that as he could not be forced to answer the last question, there seemed no reason why he should have to answer the first two. The commissaries agreed, and Clanranald did not fight their decision, as there was more than enough other evidence to prove her adultery.[34]

We do not know the specific reason for Captain Payne's objecting to testifying, but in some cases it was fear of the consequences. Although there was no such thing as 'criminal conversation' in Scottish law, a husband could nevertheless sue a 'seducer' of his wife for damages. In the 1794 case of William Darling, manufacturer in Calton of Glasgow, against Janet Watt, a material witness deponed that Janet's lover, George Dobson (another manufacturer in Calton of Glasgow) gave him money to leave the country but the witness then received a letter advising him 'that Dobson had got a line from the Pursuer declaring that he would not insist for damages against Dobson in case he the Deponent would return to the country which Dobson wished him now to do'. Then there was the 1802 case of Alexander Moubray, mariner in Limekilns, Fife, against Janet Scott, guilty of adultery with William Hutton, who fathered her child while her husband was away at sea. When she tried to put up defences, his lawyer answered that there was plenty of evidence that Hutton was the father of her child: 'Nay so conscious is Mr Hutton of his guilt, with the Defender Janet Scott, that he has offered to compromise an action of damages brought against him before this court at the instance of Mr Moubray and his attorney'. Finally, in the 1828 case of Alexander Dingwall Jr, merchant in Aberdeen, against Isabella Mathieson, one of her lovers, Alexander Milne Jr, merchant, admitted meeting her in houses of bad fame. After being cautioned and asked about connection with her in those houses he 'declared that he was not very willing to answer it for fear of being brought to trouble, and upon being shown a letter from the pursuer to his agents authorising them to pass from all claim of damages against any witnesses in a similar predicament, The witness signified his willingness to answer the question and Depones that he had connection with her in those different houses.'[35]

Most male paramours called as witnesses had no hesitation in utilising some version of the standard wording and answering the question, as in the 1789 case of Peter Williamson, printer in Edinburgh, against Jean Wilson. David Stephens, trunk maker, deponed 'That it consists with the deponents knowledge that Mrs Williamson the Defender has had carnal knowledge of a man different from her husband and Depones that his knowledge of the above circumstance is not derived from the information of others'. Or, in the 1795 case of John Hepburn, blacksmith in Kirkland near Leven, against Janet Hunter, Charles Monro, thread manufacturer in Canongate, deponed that 'it consists with the knowledge of the witness that within these two years a man different from the pursuer has had a carnal connection with the Defender, That he knows the Defender within these two years was delivered of a child, and that the man above alluded to, acknowledged himself to be the father of the child and has hitherto given it maintenance.' (Monro himself was, of course, that man.)[36]

A less sophisticated witness was James Walker in the 1817 case of Walter Henderson, block maker in Kincardine, against Janet Hamilton. Asked if he had been in the practice of visiting Janet he deponed, 'Ay, I have seen her o'er and o'er'. He admitted that her child was 'laid to me', and when asked if he knew that she had had carnal connection with a man different from the pursuer, he said, 'Yes I know she has had it with my self, but don't know that she has had it with any person else.' As time went on more witnesses answered the question straightforwardly. In the 1822 case of Alexander McBean, in Inverness-shire, against Ann Balfour, John McLean, wright, 'Interrogated if he the deponent had Carnal Connection with her Depones and answers I cannot deny but I entered her Bed Interrogated If the defender was in her Bed at the time Depones Affirmative'. And, finally, in the 1830 case of John Newbigging, gold beater in Canongate, against Margaret Walker, Sergeant Alexander McLeod said 'I know that I am at liberty to decline answering the question, but I do not decline acknowledging that I was in bed with the woman mentioned, and had twice connection with her before leaving the house next morning'.[37]

What about women paramours? Some did object to testifying. In the 1773 case of Euphemia Hepburn against Matthew Poole, baker in Canongate, it was proven by various witnesses that he had had a longstanding affair with Peggy Hawkins. When Peggy appeared before the court and was asked 'whether she knew that the defender during the Time Lybelled had Carnall dealings with a woman different from the Pursuer', she wanted 'to know who is the Person meant in the question and whether she the witness herself is comprehended under the Generality of a woman different from the Pursuer and if this last be the meaning of the Question declines answering the same and says she came here not to accuse herself'.[38] But this was quite unusual.

If a woman was well known to be cohabiting with a married man, then appearing in court to testify to this could do her no further harm. If she was a servant who had been exploited by him she might have been only too pleased to testify against him. And many women in such a situation would have borne a child to the man.

Prostitutes were frequently witnesses against clients. The testimony of Mary McLeod in Greenock must have been particularly galling for David Monro in the 1828 case of Agnes Smith against him. According to her statement, after she agreed to go to bed with him he 'took down his clothes and attempted to have knowledge of her person but was unable'. She 'was in bed with him for about ten minutes but was at length so provoked that she rose and ran out'. (Some weeks later he was more successful.)[39]

More examples of prostitutes as witnesses can be found in Chapter 8. An example of a servant willing to testify was Elizabeth Cameron in the 1830 case of Elizabeth Morton against William Caldwell, victualler in Gorbals of Glasgow. William's wife had left him, and witnesses deponed that a few weeks after Betty Cameron entered his service she appeared to be pregnant 'and said she would be Mrs Caldwell yet'. When a neighbour 'observed that that could not be as Caldwell was a married man . . . Betty Cameron appeared to be much struck and confused with this information'. When Betty appeared before the court she said that when she 'went to Caldwell's service she did not know that he was a married man and he expressly stated to her that he was not so – and that she did not know he was a married man at the time she first had connexion with him'. She had raised an action against him for inlying expenses and aliment for the child, which he had settled with her out of court, so she had nothing to lose by testifying.[40]

By 1809 (in the case of Mary Blair against Thomas Douglas) it had already been stated that 'if the persons with whom the party is accused of being guilty were not allowed to be brought forward as evidences the Pursuer may be bold to say that not one Divorce among ten would ever be proved'.[41] The statement is something of an exaggeration, but they were certainly key witnesses in many cases. However, the testimony of what witnesses had seen, heard or done was not the only evidence used to prove adultery, and in the next chapter we turn to other types.

NOTES

All CC references are in the Scottish Record Office.
1. Patrick Fraser, *Treatise on the Law of Scotland as applicable to The Personal and Domestic Relations* (Edinburgh, 1846), vol.1, 663.
2. cc8/5/2.
3. cc8/5/17; cc8/5/26.
4. cc8/5/37.
5. cc8/5/41.
6. Lawrence Stone, *Road to Divorce – England 1530–1987* (Oxford, 1992), 213–4.

7. cc8/5/3. Patrick did not confine his attentions to one woman. Another witness, Margaret Bowie, had 'been frequently assaulted with the defender for a Kiss of her and other favours . . . one night particularly without the house while it was Dark he took hold of her and strugled with her'. On another occasion he 'attempted to kiss her and putt his tongue in her mouth'.

8. cc8/5/6. Anne also came upon Isobell in the barn with another man, Robert Finlayson. He 'Immediatly got up, holding his Breetches in his hand which had been let down, and the Defender continued lying on her back with her cloaths up and the Deponent saw her Thighs and Legs naked'. Finlayson 'Turning to the Deponent spoke a great deal of filthy Language to her Telling the deponent he was ready for her'.

9. cc8/5/15.

10. cc8/6/49.

11. Stone, *Road to Divorce*, 217; Marjorie Plant, 'The Servant Problem in Eighteenth Century Scotland', *Scottish Historical Review*, vol.29 (1950), 143.

12. A somewhat different pattern appears in some aristocratic and upper gentry households, where a servant might have worked his or her way up from a lowly position to that of housekeeper or butler; such witnesses appear in later chapters and case studies.

13. cc8/5/3.

14. cc8/5/4.

15. cc8/5/19.

16. After plundering the house Isabel fled with Ireland and was known to have borne him two children in England. A neighbour deponed that 'on the day on which Isobell Carson and Ireland deserted the deponent thought in his own mind that an odd event was intended as he saw Ireland exposing his two Milk Cows at an improper time and at an under value he having provided provender for them during winter and his wife and numerous family having great need for them That the instant the rumour arose that the pursuer's wife was fled the deponent hastily said to John Ireland a brother of the said James Ireland with whom the deponent was in company that he would wager a guinea the pursuer's wife and James Ireland were fled off in company together and that they would never see their faces more'.

17. cc8/5/31.

18. A *neighbouring* servant added more damning evidence. Hannah Yeoman, 16, said that her mistress's kitchen window 'faced the window of the Back bed room of the Pursuer's house so that it was possible for a person to see from said kitchen into said bed room so as to observe distinctly any thing that was passing there'. One Sunday forenoon when she knew that Mr Mccall was at church she saw a man at the bedroom window 'with his breeches down & washing his privy parts.' She did not see Mrs Maccall in the room 'while the Gentleman was washing himself as above mentioned, but that she saw her come immediately after and carry away the Bason which the Gentleman had been using'. He was 'a fat tall man', and subsequently Mr Meek, 'a fat stout man', was pointed out to her, and he was 'apparently like the man whom she saw in the Pursuer's back bed room as above deponed to.' (Another witness deponed that Meek's 'nickname' was 'Mukle George'.)

19. cc8/6/164.

20. Neighbours were also the crucial witnesses in eighteenth-century Massachusetts, as demonstrated by Nancy F. Cott, 'Eighteenth-Century Family and Social Life Revealed in Massachusetts Divorce Records', *Journal of Social History* 10 (1976), 22–5.

21. cc8/6/35.

22. cc8/5/20.

23. cc8/5/28.

24. cc8/5/37.

25. cc8/5/9.

26. Ibid. Aitken was by no means the only witness against Emelia, for 'she attempted several times to entice the pursuers servants to have had carnal knowledge of her particularly Alexander Miller when riding severall times before her, she attempted to put her hand into his breeches, upon which he told her he would come off the horse in case she insisted', and 'she told Archibald Muir another of the pursuers servants, That he had got a word of being very kind to the women, and to be very good at it, And that it would be as good to deal with her as any woman, and she took up her coats to entice him.' And Alexander Godsman, travelling chapman in Glasgow, 42, once saw her 'in Company with a very young man, and that he and she and the deponent came out of the said house together and walked down the street together untill they came near the Cross when the young man and she parted, and the young man (it being in the dusk of the evening) touched upon the deponent, and turning aside his Coats showed the deponent his breeches open, and shirt out, and his privities exposed, Upon which he said to the deponent "She has been holding me by the prick, all the way we walked from the forsaid house".'

27. cc8/5/11. The witness declared that she 'received thanks from Mr George Chalmers but no other good deed or promise of good deed or Reward.'

28. cc8/5/20.

29. cc8/6/12.

30. cc8/6/14.

31. cc8/5/13.

32. cc8/5/16. John Macklean also declared that Ann had had intercourse with some of the men servants and 'likewise at different times asked the deponent to go to bed with her'. The case was nevertheless bitterly contested.

33. cc8/5/19. The content of the letter is revealed in the next chapter.

34. cc8/5/20.

35. cc8/5/21; cc8/5/26; cc8/6/157.

36. cc8/5/19; cc8/5/23.

37. cc8/6/113; cc8/6/133; cc8/6/166.

38. cc8/5/13.

39. cc8/6/157.

40. cc8/6/167.

41. cc8/5/30.

DUNDAS VS RANNIE – THE DESPOT DECEIVED

In 1778 Henry Dundas was Lord Advocate of Scotland, and in the years that followed he became the most powerful man in the country.[1] He married Elizabeth Rannie in 1765 when she was only fifteen, and his closest friend, Archibald Cockburn of Cockpen, married her sister three years later. They had several children, and though Elizabeth apparently complained of neglect by her husband there is no other indication that the marriage was not a stable one until, as a bolt from the blue, Dundas received a letter from his wife confessing infidelity.

On 11 October he was breakfasting at Arniston, his stepbrother's country house, with a fellow lawyer, James Newbigging, when the letter was delivered to him. He seemed to Newbigging 'to be in great agitation and having recovered himself a little read from part of the letter':

'Sir How much will you be amazed when on reading this Letter, you find it comes from one who is undeserving of being your wife or the mother to your unhappy Children – the Crime which I have committed and the Consciousness of my Guilt (which I know cannot be hid) now Compells me to leave you and my Children for ever; – before this reaches you I shall be far from home, where I beg you may not pursue me as I never can again live with you as your wife, it will be of little or no consequence to bring me back: – if Sir you wish to know the whole circumstances of this unhappy story Mr Colt at Inveresk will inform you of *every particular*: – The distracted situation of my mind, and the horrors of what I have done has now drove me to despair: I bid you an Eternal Adieu think Sir no more of a wretch, whose ingratitude to you is sufficiently punished by the Guiltiness of her Conscience; which must ever torment and embitter every moment of her Life. Every soft word or look which you gave or said to me since I came home only served to aggravate my crime and drive a thousand daggers to my heart – and whilst I viewed you with horror I wondered at myself how I could carry on the deceit with such seeming composure and cheerfulness – I now go Sir thrown out with infamy upon the wide world, without friends, or assistance of any kind – God only knows what is to become of me, or where I am going to: – farewell farewell I can write no more'.

Elizabeth certainly had a taste for self-dramatisation, but at the time her husband received the letter she was, in fact, still in their Edinburgh town house in George

Square, so before going on to discover what happened at Mr Colt's house we will continue with the events of 11 October after the delivery of the letter. Elizabeth told Robert Moffat, the butler, about the letter and asked him 'to go and take a room for her', because she feared that when he received the letter her husband would come to Edinburgh, and she was afraid to see him. Moffat had heard from his wife, who was Elizabeth's maid, what had happened at the Colts, so he understood why his mistress 'appeared to be in Confusion', but 'he declined to hire the room saying that he did not know whether it would be right to do so but that he would inform Mr Cockburn the sheriff as her nearest relation and desire him to come and speak with her'. Elizabeth 'said that Mr Cockburn was in the country and she did not want to see him'.

Moffat, showing a good deal of initiative, went to Archibald Cockburn's house (he was not in the country) and told him that Elizabeth was going to send for a post chaise to carry her off. Cockburn 'immediately got out of bed hurried on his cloaths' and rushed round to George Square, 'with a resolution to prevent her if she was not gone and to follow her and bring her back if she was'. He went directly upstairs to her dressing room where he found her with her hat on taking a cup of tea. When he entered the room she 'said My God Mr Cockburn and seemed greatly surprised and disconcerted.' Cockburn 'after putting a little girl of the name of Marie out of the room' told Elizabeth that 'he was informed she was going to leave her house and begged to know the reason of it'. Elizabeth 'answered that she would not tell him'. Cockburn said that the previous evening Mr Newbigging had told him 'the reports that were going and therefore he would by no means Insist from her for a recital of a story which would be very disagreeable but he supposed these reports were the Cause of her Intention to leave her family'.

Elizabeth admitted that he 'was right in his conjecture'. Cockburn 'told her that it was highly improper for her to attempt any such thing and that she ought not to think of it'. Elizabeth was 'angry and said she had taken her resolution and all the world should not prevent her'. 'She seemed determined', so Cockburn 'told her that if she was Innocent her flying from her family would be highly injurious to herself and that if she was guilty her being permitted to do so might be productive of the greatest trouble and distress to her husband and all her connections'. Therefore he, Cockburn, 'was under the disagreeable necessity of letting her know that she would not be allowed to leave her house' if he 'could prevent it and therefore she had better lay aside all thoughts of any such scheme'. Elizabeth 'flung herself into her bed chamber seemingly in great rage', and bolted the door.

Eventually, by mentioning her sister's name, Cockburn managed to gain access and told her that 'he looked upon himself as placed in a very delicate and distressing situation that he was the husband of her sister and of consequence the person she would most naturally look to for advice but he was at the same time the near relation and most Intimate friend and companion of her husband'. 'On this occasion however' he 'would renounce his connection' with her husband 'and act only the capacity of her friend'. If she could furnish him 'with any defences sufficient to remove the appearances that were said to be against her he would strain every nerve for her protection'. Elizabeth 'said she had no defence and could look for no protection'. Cockburn then asked her 'in what manner this shocking business could be communicated to her husband', and she told him that she had already sent a letter in which she confessed and referred him to Mr Colt for more information.

Obviously Elizabeth was not going to contest a divorce action, and agreement was reached that her lover's name would not be mentioned so that she would be able to marry him afterwards. (Twenty years later the commissaries would not have allowed them to get away with that so easily.) He was in fact a Captain Faukener (referred to in the action simply as 'the officer'), about whom nothing further is known. Nor do we get any insights into the relationship between them, except that it had been going on for some months. During the summer Elizabeth had been on a ten-day jaunt around East Lothian, and 'the officer' had stayed at every house where Elizabeth stayed. Barbara McKinles, wife of Robert Moffat and maid to Elizabeth, carried letters from her mistress to the officer. On the crucial night she tried to prevent Elizabeth from writing by claiming, falsely, to have no wax to seal a letter.

The event that night was the second of two balls at Musselburgh. Elizabeth was to sleep at the house of Oliver Colt of Aldhame, and the Honourable Mrs Helen Stewart, his wife, deponed that on the previous day the officer had called and asked if she could put him up on the night of the ball, and Mrs Colt 'agreed to give him a bed for the following night'. She was then informed by some of her younger daughters that before she and the company had returned from the ball, the officer had been trying to establish where all the guests were to sleep, 'and the young ladys said bless me Mama that officer expressed great curiosity to see all the rooms up stairs and they told her That he had been in all the different rooms and had asked who was to sleep in each of them'. Naturally this crass behaviour created suspicion, and 'Mademoiselle Pasque who lived in Mr Colt's family', 'having taken an alarm from some circumstances that had past at supper and from the officer above mentioned enquiring at some of the younger Miss Colts where the different persons in company were to sleep', she and some of the other guests went into the room opposite Elizabeth's, and kept a lookout: 'a little after two in the morning they saw the above officer in his night gown and slippers with a candle in his hand' go into Elizabeth's room.

Mrs Colt's sister, the Honourable Miss Margaret Stewart, had been told about the girls being asked by the officer to see all the rooms, 'which Mrs Colt thought was impertinent and was surprised at it'. After leaving Mrs Colt in her room Miss Stewart had gone to Miss Colt's room in the attic and on the way back she 'observed the light of a candle in the principal stair upon which the deponent started back being in ane undress'. 'The light approached', and she 'saw a person in a white dress like a night gown with untied hair with a candle in one hand and holding up the night gown with the other as if to intercept the light'. In the morning 'some of the children came into her room and said that some of the maids had seen a man in a white gown upon the stair or in the passage in the morning after they were gone to work,' but Miss Stewart 'did not chuse to ask the children questions upon the subject'. 'Upon comparing all circumstances' she was afraid that the man had gone into Elizabeth's room, 'tho' she had no certainty for her suspicion' and did not know either of them. But the chambermaids testified to their knowledge that the officer had spent the night with Elizabeth. Mrs Niccol, the cook, saw him at 5.30 in the morning and said 'addressing herself to the officer by name Is it you Captain I am sure you was to have slept below stairs to which he made no answer but went into his bed chamber'.

Later the same morning, in the coach on the way to Arniston, Elizabeth complained to her maid, Barbara, 'that it was the noisiest house she ever had been in for that she believed they had been sweeping the passage since five in the morning'. 'Taking Occasion from this', Barbara gave her mistress 'the Information she had got from Madam Pasque'. 'Good God watching me they were very Impertinent', responded Elizabeth, insisting that the officer 'did not come into my Room till about five o'Clock and did not stay above ten minutes adding that she had told him his coming there was very improper that he had come there to speak to her about some particular business and wished she would write to him concerning it'. She added that 'in going out of the room the officer started back and said he saw some body watching there', to which Barbara answered, 'Madam they will not tell they saw him when he went in and when he came out', and no more was said on the subject. But the next morning Elizabeth was up at five in the morning writing to the officer, and the following Sunday she gave Barbara a sealed letter addressed to her husband. After the letter was dispatched Elizabeth asked her maid 'whether she could get a Lodging to take on a Sunday', and when Barbara asked 'what she meant by enquiring for a Lodging' she said that she had written to her husband, 'and that as he would be home instantly she wished to get out of the way'. After which Moffat went to get Cockburn, and the rest we know. The case lasted only five weeks, and Dundas was granted his divorce on 21 November.

He took it badly, writing to a friend on the 24th, 'I know not what time and business may do, but at present I feel nothing upon my mind but a settled gloom and melancholy.' He did eventually remarry, but not for another thirteen years. As the injured party he had all the sympathy. Sir Alexander Dick noted in his diary on the 29th: 'Lord Advocate divorced last week from his criminal wife, and she married soon after to the man who caused it, a vile scandalous affair on her part and his, who is now saddled with her and will probably soon suffer by her.'[2]

We do not know if Captain Faukener suffered, but Elizabeth Rannie certainly did. Six years later, in November 1784, she wrote from Berkeley Square, London, to her son's tutor, Professor Bruce: 'after I have been a little while at Bath and recovered my health, I mean to dismiss my servants, come back to Town, and put myself as an apprentice to some Mantua-maker, or Milliner'. She knew that he would 'think me mad after reading this letter, but is it not better to work for my daily bread, than submit to live with a brute!' She planned to leave Captain Faukener soon, and looked forward to it 'with as much eagerness, as a school boy does, to the day he is to leave school'. Having signed the letter 'ER', she added: 'You see I have not signed EF which I shall never to do again'.

She spent the next two years in Paris and then wrote to Professor Bruce during a brief visit to London of her wish to settle in England, 'but Mr D won't hear of it': 'Upon my complaining to the Duke of B[uccleuch] of the treatment I had met with, from those who should have done everything in their power to make me easy and happy, he answered with a sort of triumph and contempt had you followed my advice and never left your house in Berkeley Sq, your situation would have been different; now you must make the best of it you can; you may exist upon your income, but as for enjoying any degree of comfort thats totally impossible – such a speech as this, I own cut me to the heart and soul, and now I so sincerely repent my going abroad, that I am often tempted to try and return to those with whom I used to live. If I do anything that is wrong, or derogatory to that character which I wish to maintain on account of my children, they have nobody to blame but themselves; necessity will in all probability force me into a very different line of life, especially as the D of B let me understand, that I need not apply again to any of my friends, as they were quite determined to give me no further support – What I have done to deserve this cruel change God only knows.'[3]

It is hard to feel much sympathy for such a silly woman. It says much for Dundas that in spite of her deceiving him with another man, and a divorce which pronounced her legally dead, her ex-husband was still giving her money. Presumably he allowed her to return to Britain when the French wars began, and in fact she long outlived him. In 1838 when her great-grandson, Sir Robert Dundas of Arniston, succeeded to the estate, he noticed that an annuity was paid to a Mrs Faukener in Cornwall. There Elizabeth Rannie had spent the remainder of her life, never seeing her husband or children again. Sir Robert continued the payment of her annuity until her death in 1847, aged 98.[4]

cc8/5/15

1. See Michael Fry, *The Dundas Despotism* (Edinburgh 1992).
2. Cyril Matheson, *The Life of Henry Dundas First Viscount Melville 1742–1811* (London 1933), 51.
3. Letters of Elizabeth Rannie to Professor Bruce, Scottish Record Office GD152/104/15/1 and 5. I am grateful to David Brown for advising me of the existence of those letters.
4. Matheson, *The Life of Henry Dundas*, 51.

CHAPTER 3

PROVING ADULTERY – OTHER TYPES OF EVIDENCE

The mainstay of any divorce action was what witnesses saw and heard, but four other kinds of evidence appear frequently enough to deserve a chapter to themselves. These are: 1. a confession of adultery, 2. revealing letters to or from the adulterous parties, 3. the birth of a child, and 4. venereal disease.

CONFESSIONS

'Confession alone is not sufficient evidence of the fact of adultery', wrote Patrick Fraser; 'without this restriction, there would be no check to the collusion and imposition that might be practised on the Court.'[1] But, of course, confession always appeared in conjunction with other evidence. Formal confessions are almost entirely a feature of the early period, when kirk sessions were still active, and the striking thing about them is not the possibility that they might have been collusive, but the way in which parties contesting a divorce tried to argue away such crucial evidence.

This is shown in one of the first cases in the records, that of John Ker, merchant burgess of Edinburgh, against Cecill Scott, in 1691.[2] When they married, in September 1690, Cecill was already 'five moneths and three weeks gone with Child to John Lesley writer in Edinburgh', and she continued to meet her lover afterwards. On 24 January 1691 in presence of a baillie, two ministers, two elders of the North Kirk session and the session clerk, she confessed that Lesley was the father of her child, and that she had committed adultery with him. Although they had had secret meetings, they had never been seen in the act, so her lawyers fought back hard. They said that

No regard ought to be had to the said pretended Confession, because it is altogether extrajudiciall, as being made by the Petitioner only before ane Baillie of Edinburgh, and some Neighbours in the said John Ker his own house, where he was personally present, against all law, reason and custome, which was done by him some few dayes after the Petitioner was brought to bed; for no man who understands law, will say it was in the power of John Ker a privat Citizen to erect a judicial Court in his own house for examining his wife's imaginary guilt of Adultery; That upon her Confession she might be found guilty of the same and he Divorced from her.

They also claimed that the 'pretended' confession had been extorted from her 'partly by her husband's fair words, and partly by his threatnings' at a time when she had not fully recovered from childbirth. After the birth 'she was sett to an outter cold Room, by ane unnatural and more than brutish Cruelty upon the seventh or eight day after her delivery; she was watched as a witch, and tortured by the hourly terrors of his rage. So that if threatnings, loss of liberty, bad usage, superadded to maritall reverence, be just Causes of fear, then here was the most powerfull concussion imaginable.'

Ker's lawyers refuted the arguments and denied those allegations. The confession had been sworn under oath before a baillie and two elders who had been delegated by the kirk session for that purpose, which made it 'as solemne and effectual as if made befor the Kirk Session or presbytery seeing it is the Judge and Clerk, and their Assistants, and not the bare place or bank that makes a Confession Judiciall'. Far from torturing her after the birth, Ker treated her 'with greater Indulgence than could have been expected, for what severity both the law of God and the Civill law do allow to a husband against a wife, whom he married for a maid, and finds to be a whore, is notourly known'. Yet 'the most he did, was to separat her, not out of his house, but to another Chamber from his bed and Company. And all the promises he ever made to her were to Invite her to Confess her sin, upon which if she would Confess within Doors, it might have been told her, that he should not bring her publickly befor the Church, which was both fair and reasonable.' The commissaries found the allegations of threats or force 'not sufficient and relevant to infer a just fear' and allowed the case to proceed. There was sufficient additional evidence to convince the commissaries that she was guilty, and to grant Ker his divorce.

In the last chapter we saw the evidence of witnesses in the 1737 case of Peter Rolland, merchant and late baillie of Dunfermline, against Christian Dalgleish, guilty of adultery with James Beatie, tobacconist, but there was also a confession by her, and her lover, before both the regality court and kirk session.[3] Her lawyer argued in a similar fashion to the earlier one, that her husband

had partly by severe threats and menaces partly by the grossest Imposition upon the petitioner who was a poor weak woman prevailed upon her indeed rashly to sign a confession clandestinely in her own house at a meeting of the session and likeways of the Regality Court held there pro re nata That although the petitioner was assured a Thousand times in the most solemn manner by her husband that he wanted that confession only to pacifie his rage and that it should never operate against her in any manner whatsomever and that indeed she consented principally upon Misinformation of the nature of the thing and to prevent the threats of his passion which had grown the length of madness.

Rolland's procurator pointed out that Rolland was actually away from home when the confession was made before the kirk session. And secondly,

> By what compulsion was Mr Beaty her Gallant brought to concurr with her in that fable He at that time had beyond expectation been settled in a house in the Toun of Dunfermline had got a considerable stock of Tobaccos upon hand with a ware house and other conveniencys for manufactoring and vending the same and yet he in that raising and floorishing situation out of a sense of his guilt and ingratitude to his former master confessed his crime with a seeming penitence removed his goods in a secret and clandestine manner from his house and fled from and abandoned his country and the comfortable settlement he had in that Town of Dunfermline.

And, as we saw in the previous chapter, witnesses had seen and heard more than enough to convince the commissaries that the confession was genuine and adultery had been committed.

The Church insisted on confession and repentance in order to 'purge' a sin. The extent to which this became internalised is graphically illustrated in the 1752 case of Archibald Park, tenant in Berwickshire, against Marion Inglis. Marion, who no longer slept with her husband, found herself pregnant by her lover, John Wightman, and tried to procure herbs to abort the child. When that failed she decided to flee, but before doing so she told her servant, Isobell Mercer, 'that she could not go away untill she got the session clerk to make her Confession to him'. Isobell brought the session clerk, but after she confessed to him he 'told her he could not be answerable to let her go untill she appeared and made her Confession before the Kirk session, and Immediately thereafter the same day she being called before the Kirk session, she Compeared in the Ministers Manse before two Elders . . . and Repeated her said Confession, which was wrote by the said session clerk'.[4]

Later in the century the system of church discipline fell apart, and therefore formal confessions before a court no longer formed part of the evidence, but written confessions still cropped up from time to time, as in the 1780 case of Peter Dalgliesh, distiller at Finniestown near Glasgow, against Christian McMurtrie. Her lover, Charles Tweedale, had fled when their affair became known, and her husband 'proposed her signing an acknowledgment of her Guilt to which she agreed'. When it was drawn up and she came to sign it 'she appeared unwilling and gave for reason that she was affraid it might hurt her but signed it upon her Brother in law's saying that he should be Caution it would not hurt her'. Peter 'said to her that it would make it easier for him as to the proof in the process of Divorce', and the money that he reckoned her signing the paper would save him he gave her instead. This civilised behaviour was not considered collusive since the adultery had long since been committed, so that simply facilitating a divorce process was acceptable, though obviously there was other evidence as well.[5]

Such formal written confessions are rare, but as a form of evidence they are not very different from letters written by the guilty spouse admitting the adultery, and those are relatively common.

LETTERS

Letters – to husbands, wives, or lovers – are transcribed in full in the records and are quoted from extensively in this book, because they contain the original words, unfiltered through the court's clerk, of those who wrote them.

Letters from wives to husbands after their adultery was discovered are amongst the most poignant. In 1788 Veronica Hay, whose adultery with Mr Renton was so much disapproved of by the servants in the last chapter, wrote to her husband, William Ker: 'My tears fall so fast that I can hardly hold the pen – tomorrow I shall bid you adieu for ever May you be happy, God bless my dear Children'. (After leaving she wrote to one of the servants: 'does my sweet Children ever speak of their unhappy mother they never are one moment absent from my thoughts – how does your master hold out, give my best wishes to the rest of the servants tell them I wish them more happiness than has fallen to the share of your late Mistress.')[6]

In a case of 1811, while Andrew Bogle Esquire, merchant in Kingston, Jamaica, was away in the West Indies, his wife, Mary Stirling, was guilty of adultery with the Honourable Henry Stanhope, son of the Earl of Harrington. The servants all came to know of it, so Mary left Scotland for Cheltenham with the children before her husband's arrival home, and wrote him a lengthy letter at that time. A few extracts will give the flavour, which is clearly derived from the popular sentimental novels of the time, however sincerely felt:

> The dreadful hour is come – the last sad duty I have now to perform ere I quit this house for ever is to write you. Oh! God – will not my trembling hand refuse to trace these lines? will not my heart quite break as I pronounce the fatal words which cast me off from you for ever? . . . Some other pen than mine must tell my dreadful story – but none shall *accuse* me to you before *myself* . . . Your children are safe and well – and happy. Once I was all they are, and I too was innocent – Oh! God oh! God do not let a wretch like me murder your peace for ever – you have comforts, *many* joys in store for you in our children – live for *them* – support existence for their sakes – they will reward you oh! most amply and think of their unprotected state – they can have no *mother* now – O! God and who has robbed them of a fond a doating one – She, she herself – even nature shrinks from guilt like hers.[7]

By this time many Scotswomen at lower social levels were literate and capable of writing letters, though their spelling would be more erratic and they would naturally write in simpler terms. In a case of 1814 Janet Forrest fell pregnant while her husband, William Dobie, was away as a private soldier, and he brought a divorce action on the poor's roll. She wrote him a letter as soon as she knew she was pregnant, telling him how it happened. The man had been her first foot at Hogmanay, and he and two others stayed for hours. At five in the morning

> the subtill villain pretended to fall asleep and his wife begged I would let him stay till he awaked I have too much occation to reflect upon and will while I live but I never had the smallest suspistion that the Wrech intended any Evil towards me till it is now too late and God only knows what I suffered in my Mind before I knew the miserable condition I am in which the thought of is like to drive me to Distraction.

In a second letter she wrote: 'all I can say it never was my Incklination nor out of my Disregard to you it happened whatever you may think I beg of you my Deir Husband to Pardon and forgive what is past which if you do not I may safely say there is not a more miserable Wrech on Earth'.[8]

In an 1818 case, while Thomas Thomson, butler, was abroad serving his master, his wife, Catharine Janet Gasson, became pregnant by a fellow servant. Afterwards she wrote to her husband:

> I have long felt the greatest desire to write to you yet scarcely know how to address you or how to implore that pardon I am so anxious to obtain I am ashamed and truly sensible of my misconduct and guilt but could you have known what I have suffered and what I still do and ever must suffer I am sure you would feel compassion for me . . . however long I may live I shall never again know happiness Oh then take pity on me and say you forgive me to obtain your forgiveness is the first wish of my heart and there is nothing I would not do to obtain it . . . I conjure you by the affection you formerly bore me by the affection you feel for *our* Child not only to pity but to forgive me . . . I take every care possible of our Child who is indeed my only comfort, yet dearly as I love him the sight of him generally causes me the deepest sorrow and fruitless regret.[9]

What about men? Did their letters ever feature in the evidence? Yes, very occasionally they did, but the tone was always very different from those of women.

For example, Donald MacDonald, who had been servant to the Earl of Kellie, impregnated a fellow servant, Betty Brown. (Betty deponed that 'she did not know till very lately' that Donald was a married man.). His letter to his wife Jean began by explaining that he would have written sooner but had expected to be in Edinburgh, and then asked how she 'and Little Mary' were. He promised to send 'whatever money you want'. And by the way: 'I was engaged with Mr Erskine till Martinmas next But I am sorry to inform you I got one of the maids with Child and on that account I expect to be put off at the term I hope you will be so good as let none of your friends know nothing about this'. However, others clearly did already know, for Donald added that he had received a letter from her brother who 'could not [have] used me worse though I had been a tin seler'. He did not contest Jean's divorce action in 1799.[10]

Then there were the letters of John Cobban to his wife, Robina Hill, in an 1830 case. After they were married in Dunfermline in 1824 they agreed not to cohabit until John had found himself a good position. He went to England and wrote affectionate letters to her, and when he returned in 1827 they cohabited for a few weeks. He then told her that he had to return briefly to England and when he 'was about to step on board the smack at Leith for London, he disclosed to the Complainer a fact which he had previously concealed Viz[t] that he had, since his marriage, been carrying on an adulterous intercourse with another woman in London . . . by whom he had or was about to have, a child begotten and born in adultery'. When he was back in England he wrote:

> There is one I have injured that I esteem one hair of her head of more value than all your body. She has been truly kind to me and I shall return it as far as lies in my power, for I love her as I do my life, which is as much as to say I have no love for you and really I have not, for what little I did have for you, your vile temper has completely blasted. Therefore I am resolved not to live with you, for I would live a most uncomfortable life with you, and were you to press me to live with you I should never sleep with you, for I have taken an oath never to sleep with you till I have brought up my child, and even then nothing but force could make me live with you, but you should never force me to sleep with you.[11]

After Robina brought her action before the commissary court John apparently expressed contrition and asked her forgiveness (which she did not grant). But these sentiments were nowhere reflected in his letters, nor in any example of a man's letter, in contrast to the many pleas and repentances penned by wives.

A different kind of evidence used in divorce actions was the intercepted love letter. 'The letters of the parties are important adminicles of evidence,' wrote Fraser, 'and are frequently the means by which a key can be given to suspicious and equivocal proceedings.'[12] What he meant was evidence to the court – but they were even more powerful instruments of evidence to suspicious or unsuspecting husbands.

In the 1788 case of William Ker against Veronica Hay, featured earlier in this section and also in the previous chapter, the adulterous couple used a local man to deliver their letters, for which he received from Veronica 'a trifle of money and a few shillings from Mr Renton'. His conscience bothered him, so he held on to one letter, telling Veronica that he had burnt it, and 'went to Captain Smith at Hare', who was a friend of Ker's, 'to whom he imparted his receiving the letter', and at same time told Captain Smith 'all he knew relating to the intercourse' between Veronica and Mr Renton. Captain Smith approved of his intention of delivering the letter to Ker – and the game was up. All that the letter said was: 'my Love Ruin is certain we have been both seen and my staying so late has been the Cause, My Servants on the watch, how often did I beg you to let me go, yet still your love got the better of your prudence'.[13]

Love letters are of particular interest when tied in with other evidence about the individuals and relationships in question, and therefore feature in various cases covered in later chapters (and see Case Studies 2 and 9). But an example that is not featured anywhere else appears in the case of George Prestoun, chirugeon (surgeon) in Edinburgh against Mary Boghurst. As it was one of the earliest cases – 1696 – Mary's language to her lover, Charles Campbell (son of the late Earl of Argyll), is archaic, but the sentiments are echoed by countless later women. 'My Dear', she wrote, 'thou fillest my soul with raptures of joy inexpressable, and gives me life, who without thee cannot live . . . a thousand times this night I wisht thee in my arms, but alace in vain I sought for heaven . . . Tho' within this prison my body is confined for a time, my heart is ever with thee, that can nothing separate till I cease to be no more, thou art in my thoughts all day, and dreams all night'.[14]

It was virtually always in male-initiated divorce cases that love letters were used as evidence. In the 1809 case of Andrew Handyside, merchant in Edinburgh, against Isabella Pender, her lover wrote her only one letter, but it was her downfall.[15] During the summer, while Isabella's husband was in London, Isabella began an affair with an advocate, Mr William Rose Robinson. She would even call her servant to the window when he passed, saying he was her 'beau', and one day she 'took a visiting Card out of her pocket on which there was the name of Robinson and having kissed the Card said it was a Sweet Card to her.' On the nights she went to meet her lover she 'dressed herself particularly well and used to rouge and paint'. In the autumn Mr Robinson wrote her a letter to let her know that he had to go to the north. Isabella 'frequently read it and shewed it' to her servant, and 'said it was a sweet letter.' Some time later the letter went missing, and she was very anxious about it.

Her anxiety proved well-founded, for her husband, having read it, asked friends to watch her movements. After her next rendezvous with her lover she returned very agitated and said to her servant, 'Bell I'll not be long your Mistress now I have been detected by eight ruffians with Mr Robinson in a bed room in a house at the head of the Canongate.' She 'expressed great distress but said she was not so sorry for herself as for Mr Robinson as it would ruin him in the way of his business and that he had said to her "I told you always Isabella that that letter would play damnation with me if you did not burn it".' She also told another servant that the missing letter was obviously 'the cause of her being detected . . . that Mr Robinson had often told her to put it away but she could not think of doing it.' And what did the letter say? Unlike the one above (and those featured in later chapters), it was not particularly passionate. He began by advising her that he would have to go to the north for three or four weeks:

I know not Isabella how you measure time but with me it either gallops or stands still according to existing Circumstances Now I do protest that these self same three or four weeks have a very formidable appearance and I must e'en muster all my stock of patience, a virtue with which it unfortunately happens, I am but scantily endowed . . . Do write me like a sweet girl and I hereby promise you never to 'flatter' you (as you call it) I shall never tell you that you are handsome nor sweet nor anything of the sort This I am sure will please you and all that I ask in return is that you will let me know how you are and what you are about . . . When I have read your letter (if you honour me so far) I shall burn it to prevent accidents and it will be right that you use a similar precaution as to this.

But, of course, she did not, and one can understand why, for to a woman in love that really would have been a very 'sweet' letter.

If letters were used as evidence mainly in male-initiated cases, one might have supposed the same to be true of children conceived in adultery, and indeed we have seen earlier in this chapter examples of wives in that situation. However, as we saw in the last chapter, the mothers of married men's bastards did not scruple to testify against them, so in fact that form of evidence was much more evenly distributed between the sexes.

CHILDREN

Maurice Lothian, a legal commentator, cited several cases where a man returned from abroad to find his wife either pregnant or with a new child, which was conclusive evidence of adultery.[16] As far as kirk sessions were concerned, unless a couple were actually seen in the act by a number of concurring witnesses, a pregnancy was the *only* proof of adultery. Legally a child borne by a married woman was not a bastard, and some men and women tried to argue from that point.[17] But whenever it was proved that the husband could not have fathered the child, a divorce was always granted.

Out of the 367 successful male-initiated cases, 105 – 29 per cent – involved the wife bearing another man's child. Particularly during the war years many of those cases involved the classic scenario of a husband coming home to find his wife with a child. But there were also a number of cases where the couple had been separated for years, the wife cohabiting and bearing a family to another man. When the husband wanted to remarry he could point to the second family as proof that his wife had been unfaithful to him. Bastard children fathered by adulterous husbands featured in 102 cases out of the 290 female-initiated actions, at 35 per cent a higher proportion of the whole. Many of those were men impregnating their servants, but there were also some in stable second relationships.

The unusual aspect of the 1769–70 case of John Pierie against Isabella Backie was that Isabella was a 'lady', the daughter of William Backie of Hoy, in Orkney, and that her adultery was committed with James Frazer from Caithness, 'a Tinker or Smith who wrought in Silver and Copper'. A witness deponed that she had challenged Isabella 'smartly why she that was a Gentlewoman was so silly as to allow Donald Frazer the Liberty of Breakfasting dining and supping with her', but the witness had not then realised that Isabella was with child. She, 'to conceal her shame among her Friends left the Orkneys and came to the Town of Peterhead', where she had her child. John was a master's mate and was able to produce certificates of the ships he served on all through that period, proving that 'the said Child must of necessity be an adulterous Bastard'. When he returned home he went to Peterhead in search of his wife; afterwards Isabella told her landlady that her husband 'needed not have come to see her for she had wrote him long before that the child was not his and of her whole Misfortune'.[18]

An 1805 case with the classic scenario is that of Joseph Green against Elizabeth Nisbet. Joseph was a surgeon, and he too served on board ship. He returned home 'with the single intention of visiting his wife and settling her comfortably during his absence on another voyage which he is soon to set out upon; but to his distress and mortification found that she was great with child and upon the point of delivery.' She had been living with her father in Musselburgh and apparently 'had been seduced' by one of the officers stationed there. (He was, in fact, a Major Sibbald, and maintained the child from the time of its birth.) David Tait, a friend, deponed that when Joseph arrived back in Musselburgh 'he sent for the deponent to the house of one Moir a vintner in Musselburgh' and asked him to bring his wife there, 'as he declined going to the house himself on account of some bad usage he had formerly received' from Elizabeth's mother. Tait went to Elizabeth, and when he informed her of her husband's arrival 'she said God forbid and refused to go to him'. Tait therefore returned to Joseph and 'reluctantly informed' him that his wife was pregnant. Joseph 'received this account with great emotion, and was with much difficulty prevailed on to go and see her.' He raised the divorce action immediately after that.[19]

What about men who fathered bastard children? We will see many of those in Chapter 8 – and also in Case Studies 3 and 12 – but some examples may be given here. In the 1813 case of Margaret Hay against James Herbertson, wright in Glasgow, the key witness was 19-year-old Elizabeth Cairns, who deponed that 'a carnal connection took place between them', in consequence of which she became pregnant and had a child. After that she tried to get him 'to take away the Child and put it to nurse but he rather declined this and urged the deponent to nurse it herself and promised to give her money when necessary'. Elizabeth's father 'caused a process to be raised in her name' against James, and she was informed that a decreet had been obtained against him. 'Being further interrogated whether she has had any carnal intercourse with . . . James Herbertson since the birth of the foresaid Child?', she replied that 'she has had such connection and that she has been living in family with him and keeping his house since the month of February last and further depones that she left her fathers house when said Child was about five months old and the Child continues to be kept in her fathers house and the defender pays aliment for the Child to her father.'[20]

A more typical example of a man who had set up a second household can be seen in the 1822 case of Catherine Waddell Boyd against James Shortridge, baker in Maxwelton. The couple, having married in 1810, had actually separated in 1813, since which time he had been living with Susan McLachlan, who had borne him three children. Catherine was able to provide details of the births of the children, who were 'known and called by the name of Shortridge and on such footing did the Defender live with the said Susan McLachlan that she was occasionally believed to be Mrs Shortridge the wife of the Defender and so truly did the Defender himself believe that he was the Father of these Children, that he was in use to call the attention of various persons to the likeness, particularly of the boy, to himself.'[21]

In the days before adequate contraception, adultery always carried the risk of begetting a child. It also carried another risk, one which also affected both sexes in divorce cases.

VENEREAL DISEASE

Legal commentators did not refer to this form of evidence as one of the proofs of adultery, but it cropped up in thirty-six different cases in our period. Bill Bynum writes that urethral or vaginal discharges, gonorrhoea and syphilis 'were often assumed to be either stages in, or varieties of, what was the same category of disease', and that 'most writing in the period referred simply to "the venereal disease" as a blanket category to describe all of these conditions,' although it *was* known that syphilis, or the 'pox', could be cured by mercury.[22] Bynum's comments are entirely applicable to the evidence in divorce records.

In the 1766 case of Isobell Thomson against John Lawrie, flesher in Edinburgh, Lawrie admitted that both he and his wife were 'affected with a Distemper which the pursuer is pleased to call Venereal' but tried to argue that it should

> not be inferred from thence that the Defender contracted the same by Adulterous Converse with other Lewd and Wicked Women or afford any Foundation for a Process of Divorce against the Husband because in such cases it is possible that the husband has catched the Distemper from his Wife as that she was Infected by him besides it is well known that there is a Possibility of being infected with a venereal Distemper otherwise than by Carnall dealings so this is but a flimzy Foundation for Pretending to dissolve the Marriage on the head of Adultery.

Isobell's lawyer agreed that it was not in itself sufficient evidence, 'but when it is Joined with other Facts and Circumstances sett furth in the Lybell which the pursuer undertakes to Prove there cannot then remain the least doubt of the Defenders Adultery and that it was by these Adulterous Practises that he gott the Distemper'. The proof was not difficult, as witnesses had seen him in bed with another woman, and he told them that she 'had given him the Clapp and wished that he had never seen her Face for that she was the Ruin of his Family'. Isobell got her divorce.[23]

When venereal disease was part of the evidence, doctors were invariably called to testify. In the 1774 case of Rachel Forbes against John Sharp, John Shiells, surgeon in Edinburgh, when consulted by Sharp to cure him of the venereal disease was told that 'he had been engaged in some unlawfull amours in which he had got the venereal infection'. Alexander Bruce, surgeon in Musselburgh, had been consulted by Rachel, but when she first came to him 'she seemed to be ignorant what her distemper was'. (Sharp also infected a servant woman, who 'upon that account went to the Royal Infirmary where she was cured of the said disease'.) In the 1807 case of Agnes Peacock against Alexander Teviotdale, an apothecary testified that Alexander had asked him to attend his wife. She 'was at that time under a course of mercury which her husband informed the Deponent he had procured from an acquaintance and given her in pills', and, 'having taken too great a quantity incautiously her face became swelled and a discharge of saliva from the mouth and she was almost speechless when the deponent was called in.' Alexander told him 'he had had the venereal disease himself and had given it to his wife for which he gave her these pills as they had cured himself.' When the apothecary saw her 'the disease for which the pills were given had been checked and the Deponents prescriptions were those that were required to remove the illness caused by the over quantity of mercury.' Another wife infected was Agnes Young who, in 1827, brought a divorce action against her husband, James Wilson; the surgeon deponed that her child died as a consequence of the disease.[24]

However, it was not only adulterous husbands who were infected, for adulterous wives ran the same risk. In the 1780 case of Ebenezer Whyte, weaver in Paisley, against Elizabeth Kennedy, the surgeon (John Shiells again) said that Elizabeth 'had a sore throat which the deponent considered as venereal and ordered for her mercurial pills and other proper medicines which were continued for some time', and that her child was also infected. Her landlady deponed that Elizabeth told her the 'distemper had been communicated to her' by her lover, John Pattison, 'who had got it in England'. Elizabeth 'acknowledged to her that Mr Pattison was the first who ever had carnal knowledge of her besides her husband after her marriage'. In this case the effects were grave, for 'having left Edinburgh and returned to Paisley before her cure was affected the strength of the distemper increased to such a degree that she soon thereafter lost her sight and has been blind ever since.'[25]

In the 1789 case of Peter Williamson, printer in Edinburgh, against Jean Wilson, the surgeon deponed that Jean 'complained to him that she was not well and had sores about her private parts which on inspection the deponent immediately perceived to be venereal shankers'. He 'immediately put her under a course of mercury', and six weeks later she declared that 'she was completely cured'. He added that she 'seemed exceedingly unwilling to believe that her disorder could possibly be venereal'. A servant was told by a friend not 'to allow any of the children to drink or take any thing out of the same cup' as Jean, and also said that the 'illness rendered her [Jean] both deaf and hoarse for a considerable time'. Another infected wife was Helen Fisher in Perthshire who, in 1791, was divorced by her husband, David Craw. Her lover, Robert Kinnear, farmer at Kinnaird, told an acquaintance that 'he had had carnal knowledge of Mrs Craw and had given her the bad disorder'. Craw was heard to say 'in presence of his wife that he bore the effects of her Connection with other men'. At any rate, he had no difficulty in obtaining his divorce.[26]

We have now had examples of the different kinds of evidence that made up the proof in a divorce case. But no matter how damning the evidence was, there were always lawyers willing to defend guilty partners. How they attempted to do so forms the subject of the next chapter.

NOTES

All cc references are in the Scottish Record Office.

1. Patrick Fraser, *Treatise on the Law of Scotland as applicable to The Personal and Domestic Relations* (Edinburgh 1846), vol.i, 662.
2. cc8/5/1.
3. cc8/5/4.
4. cc8/5/9. As with previous confessions, there was plenty of other evidence as well, including the fact that 'the defender was several times seen to put her hands into Wightmans Breeches, and draw out his Privities and sometimes pull down his Breeches.'
5. cc8/5/16.
6. cc8/5/19.
7. cc8/5/31.
8. cc8/5/33. After her child was delivered, Janet went 'into the Charity Work house of the Parish of Saint Cuthberts to reside' and was still there when the divorce action was brought.
9. cc8/5/36.
10. cc8/5/25.
11. cc8/6/167.
12. Fraser, *Treatise on the Law of Scotland*, 662.
13. cc8/5/19.
14. cc8/5/1.
15. cc8/5/30.
16. Maurice Lothian, *The Law, Practice and Style Peculiar to the Consistorial Actions Transferred to the Court of Session* (Edinburgh 1830), 175–6.
17. In the 1825 case of James Cairns against Ann Brooks, when Ann raised an action against her lover, a lawyer, for aliment for the child, he did not deny carnal connection with her, 'but rested on a preliminary plea in law, that as she was a married woman she was not entitled to maintain in law that any other person than her husband was the father of the said child, while the said Ann Brooks maintained that she had not been in company with or cohabited with the pursuer her said husband for four years prior to the said date of her said action.' cc8/6/145.

18. cc8/5/12.
19. cc8/5/28.
20. cc8/5/33.
21. cc8/5/40.
22. W. F. Bynum, 'Treating the Wages of Sin: Venereal Disease and Specialism in Eighteenth-Century Britain', in W. F. Bynum and R. Porter (eds), *Medical Fringe and Medical Orthodoxy, 1750–1850* (London, 1987), 13, 15.
23. cc8/5/11. An unusual feature of this case is that Isobell had previously obtained a legal separation from her husband in the commissary court. She said that at the time she had not known of his adultery; it seems much likelier that she had now met someone else she wished to marry.
24. cc8/5/14; cc8/5/29; cc8/6/154.
25. cc8/5/16.
26. cc8/5/19; cc8/5/20.

LOCKHART WISHART VS MURRAY – LETTERS AND SIGHTINGS

Mary Anne Murray was only sixteen and General James Lockhart Wishart of Lee and Carnwath over fifty when they married in 1770, so that when he brought his divorce action against her in June 1783 she had spent nearly half her life married to him. From a letter quoted below we know that she had children, but they do not figure in this case.

She (or, at any rate, her lawyer) declared: 'In paying his addresses to her he had the art to impress her with the notion that he tenderly loved her and on that account notwithstanding the inequality of their ages she formed to herself the prospect of living a happy life with him. In a short time however she found herself miserably disappointed. While he was acting the part of a lover he had assumed a temper by no means natural to him and it was with astonishment she discovered she had been deceived in this particular. She had believed him calm and placid but when his real temper appeared it was boisterous and ungovernable particularly towards his wife so that the whole period of the marriage has been a series of miserys and disquietude to her.'

She gave this example: 'Immediately after their marriage they went to make a visit to a Brother of the Generals who lives in Kintyre where the General fell into a violent fitt of passion with her leaving her in the hands of strangers whom she had never before seen when they had not been a week married. The reason of this proceeding was no other than his taking some exceptions at the stile of a letter which he himself had desired her to write, not many weeks after this the General thought proper to take a separate Bed from hers and from that time to this they have never slept in the same bed. He also deprived her totally of the management of her house so as not to leave her the power of giving directions to her servants in family affairs but took the whole upon himself or delegated them to others'.

The General denied mistreating her but not the substance of her allegations. 'In vain', declared Mary, 'did she endeavour to gain his affection by gentle behaviour and showing the greatest submission to him – the more she endeavoured to approach him the more distant he grew – In short after living a course of years in this manner her spirits has been quite broke her nerves destroyed and her health totally ruined'. In fact, she drowned her miseries with alcohol and drugs. Her lawyer tried to have everything connected with her drinking struck out of the record as irrelevant to the divorce; his lawyer responded that being drunk 'might be an additional motive or inducement in those who had a design upon her virtue to take advantage of her situation', and that drunkenness had featured as an ingredient in a number of other divorce cases. After an appeal by her to the Court of Session that court ruled that witnesses were not to be examined regarding drunkenness.

However, Mary's letters were retained as part of the evidence, and the two she wrote to her husband in April and August 1782 expressed penitence for her misconduct. In the first she promised never again to 'taste any sort of liquors but at table and in your presence and then very sparingly I had made this resolution before and now bind myself once more by every sacred tie should you again restore us to happiness'. She did not keep it, and her second letter is much more painful to read: 'I am sensible to what an abject state I have brought myself spurned by you detested by my acquaintances and ridiculed by my servants I have no hopes but you to regain my Character Have therefore pity on me . . . I supplicate you in the names of your son your heir and of my daughter to soften towards their mother. I know after having broke the most sacred ties of honour you have no occasion to believe me that after the many scenes of drunkenness I have most unfortunately fallen into I have by my late infamous behaviour merited your hatred and disdain yet I dare once more entreat and supplicate you to lend me an assisting hand I despair of ever regaining your friendship or your affection. I have justly forfeited my right to both but yet do not leave me in this Sea of infamy to which I have Exposed myself accept my following vows and if ever I swerve from them may misery be my fate in the world and my hopes in this life hereafter be forever blasted If ever I taste spirituous liquors of any kind wines of any sort unless one or two Glasses at a time a meal If ever I use peppermint Laudanum or any such somniferous stupifying liquids may I be for ever miserable shut lock me up with the lowest groveling race and never restore me more to favour or to the world . . . I ask not your affections untill by penitence and a new behaviour I gain a title to them but restore me to some tranquillity procured by allowing me to appear and act as your wife to establish my lost reputation as I keep my word or break it may heaven pour down its Curses on the head of your once beloved but now miserably rejected wife'.

What is not at all clear is why the General brought his divorce action against his wife in 1783. The affair which formed the grounds for it occurred between 1775 and 1777 (on the Continent), and a second affair (for which there was much less evidence) apparently occurred in 1779. It is possible that the four crucial letters, which were found in her bedchamber, were only discovered at that time, and that the General, with such written evidence in his hands, then made enquiries and learned all about his wife's infidelity. It is also possible that he had had enough of her drinking and therefore used her adultery as a means of ridding himself of her. But this can only be conjecture.

The damning letters, unsigned and undated, were in the handwriting of Captain

Ewan Baillie, in the service of the East India Company, and her keeping such damning evidence for so many years is a good example of a woman's sentimental attachment to a lover's words in writing. Her lawyer claimed that 'The gentleman to whom these Letters are attributed . . . was a great acquaintance and constant companion of General Lockhart himself who invited him to stay with him for some time at his house at Dryden . . . She could not refuse to treat the friend of her husband with that attention that every Gentleman expects to be treated with'. Any other imputation was denied, a difficult claim to sustain in view of the contents of the letters.

In the first he wrote, 'Oh Mary disconsolate and inconsolable as I am what relieff could I not find in the arms of her who is so much Calculate for my Bliss and so capable herself of receiving enjoyment from the society of her Lover'. In the second: 'Mary my own Mary it is not in the power of human things ever to destroy our mutual confidence nor can ought but death ever interrupt our union it is for that I hope to live and for that I condescend to bear the hardships of fate and destiny otherwise otherwise Oh God – no more'. In the third: 'Mary it must be and for a time we must part our lott is prescribed prudence safety and self preservation on your part all, all require it and tear down natures Laws you wished to see me again and perhaps I might have promised it, but oh Mary I know your feelings I dread my own we should not and I dare not venture such an interview . . . oh sweet woman think of me as one who saw you with pleasure and has quit you with pain who lives for you and whose peace will be directed by your welfare'. When Captain Baillie went to India he gave her directions on where to write to him and where he would write to her and poured out his anguish at leaving her: 'I am ashamed to show you so bad an example of fortitude but tis not in my power to do otherwise one consolation to me from it is, the certainty that I love and live for you'.

Mary's lawyer argued that 'receiving or writing Letters are very different acts from those of infidelity to the marriage bed and therefore cannot found an action of Divorce,' and, moreover, that no letters were produced from Mary. But, in fact, a witness, Nicolas Lenain, who had been the General's cook (and whose evidence was interpreted by a French teacher in Edinburgh), deponed that a fellow servant, mysteriously known as L'Orange, showed him letters from Mrs Lockhart to Captain Baillie. The 'reason he gave for doing so was that the letters were written partly in French and partly in English and that he wanted the deponent to explain the English to him which he did not then understand'. It was 'from Captain Baillies imprudence in leaving his letters open about the room L'Orange got access to them', and Lenain remembered that 'the Letters contained strong Expressions of Love and the Expressions of my Love both in French and English and also complaints of the red Boy by whom he supposed the General was meant because he had often heard the same expression used . . . in these letters Mrs Lockhart Expressed her hopes to be happier some time than she was then'.

Nor were letters the only evidence, for curious servants had been watching the lovers. Katharine Stenton, Mary's maid, said that her mistress met Captain Baillie in Brussels, and that 'on this occasion she spoke very much in his favour and that he had paid her very particular attentions'. After their first meeting he would visit her daily, and he went with them when they moved on to Aix La Chapelle. The General was indisposed with gout at that time and often stayed home while his wife 'attended the public places every Evening when they were open', usually accompanied by Captain Baillie. When they returned home, and the General was in bed, they supped alone together. There was a crack in the maid's room from which the maid 'could very plainly see what past in the dinning room when the Candles were lighted'. Katharine 'often had the Curiosity to look through the crevice of the door and has seen Captain Baillie and Mrs Lockhart embracing one another Has seen his hands about her neck and her hands in the Bosom of his shirt'. On one such occasion she 'saw him unloose his waistcoat and take his watch out of his pocket and laid it down upon the table That he then put his hand about her waist and half led and half carried her towards a settee'. Katharine 'retired from the door so soon as she saw them going towards the settee'. However, a fellow servant, George Montgomery, continued looking through the crevice and 'saw Captain Baillie and Mrs Lockharts legs lying mixed upon the couch her toes pointed up and his down'.

Captain Baillie's servant, Nicolas Lavell, he of the odd nickname *L'Orange*, also appeared as a witness, interpreted by the French teacher. In Brussels he carried letters from his master to Mrs Lockhart. He described to the court the Captain obtaining a rope and on one occasion making his escape from Mrs Lockhart's room with it. On the journey to London, 'when at Lille the General being indisposed the deponent coming from his room saw Mrs Lockhart and Captain Baillie in a kind of Gallery or Coredore That he had an arm around her waist and that she had hold of his Privy member with her hand'. When travelling north, in Morpeth, while *L'Orange* 'was at supper with the other servants of General Lockhart . . . thinking he heard his Master call him by his name *L'Orange* he opened the door where Mrs Lockhart and Captain Baillie were and saw the Captain above Mrs Lockhart on a Canope That the Captain then got up and his Breeches were down and he desired the deponent in a huff to go about his Business'.

In the course of the divorce action Mary's lawyer tried to get as much money as possible out of the General, and also the jewels which had been given her at the time of her marriage. As for the latter, the General stated that 'they belonged to the family and never were the property of Mrs Lockhart'. He declared his willingness to pay whatever the court decided was appropriate for her aliment and expenses, and the commissaries ordered him to pay her £100 for aliment and a further £50 for expenses. Subsequently she petitioned for more money, when the General answered that he had 'not till now had any Experience of the Commissary Court and therefore he cannot say whether every process before this Court is equally Expensive but he supposed that it cannot well be the case otherways no person of ordinary fortune could possibly afford to enter these walls and it very much becomes the honour of the Court to advert to the charges which are here made and to consider whether they are Just and moderate'. The commissaries found her account of expenses to be 'in the highest degree Extravagant and oppressive and that the defender has indulged in the most profuse wanton and unnecessary expence', so they refused her petition. But later, after an appeal to the Court of Session, the General had to pay her £200 for aliment between July and December, £60 for expenses plus a further £30 for future expenses, as well as £28. 10s. for her counter process (but the £150 already paid was deducted).

In view of the damning proof of Mary's infidelity, the counter process – on the grounds of his alleged adultery with prostitutes – was her only hope of salvaging anything, but it backfired. One of her witnesses, Janet Lockhart, declared that two months earlier Henry Crichton, 'Cadie or running Stationer in Edinburgh' (i.e. messenger), came to her and described General Lockhart as 'a tall Elderly man with a blue and red ribbon through the button hole of his Coat', so that she could say that she had had intercourse with him. She was to go to Alexander Tap, 'a Chairmaster', and tell him that 'a young man had broke open the door and caught the deponent and General Lockhart together'. However, she told the court that 'this never happened, nor did this young man ever catch the deponent with any man whatever'. As Tap had promised her 'that she should be handsomely rewarded', she 'did as Tap desired her and that what she said was taken down in writing by a young Lad whose name is Spence whom the deponent now sees in Court. That the writing was read over to the deponent in presence of Tap but she did not sign it nor was desired to do so, and that she did not understand well the sense of what she was about'. Another witness deponed likewise. (It does not seem likely that a belated pang of conscience smote these witnesses; presumably the General's agents gave them money to retract their statements.) The commissaries suspected Crichton and Tap to be 'guilty of improper practices in endeavouring to Suborn these and other witnesses to give false evidence', but as neither had been 'examined as witnesses, nor otherways appeared in the Cause, They recommend to the Clerk to lay the above mentioned depositions before the Agent for the Crown for the consideration of his Majestys Advocate.'

In December the commissaries granted the General his divorce and a decreet absolving him from the counter process.

cc8/5/17 and cc8/6/42

TURNER VS BAMBOROUGH – THE COMPLICATIONS OF CONCEALMENT

Robert Bamborough, vintner in Leith, did his best to prevent his wife, Mary Turner, from discovering that another woman had borne a bastard to him in December 1796. He was unlucky in two ways: first, the midwife who delivered the child was a woman of probity and, second, the husband of the wetnurse was a greedy wretch.

Jean Jack, the midwife, refused to deliver Ann West's child until Ann named the father. Immediately the child was born Jean wrote to Bamborough, advising him that Ann had named him as father. Bamborough was agitated by this news, rushing right round to the midwife's house, and getting her out of bed (this clearly stuck in her mind for her to have mentioned it in her testimony), and he 'seemed to be very vexed and at a great loss in what manner to dispose of the Child'. Jean told him that Ann 'was in great poverty and in great distress and that the wisest thing he could do was to acquaint Mrs Bamborough with the whole affair, to which he answered he could not do that for it would ruin the peace of her family'. In that case, she advised, 'the wisest course he could take was to give out the Child to nurse'. It is not clear why he could not simply have given Ann money to subsist on. She was described as a 'woman of bad character', and the child had been conceived in a house of bad fame, but Bamborough would hardly have been so ready to acknowledge paternity if she had been a prostitute. In any case, after three weeks she never saw either the child or Bamborough again. Meanwhile, Jean found a wetnurse, a Mrs Begg, and paid her, having been given the money by Bamborough.

Unfortunately for Bamborough, James Begg refused to allow his wife to nurse the child until he knew who the father was. After that he 'was in the use of hanging about Mr Bamboroughs door and dunning him for money'. Begg also wrote to him a few times, and the last letter was seen by Mary. Bamborough then wrote to Jean Jack: 'James Begg sent a letter last night which has fallen into my wifes hands, and she wants to know where it came from, which if she does will prove my ruin, You will please therefore as soon as possible endeavour to do what you can to stop it as he wrote about money But she does not know what it is for. I beg as a particular favour you will lose no time for you know the consequence of it I will see you soon, You must make Begg make some excuse for the letter he sent if it be found where the letter came from.'

Jean Jack went round to Begg's house, and asked Mrs Begg why she was always pestering Mr Bambrough for money'. Begg, 'who was in bed', 'cried out he would do for' her 'when he came out'. Jean 'thereupon left the house and thought it full time to acquaint Mrs Bamborough with the whole affair and to save her and her husband from being imposed upon by the nurse and her husband'. She wrote to Mary: 'Mrs Bamborough This is to inform you that your husband has a Child at the nursing, the Child is a Girl and your husband pays fifteen shillings sterling a quarter for her, and the people wants a sum of money from him and I think it proper that you should know of it. I know that the mother can make him pay for the Child for ten years therefore I would have you take care how you pay your money'.

The secret was out, and Mary then searched for and found the various letters from Begg to her husband in a drawer. But Bamborough still fought the case, on the grounds that she had continued to cohabit with him for a further nine months after she knew of his adultery, implying she forgave him. She told the court that she had never slept in the same bed as him again but had considered it necessary to stay in the house until the debts were settled, as it was she who was in charge of the tavern part of the business. He denied this, and produced accounts to show that there were still plenty of debts outstanding when she did leave. She replied that she had never said that all the debts had been settled before she left, and added: 'Tho' no ways material to the question at issue, as this subject has been improperly introduced by the Defender, it may be only further mentioned, that upon her thus removing from the house and as every thing from that circumstance must have gone into perfect confusion the proprietors saw the necessity of securing their rents by sequestration, and at length took possession of the whole property and committed the management of the Tavern for its preservation to the pursuer who now acts under them exclusive of her husband'.

The commissaries repelled the defence of reconciliation, and Bamborough lost both wife and business. But at least the Beggs could no longer blackmail him.

cc8/5/24

CHAPTER 4

CONTESTED CASES

This chapter is concerned with cases where an adulterous defender brought other defences besides denying the adultery. We will look at each of these defences in turn. Lawyers also invented some novel defences which will not be found in any legal manual, and we will look at a selection of those as well. The key tactic was to drag the case out as long as possible, in hopes that the pursuer would be financially (or even emotionally) unable to see it through. Objecting to witnesses was one means of doing this, and we will also look at others.

LIBEL TOO VAGUE

Out of the 200 contested cases brought to a conclusion of divorce, 72 (36 per cent) utilised this defence. Indeed, it was deployed in the very first case in the volumes of decreets – William, Earl of Monteith and Airth against Anna, Countess of Monteith, in 1684. Before proceeding to details of the alleged adultery, all libels contained standard wording to the effect that the defender had given his or her body to various lewd or wicked men or women. In this case, as in some later ones, the Earl's lawyers argued that this was 'absurd and rediculous [sic]' as only one name had been given. They also argued that the name of the paramour, Ross of Auchlossen, was insufficient as his Christian name was not given, 'seeing it was nottour and was offered positively to be proven that there were more persons than one of the surname of Ross to whom the designation and title of Auchlossen is proper and competent and who actually and commonly pass under the same title'. The commissaries demanded the Christian name (it was Robert Ross, younger of Auchlossen) but once it was given paid no more heed to that defence.[1]

In the bitterly fought action of Francis Carruthers of Dormont against Margaret Maxwell in 1741, the commissaries initially repelled the defence that the libel was too vague and general, but on appeal to the Court of Session the higher court instructed that the pursuer must 'give in a more special condescendance of the places where and times when the crimes libelled were committed with a condescendance of the persons with whom if known to the witnesses, and some marks distinguishing them if unknown to them'. He was able to do this and was granted his divorce.[2]

The defence was also used in the 1766 case of James Chalmers, planter in Jamaica, against Margaret Marr. The commissaries demanded that he provide the dates and places where the adultery had occurred. After this was done Margaret petitioned that the libel was still too vague and general as the names of the men with whom she committed adultery had not been supplied. By this time Chalmers' investigators had managed to obtain more information. The first man 'was a Clerk on Board the Phoenix or Feniwick ship of war then lying in the Road of Leith that he went by the Name of John Hucklie and lived with her for a month or six weeks in the house of Archibald Stevenson a Porter in Leith'. A second man 'was given out by the Defender to be a smuggler while she lived with him in the house of widow Brymer or Rymer in Brughton and a singular Circumstance happened to this Paramour of the Defenders at this Period for when he was living with the Defender in that House he was taken up for stealing horse Graith [harness and trappings]'. Chalmers was allowed to prove his case, did so, and was granted a divorce.[3]

However, though the libel in the case of Georgina Lindesay against Frederick Carmichael in 1802 did not name names, when this was objected to, her procurator called it 'sufficiently articulate in the circumstances of the case, for it is not one particular act of guilt [with] which he is charged but unhappily for the pursuer, she has too good reason to say that her husband had during the period Lybelled lived in a most profligate manner having carnal dealings with lewd women as often as opportunities occurred':

> When a person loses sight so much of the principles of religion and morality as to commit transgressions in every place and on every opportunity which occurs, any one of which would convict him, he is not entitled to call for a Condescendence of any specific act of adultery, to permit him to do so would be giving him a manifest advantage from the frequency of his guilt, because the pursuer may fix upon one act and fail in establishing it, while the defender tho guilty of five hundred other acts of adultery, would from the failure of proving the single one condescended upon come off as innocent.

Furthermore, there was 'the great difficulty of a Lady's condescending upon the particulars of her husbands guilt – she of all others being the person from whom it is to be concealed, while the indelicacy of investigating the facts prevents her from making those researches which are necessary'. In this case the standard rubric was actually true, and the commissaries 'Found that the Lybel contained a specification of facts sufficiently articulate and special', allowed her a proof of her libel, and subsequently a divorce.[4]

When the commissaries agreed that a libel was too vague and general they would demand a 'special and articulate condescendence' of the facts to be proven (and names of witnesses). Finally, in the early nineteenth century, the special condescendence became standard practice, so in the long term this defence was responsible for tightening up divorce procedures. In the early period the defence might have forced pursuers' agents to do more work in ferreting out the facts than they might have anticipated. It could have been a way of 'fishing' to see how much the pursuer actually knew or could substantiate, but it seems to have been largely a delaying tactic. No surviving case was dismissed because the libel was too vague and general.

RECRIMINATION

In accordance with Roman and Canon laws, it was for a long time the law in Scotland (as it remained in England) that recrimination, or mutual guilt, was an absolute bar to divorce.[5] It was brought forward as a defence in 25 (12 per cent) of contested cases, but in most of those cases a counter process was raised, and during the eighteenth century there was no case in which the guilt of the pursuer was proven, so the legal consequences of recrimination were uncertain. In the case of Captain William Jardine of Applegirth against Barberie de la Motte in 1786–7, after the proof of adultery had been brought, the defender gave in a new defence of recrimination. The Captain objected that recrimination 'was not admissible by way of defence', and that she would have to raise a counter process against him; also, that even if she proved her case it would not bar his divorce, though it would entitle her to divorce him at the same time. The commissaries allowed her a proof of her additional defence, but when Captain Jardine appealed to the Court of Session that court insisted on a counter process being raised, which formed a precedent for future cases. The question of whether proof of his guilt would bar his divorcing her was not resolved as she failed to prove him guilty.[6]

After William Ramsay, spirit dealer in Dunfermline, proved the adultery of his wife, Janet Muir, in an action brought in October 1788, she brought a defence of recrimination on the grounds that Ramsay had fathered at least two bastard children. The commissaries insisted on a counter process being brought, but this was for separation and aliment, not divorce. She also petitioned for money to conduct her new process, and the commissaries ordered Ramsay to pay her. Ramsay pleaded that it was unfair to make him pay for her case when he had already proved his own, but in view of her right to appeal against the commissaries' decision, his petition was refused. He then craved to be admitted to the poor's roll; the commissaries refused, and the case 'fell asleep' until October 1792, when, as Janet had brought no proof of his guilt, he was granted his divorce. In 1797 Margaret Marshall's counter process against John Craig was not for divorce but simply one of recrimination. (He responded: 'A Lybel of recrimination from the keeper of an open Bagnio, from a woman living in constant public adultery is really an insult to the dignity and sacred nature of the Court'.) It is difficult to know what the legal consequences of such a judgment would have been, but once again there was no proof of the pursuer's adultery.[7]

In a complicated case of 1798–9 (Lockhart against Henderson) it was stated that the question of whether a plea of recrimination, when proved, could prevent a divorce or whether it had to be pleaded in a counter process, affecting only the financial effects of the action, 'has never been reduced to fixed principles either by our lawyers or the decisions of the Court.' However, it had always been found 'that this plea is not competent unless it is brought forward in a counter-action'. The commissaries repelled the defence of recrimination (and the counter process had already been thrown out on the grounds of *remissio injuriae*, i.e. forgiveness), so the pursuer got her divorce. That case established that recrimination would not prevent a divorce, i.e. if both parties were guilty that was not a reason why they should have to remain locked together in marriage, though neither party could then claim the other's estate.[8]

A case finally came up, in 1819–20, when both parties, Andrew Heggie and his wife, Catherine Simpson, were able to prove each other's guilt, and the court had no hesitation in stating that 'mutual guilt is no Bar to Divorce' and granting them both their freedom.[9]

LENOCINIUM

One legal commentator described this as 'where the husband becomes the pander to his own dishonour, by conniving at his wife's adultery, or inciting her, directly or indirectly, to the perpetration of the crime.' Another defined it as 'the husband's lending himself to his own disgrace, either directly, or by the countenance or encouragement he may give to others'. He described a case where 'a husband, inebriated at a bachannalian feast, offered, in revolting jocularity, to sell to the highest bidder permission to attempt his wife's chastity'. The wife apparently committed adultery subsequently with a man who had been at table on that occasion, and the husband 'on finding that she had discovered this disgusting scene, abandoned the process without even making up a record, satisfied from the advice which he received, that it formed a sufficient bar to his action'.[10]

In one of the earliest cases in the volumes of decreets (February 1692) the procurators for Elisabeth Wilhelmina Van Ghent, wife of Colonel George Lawder of Restalrig, defending her against the accusation of adultery with Sergeant Mcghie, claimed that 'her husband did induce, prompt, hire and hound out Serjand Mcghie and others to ly with the Petitioner', but they were unable to prove this, and the divorce was granted. In the case of Colin Mackenzie against Katherine Mckenzie in 1744, it was stated that her husband was instrumental in any bad behaviour of hers by 'making her to Drink aquavite and other strong Liquors, hindering her from going to Church obliding her to come into company with his Companions and Guests and then in their presence intertaining the Defender with most obscene Language and exposing her Nakedness in the presence of the Company, and causing them for their Diversion pull the hairs from her pudenda or by doing it himself in their presence.' All of which he denied and which was never put to the proof.[11]

The defence was also used in the 1779 case of Thomas Scott against Margaret Kerr, who ran off with an actor, John Townsend, when it was alleged that Scott had offered Townsend money. Scott was questioned and declared that the only time he had seen the man was when he discovered him in a compromising position with his wife, and the defence did not succeed.[12]

A defence which was not termed lenocinium but which was closely related alleged a plot by the pursuer to place the defender in a compromising position, as in the case of Thomas Hally, watchmaker, against Margaret Telfer in 1741. In response to the charge that she had been found in bed with a soldier in a bawdy house, she claimed that she had gone to the house, where she had never been before, to settle a debt, and that

> a person with a red coat came into the Room, and fell a struggling with the Defender, and endeavoured to push her into the bed, whereupon the Defender immediately called out so loud, That sundry persons came into the Room to her Relief, some of whom it seemed had been upon the plot, For by the consequence it appeared that it had been a plot laid by her husband, or some of his Emissaries, for that fellow to Invade the Defenders chastity.[13]

But John Simpson, an elder of the parish, who had gathered together witnesses and entered the room because he suspected there was 'lewd company', testified to his shock at discovering who the woman was, so her defence failed.

Similarly, in the case of William Ramsay against Janet Muir (1788–92), she claimed that her husband had formed a 'diabolical scheme'. He 'had taken some worthless man a hawker or showman' into the house, who 'came into her room and without speaking came straight to the Defenders bedside and offered to violate her honour Upon which the Defender summoned what resolution she had to repell the attack of the scoundrel', but her husband and his brother rushed in and found them together. In this case witnesses had actually overheard her speaking to the man and agreeing 'to yield to his embraces if he paid her eighteen pence or twenty pence'.[14]

However, such a plot *could* be hatched, for in the case of Thomas Prophet, fish dealer in Edinburgh, against Mary Ross, in 1826, a witness admitted that the pursuer 'promised me some money if I would get the Defender made the worse of liquor and then procure some person to go to bed with her or go with her myself', and the case fell.[15] That was a rare case in which such a defence stood up.

RECONCILIATION

Continuing to cohabit with a spouse in the knowledge that he or she had been guilty of adultery was considered tantamount to forgiveness (*remissio injuriae*), which barred a future action for divorce on the ground of that adultery, and hence formed a valid defence. However, the law treated men and women differently, for from a wife the court looked for 'long suffering and patience, not expected or tolerated in a husband.' Apart from the ideological double standard, there were also the practicalities. A woman might not be in a financial situation to leave her husband, or might have children, so her remaining in the same house after she knew of his guilt would not necessarily be construed as forgiving the wrong, as it would most likely be for a man. This double standard was to women's benefit in law; the man's legal case was weakened if he did not act immediately, the woman's much less so. Rather surprisingly, it was possible to run a defence of reconciliation while continuing to protest innocence. 'The accused party may plead, "I am not guilty; but though I were, I am forgiven." . . . Actual *knowledge* of guilt . . . is not indeed required, because there can be no actual knowledge of what may *not* exist, but there must be a complete and perfect *belief*'.[16]

A particularly interesting case is that of Dame Alice Paterson against Sir Alexander Dalmahoy of that Ilk in 1720.[17] The libel alleged acts of adultery over a number of years, and his procurators claimed that she had known of these at the time and continued to cohabit with him. In evidence they claimed 'words emitted by her in severall places and before severall persones Importing her knowledge of the facts Lybelled . . . her often upbraiding him with the name Adulterer' – and more. For when Agnes Robertson (the servant with whom he had committed adultery) left the parish Lady Dalmahoy had told the minister at Ratho 'that she suspected Sir Alexander was guilty of baseness with her' so Agnes was denied a testimonial of good conduct. After that, Lady Dalmahoy discovered that her husband met Agnes in the West Kirk parish so she asked the ministers there to expel Agnes from that parish, which they did. Some years later she traced Agnes to Corstorphine parish (where her husband was apparently still seeing her) and wrote to the minister to put her out of that parish as well. The minister at Ratho testified to receiving letters in which 'My ladie shewed her suspitione and Jealousie of Sir Alexanders being base with the said Agnes Robertsone . . . And further adds that he received a letter from my Lady since the Commencement of this process, Importing that he should destroy all former letters wrote by My Lady to the Deponent upon this Subject'. Ultimately, when Agnes was committed to the city guard as 'a light woman', Lady Dalmahoy had put pressure on the authorities to have Agnes 'transported to the plantationes'. In spite of all this, and more, her lawyers argued: 'A very strong Jealousy she had of Sir Alexanders guilt but no legall proof And therefore she chose by writing to ministers and others who could help her to Cure her self of the uneasyness, and him of his bad practices, by banishing that harlot who it seems seduced him.'

The commissaries found that the defender's proofs 'did not prove nor necessarily infer the pursuers knowledge of the defenders said guilt while she Cohabited'. Dame Alice obviously did know perfectly well what her husband was up to, and feared that the letters proved the fact, but because she had done everything in her power to put a stop to the affair and protect the marriage the defence did not succeed. Thus, though the position according to law was that an innocent spouse who continued to cohabit with a guilty one after knowing of the adultery was presumed to have forgiven that adultery and therefore was not entitled to a divorce, we can see such a defence was not sustained when the pursuer was a wife who had gone to such lengths.

For a situation in which this defence added greatly to the bitterness of the divorce action, see Case Study 4.

Matthew Poole, baker in Canongate, had kept a mistress since his marriage to Euphemia Hepburn, and begotten two children on her, but Euphemia did not raise a divorce action until several years afterwards (1772), so his procurator pleaded *remissio injuriae*. Euphemia was examined by the commissaries and testified to her increasing suspicions over the years but insisted that she had not believed in his guilt. It was only when she discovered that her husband was infected with venereal disease that she left his bed, 'tho upon another pretence as the Declarant was ashamed to own the real cause but gave out that it was on account of Buggs that was in the Bed'. She did not leave the house until she had managed to trace the woman he had been writing to, four months later. In spite of an appeal to the Court of Session by the defender, the defence of reconciliation was repelled.[18]

When Robert Sutherland of Langwall, who had fathered children on two or more of the servants, pleaded this defence against his wife in 1773, her procurator answered:

There are various instances in the Records of the Commissary Court, where this defence of Reconciliation has been pleaded, but it never was sustained as relevant . . . Indeed a more ungracious defence could not well be supposed where the Husband was the Defender, for it amounted to this, that because he had made use of that Influence and power which every husband must naturally have, over his wife, to prevaill with her for a time to submit to his irregularities, she must therefore be debarred forever from demanding redress however intolerable and unjustifiable his Conduct might be.

The commissaries agreed.[19]

In a case of 1778, Alexander McLaurin's wife, May Watson, insisted that he had had carnal knowledge of her after the date of the divorce summons, which would bar his action. McLaurin offered to deny this upon oath, at which point the Defence backtracked, saying that it was not necessary to prove carnal dealing in order to prove reconciliation, for his visits to her, which were neither necessary nor accidental, in which they ate and drank and laughed together, were inconsistent 'with the feelings of a husband who believed his wife to be an adulteress'. The commissaries did not agree, and when McLarin swore on oath that he had not had carnal knowledge of his wife since knowing of her adultery, they repelled the defence of reconciliation.[20]

In the next chapter we will see cases where this defence succeeded, but this occurred in only five of the 44 cases dismissed by the commissaries, whereas it was deployed *unsuccessfully* in 52 of the contested cases which resulted in divorce decreets.

OTHER DEFENCES

If no marriage had taken place, then no divorce could be granted. The case of
Charlotte Armstrong against John Elliot in 1760 was for declarator of marriage,
legitimacy and divorce. Simultaneously, another declarator of marriage action was
raised by Janet Boston, whom he had subsequently married bigamously. Elliot denied
marrying Charlotte, but the marriage was proven by witnesses, and as his bigamous
marriage to Janet was also proven, Charlotte was granted her divorce on the grounds
of his adultery with her.[21]

A defence which would immediately bar an action, if proven, was *battery pendente
lite*, assault during the course of the action, and some wives even tried to provoke their
husbands to violence in hopes of stopping the divorce action. Christian Wilson's
lawyer (1775) claimed that when she went to the house of her husband, William Fife,
to deliver a message, 'he damned her for a bitch and whore, sent his Landlord for a
party of the guard who dragged her along in a barbarous and infamous manner'. Fife's
version was that she had battered at the door at midnight and created a furore which
was why the landlord called the party of the guard 'and lodged her in the guard as a
disturber of his family and neighbourhood'. Before this she had called to her husband
for help, and he had risen from bed and asked the guard 'to use her as decently as
possible'. But that was not what she wanted, for 'she clenched her arm about the
Respondents neck' (and he asked the judges to note that he 'was by far the weaker
party') and dragged him along with her to the guard door 'where the party extricated
him from her hold.' He reckoned that she 'by this unseasonable visit to the
Respondents abode had two things in view first to endeavour either to get into
bed with her Husband in the place where he was or to get him home with her or else to
endeavour to provoke him to such a degree, as if possible to make him use her with
violence, either of which events might have proved fatal to the Respondents plea'.
Witnesses bore out his story, Christian's procurator withdrew the defence, and Fife
obtained his divorce.[22]

Insanity was not a ground for divorce, but it was occasionally pleaded as a defence
with the claim that the defender was not responsible for his or her actions. In the case
of Robert Allan, surgeon in Edinburgh, against his wife, Anna Scott, in 1817, her
father claimed that she was not responsible for her actions, being deranged, and he
had himself appointed *tutor ad litem* by the court. The basis of his claim was a letter
written to him by Allan just before the couple separated, in which he stated, 'From
your daughter Mrs Allan being occasionally subject to fits of mental derangement my
house repeatedly becomes a scene of riot which is destructive to my peace of mind and
ruinous to my business.' Allan insisted that this turn of phrase was not meant literally,
and that when they separated she had not been committed to a lunatic asylum but was
even permitted to have one of their children with her. Nevertheless, her father was
allowed to claim expenses for this defence. In the course of the acrimonious battle,

Allan went to see his wife, who refused to accept any money for her child, which she admitted was not his, and called in witnesses to see her put this in writing. The father's response to this in court was that 'if the writing produced was the holograph the Commissaries would hardly require a stronger proof of insanity than granting such a writing.' Fortunately, when she herself appeared in court the commissaries found her mental faculties to be perfectly in order. They therefore revoked her father's powers as *tutor ad litem* and spared Allen his costs.[23]

There are various defences which could be called 'a nice try'. The year after the Union of 1707, the Countess of Wigton claimed that the court had no jurisdiction because she was a British peeress who could only be tried by the House of Lords. But since divorce did not exist in England the commissaries repelled the plea. David Sime, defending himself against his wife Grizel McInroy in 1762, argued that his adultery was actually justified. His mother-in-law, he said, had insinuated that 'my marriage was voidable and that my wife had deserted me on Account of impotency', so to disprove this allegation after his wife left him, 'he lay with his maid and got her with child.' He thought himself very hard done by that his mother-in-law 'with a very bad Grace brings an Action of Divorce against him for adultery, tho formerly she openly accused him of Impotence'. The commissaries did not accept his logic and granted Grizel a divorce.[24]

Lieutenant General Henry Fletcher of Salton declared with his defences in 1781:

> when he went to bed with the Pursuer on the night of their marriage she refused to allow him any communication with her and had herself wrapped up and swaddled with different cloaths and bandages to prevent him in which extraordinary conduct she persisted for a considerable time nor would she ever permit the Pursuers embraces except after a violent struggle and even then but seldom.

He seemed to think that this might bar her action for divorce, but her procurator answered:

> As to the Pursuers conduct on the wedding night she only observes that she is yet to learn that the Laws of the Land prescribe any method in which brides are bound to receive their Bridegrooms on that occasion and she has allways understood that this was a matter left to be regulated by the feelings and delicacy of the parties, accustomed as the defender may have been to the Passive virtues of such damsels as those who passed in review before your Lordships at the prooff he may not have relished the reluctance with which the Pursuers youth and innocence made her admit the first embraces of a Husband, But it is believed that this conduct will not meet with any reprehension from your Lordships or far less be thought an Excuse for the Defenders adultery sufficient to bar a Divorce.[25]

However 'seldom' his wife might have allowed intercourse, there was no pretence that the marriage was unconsummated, so the defence did not succeed.

Further examples of unusual defences could be given, but with the onus of proof on the pursuer, there was a more promising tactic for defence lawyers to deploy.

OBJECTING TO WITNESSES

Witnesses were objected to in 33 (17 per cent) of contested cases resulting in divorce. In early cases the grounds were often that the witness was *mala fama*. In the case of a whore, 'It is for money that she prostitutes herselfe and the Law therefore presumes that she is not proof against the meanest bribe'. The answer was that in difficult cases like adultery such witnesses were admitted, 'For otherwayes Adultery may in many cases pass unpunished if such persons were not received witnesses, women of that Character and they only being for the most part present where such Criminall Transactions are carried on especially in populus Citys where lewd houses can be had'.[26] As the commissaries always adhered to this line, the ground of bad character stopped being used in the course of our period, and an allegation of malice became the usual objection.

In fact, every witness who appeared in court had to swear that they had not received either a 'present' or the promise of one and that they would not give malicious or 'partial' council. As their testimony was thus considered to have been 'purged' of malice by their oath, a simple allegation of ill will was rarely allowed further proof. Nevertheless, defenders tried it on.

For example, in the case of Dougald Campbell of Ederline against his wife, in 1727, she claimed that his servant, John Black

> Intertained Deadly malice against the Lady in as far as the Lady having had occasion to Reprove him for certain misdemeanours committed by him while a servant in the Family he did vow and swear revenge agt her, and thereupon he went to the said Dougald Campbell and most Groundlessly and maliciously Informed him That his Lady was Guilty of Adultery and offered to be a witness against her.

It was answered that 'the manner of his executing his Threatned Revenge did not show Capitall Enmety or even any malice at all, It was in exoneration of his Conscience in acting the part of a faithfull servant to Inform him of the wicked practises of the Defender whereby his master was Injured in the highest manner'. The court repelled the objection.[27]

However, malice was one thing; active connivance was another. In the case of Walter Welsh of Lochquharet against his wife in 1733, she alleged that three of the proposed witnesses, Mrs Reid, her daughter and son in law, 'had for some time past been busie and active in serving and agenting for Lochquharret against the defender by makeing inquiry after and tampering with others to be witnesses against her and by directing them to be cited as such'. The court found the objections against Mrs Reid proven and allowed the defender to adduce proof as to the rest.[28]

However, when the commissaries sustained the objections to Jean Mckay, as a witness in the case of Margaret Taylor against William Adie in 1780, on the grounds that she was 'of Infamous Character', and 'besides she has been employed and found out Evidence in this Cause and has been paid or at least promised payment for her trouble', the pursuer appealed to the Court of Session, which instructed that she be examined, 'reserving all objections to her Credibility'.[29]

Defenders sometimes objected to witnesses as being under age, but there was no strict cut off date; if a boy or girl in their teens demonstrated to the court that they understood the nature of an oath they would be admitted. Another ground for objecting to witnesses was near relationship. In a 1746 case Isobell Bryce objected to her father-in-law, James Dun senior, and other relatives of the pursuer's, as witnesses. It was answered that 'tho' a near Relation may be an Objection to a witness in Ordinary cases Yet in occult Crimes which cannot be otherways discovered, such Relations must ex necessitate be admitted', an argument which the commissaries generally sustained.[30]

Objecting to witnesses may have been a key strategy in most contested cases, and it certainly helped to drag them out. But a pursuer was never denied a divorce because a key witness had been prevented from appearing, so ultimately it was not a successful strategy for the defender, though it would have added to the costs and thereby to the lawyer's fee.

OTHER DELAYING TACTICS

It goes without saying that any strenuously defended case did not rely on any one defence, but used every available one as well as objecting to witnesses. Some began as they meant to go on, by claiming that a legal technicality was incorrect in the libel, which should invalidate the whole action. But there were also some more unusual ways of dragging out a case.

Thomas Tulloch, merchant in Edinburgh, brought his suit against Margaret Falconer in December 1753, and she was allowed to adduce proof for her exculpation. As she 'had carried on her Criminall Correspondence in Different Places under the Disguise of Borrowed Names, and endeavouring to conceal her Character as being the pursuers Wife', Tulloch considered it necessary for her to appear in court to be identified by witnesses, and the commissaries ordered her to attend personally. She appealed to the Court of Session, but her bill was refused. Her procurator claimed that she was in the country near Glasgow, and that he would produce her, but when the time came she did not appear, and three months later he claimed that she was in

London and unable to travel to Edinburgh; the pursuer doubted this; she provided affidavits which he claimed were forged. By this time his witnesses had deponed (damningly), so she then claimed that there was no longer any reason for her to travel to Edinburgh, and the case dragged on with more appeals to the Court of Session. Ultimately, the commissaries found her adultery proven and granted the divorce, but that was not until February 1757, more than three years after the summons.[31]

Endless petitions certainly helped to drag out a process. A good example is the case of Burnside against Paterson, which ran from January 1804 to February 1807 and beyond. Even after her lover had deponed as to his carnal connection with the defender, corroborated by other witnesses, she gave in a 'condescendence' that no such meeting as described had taken place. The commissaries found the proof which she offered irrelevant and inadmissible; she petitioned, asking them to review their interlocutor and withdraw it; they refused; she petitioned again; they refused again and prohibited the clerk to receive any more petitions from her. Nothing daunted, she appealed to the Court of Session; after the pursuer's answers her bill was refused. Even after the divorce decreet was issued, she presented two more petitions until, in June 1807, the commissaries again refused to accept any more.[32]

SKULDUGGERY

In the case of Carruthers of Dormont against Margaret Maxwell (1741–2), one of the witnesses was alleged to have said that 'If people of Creditt could not be got to Depone against the Lady, and since bribing was in fashion, we could bribe witnesses to Depone as well as others'.[33] In long, bitter, contested cases bribery, threats and leaning on witnesses were not uncommon. A servant maid to Margaret Cassa, defending herself against her husband, George Young (1749–50), deponed that a few days before her appearance in court she 'met with Margareta Cassa and her mother upon the street, who asked her what she was to witness That she the compearant answered That she knew not but when she was asked she would witness the truth, and that both of them had offered her a present if she the compearant would not witness any thing against her'.[34]

When Cecilia Smith won her divorce from John White in 1802, his procurator argued that her claim for expenses was too high. Her lawyer described the difficulties he had had in finding the witnesses: no sooner had the list been produced than the defender 'and his associates set to work':

Some of the witnesses, though in Town [when] the List was produced in Court could not again be found while the cause depended Yet they are now as easily found as formerly – Some of them he wished to conceal . . . Some of the poor girls who would not condescend to oblige him, he openly attacked on the streets, obliging them to fly to the Cadies and Chair men for protection at Mid

day and his influence over others, was but too evident in the Examination of
Ann Clifford . . . who even admitted in the Commissaries presence that she had
committed perjury 'not liking to say' what might be hurtful to the Defender.[35]

Case Study 5 shows one of the most brazen attempts at perverting the course of
justice. As with some of the more legitimate defences, skulduggery helped to drag a
case out, but it does not appear to have prevented a divorce.

All of the defences and other tactics outlined in this chapter failed far more often
than they succeeded, but not everyone who raised a divorce action could have
afforded the financial and emotional costs of a lengthy fight.

NOTES

All CC references are in the Scottish Record Office.
1. cc8/5/1.
2. cc8/5/7.
3. cc8/5/11. In bringing the defence of too vague and general a libel in this case, it was argued
   that the names of the persons with whom the defender was alleged to have committed
   adultery had to be stated, 'as was determined by the Court of Session in the late cause at the
   instance of Alexander Cunningham against his Wife'. No such case has been found in the
   commissary court records, so this is presumably an example of lawyers borrowing process
   papers and never returning them.
4. cc8/5/27.
5. Patrick Fraser, *Treatise on the Law of Scotland as applicable to The Personal and Domestic
   Relations* (Edinburgh 1846), vol.I, 672.
6. cc8/6/49.
7. cc8/5/22; cc8/5/23.
8. cc8/6/32.
9. cc8/5/38.
10. Fraser, *Treatise*, 670; Maurice Lothian, *The Law, Practice and Style Peculiar to the
    Consistorial Actions Transferred to the Court of Session* (Edinburgh 1830), 165–6.
11. cc8/5/1; cc8/6/14. Her other defences were reconciliation and recrimination. There are
    process papers for the case from January 1744 to March 1745 but no decreet.
12. cc8/5/16.
13. cc8/5/7.
14. cc8/5/22.
15. cc8/6/169.
16. Fraser, *Treatise*, 666–9; Lothian, *The Law, Practice and Style*, 158–60.
17. cc8/5/2.
18. cc8/5/13.
19. cc8/5/14.
20. cc8/5/25.
21. cc8/5/11. 'In respect from the proof in this Cause it appeared John Elliot had been guilty of
    high offences', the commissaries 'recommended to his majesties advocate to Enquire
    particularly into the Circumstances of this case & consider if it would not be proper that
    John Elliot should be Criminally prosecuted for his Conduct'.
22. cc8/5/14.
23. cc8/5/36.

24. cc8/5/1; cc8/5/9.
25. cc8/5/27.
26. Campbell vs Lamond, 1725–8, cc8/5/3.
27. Ibid.
28. cc8/5/4
29. cc8/5/16.
30. cc8/5/6.
31. cc8/6/22.
32. cc8/6/84.
33. cc8/5/7.
34. cc8/5/9. An in-depth look at this complex case can be had in R. A. Houston and Manon van der Heijden, 'Hands Across the Water: The Making and Breaking of Marriage Between Dutch and Scots in the Mid-Eighteenth Century', *Law and History Review* 15, 2 (Fall 1997).
35. cc8/5/26.

STEEDMAN VS STEEDMAN – THE BITTERNESS OF KINDNESS

Unlike a great many divorce cases, where the marriage had clearly broken down irretrievably before adultery was committed, in this one the couple continued to live together and exhibit fondness for each other even after the divorce summons was delivered, and it was her lawyer's bringing the defence of reconciliation that embittered the relationship beyond endurance. It was unusual too in the way the husband rushed off to get a divorce summons the moment he learned of his wife's infidelity.

James Steedman and his wife, Janet, kept a small shop in Kinross, attached to their house. In July 1741, when the action was brought, the couple had been married for thirteen years, and Janet had borne six children, of whom two were alive. (Janet's surname being the same as her husband's was simply because the name 'Steedman' or 'Steadman' was common in Kinross; we will meet others in the course of the process.)

Janet's lover was Charles Cooper, sheriff clerk of Kinross, who is a shadowy figure. (This was before the era when paramours were called as witnesses.) Janet did not accompany her husband to church, and from autumn 1739, Cooper was seen going into the house every Sunday after James had left. They were also seen together in the 'parks of Kinross'. In May 1740 they were heard and seen in bed together; she was pregnant at the time, and the child she had in June died shortly afterwards, when 'the Common Bruit and Report of the neighbourhood was that the child had got hurt by the said Charles Cooper and the defender their poultring together.' The rumours were backed up by various witnesses, so it was a classic case of the husband being the last to know, and James's rush off to Edinburgh to initiate a divorce – in an era when divorce was still very rare – presumably reflected his humiliation at discovering what everyone in the town had known for a good two years.

There is no indication of how the discovery was made, but in spite of James obtaining a summons for divorce, in the following days and weeks Janet continued looking after the house and shop, and witnesses deponed that the couple's treatment of one another had not visibly altered. Various friends and relations attempted to reconcile them. The first was John Steedman, a schoolmaster, who was called over to the house on the evening of the day on which James had executed the divorce summons. He found Janet 'in a passion', and she asked him if 'he had said he had seen undecencies betwixt her and Charles Coopar'. When he denied having doing so, Janet turned to her husband and demanded to know why his mother had told him that the schoolmaster had seen such things, calling her mother-in-law 'bad names . . . such as Jade'. James answered that his mother had not said such a thing, only that John 'was concerned to hear such Reports about them in the Town'. Janet said to John that if she had realised that was all she would never have asked him to come round.

After that 'the conversation turned upon the summons of divorce', and James 'protested in a solemn manner, that his only view in that was to clear her character and that he would willingly give all that he was worth to have it cleared to his satisfaction.' At some point Janet remarked to James 'that while her blood was warm she would never love him'. She 'appeared to be in a great passion' with her husband, said John. He put it to James that he 'had taken a harsh way to clear his wifes character and wished some other expedient could be taken for that purpose,' James agreed, so John 'proposed the taking a precognition before the church session'. This seemed acceptable to James, but Janet cried out that 'she would not allow her name to stand Recorded in any church Register, and that if any Starks in Scotland meaning the minister . . . should send her a summons to appear before the church session, she would put a pair of Bullets through his head.' (So Janet's non-attendance at church was more than just a connivance; she was actively anti-clerical.) John also said that Janet 'severall times blamed' her mother-in-law 'as the person who had advised him to the methods he was then following,' and said that he 'took too much of her advice'.

Alexander Walker of St Foord was another friend who became involved. James told him that 'he had good reason to apprehend' his wife 'had been unfair to him with respect to her chastity', and 'that he designed to prosecute a divorce against her, for he could not think of living with her as her husband, after the Injury she had done him in that way'. Alexander suggested to James that 'possibly he might faill in the proof', and that it would 'bring an Infamy upon his wife and children,' and told James that in his opinion 'it was more eligible for him to agree to a separation from her and settle some aliment upon her'. At that stage James 'showed no aversion to that proposall', as long as he could be sure that his wife 'after the separation in this manner did not have children which might be Imposed upon him, but that he would take advice in it before he determined himself'. Subsequently James told Alexander that 'he had got advice that the separation formerly talked of . . . was impracticable and that he intended to go on in his process, and that he could have no security by such a separation against children to be borne afterwards by the defender'. Alexander was asked by Janet's uncle 'to endeavour an accommodation', but James's 'Mother and brothers were absolutely against it'.

The minister, Mr Robert Stark, also attempted to effect a reconciliation. He spoke to James about 'the consequences and difficulties which might attend such a way of Redress' and thought that James 'was very much Impressed with it, and said he had no other Intention by that process of divorce, but to clear his wifes character and give ease to his own mind'. The minister then spoke to Janet and 'found her in a very high temper and much irritated because of the summonds of divorce she had got at her husbands instance', but after the minister 'had reasoned some time with her, she cool'd much in her temper and expressed herself to this purpose "That nothing gave her so much pain as her husbands uneasiness" ', which the minister took to mean that 'the observation by neighbours upon what had happened and the attacks made upon her character did not trouble her so much as that, adding that if it was not for giving the pursuer more pain she would walk in Mr Coopars arms from Baillie Whites by the old Mistress's (meaning the pursuers mother) her door to Deacon Hudsons' to upset her because she 'was the Instigator of this process'.

The minister then spoke to them together, and James said that 'he could wish the happy man would be found who could fall upon an expedient' to clear his wife's character 'and give ease to his mind without going to extremities'. He turned to Janet saying 'O Jeannie I have no Intention by what is done but to clear thy character and give ease to my own mind and I would give the half if not the whole of what I am worth to reach these ends'. The minister then suggested that 'an easier method might be fallen upon than the prosecution of a divorce by taking a precognition before the Kirk session of Kinross'. But Janet 'turned high in her temper' and refused to consider such a thing, adding that 'if she happened to be assoilzied [absolved] from this process by the Commissaries she would not live with him for she could not love him, but hate him while blood ran in her veins for the treatment he had given her . . . and furder added You tricked me in my Marriage, the old Jade your Mother has abused me all along . . . and furder said You think you have given me a great deall of pain by what you are doing, but you do me pleasure, that I can be an Instrument of bringing disgrace upon your Mother'. James then 'stood up and said, Since that is the case I'll be at the bottom of it and nothing shall stop me cost what it will.'

A few days later an accident brought them close again. The Duke of Hamilton, 'with a numerous company', was passing through Kinross on horseback, and ran over a child of theirs. Mr Stark, the minister, heard the news (he was 'informed that the pursuers eldest son James was killed by the stroake of a horse', but from later testimony, it appears that the child was injured, not killed) and went to see them. He found them 'sitting in a Room together beside the child who was then in bed and thought their Behaviour was decent and suitable to the Melancholy Occasion'. A servant, Bessie Arnott, said that 'when the child got the hurt by the horse upon the street, and the defender seemed uneasy and cried out, the pursuer said to her, hold your tongue my Dear and compose yourself, and he and another man having taken her each by an arm, helped her down the street to the pursuers house'. Bessie had known the couple before the divorce action and was one of those who 'observed no alteration since in the pursuers carriage to the defender but that they behaved to one another as man and wife in the same way as formerly upon the occasions above-mentioned.'

The reason for all these witnesses testifying about the relationship was that Janet's procurator raised a defence of *remissio injuriae*. As soon as this happened James threw her out of the house, and his lawyer protested: 'the pursuer upon his coming up to such a degree of suspicion as gave him ground to raise this process, did not barbarously thrust the defender out of his house and expose her to the world, but allowed her to continue there as he still did untill triall of her Guilt, surely his so allowing her to remain in his house could never Inferr a renunciation of this process especially when he had acted in the most explicit manner to the contrary by carrying on the same in the most expeditious manner'. Her procurators argued against this, claiming that 'the pursuer had gone into the defenders Room when she was lying a bed and shutt the door upon them, that he still continued to treat her as his wife, acknowledging her as such, shewing her signs of kindness and affection, and employing her as formerly in the management of his house and of his shop, giving her money to lay out for the necessaries of the family'.

Her lawyers also asked for money for aliment and expenses, as her husband 'turned her and her servant out of doors, without any order of law and without money or any of the necessaries of life to support them . . . so that ever since that time they had been supported, upon credit, by good Neighbours and acquaintances who pitied her miserable condition'. James objected strongly: 'It was humbly submitted to their Lordships, if he had not a just call and provocation for doing so, after the false and treacherous construction her procurator in her defences had endeavoured to put upon the Respondents not thrusting her out of his house'. But the commissaries found him liable to pay her £10, 'and to deliver to her, her Chest of Drawers wearing apparell'. However, they allowed her to attempt a proof of her defence of reconciliation before hearing evidence of adultery.

The layout of the house was important: the main bedroom was between the kitchen and the shop, so although James moved his things to another bedroom, he inevitably had to pass through hers at times. Her procurators tried to make this out as reconciliation, but it was no such thing, and the defence failed.

It was not difficult to prove the adultery. Elizabeth Robertson, a servant, was one of several who had seen Janet and Cooper in the act, by peering through a 'hole in the Room door from the kitchen'. The first time she 'had any apprehensions of the defenders immodesty' was one day when James was out and 'Mr Coopar came into the house and went straight into the defenders bed chamber'. James 'came home and tried to get into the bed chamber by the door which leads from the shop but finding it bolted he came to the kitchen to go in by the door that led from the kitchen whereupon the defender unbolted the door and came out to the kitchen, and she appeared to the deponent to be in such confusion that she could scarce speak to the pursuer and she dissuaded him from going into the Room at that time alledging they would be disturbed in their dining by people coming in there, and that it was better for him to dine upstairs which the pursuer complied with, and a little after the deponent saw Mr Coopar go out by the shop door.'

Elizabeth Robertson was not the only material witness, but the pursuer's side were worried about having enough firm testimony to back up the common gossip of adultery, and were offering inducements – and threats – to witnesses. For instance, Elizabeth Selkirk was offered the 'discharge of a debt she owed to James Steedman, and likewise to procure her the friendship and favours of old Mrs Steedman all her lifetime and assured her that the said Mrs Steedman would give her considerable rewards' if she would testify in accordance with their wishes. When she told Steedman that 'she had no letters and could say nothing against the character of Mr Coopar or Mrs Steedman he offered to beat her with his whip and would had done so, if her Lady had not interposed'. She added that 'it was a common clash' in the town of Kinross that James's mother and brother 'had been Bribing the whole Town of Kinross'.

Because of this, Janet's lawyers appealed to the Court of Session. That court found that even if she could prove bribery 'it could not avail her seeing none of the witnesses said to have been practised upon by the pursuer had deponed any thing materiall against the defender', so the appeal was unsuccessful. They then appealed to the House of Lords, which upheld the earlier decisions, and the divorce was finally granted in July 1742.

Janet comes across as a hot-tempered woman with a strong personality. Her mother-in-law was clearly another dominating personality, and the two clashed. James seems to have been remarkably weak and pliable, always accepting the suggestions of the last person he spoke to. It seems his mother goaded him into the divorce, and then did everything she could to make certain it went through; left to himself, James would probably have continued to cohabit with his unfaithful wife. The truly corrosive bitterness was created by her lawyers twisting his forbearance toward her into a handle to try and prevent him achieving his divorce.

cc8/5/7

DAVIE VS GRANT – UNSCRUPULOUS TACTICS

This action lasted some six years, so only a brief summary can be given here, but it shows the depths which an adulterous husband might plumb in attempting to avoid the financial consequences of being divorced.

Helen Davie was the widow of Mr Wilson, a mason in Edinburgh. He cannot have been a young man, and had been married before, for he left his grandchildren in her charge. In December 1776 she married her late husband's lawyer, John Grant Junior. He was younger than her, and perhaps she sought with him the sexual passion missing from her first marriage. But Grant had married her for her late husband's money, and he already had a pregnant mistress. He also frequented bawdy houses and contracted venereal disease. A year after the marriage Helen brought a divorce suit against him.

Right from the start of the marriage, according to Helen, his behaviour was cold and distant, and then became abusive. She discovered that he was still seeing his mistress, Nancy Cumming, and going to bawdy houses. Grant responded by painting Helen as a raddled, poxy old bitch: 'The pursuer was not only much given to liquor but an extraordinary warmth of Constitution led her to a very rigorous and immoderate exaction of the debutum conjugal which the defender tho in the vigour of youth found it was no easy matter to gratify . . . Jealousy the natural consequence of such a disposition soon took place and triffles light as straws were held up by her as Confirmations strong like prooff from Holy writ'. Indeed, 'he claimed, 'independent of her being a strange compound of Laziness and dirtiness and perpetually having the tobacco pipe or the dram glass in her hand an immoderate use of spirits inflamed the pursuers Blood and rendered a Constitution otherways naturally warm so full of desires and passions that it required a man of more than ordinary abilities to gratify her expectations – a disappointment in this respect made the pursuers temper peevish childish and uneven'. (By contrast, of course, Nancy Cumming, was 'a young Lady of a most amiable disposition of respectfull parents and of a most irreproachable Character'.) When the case later went to the Court of Session, that court was so shocked by such 'indelicate' and 'indecent' language that both parties were fined, in spite of the protest by Helen's procurator that 'if indelicate and indecent expressions according to the ordinary acceptation of these terms are to be removed from a Process of Divorce on the head of adultery it cannot well be done but by destroying the process altogether'.

The court perhaps felt more comfortable when the arguments came back to money. Helen had an income of £70 per annum left to her by her first husband and was also guardian of his five grandchildren. Grant, she alleged, was not only after her own money but sought to defraud the grandchildren; he had sent Nancy Cumming (pregnant) off to London, promising to join her there as soon as he had seized the fruits of his mercenary plan.

Grant first attempted the defence of reconciliation, on the grounds that his wife had continued to cohabit with him, but this tactic was rebuffed when she swore that she 'never admitted the defender to the priviledges of a husband nor cohabited with him' after she knew of his adultery. It was much harder for her to go on to prove that adultery. Only one witness, a former servant, was prepared to testify to 'indecent freedoms' between Grant and Miss Cumming; other witnesses denied seeing any such thing. In desperation Helen's agent sent someone round Edinburgh's bawdy houses offering 'a Guinea to any woman that would swear that she had a Criminal correspondence with Mr Grant'.

One such witness was Isobell Cruickshanks, servant to one Margaret Stewart, who had often been visited by Grant. At those times they would be shut up in a room alone together sometimes for two hours, and Isobell would hear 'the Bed Cracking', which she 'imputed to their having carnal dealings together', and when Margaret emerged her head dress would be 'disordered'. The obvious problem with this sort of witness that was it was too easy for the other side to denigrate her character and evidence. According to Grant, Isobell Cruickshanks was a common prostitute. 'Mrs Stewart a lady whose character according to her station in life is unexceptionably good' had dismissed her servant and the latter 'partly from resentment, . . . and partly influenced by promise of reward . . . has sworn to a great variety of conjectures and suspicions of intimacy betwixt Mrs Stewart and the defender'.

But the next witness, Jean Nottress, had herself had sex with Grant, though she hid behind the standard euphemism that 'it consisted with her knowledge that the defender had carnal dealings with a woman at Mrs Bell's house'. She described Helen Davie visiting the bawdy house where she worked with a Mrs Aitken in search of witnesses, when one of the girls said that 'she had given occasion to Sir Thomas Wallaces Divorce and that she had got a Guinea for Divorcing Sir Thomas'. Mrs Aitken 'then said that the person who would declare the truth in this divorce would also get a guinea'. However, Jean Nottress denied that she herself had been offered money to testify. This trawl of bawdy houses in an attempt to find women who had slept with Grant seems to have been legally acceptable because they were persuading witnesses to testify, not bribing them to lie or distort.

Grant then made the first of many appeals to the Court of Session, claiming that Helen had 'been guilty of most undue practices in order to induce some of the witnesses already examined to give false evidence in this cause and that she herself is a notorious drunkard and has been guilty of the very Crime of Adultery with which she charges the defender'. As a counter-process was necessary in order to prove such a charge, he initiated a divorce action against her. He also repeated his charge of her inordinate sexual appetite, and following the Court of Session's line, the commissaries fined him ten shillings for his 'improper and indecent Expressions'.

Helen petitioned for £50 to defend herself against his counter action; the commissaries ordered him to pay her £5; he petitioned against giving her anything at all, adding the irrelevant observation that 'during the whole course of this Ladys life before the date of her marriage to Mr Wilson she never exceeded the station of a menial servant'. The commissaries confirmed their order, and Grant appealed to the Court of Session. The higher court ordered him to pay her the £5, but he did not do so. At this stage Miss Cumming appeared as a witness and denied any knowledge of Grant's carnal knowledge of a woman other than his wife. Her willingness to lie so boldly shows the difficulty that Helen would have had in procuring her divorce if she had had to rely on this one relationship only.

But there was his adultery with Jean Nottress, and the commissaries prepared to conclude the case. Grant vigorously objected. He had not been allowed to proceed with his counter-action because he had not paid his wife the £5. That sum was supposed to be for her to defend herself against the counter-process that had not yet been brought, so he had a point, but not a point relevant to the proof of his adultery. The argument raged on with more petitions and answers, until the exasperated commissaries again held the proof as concluded and prepared to issue the decreet, at which point Grant once more appealed to the Court of Session. That court repelled his defence of reconciliation but allowed him to prove recrimination, i.e. that his wife was also guilty of adultery.

Grant's libel was so vague and general that he was ordered to produce something more specific. The best he could do was 'an Eneas or Angus Fraser who happens to be in the East Indies and a John Caddell living in the West Indies the purpose of which is evidently by adducing these witnesses to throw the Cause aside for years hunting after Evidence in the East and West Indies'.

Grant also continued to insist that Helen's witnesses had been tampered with. However, his attempts to prove bribery were not successful. One witness, Rachel Brown, declared that 'Jean Nottress had not a Baubie'. Nor was he at all successful in proving his wife's alleged bad character, for she was able to produce witnesses who swore that Helen 'never associated with any loose company but led a sober Regular and decent life'.

Further arguments raged over the admissibility of various witnesses, with more appeals to the Court of Session. Finally Grant attempted to prove the adultery of his wife by means of prostitutes who swore they had seen her in a bawdy house with a man in a white wig. The first of these, called Margaret Fraser or Mrs Purcell, claimed that she had kept a house of assignation visited by Helen, but her testimony was incoherent and contradictory. The next, Isabell Cameron, admitted that she had been drummed through the town as a common prostitute, but the commissaries agreed to hear her story. She was resident at a bawdy house and said that she saw Helen several times in that house at night, 'attended by a middle aged Gentleman with Black Cloaths and a white wig . . . that they were in a Back room where was a Bed'.

The whole thing was nonsense. Mrs Purcell subsequently acknowledged herself 'to have been intoxicated with liquor to a degree of stupification at the time of her Examination and that she is now willing to approach the Seat of Justice and confess her Error as well as to bear Evidence of her being suborned by the defender John Grant and instructed previously by him in what she was to swear'. The defence added that 'altho she is a woman of infamous Character yet if her testimony is confirmed by others it will open a scene of perjury and subornation that has taken place in this Cause on the part of Mr Grant and others employed by him'. The commissaries ordered that Mrs Purcell and two other witnesses, Nelly Black and Elizabeth Carmichael, be cited the next day, and Grant was to attend. He again appealed to the Court of Session, which upheld the commissaries' order.

The evidence of Elizabeth Carmichael (aged 26) could not have been more damning. A fortnight earlier, after John Mcara, flesher in Edinburgh, had prepared a room, John Grant came to Mrs Purcell's house. 'A mutchken of whisky Punch and a pound of cheese was ordered by Mr Grant'; 'the company who partook of this fare' comprised Grant, Mcara, Mrs Purcell, Nelly Black – and Elizabeth. 'When this company were together Mr Grant took a small writen Book out of his pocket and addressing himself to Mrs Purcell and Nelly Black told them that they were to get a charge to attend the Commissary Court next day as witnesses'. Sums of money were mentioned in the course of the conversation, though Grant commented that he could not give out any money 'at that time Because if he did it would be thought bribery'. Mr Grant, said Elizabeth, 'described his wife very particularly as a middle sized woman much marked with the small pox and that his reason for giving them this description of her was that they might know her again when they saw her in Court'.

At that meeting Elizabeth was asked by Mrs Purcell, Mcara, and Nelly Black 'if she had ever seen Mrs Grant in Mrs Purcells house to which she answered that she never did – she was then desired by these persons to say as they said when brought in Evidence for that she knew the person of Mrs Grant as well as they'. To which Elizabeth had replied 'they were liars and that she would not swear against her conscience to skreen any person whatever . . . Mcara called her a damned Bitch for if she would be a witness and not tell any tales it would be better to her than a silk handkerchief'.

It was now revealed that all of the witnesses had given false names, a necessity because Grant had previously had to provide the court with a list of the witnesses whom he would be calling, so the names of those who actually appeared had to conform to that list. The witness who had testified as Isabel Cameron told the court that her name was Tibby Mckinnon and that she had never been known by any other name. Similarly, Mrs Purcell was never known as Margaret Fraser 'till the night of the punch drinking'.

After this collapse of former witnesses, Nelly Black also told the truth. The day after they had drunk the punch she and Mrs Purcell were sent for by Mr Grant who 'then directed the deponent to swear that Mrs Grant his wife had been seen in Bed in the house of Mrs Purcell with a man who wore a white wig – the answer of the deponent to this request of Mr Grant was an assent to do what she was desired at the same time she knew very well and was conscious to herself that what Mr Grant desired her to swear was a falsehood'. She deponed that she was never offered a bribe or present 'But when she agreed to swear falsely . . . she must have been actuated by the Expectation of a future reward from Mr Grant'. Mrs Purcell had similarly agreed to his request that evening. Mr Grant had described his wife 'as a woman of a Bold look pretty much marked with the small Pox and dressed all in Black that they might know her from the description when they came to be examined in Court and might swear to her being the same person whom they had seen in Mrs Purcells house in Bed with the man in the white wig'.

Mrs Purcell was not the only one to acknowledge that 'she had been very much intoxicated with liquor when she was examined in court'. Mary Neilson, who had appeared as a witness under the name of Miss Groves, also said that 'she was intoxicated with liquor when she came formerly to be Examined in Court'. In response to Grant's objections to all of this, Helen's procurator stated that 'the whole plot was accidentally and voluntarily discovered by Carmichael who was not in view or heard of by the pursuer at the time. It seems Mr Grant had attempted to lead her into the paths of perjury and subornation but in vain, and as soon as Mrs Purcell and Black learned they had made a discovery of their whole transactions with the defender they confessed and Mrs Purcell alledged that at her Examination she was so drunk that she did not well know what she was saying or doing this fact indeed was conspicuous to every person present at her Examination and will occur to Everyone who reads her deposition'. Mrs Purcell, when she appeared again in court, confirmed this; when asked how she could swear that Helen was the person in bed with the man in the white wig, an 'absolute falsehood', she declared that 'her senses were entirely stupified with drink'.

Grant did not yet give up. He made much of the fact that the women had all declared that no bribe had been offered. Furthermore, he still insisted he could prove that he himself had not been guilty of adultery. Helen's procurator answered: 'If there is no direct Evidence of Bribes being given there are still the strongest that rewards were promised', and the defender had been 'proven guilty of and accessory to the Crimes of perjury and subornation'. And the pursuer 'cannot help Expressing her astonishment at the defenders confidence in talking of reprobating the Charge of adultery against him in any respect as it is a known fact to all the world, that for several years past he lived openly with a woman in family together and that he has had several children by her.'

Nothing daunted, Grant petitioned again, craving that he might be allowed to give in a document proving that 'the evidence of these witnesses in place of militating against him will fall to be expunged from the record'. The commissaries allowed him to do so, but after reading it they found that 'the coincidence of the testimonies of the witnesses is such as to afford strong ground to believe that the said John Grant has been guilty of subornation of perjury by giving or promising Bribes to the said witnesses and that some of them did in consequence thereof actually appear before this Court and assuming false names suggested to them by the said John Grant in order that they might correspond with his list of witnesses deponed to falsehoods likewise suggested by him'. In respect of 'the Criminal nature of the above facts grant warrant to a Macer of Court to apprehend the said John Grant and incarcerate him in the tolbooth of Edinburgh therein to remain untill liberated in due course of Law'.

Grant *still* did not give up, and astonishingly the commissaries allowed the examination of more witnesses adduced by him. At this stage it was Helen's procurator who appealed to the Court of Session, and that court instructed that the case come to an end, and the commissaries pronounce judgment. In January 1784 Helen was at long last granted her divorce, and Grant had to pay her expenses of £150, a surprisingly small amount for a process that went on for six years. One hopes that Grant was punished by the criminal court, but such a slippery character may well have wriggled out of it.

cc8/5/17

CHAPTER 5

UNSUCCESSFUL CASES

Documents have survived for 147 divorce actions that did not result in a decreet of divorce. Out of those, 44 were dismissed, and the rest were seemingly abandoned. Ten decreets assoilzing (absolving) the defender were recorded in the volumes of decreets; the rest survive only as process papers. Most unextracted decreets consisted only of a scribbled note on one of the existing documents, and by the end of the period this was almost always the witnesses' depositions. If the only document to survive was the libel, there is no way of knowing if the case really was abandoned, or if a divorce was in fact granted. However, it is clear from the surviving papers of various cases that lack of means was the usual reason for abandoning an action.

Only one case was dismissed because of suspected collusion, and even for that one the grounds were rather dubious. Four were dismissed because the marriage was not proven, nineteen because the adultery was not proven, and five because *remissio injuriae* was proved. Three others were dismissed because the defender's domicile was not in Scotland. We will look at examples of all of those categories.

COLLUSION – AND MARRIAGE NOT PROVEN

As we will see particularly in Chapter 11, collusive divorces were not difficult to get away with, as the Court of Session severely limited the commissaries' powers to delve into the question. The one and only case dismissed on that ground is an oddity. In 1790 Catherine Taylor brought a divorce action against Thomas Watt. Initially the marriage had simply been an agreement between them and was kept secret (because Catherine 'knew her Mother would be offended at the Marriage on account of Thomas Watt being so young and not having where with all to keep a house'), but after she bore his daughter in 1786 they were married in the presence of witnesses. They were both servants, in different households, and in August 1790 a suit of declarator of marriage was brought by Ann Ralston, alleging that she and Watt had been fellow servants from Martinmas 1788 to Whitsunday 1790, that they had been married 'by *mutual consent*', and she had borne his child. This formed the ground of Catherine's divorce action.[1]

In the first instance Catherine consulted a lawyer not for a divorce but because she thought her husband 'did not give her so much money for her Maintainance as he might have spared'. The matter was dropped, but some months later Thomas told Catherine that 'Ann Ralston was naming him as a husband and that if she did not also put in her Claim it would be against her.' It was at that point that Catherine raised the action, 'at the desire of her Friends', she said, and then 'afterwards departed from it and rather chused to continue the Wife of Thomas Watt than be separate from him'. The commissaries found sufficient evidence of collusion and dismissed the action, 'reserving to her, if she sees Cause to insist in a proper action of declarator of Marriage at her instance' (which would have secured her the aliment she was wanting as well as seeing off Ann Ralson's claim to be his wife). They clearly believed the divorce action had been agreed on so that Thomas could marry the second woman who claimed him as her husband, but in any case it looks as though Catherine was pressured into the action and did not really want a divorce at all.

Because of the profound financial implications of a divorce, the first step in all cases was to prove that the couple were legally married. As an agreement to marry followed by intercourse was a legal marriage, without the need for witnesses, this was not always straightforward. The evidence of friends and neighbours that the couple were considered to be married persons, and behaved towards one another as such, was as important as the subsequent evidence of adultery. Several pursuers who were successful in proving adultery had to provide additional evidence of a legal marriage before the commissaries would grant them a divorce. And some actions were dismissed on that ground.

In the 1713 case of Agnes Fleeming against Laurence Charters, merchant burgess of Edinburgh, on the grounds of his cohabitation with a Dutch woman at Breda, Charters declared that when Agnes had his child she did not claim it was 'begot in a married state but in fornication' and that he had never married her. Agnes said that after her child was born the Tron kirk session 'having inquired anent the same found no fornication in the caice . . . And that she hes bein blameles and free of any scandall'. She produced a marriage certificate which Charters said was forged. He told the commissaries that he could prove that the kirk treasurer and his servant, on hearing of Agnes's pregnancy, 'did expressly examine her whether she was married to the Defender which she altogether Denyed'. As for the Tron kirk finding her blameless, this was obviously because of the forged marriage certificate, which, since he was not there to object to it, could not 'in the Least Instruct the marriage lybelled'. The commissaries allowed Agnes to produce witnesses to the marriage, but after hearing them they found 'actuall marriage not proven nor such cohabitation as is sufficient to Inferr the pursuer and defender to be Man and Wife', so the case was thrown out.[2]

Then there was Mary Allan, who sought a divorce in 1765. She claimed to have married Matthew Johnston, journeyman mason in Edinburgh, in 1761. Matthew declared that at that time he was living with his father in Queensferry, and that he, 'then a weak tender boy was seized with a temporary delirium or madness which made him without the least cause desert his fathers family and range over the Country for several weeks in a disorderly manner'. 'While labouring under this severe malady', he said, it was his 'misfortune to fall into the hands of this pursuer an artful designing woman of more than double his age who . . . so far imposed upon him as to carry him to Edinburgh with her to the house of James Finlay her brother'. He could not 'more positively say' what happened there, 'But Certain he is that no marriage was solemnized as is alleadged by the pursuer nor did he ever Cohabite with the pursuer as his wife, nor were they ever habite and repute as husband and wife.' When he recovered his reason he blamed her 'for her behaviour towards him when his mind was disordered and desired never again for to see her face. He afterwards entered into Indentures as an apprentice with Deacon Jamison mason in Edinburgh'. A year before this action was raised he was married to another woman; Mary knew about the marriage and had made no claim on him, and in fact for the past year had been cohabiting with another man, who was habit and repute by the neighbourhood to be her husband. Mary was unable to provide any evidence of a marriage with Matthew so her case failed.[3]

The above were both cases of a woman bringing a divorce action on the basis of a supposed marriage, but men were capable of doing the same. James Tassie, in Newlands of Cathcart, claimed to have been married to Mary Smith in March 1786, the month before he raised the divorce action, on the grounds that within a few days of the marriage she was guilty of adultery with Matthew Waddell and had been cohabiting with him ever since. Mary declared that she had never married Tassie and that she was Waddell's lawful wife:

> The defender is a young woman at present not much more than 16 years of age, and in the view of possessing himself of a small triffle of money that belonged to her, the pursuer for sometime plagued and teased her with his addresses, nay he even spirited her away from her friends and carried her to the house of Crawford the person mentioned in the Lybell, who is his near relation where he detained her for some days, and artfully endeavoured to procure her to acknowledge him her husband; but as before noticed, they never were married nor Connected together, and the defender having effected her escape, did marry Matthew Waddle her present husband.

The case lasted a year, with two appeals to the Court of Session, but Tassie did not succeed in proving a marriage, so he too failed to obtain a divorce.[4]

ADULTERY NOT PROVEN

The majority of cases which failed because adultery was not proved were counter-actions, in which defence lawyers alleged the pursuer's guilt so that even if a divorce were granted the guilty spouse would not suffer financially. Examples can be seen in Case Studies 2 and 9. Another example comes from the 1787 counter-process of Barberie de la Motte against Captain William Jardine. The women alleged to have been guilty with the Captain were Bett Crow and Jean Geddes, servants. Ann McAndrew, another servant, deponed that Bett had been dismissed because of Mrs Jardine's suspicions. Ann saw Bett snap her fingers in Mrs Jardine's face 'and say that she did not care a Damn for her that she regarded the Captain who was a good Man and that her Mrs Jardine's proceedings were very low'. According to Ann, 'Bett Crow when speaking of the Captain said he was a Good Man', but Ann 'never heard Bett Crow acknowledge any improper Intimacy to have subsisted between her and Captain Jardine and that Bett Crow was a free and out spoken Woman'. Bett's aunt told the court that after her niece was dismissed her uncle considered her 'an Injured woman [and] was resolved to espouse her cause'. Nor did any servants suspect anything 'indecent' between the Captain and Jean Geddes, though she 'was in the use of behaving with great Insolence to her Mistress and fellow servants'. There were forty-five pages of depositions in similar vein, but it did not add up to much and the commissaries dismissed this counter-action, while granting the Captain a divorce against his wife.[5]

More unusual was the 1725 case of David Thom, merchant in Kilsyth and then Edinburgh, against Janet Stark. Janet had raised an action of separation and aliment against him on the grounds of his brutality to her over a number of years. By this time they were living separately, but he would turn up at her house to abuse and threaten her. There was plenty of proof of his maltreatment, so in hopes of avoiding having to pay her any aliment, he raised a divorce action against her on the grounds of adultery. He produced a string of witnesses, but none of them had anything relevant to say, and the case was dismissed. (Janet obtained her legal separation.)[6]

However, there were also cases which were not counter-actions. A messy one was that of John Duncan (latterly residing in Dundee, later wool stapler in Huddersfield) against Elizabeth Maitland in 1806. He alleged that she was guilty with several men, but when one of them, John Mill, gardener, was asked if it consisted with his knowledge that Elizabeth had had carnal dealings with a man other than her husband he said no. Another man, William Moncrieff, Town Officer of Dundee, was cited by Elizabeth, and he declared that since he had been brought to Edinburgh by the pursuer he had 'been repeatedly offered by one Mungo Shepherd Grocer in Dundee Ten Guineas which he said he was desired in a letter from the pursuer to offer the deponent if he would give such evidence as would convict the defender of adultery, which he refused to do, but that he got no reward or promise of reward from the defender'. Being asked if 'it consists with his knowledge that the defender has had carnal Connection with any man different from the pursuer her husband? Depones *negative*.' A curious twist to this case is that the commissaries did not believe him and felt that there was enough proof of adultery to grant the divorce, but when Elizabeth appealed to the Court of Session that court reversed the judgment.[7]

The marriage of David Walker, excise officer in Leith, and Elizabeth Gray was apparently an unhappy one from the start. According to Elizabeth, a few years after the marriage his stock

> was sequestrated for payment of the rent, and he himself turned out of the possession. His temper then became gradually peevish and his mind imbibed all the Evils of penury and avarice, which frequently fell with severity on his innocent Wife. This had the effect of perhaps rendering her less anxious to please him; and at last his violence increased so as to thrust his Wife to the Street in the Town of Leith about the 1st May 1808 without a penny in her pocket, and almost without cloathing.

A contract of separation was drawn up, by which he agreed to pay her £16 per annum in quarterly instalments, but he allowed it to run into arrears, and when pressed for it he raised a divorce action (in January 1810). Did he genuinely believe her guilty with George Clark in Dundee? Clark deponed that one night in June 1809 Elizabeth took him into a public house in Leith and showed him some papers, which he thought were to do with the articles of separation. He told the court that he was never in bed with her and did not know of her having carnal intercourse with any man. In December 1811 the commissaries found 'there is no sufficient evidence appearing from the proof that the Defender was guilty of the Crime of Adultery', and therefore assoilzied her.[8]

And did Alexander Henderson in Berwickshire really believe that his wife, Jean Edmond, was guilty with Francis Louis Beens, a midshipman in the French service, and prisoner of war on parole at Lauder, in 1813? She had been living separately from her husband for some months, and had recently borne his child; he seems to have thought the child was not his, but none of the witnesses saw 'any incorrectness of behaviour or impropriety of conduct' between Jean and the Frenchman, and the commissaries 'having considered the proof adduced by the pursuer and whole Cause', found the pursuer had 'failed to prove his Lybel', and assoilzied her. In 1829 Alexander Burton, thatcher in Carvington, must have believed that his wife, Janet Matthew, was guilty, as he successfully applied to bring his action on the poor's roll. But it hinged on the testimony of only one witness, Mary Mitchell, a servant, who declared that one night when Burton was away James Smith, labourer, stayed the night. Mary saw him in bed with Janet and believed that they had carnal connection. She declared that after he went away Janet said to her that 'she had played the loon, but she hoped the deponent would not tell.' About six months later Mary 'told it in secret to her sister, and she supposed that it was in this way it came out.' But the sister told the commissaries that she arrived in the morning to find Smith in the bed but fully clothed; she did not see anything untoward and claimed that her sister never told her that anything had happened. Smith had long since left the area and could not be traced. In April 1830 the commissaries found that the proof was 'not sufficient to establish the allegation in the Lybel' and assoilzied Janet.[9]

Even when adultery was proved there were, as we saw in the last chapter, various defences that could be put forward, and we turn now to some of those.

REMISSIO INJURIAE

We saw in the last chapter that because an innocent spouse, through ignorance or necessity, might remain with the guilty party after adultery was committed, this defence was frequently used in contested cases. Every once in a while the commissaries believed that a genuine reconciliation had taken place and therefore dismissed the action.

For example, in the 1780–1 case of Andrew Wilson, sometime baker in Edinburgh, against Janet McPhell, she stated that after he returned from abroad 'he met with her sundry times and on these occasions exprest his Love and affection for her telling her what was done in the present action was much against his inclination and only done to please his father.' Not only that, but after he had instigated the process of divorce, 'they eat drank and behaved to one another in a Loving and affectionate manner' – and ended up in bed together, where they were seen by various witnesses. Wilson had no answer to this, so Janet was assoilzied.[10]

The case of James Nimmo, smith in Linlithgow, against Marion Pettygrew was messier. When Nimmo instigated the divorce process in November 1797 the couple had been married for nearly thirty years. Nimmo actually caught her in the act with Thomas Veitch, after which he made 'strict inquiries into the Conduct of his Wife And to his utter astonishment he found that it was no new affair for her and Veitch to have carnal connection together, as they had been practising such a course of criminal correspondence for many years back.' The case was vigorously contested, with objections raised to various witnesses. Then, in August 1798 her lawyer stated that Nimmo had 'barred himself', for he had taken his wife back, 'And had for sometime past and was at present cohabiting with her'. Nimmo called this a 'gross fabrication', and said it could only arise from the fact that when he was at work in his workshop, leaving the young children at home, she had 'repeatedly intruded herself into the house and he has been as often as he came home obliged forcibly to turn her out.' The commissaries allowed her to bring proof of her allegation. Witnesses deponed about quarrels between them, that he once threw her out of the house, and she threw stones at him in the street, but also about their recently having apparently 'agreed again' and lived together as husband and wife. In June 1799 the commissaries assoilzied her on the grounds of reconciliation.[11] .

Another messy case was that of Matthew Hutchison, flesher in Leith, against Jean Hutchison, which ran from October 1806 until March 1808.[12] Jean had confessed to him, in presence of her aunt and others, her adultery with James McAlpine, journeyman flesher. Matthew sent her to her aunt's in Leith and then, at her own request, to London. 'Other enquiries', he said, 'led to the information that

McAlpine and his Wife's intercourse had subsisted for a considerable time back and that she was so abandoned to all sense of feeling and shame as to introduce McAlpine to her husbands house and bed when he was absent in the Country in the course of his business.' According to Hutchison, after the summons of divorce was served on her, 'Every means were used by the Petitioners Uncle Mr Robert Chisholm at Tranent and by her Mother to obtain the pursuer to depart from his action of Divorce', threatening that if he persisted they 'would put him to every expence in their power by defending the petitioner in the action of Divorce.' Hutchison 'without hesitation rejected the proposal.'

All this may have been true, and the case was vigorously contested, with frequent demands for aliment and subsistence for Jean in London, but Matthew had provided plenty of ammunition for a defence of *remissio injuriae*, for after the disclosure of her adultery, while she was at her aunt's, he paid her frequent visits. Janet claimed that he enjoyed 'the priviledge of a husband several times'. Hutchison said that he called because 'he was anxious to know the extent of her guilt and he was no less anxious to have her removed from Leith, from under the influence and power of McAlpine to whom her affection seemed to be rivetted in a most uncommon degree . . . The *incredible* assertion that the Pursuer at these meetings used the priviledges of a husband with the Defender is most positively denied'.

No one saw them having intercourse. But a witness, a servant of Janet's aunt, said that the first night Hutchison called, when he saw Janet weeping he 'took her kindly by both hands', and the deponent heard him say to her that she 'would remember him when she was far from him.' Two cousins admitted that he seemed very much affected at parting with her when he saw her off on the boat to London. It seems unlikely that Hutchison had intercourse with his wife while she was at her aunt's, but he had failed to play the expected role of a betrayed husband, and the commissaries sustained the objection of *remissio injuriae* and assoilzied her. He appealed to the Court of Session, but the higher court sustained the commissaries' decision.

DOMICILE NOT IN SCOTLAND

In Chapter 11 we look at English couples who came to Scotland for their divorces, and the issue of domicile and jurisdiction dominated most of those cases. But it appeared in others as well, for example that of Charles Colin Campbell, Captain in the 74th Regiment of Foot, serving in the East Indies, against Harriet Fraser, daughter of Colonel Charles Fraser in the East India Company, in 1793–4.[13] Her procurator pointed out that Captain Campbell, 'the son of a Scotsman and a lady of Portuguese extraction, a native of India, was himself born in India.' Harriet's mother and father were both Scottish, 'but she was born in London and Educated in England where she resided till the year 1783 when she came to Edinburgh to live with her Mother her father being dead'. In 1786 she married the Captain, and they resided in Scotland from February to September of that year, after which they never went back. To sum up: 'This action has been brought by the Pursuer a native of India having an aversion to and no property in Scotland against the Defender a native of England and possessed of no property in Scotland before the Commissarys on account of acts alleged to have been committed in England.'

Her procurator also pointed out the 'clandestine' nature of the proceedings. Both parties were residing in England, and her husband knew perfectly well where she was, but instead of having the summons served on her personally he had it executed edictally (i.e. called out at the mercat cross of Edinburgh and pier and shore of Leith), so that he had got as far as concluding his proof before she even heard about it, by accident. She declined the jurisdiction of this court, assuring the commissaries that she was only too eager to prove her innocence but 'in the proper Court in England (in which she dares the Pursuer to bring his action) where the acts are alleged to have been Committed, where the witnesses by whom the facts will fall to be proved and the witnesses to be adduced by her reside, and where a Compulsation to force their attendance can be had, which Cannot be obtained in Consequence of any Commission from the Commissarys.' No answer was given in, and the process was dismissed.

In the early nineteenth century arguments over domicile and jurisdiction came up again and again, brought up in the course of the series of cases of English couples, and the commissaries got much tighter over the whole question. In the eighteenth century successful actions were raised from as far afield as Jamaica and India, the pursuer not appearing personally but having given his mandate to someone in Scotland to act for him.[14] And a number of husbands and wives were granted divorces from spouses residing in England. But in 1827 when Agnes Morris, daughter of a merchant in Glasgow brought an action against Alexander Colquhoun Jaffray, surgeon, who had gone off with another woman, with whom he still cohabited in Liverpool, the commissaries decided that they had no jurisdiction.[15]

OTHER REASONS FOR DISMISSAL

We saw in the last chapter that insanity was sometimes brought as an unsuccessful defence; in one case the insanity of a pursuer was genuine. In 1789 Margaret Sheddan, daughter of William Sheddan of Lochy, sought to divorce John Sheddan, hammerman in Perth.[16] John produced a certificate signed by the minister at Auchterarder and one of the elders attesting that Margaret was sometimes so 'remarkably insane' that she had to be put under the care of a keeper. A cousin of John's commented that 'she was insane and so much so that to prevent her from doing violence to him and his family or from hurting herself he with the consent and approbation of her father and husband kept her bound in Iron chains That by some means she got the chains broken and one morning about twenty one months ago got out and run away since which time she had not been under his charge'. Since then 'she had been wandering from place to place'. John's procurator argued that Margaret had evidently 'by the plausible and artful manner which her cousin attests she put on to strangers must have deceived the men of business who appear on her behalf so as to procure the present extraordinary Summons'.

Margaret's procurator naturally argued that this was untrue, and the commissaries cited her to appear before them. In the course of the examination she 'produced a certificate under the hands of the minister of Muthil and being interrogated who was meant by Lady Margaret Sheddan of Lochie and Broadgate written among other things on the back of the said certificate Declared that this and the other things were of her hand writing and that she meant to describe herself by the name Lady Margaret Sheddan for that two ploughgates of Lochie were the property [of the] Declarant'. She also said that while she was confined 'with hand cuffs and Iron fetters around her legs', she 'behaved to every body that came in more discreetly than any body about the house could do as she had a better education'. The commissaries 'Found from the said Declaration as well as the productions ultroniously made by her in the course thereof and her manner and appearance when examined in presence of the whole Commissaries that she was in such a state of mind as that the oath of calumny and collusion could not with propriety be put to her. Therefore Found that the process could not proceed and Dismissed the same'.

During the period when church courts were still very active, a kirk session intervened in one divorce process. This was in 1757 when Anna Marshall brought an action against John Macmillan.[17] She was able to prove that he had cohabited with another woman, first in Scotland and then in England, and the commissaries had got as far as writing out the divorce decreet when the minister and kirk session of Bothwell petitioned the court.

About three years earlier Anna had married a farmer named Richard Budel, and bore him a child. As there was no evidence of the death of John Macmillan, her former husband, she was called before the kirk session of Shotts, where she then lived, but 'before the Cause was brought any length she removed to Glasgow'. The session there took up the case, but it was left unfinished because the couple then moved to Bothwell parish. By this time 'there was a loud Fama clamosa that her former husband was still alive', and the session was at last 'credibly informed' of this 'by some of our Neighbours who had been at London and been acquainted with Mcmillan and knew that he resided at London.' When Anna appeared before the session she 'denyed that John Mcmillan was alive yea offered to prove his death.' She was then referred to the presbytery which raised an action against her for adultery and bigamy.

It was at this stage that she raised her divorce action. Toward the end of the proceedings the minister and session learned of her action against Macmillan before this court 'upon the pretence that he had been guilty of Adultery with some other woman with whom he had gone off and this is done no doubt with a view to Justify her present Marriage with Richard Budel which however your petitioners are advised will not do in Law seeing she has married Budel before any divorce was obtain'd against John Mcmillan'.

The petitioners understood that civil and ecclesiastical courts were independent of one another, but ecclesiastical courts would suspend procedure when they learned that the commissary court was hearing a case, and as the trial of Anna Marshal had begun in the ecclesiastical courts they hoped that this case might be suspended in the same way. The 'Principal design of bringing a divorce by a woman against her husband as guilty of Adultery is to have the marriage dissolved and her declared at liberty to marry another so if it be fact (as can be instructed) that she has already married another man at her own hand then the reason of giveing legal divorce ceases.' Anna's procurator declared that the petition was 'officious and impertinent, Because it does not belong to a Minister and Kirk session to interfere in a process, in which they have no Concern, and altogether incompetent as they are not parties to the said process'. However, when the commissaries ordered Anna to appear before them in Court to 'answer to such questions as shall be put to her anent the matters mentioned in the petition', there was no response, so that was the end of the divorce case. (We will see more civil–ecclesiastical interchange in Chapter 12.)

After looking at these various reasons for a case to be dismissed we are still left with some puzzles. For example, in August 1772 Joseph Cowan, carpenter in Leith, brought an action against Agnes Hardie, whom he had married in June 1769. After eighteen months' cohabitation he went on a voyage to North America and when he returned in July 1772 he found that his wife had borne a child in March. After petitioning, he was admitted to the benefit of the poors' roll. He swore his oath of calumny, and in January was allowed to adduce proof; in April witnesses deponed about the delivery of the child. But in July the commissaries found the 'procedure highly irregular and therefore dismiss the process'.[18] There is no indication at all what was irregular about it, and a few other cases fall into this category as well.

Of course, the inexplicable features even more prominently in cases which were abandoned, but where the documents do provide a reason, that reason was always lack of means.[19] The strongest evidence of this comes from the case of Martin Turfie Junior, sailor in Kinghorn, who brought an action against his wife in May 1806. She petitioned for interim aliment and expenses, and the commissaries ordered him to pay her 10, at which point the case was abandoned. He brought a new action in January 1808, and once again she petitioned for money. The commissaries again ordered him to pay her £10, and he protested: 'the present application has been made with no other view than that of obtaining delay and in the hopes that by harassing him with unnecessary expences which he is ill able to bear he would be obliged to relinquish the present process as he did a former and for want of money to carry it on'. He then petitioned to be admitted to the poor's roll, was so admitted, and was able to present his proof and obtain his divorce.[20]

Worst off were pursuers in contested cases who were not indigent enough to hope for the benefit of the poor's roll but not affluent enough to carry on prolonged litigation, particularly in the early nineteenth century when the commissaries became increasingly reluctant to allow witnesses to be examined locally.

Occasionally material from an unsuccessful case is used to illustrate a point in later chapters, but for the most part the remainder of the book is concerned with cases that did result in a divorce.

NOTES

All CC references are in the Scottish Record Office.
 1. cc8/6/53.
 2. cc8/6/6.
 3. cc8/6/25.
 4. cc8/6/48.
 5. cc8/6/49.
 6. cc8/5/2 for her action against him; cc6/8/8 for his against her.
 7. cc8/6/82.
 8. cc8/6/91.
 9. cc8/6/99; cc8/6/164.
10. cc8/6/39.
11. cc8/6/66.
12. cc8/6/81.
13. cc8/5/21.
14. Chalmers vs Marr, 1766, cc8/5/11; Campbell vs Campbell, 1790, cc8/5/3; Fortune vs Crawford, 1798, cc8/5/24.
15. cc8/6/158.
16. cc8/5/22.
17. cc8/6/21.
18. cc8/6/31.
19. Examples include Kelly vs Morrison, 1734, cc8/6/10; Anderson against Neish, 1765, cc8/6/24; White vs Irons, 1814, cc8/6/109.
20. cc8/6/81; cc8/6/87.

WAUGH VS BALLANTYNE – TRUE MADNESS

The marriage in June 1787 of Thomas Waugh, writer (lawyer) in Jedburgh, and Jean Ballantyne, daughter of Thomas Ballantyne of Hollylie, was doomed from the start. Jean, a timid 18-year-old, was tyrannised by her jealous bully of a husband for ten years before the incident that brought matters to a head, though she then had to endure a further six years of litigation before she was finally freed from him by a decreet of separation. When he brought his divorce action against his wife, Waugh was utterly convinced of her guilt, having found the man whom he had long suspected to be her paramour concealed in the house at an early hour of the morning of 25 August 1797. The alleged lover, however, was shortly afterwards confined to a madhouse, and it was on the question of his sanity or insanity on the night in question that the case hinged.

According to Waugh's libel, within four months of the marriage Jean attempted to leave him, 'ultimately returning with reluctance in consequence of his having commenced a process of adherence against her'. Her response was that 'she trusts to prove not only by her own servants, but by the most respectable Inhabitants of that Town that her conduct has been exámplary both for circumspection and submission to the will of her husband Had she stiled him her Lord and Master, she would have expressed herself more Correctly. For being possessed of a temper naturally jealous it increased with years and suggesting to him perpetually new suspicions turned his nature into bitterness – This led him continually from hints and surmises to insinuations, from these to the flat accusation of infidelity and from that to the grossest insult and harsh usage; so that the respondent has led a life of misery and by her husbands violence has had her constitution entirely enervated.'

Apart from the final incident, Waugh's only specific accusation was that in the summer of 1788 when he had left his wife at Holy Island (Northumberland), where he had taken her 'for the benefit of sea bathing', she was persuaded by John Rutherford Ainslie (also of Jedburgh) and his relatives to leave the island and join them, without the permission or knowledge of her husband. She replied that there was no reason why she should not have joined family friends, but 'Mr Rutherford Ainslie was then at Bath or some other place in the South of England, and the pursuer's disturbed imagination has conjured that gentleman down to Holy Island and Berwick'. It was Mr Ainslie's brother-in-law, Mr John Clunie, merchant and one-time Mayor of

Berwick who, on a family excursion to Holy Island, discovered Jean 'all alone in a lodging quite retired', and persuaded her to join them in Berwick. His sister, Miss Mary Rutherford, told the court that after Waugh returned to Holy Island and found that his wife was not there, he 'expressed himself to others . . . in terms of such anger and reproach for having carried away his wife without his knowledge and threw out so many reflections against Mr and Mrs Clunie and the deponent for having done so as naturally produced a coolness between the families . . . at this time Mr Rutherford Ainslie the deponent's brother was either at London or Bath.'

This was the only specific accusation until the final one, but he claimed that his wife had carried on a longstanding adulterous affair with John Rutherford Ainslie. He forbade his wife to receive visits from the man, yet according to their servant, Margaret Smith, during her first year of service (1793) Mr Rutherford Ainslie frequently called on Mrs Waugh when her husband was away. Other witnesses once saw Jean and Rutherford Ainslie walking 'privately' together, which was taken notice of since it was known in Jedburgh that Mr Waugh had forbidden Mr Ainslie his house. But not a single witness claimed to have seen anything 'improper' between them, or to have suspected a love affair. One may surmise friendship, or even an attraction, between them, otherwise Jean, who was so afraid of her husband, would not have defied him by secret meetings, but in a small town like Jedburgh where the characters were well known, and gossip was rife, the concurrence of all witnesses in disbelieving Jean guilty is striking.

So to the crucial events of 25 August when Waugh told a witness, Thomas Miller, 'he had found Mr Rutherford Ainslie with his, Mr Waugh's wife and showed the deponent a hat which he said was Mr Ainslies' and 'said, "Who would not pity my case this morning. I have often suspected Mr Rutherford Ainslie with my wife, but now I have found it out".' Waugh said 'he had found him in the house and in a room up stairs the door of which was bolted so that Mr Waugh could not get in and that he had gone to get something wherewith to break upon the door but when he returned he found the door open and when he went into the room he said that he found Mr Ainslie concealed in the bed . . . Mr Waugh said that Mrs Waugh at that time had on a petticoat but had not the rest of her cloaths'. Andrew Turnbull, a 29-year-old weaver, was standing outside Waugh's door that morning, when Waugh emerged 'and said "I have catched Rutherford Ainslie in bed with my wife this morning and there is his hat"'. Immediately after that Turnbull met up with John Thomson, the Town Clerk, who asked him 'what was on hand,' to which he 'was shy in making an answer', but eventually 'said that Mr Waugh had caught Mr Rutherford Ainslie in bed with his wife that morning, and Mr Thomson answered "Tut that's nonsense it would be the maid".'

Waugh called witnesses – James Wintrope, wright, Provost Billerwell, Captain Ormiston, Thomas Wood and Mr Rutherford, writer – 'to look at a room in his house in which he said Mr Rutherford Ainslie had been found under the tyke of the bed'. So these gentlemen stood and looked at the bed. But did anything go on in that bed?

According to Katharine Wilson, their servant at the time, 'Mr Waugh slept in the parlour in one bed while Mrs Waugh and the deponent slept in another bed in the same room' – which seems an extraordinary arrangement. On the morning in question Katharine awoke to find her mistress missing, and 'thought Mrs Waugh had been taken ill as she was often in the night time'. Katharine went out to the well for water and when she returned Mr Waugh came down with a hat in his hand, and 'repeatedly called Mrs Waugh a whore and swore at her'. Katharine did 'not recollect that Mrs Waugh denied the charge of being a whore, indeed she was crying so bitterly that the deponent did not understand and certainly does not recollect any thing she said upon the occasion'. Katharine 'was herself much agitated and shedding tears at the time occasioned by seeing her mistress's agony and her master's violence'.

When Mr Waugh went out to the street Mrs Waugh 'immediately went into the parlour and flung herself upon the bed'. Katharine 'followed her into the room and found her so agitated that she was afraid she would put hands to herself . . . she pulled her hands out of the deponent's and began to tear her cloaths'. Jean took some laudanum and then slept until three the next afternoon, and that evening Katharine said to her mistress, ' "Dear Mrs Waugh why didn't you cry to me when Mr Ainslie came into the house?" To which Mrs Waugh answered that she durst not as she was afraid of Mr Waugh.' Subsequently Katharine 'said to Mrs Waugh "What made you rise?" To which Mrs Waugh answered that she heard the dog barking, that she rose and went up stair to see what it was and found Mr Ainslie at the head of the stair.' She had 'urged him to go away which he refused to do'.

A further picture of a terrorised wife emerges from Katharine's testimony. On many occasions prior to this one she 'heard Mr Waugh reproach his wife both with whoredome and drunkenness. That whenever Mrs Waugh lay longer in bed than usual he would say to her that she sat up all night whoreing and drinking and that was the reason she could not get up in the morning though on most of those occasions the deponent was conscious that Mrs Waugh had been in bed with her the whole of the preceding night, the deponent having frequently been kept awake most part of the night by her mistress's bad health.' The illnesses, she added 'were nervous and the Doctors called them hysterical fits, and she was very subject to them before this . . . when any thing agitated Mrs Waugh she was subject to these fits. And being interrogated if she was timorous in her nature and easy frightened? Depones that she was most terribly so,' and from that Saturday morning until Tuesday evening 'she was out of one hysteric fit into another, and not in a situation to keep up a continued rational conversation with any person'.

Isobel Wood, a cousin of Jean's, told the court of Jean's begging for her husband's forgiveness, though at the same time saying that she was innocent. Striking evidence of the town taking sides comes from Isobel's statement that Jean 'was during the above time visited by different Ladies among others by Mrs Thomson wife of Mr Thomson Town Clerk of Jedburgh, Mrs Somerville the Ministers wife, Mrs Jardine of Wrens nest, Mrs Ormiston the pursuers daughter, Miss Chatto of Mainhouse, Mrs Borthwick wife of Baillie Borthwick and Miss Somerville the ministers daughter'. Miss Chatto subsequently deponed that 'in the course of her acquaintance with Mrs

Waugh she never remarked the smallest levity or impropriety of behaviour in that lady but on the Contrary her Conduct appeared to the deponent to be uncommonly guarded for so young a woman'. The only criticism such ladies had of Jean's conduct on the occasion in question had been her failure to call out when she first discovered Mr Ainslie in the house, but to all of them she had said that 'she had been afraid of Mr Waugh and wished on that account to get Mr Ainslie privately out of the house'.

Some of the confusion arose from the fact that the front door was bolted and the windows screwed shut, so Waugh alleged that Ainslie could not have entered the house without inside help, but at least one witness claimed that an upstairs window was sometimes left open. The major legal battle was over the question of whether witnesses should be allowed to testify about what Ainslie had told them on the morning in question. He was again locked up in an asylum, and so could not be called as a witness himself, but Waugh contended that he had been perfectly sane on the morning in question, so that interrogating witnesses on his comments was perfectly legitimate. The Defence brought a mass of evidence as to the man's mental state: we would call him a manic.

When he had his fits, 'probably fancying that he is playing the character of Ranger he amuses himself by breaking into the houses of the Town's people in hopes to meet with their servant maids'. (See the Introduction to this book for an explanation of 'Ranger'.) Alexander Simpson, a teller at the Royal Bank in Edinburgh, knew that in July 1795 Mr Ainslie 'was in a state of derangement' and 'was sent to a private madhouse', and in September 1797 he was again 'brought to Edinburgh in a state of derangement and conveyed to the madhouse'. On all those occasions 'the case and turn of Mr Ainslies conduct and conversation were similar. That this cast consisted chiefly in vanity and supposing himself a great man That in 1794 he talked of raising regiments and at the other period before deponed to he discoursed in the same manner and likewise boasted of his riches and talked of buying land.' Other witnesses knew that Mr Ainslie 'wished to put into the newspapers ridiculous advertisements, and wished to circulate hand bills to the same purpose and desired the printers of the newspaper to insert paragraphs containing accounts of his family Connections with the Lord Chancellor and other great men'.

Thomas Hay, surgeon in Edinburgh, a relation of Mr Ainslie's, deponed that in 1794 'Mr Ainslie was very much deranged and as the deponent thought stark mad', and he was like that again in 1796. When he was deranged 'the general turn of his mind was vanity, and he particularly talked of his great connexions, and about military matters conceiving himself to be a very great officer and a rich and powerful man'. Hay added that 'before the first attack of his disorder and since that period during his lucid intervals Mr Ainslie always appeared to the deponent to be a plain, decent and rather shy man, and a man of veracity and honour but that when he was deranged his character was perfectly reversed'. Mr George Rutherford, merchant in Glasgow, Mr Ainslie's brother, was sent for to London when Mr Ainslie was first deranged. On the journey north, 'Mr Ainslie still continued very high and when in Company he would be as high before dinner without taking drink as the rest of the

Company were after dinner and drinking freely'. Subsequently, 'the state of his spirits was quite the reverse of what they had been when the deponent left him at Berwick as he was very low and he frequently complained to the deponent that he could not sleep and the deponent considered him as still under the influence of his disorder of which he considered the lowness of spirits merely as different symptoms from what he had observed before'.

And there was plenty of evidence of the man's entering houses. Martha Charteris, wife of Dr Somerville, minister at Jedburgh, told the story of the morning when her servant screamed and said there was a man in the house. Martha 'threw up her window and looked out to the garden which immediately adjoins the house', and 'saw Mr Rutherford Ainslie whom she knows well stepping out of the window and just getting clear of it, upon which she addressed him by his name and asked him whether she was to consider him as a house breaker or madman, to which he answered that he meant the deponent no harm, and immediately walked away slowly through the garden out of the deponents sight'. Martha added that she 'told her husband of this incident immediately on his coming home who expressed no sort of jealousy or suspicion of the deponent on this occasion.' Mr Walter Riddell, writer in Jedburgh, deponed that in August 1796 Mr Ainslie attempted to get in his house 'by means of throwing up the sash of a window of a room on the ground floor of the house. That this happened about one or two o'Clock in the morning . . . that his servant maid who slept in that room came up to the deponent in his bed room which is immediately above that room, and told him that some body was trying to get into the house, and that she believed it was Mr Ainslie'. Riddell then threw open his own window and saw Mr Ainslie 'half in and half out at the window of the room below'. He 'cried "who is there?" and getting no answer said "I see this is you Mr Ainslie what do you want?" That Mr Ainslie answered "I want you" To which the deponent replied that he did not chuse to see any body at that time of night and begged he would go away. That Mr Ainslie then walked a step or two from the window and looking up to the deponent said "Do you desire me to go home?" and the deponent having answered in the affirmative Mr Ainslie said "Well I will go away" and took off his hat and wished the deponent a good morning.' Riddell 'did not ascribe this visit to Mr Ainslie's having any business with the deponent, but to his wish to get at the maid who was a good looking girl.'

His worst spell was at the time of the militia riots in August 1797. Dr Robert Lindesay was consulted by his sister at that time about 'hiring some person to attend on and confine her brother, to which the deponent assented considering that Mr Ainslie's state of mind full warranted such procedure.' Subsequently a warrant was obtained from the sheriff depute and substitute for detaining him in confinement in his own house. 'Being specially interrogated if Mr Ainslie had distorted ideas of things?', Dr Lindesay answered that 'he thought Mr Ainslie had false ideas often and that the deponent does not think that any thing that Mr Ainslie said at that time could be depended on, though at the same time the deponent has seen letters written by Mr Ainslie at that period some of which were very sensible and pertinent and others very absurd and ridiculous. Being specially interrogated if when Mr Ainslie was in his fits of insanity the deponent has heard him boast of favours received from Ladies of character which favours the deponent altogether disbelieved to have been granted? Depones that he has heard Mr Ainslie made such boast upon one occasion but the deponent gave no credit to it.'

Ainslie's own sister, Mary, deponed that she 'considered her brother as being much deranged immediately before the Militia Riot at Jedburgh in the year 1797, and thought he was much worse in consequence of having been out that day'. She received three different messages from the inn where he was behaving riotously but was unable to persuade him to come home. He finally came in at six in the morning, but stayed only a quarter of an hour, and she 'never saw her brother so much deranged as during that quarter of an hour and there was a greater wildness in his eye than she had ever observed before.' Four days later she had him confined.

The weight of evidence was so by now so great that Waugh made no further attempt to have witnesses examined on Ainslie's words at the time he was found. But the case was far from over. After Waugh realised it was impossible to prove her adultery with Ainslie, he found a witness who claimed to have seen her in a compromising position with a servant. It was by this time some two years after the instigation of the action, and to bring in a new charge at such a stage in the proceedings was highly irregular, but Jean expressed 'her readiness to join issue in the proof', and the witness was allowed to appear.

Patrick Boswell, who was in his seventies, claimed that he had been working in the fields when he saw Jean, whom he knew 'by sight when he saw her on horseback as she was the lightest rider he ever saw on a Saddle for a woman', and Andrew Hall riding together. They stopped, dismounted and disappeared for about half an hour in a strip of firs, and when they came out he said that he saw Hall kiss Jean and pull up his breeches. Boswell was intensively questioned, and even asked to demonstrate as far as possible 'the manner in which Andrew Hall was pulling up his breeches'. Boswell 'stood up and took hold of the Waist band of his breeches with both hands, putting one of his hands to the place of each of his haunch buttons and pulled up his breeches rather like a man who was afraid his breeches would fall down through slackness than like one whose breeches had been opened for any necessary purpose, and in a manner that did not appear to bear any resemblance of a man who was or had been just buttoning up his breeches.'

We then get a glimpse of how long questioning could take, for at this stage there was some discussion about the witness's fitness to continue. It was twenty past nine at night, and his examination had started at noon. At about four he seemed to be exhausted and ill and they stopped and ordered dinner, starting again at seven. At first he seemed to have revived but later he was tired and peevish. However, he did not want to return another day so his examination continued until it was concluded. (He died soon after this.)

The Defence was able to produce convincing witnesses for Jean. For one thing, she had ridden only on the turnpike and never on the moor in question. Hall, who had been 18 or 19 at the time, 'was pitted with the small pox and a coarse country lad.' His own mother deponed that 'her son was a backward diffident lad having been brought up in a Country way.' No one other than Boswell had ever seen anything untoward between them or believed that such a thing was possible.

After this Waugh once again attempted to have Ainslie's own words brought into court, but in May 1800, nearly three years after the case began, the commissaries 'Found it proven that Mr Ainslie was occasionally afflicted with insanity or at least strong mental derangement Found that on 26 August 1797 and for sometime after he was afflicted with and acted under the influence of that disorder in such a degree as to render what he said in the opinion of those best acquainted with him unworthy of Credit'. They assoilzied the defender from the action and refused to allow another petition from the pursuer, but he appealed to the Court of Session, and when his appeal was refused he appealed against that decision. When that appeal was also refused the decision was final, but Waugh, as a canny lawyer, managed to drag out the question of financial reparation for nearly three years more.

As soon as the decision on the divorce action was final Jean's separation case against him was awakened. Her lawyer stated that it did not seem necessary to bring proof of maltreatment, since it seemed 'quite sufficient simply to refer to the proceedings in the process of Divorce, which has now terminated so honourably for the Lady in order to found her in a demand for a separation a mensa et thoro.' Waugh replied that 'without this investigation she never could have been publicly vindicated . . . This then, which was necessary for her own honour as well as that of the present defender cannot be decerned a malicious prosecution', so it could not be the basis of a separation action. The commissaries did not agree, finding 'in the process of Divorce mentioned in the minute sundry acts of maltreatment by the defender to the pursuer appearing on record which entitle her to a Decreet of separation and aliment without the necessity of any further proof in the present action'.

After granting the separation the commissaries then suspended the question of the amount of aliment he would have to pay her until the amount of expenses for the divorce case was finally settled, forcing her to rely on others for her financial support during the interminable period when he disputed all the sums put forward, with both parties appealing more than once to the Court of Session. In the end the expenses which he had to pay amounted to £1,006, an extraordinarily high amount for litigation in this court, plus an additional amount for the separation case. He also had to pay her an aliment of £200 a year.

By the time the case was over Mr Rutherford Ainslie was dead. But he hardly seems to have been the only lunatic in the case. Jean's 'hysterical fits' at least provoked compassion, but Waugh's relentless pursuit of his legal action in the face of the testimony of his wife's virtue from scores of witnesses, ranging from servants to some of the most elite members of Jedburgh's society, was true madness.

cc8/5/27

CHAPTER 6

ARISTOCRATIC DIVORCES

The lifestyles of the couples featured in this chapter (including upper gentry like baronets, as well as peers) did not have much in common with the lifestyles of the majority of the population of Scotland, but their stories are worth telling in this chapter and in some case studies. They had armies of servants, so their intimate behaviour was observed by a number of different people, enabling a large body of evidence to be presented, and revealing the relationship between masters, mistresses and those who served them. And, no matter how lofty their positions, they belonged to their time and shared both the particular and universal experiences of unhappily married people. And finally, in some cases, at least, additional information, such as ages, and whether they subsequently remarried, is available about them simply because of their rank.

GUILTY WIVES

Major Robert Lawrie, son of Sir Robert Lawrie of Maxwelton, and Elizabeth Maria Ruthven, daughter of Lord Ruthven, were married in 1763 and had two children; the divorce action was brought in 1773.[1] Her affair began in summer or autumn 1771 when the Major was with his regiment in England. Elizabeth was staying in Fisherrow with her daughter and two maids and was often visited by officers quartered at Musselburgh, and particularly Lieutenant Hatton Flood. They would go out walking and riding, unaccompanied, and 'It was taken notice of amongst the neighbours That Lieutenant Flood paid too frequent visits to her'. One of those neighbours, Margaret Bowie, a widow who kept a small garden near Fisherrow, 'remembered Lieutenant Flood quarter at Musselburgh some years before . . . when he was habite and repute a Rake'. When she saw him walking with Elizabeth, who 'wore a hatt hung down her head and said Nothing' she 'concluded her to be Wife of Lieutenant Flood' and said to him 'she was glad he had at last fixed as he had been a great Rake when formerly at Musselburgh to which he answered that a reformed Rake made a good husband'.

This was not a short, casual fling, for during the following winter when the family were in Lisbon and then Marseilles, a servant of the Major's saw letters addressed to Lieutenant Flood in Devon amongst those ready for posting. In March 1772 the Major took lodgings for his wife and family in Bristol while he was in London, and again Lieutenant Flood was a frequent visitor. At that time Elizabeth told everyone that he was her brother. Mary Irvine, a servant, had her suspicions roused after seeing her mistress in his bedchamber a few times, and before the Major returned to Bristol Elizabeth told Mary not to let him know that her brother had been there because there had been a quarrel between them. When they left Bristol and travelled to Devizes, Elizabeth's eldest brother, Captain Ruthven, joined them. Flood also turned up but not when Captain Ruthven was around. He appeared at other places on their route as well, and when he did not Mary was given letters to him to post and was told to keep this secret. Mary then accompanied her mistress to Portsmouth where they embarked for Lisbon, and Flood joined them at Guildford. In Lisbon Mary also took letters to the post addressed to him. Back in London and on the route north Flood again joined them.

It is not stated how Major Lawrie came to know of the affair but hardly surprising that he did so. The divorce was not contested, but Lieutenant Flood was named so, in theory, Elizabeth would not have been in able to marry him.

Sarah Skene, daughter of George Skene of Skene, Member of Parliament for the county of Aberdeen, also committed adultery with an officer, but he was her second lover. She was married to Thomas Macdonald, Clerk to the Signet, in June 1780, and when the divorce action was brought in June 1784 she was alleged to have been guilty for the past eight or ten months.[2] Mary Campbell (aged 20) was the first servant to testify. The previous winter she 'was frequently employed in carrying letters between Mrs Macdonald and Mr Peter Gordon', and 'Mrs Macdonald discovered a great anxiety to secret these letters from her husband and deposited them in a silk bag which she put into her pockets and the pockets below the Bolster while she was in Bed'. Mary 'often heard Mrs Macdonald speaking very warm in praises of Mr Gordon and say that he was a very handsome young man'. Mary, 'feeling in her own mind a very Strong Curiosity and having at the same time a Suspicion of her Mistress opened a letter which had been given her by Mrs Macdonald to be delivered to Gordon'. In the letter 'Mrs Macdonald informed Mr Gordon that Mr Macdonald was to go to London in a few weeks and that then they would have more opportunity of seeing one another often That Mr Macdonald was to go to the Play next night and inviting Mr Gordon to drink tea but desired that it might be past Eight before he came that Mr Macdonald might be gone'.

On that Saturday night Gordon came at about nine. An hour later the other servant maid, Juliet Maclauchlan, 'had occasion to go into the Drawing room with a candle in her hand'. She 'immediately run back into the Kitchen shut the door of the Drawing room dropt the candle and fell into a faint on the Kitchen floor'. Upon 'recovering her senses being asked . . . what had made her faint away', she said that 'she had seen Mrs Macdonald and Mr Gordon on the couch in a very undecent situation'. Mary immediately went into the drawing room with a candle and 'saw Mrs Macdonald sitting at one End of the Couch and Mr Gordon at the other'. The room was dark, and 'they seemed to be both in very great confusion'. 'Mrs Macdonald cry'd out "O fy" and appeared to be angry at the deponent for intruding'. Mary noted that Mr Gordon's breeches were 'down and his legs and thighs uncovered'. According to another servant, when Mary returned to the kitchen 'she was weeping and clasping Mrs Macdonalds daughter in her arms cried "What a poor mother you have got this night"'.

Soon after that Sarah confided to her maid that 'Mr Gordon and she had quarrelled and that she had returned him his Letters'. The couple went to London then, and when they returned Mrs Macdonald 'often talked of a Major Piget and expressed great anxiety about his arrival'. The night his regiment arrived in Edinburgh Sarah gave Mary and her fellow servant, Juliet, 'tickets to the play', and when they returned they found their mistress's door bolted. They knew perfectly well why and even 'saw him come out of the bedroom on his tiptoes'. (The first time this happened 'Juliet exclaimed "Good God what's that".') On one occasion Mary overheard the Major saying to Mrs Macdonald

That he had been dining at Fortunes or some other Tavern where he heard that she had been concerned in an affair of Gallantry with Gordon That Mrs Macdonald answered that she had no further connection with Gordon than having met with him at Duns assembly and having danced a country dance with him That he then asked her if she would swear that she never had been enjoyed by any other man except her husband and himself, That he then administered to her a solemn oath to that purpose which she took.

As she was already deceiving her husband with Piget, he was foolish if he believed her oath.

Another servant, Thomas Dunlop (aged 47), was able to provide details of various occasions when Sarah and Major Piget were alone together. Being asked by the court 'how he accounts for the accuracy of dates and recollection of minute circumstances', he replied that 'he conceived a suspicion of his Mistress which led him to take a note of the day on which any suspicious circumstance occurred which he has since very frequently perused with attention'. (Thomas also deponed that on the day after Sarah had been sent out of the house the Major sent for him and said that if he, Thomas, 'would say nothing against him in Evidence he would give him Twenty Guineas in a present when the cause was over upon his honour as an honest Man and a Gentleman'.)

The case was not contested, and from remarks made by some of the witnesses, Sarah was far from averse to being divorced and, indeed, hoped to marry Major Piget. There is no suggestion that she was maltreated in any way, but her taking two lovers in quick succession suggests that she found her husband boring. At least there were no children. (Four years later her older sister, Mary, was also divorced by her husband, the Honourable Alexander Duff of Echt.[3])

A much more painful case is that of Archibald Earl of Eglinton against Frances Twysden, daughter of Sir William Twysden in Kent. Frances was the Earl's second wife (his first died childless in 1778); they married in August 1783 when the Earl was fifty-seven. A daughter, Mary, was born in March 1787, and when the divorce action was brought in December of that year Frances was pregnant with a second, who was born in May 1788.[4]

The infant, Mary, was kept at the house of the Countess's grandfather, about fourteen miles from London (the reason for this unusual arrangement is not stated). When she went there to see her child she was visited by 'a male friend' at night. Montgomery Lawson, the Earl's servant, knew about this but did not think that her grandfather's servants were aware of it. Lawson said that the man 'had on a Great Coat on these occasions by which the Deponent supposed he meant to conceal himself'. Lawson also said that the man called frequently at Lord Eglinton's house in London during the spring and summer, when Lord Eglinton was not at home, and they would spend an hour or two in a room by themselves; this would happen even when Lord Eglinton was simply dining elsewhere. The man was 31-year-old Douglas, 8th Duke of Hamilton.

There could have been no hope of marriage with his Grace, for he was already married, but her infatuation was total. In the autumn, when the Earl was away, Frances asked Lawson 'if he would admit the Duke of Hamilton into her bed Chamber'. Lawson replied, 'it was very dangerous and he would not Chuse to do it', so Frances 'said that she could do it herself', and told Lawson that 'she had written a letter to the Duke of Hamilton inviting him to come.' Lawson asked her if 'any of the other servants were in her confidence', and she said no. He told her frequently that 'she should not write to the Duke of Hamilton for that it was imprudent in her to do so', but she paid no heed. We may pause here for a moment to consider the relationship between a young servant (he was only 24) and his aristocratic mistress. He was much closer in age to her than was her husband, was completely in her confidence, and not only did he conceal her affair from his master, but he also gave her advice on the matter.

A contrasting character was John Allan, household steward at Eglinton Castle, aged 50, unmarried, a servant of Lord Eglinton's for over twenty-five years. The previous spring in London he suspected Frances of infidelity, 'and his suspicions arose from the frequent visits paid to her by the Duke of Hamilton, particularly in the months of March, May and June, his Grace never having called in the months of April the pursuer being then confined to the house with the Gout, and when the Duke came in March, May and June as above it was when the pursuer was from home', except once: 'when his Grace called he generally passed the porter and ran up stairs to the Drawing room without asking whether my Lord or my Lady was at home, and was doing so at this time but was stopped by James Reynolds footman who told him that the Defender was in the pursuers dressing room'. 'His Grace went into the dressing room and after he left the house the pursuer said to the Deponent that this was the first visit he had had from his Grace since he came to town to which the Deponent answered that it was only the first time the pursuer had seen him there'.

Allan, unlike Lawson, was entirely his master's man, and the housekeeper, Isabel Sloan, was with him in this. (Mrs Sloan, although only twenty-seven, had also been a servant in the household for many years.) One night, when the Earl was away and Frances had a group of visitors, including the Duke, staying at the house, Mrs Sloan told the steward 'that he might now convince himself of the truth of the connection between the Defender and Duke of Hamilton as she had seen his Grace go through the Gallery downstairs and go towards the Defenders bed room'. Allan 'proposed to go for David Craig Butler to the pursuer and with his assistance to break open the door of the Defenders bedchamber, but Mrs Sloan opposed this'. So the next day Allan went to Mr Fairly of Fairly and informed him. He also 'proposed to go to Lord Cassillis and inform Lord Eglintoun but Mr Fairly said that such procedure was too precipitate and that it was better to act with caution'. After that someone sent an anonymous letter to the Earl, informing him of the affair. Frances asked Allan, and the butler, if the servants would deny the Duke's visits and they told her they would not. So the game was up.

Lawson had been right in warning of the dangers of writing letters, for one of Frances' to the Duke was intercepted, and reveals fully her infatuation:

> as long as I can persuade myself you love me, I cannot help proving to you, that I have no other pleasure but in thinking of and writing to you. To be deprived of that pleasure would indeed make your absence insupportable, at the best it is painful, and my life is only animated by the hope of our soon meeting Tho I cannot flatter myself that you feel on this subject quite as I do, yet I cannot help hoping that you find our separation long, no consolation can be so effectual to me as thinking that you participate in the painful pangs of absence.

The Duke's letter to Frances, after her husband had received the anonymous information about the affair, cannot have been any consolation at all:

> I cannot pretend to give you advice, but should desire you not to speak to me any more, I think you ought to comply, for separation is a disagreeable thing Think of little M. and the child you are now bearing . . . I trust in your good sense and generosity and sincerely hope that you will not be angry at what I have said, besides your ready compliance with his desires will convince him of your innocence, and most likely he will not insist upon it, if he should a little time will soon wear off his suspicions and all will be right again, and there is no reason that we may [not] see one another in private, tho in public we do not converse.

Unfortunately for the guilty parties, this letter was also intercepted and very likely stiffened the Earl's resolve to sue for a full divorce rather than simply a separation. It must also have intensified the Countess's anguish to have sacrificed everything for a man like that.

We conclude with extracts from a letter of 18 December 1787 from the Countess to her husband. It went on for pages, but was all on the same lines as the following:

> Every moment which draws me nearer to parting with the Child I am more and more wretched – For Gods sake consider what are my sufferings, and forgive me – If you will give up pursuing the divorce, I declare solemnly as I hope to be forgiven of all my sins, and that you will consent to live to [sic] me in the same house, I will swear never to see, hear, nay even think of any one you have reason to dislike, that I will agree to live here and never see a human face, except you the maid, and the Child . . . my whole study shall be to atone for my past faults and to be submissive and kind to you in future . . . if you could but see how wretched I am, how penitent for all my transgressions you would I think, be inclined to pardon me . . . Consider the pangs of a mother being tore from her Child; Consider how the Child must suffer in losing her.

To no avail. The Earl obtained his divorce in February 1788.[5]

The next guilty wife was Catharine MacQueen, daughter of the Lord Justice Clerk for Scotland and wife of John MacDonald of Clanranald. They were married in 1784 and had two children; her lover was Captain William Payne of the First Regiment of Dragoons; the divorce action was brought in December 1790.[6]

Isabella MacDonald, a chambermaid (aged twenty), really stirred things up, while Margaret Stewart, the housekeeper, was the most telling witness. She had been aware that some of the servants had suspicions 'of an improper Connection' between Captain Payne and Catharine, but she disregarded those suspicions 'as her heart was more inclined to doubt their oath than her Mistresses honour'. The other servants 'appeared to dislike Captain Payne', but she thought that was just because of his 'giving the servants more trouble than other Gentlemen about the house'. One night, about a week before Clanranald came home, 'Isabella McDonald Cursed Captain Payne in a particular manner which alarmed and affected' the housekeeper. A few minutes afterwards she went into the kitchen and 'heard the said Isabella McDonald again curse Captain Payne before all the servants in the same particular manner'. She was 'still more surprised and shocked at hearing her use expressions before all the servants which might create or confirm suspicions in their minds and resolved to take an early opportunity of conversing with Isabella McDonald more particularly on the subject'.

The next day the housekeeper 'asked her what she meant by Cursing Captain Payne which the said Isabella McDonald appeared very averse to communicate, at the same time using expressions and hints tending rather to confirm than destroy the suspicions which had been incited in the deponents mind by her expressions the night before particularly by this expression "Curse him, for if he is not cursed sure there never was one cursed" '.

The following morning Thomas Robertson, the house servant, told the housekeeper that 'Isabella McDonalds expressions had excited in him similar suspicions', and that 'he had asked Isabella McDonald whether Captain Payne had excited her resentment by meddling with herself or her sister, to which she had answered that it would have been more for his honour if he had'. This increased the housekeeper's uneasiness 'by pointing the suspicions directly at her mistress and made her resolve to sift the matter to the utmost and to Inform her Mistress of the Suspicions which were entertained of her Conduct.'

Margaret did speak to her mistress the next day, and Catharine asked her if she should challenge Isabella McDonald, which the housekeeper thought would be a bad idea, 'because if she was innocent it was only necessary to avoid any thing that could give rise to such suspicions'. Catharine 'observed it was hard she should be censured by her own servants and reduced thereby to such a situation that she could not walk out in safety even alone'.

It is not clear how Clanranald learned of the affair, but Captain Payne was staying as a visitor at the time. All that the housekeeper knew was that one morning the servants said that Clanranald and Catharine both 'seem'd much distressed at Breakfast'. Clanranald left the house after breakfast and Captain Payne shortly after that. Catharine sent for the housekeeper as usual, who saw that her mistress 'had been weeping'. The next morning she found her 'dressed in her riding habit and asked her if she was going to Town', to which Catharine answered that she was going away and did not think she would return to Ballencrieff'. 'A little difference had happened' between her and her husband, she said. Her husband 'had long wished to go abroad', and 'was now determined to go', leaving her 'somewhere in England but she did not know where'. She asked the housekeeper to look after her things, and 'particularly recommended to the deponent to take care of her Children during her absence'. Margaret asked her mistress 'what was to become of the Children to which she answered Mrs McDonald her Mother in law or some other person would certainly take care of them'. During the conversation Catharine 'appeared extremely pale and very much affected'.

Two days later Margaret received a letter from her 'beginning with the words "your conjectures were too just" '. In the letter she also stated that someone would be coming to Ballencrieff to interrogate the servants, and it was her 'desire that they should not conceal or deny any thing they knew and the same letter contained an anxious desire for the welfare of her Children'. Catharine had written to the housekeeper nearly every week since then 'respecting the Children and with directions for packing up the things which she had left behind her'. Catharine also wrote a letter to her husband:

> Sir Unworthy as I am of your attention to me I must with pain and in earnest entreat for your forgiveness to me (if it is possible) acknowledge the justice and

truth of your suspicions against me of my criminal Intercourse with Capt Payne. I have this only to plead in my favour that I never injured your honour as my husband with any other man than him, that I never shall be connected or attached to any other, and that altho I now find my only happiness depends on my reliance on his [?]south to me I never can forget the happiness I experienced while I was your faithful wife. Take care of my poor Children for their own sake as they deserve it and still more ought they to be regarded by you from the fate of their unfortunate mother.

Another sad case, again with children involved, was that of Sir William Murray of Ochtertyre against his wife. This was also uncontested, and again servants – who were very unhappy about her affair – provided detailed evidence. Sir William, who was born in October 1746, married Lady Augusta Mackenzie, youngest lawful daughter of the deceased Earl of Cromarty, in 1770. Between 1770 and 1781 she bore seven children, but the second to the last died as an infant, and the last at birth. The divorce action was brought in October 1791.[7]

Lady Augusta's lover was in a lower social bracket but not enough to cause surprise at his frequent visits. He was Robert Harrup, surgeon in Crieff whose appearances were 'on pretence of visiting and attending . . . the defender in the way of his profession as a surgeon'. He came to Crieff in spring 1790, and servants noted that Lady Augusta 'paid particular attention to Mr Harrup from the time he came to the Country', and Mr Harrup usually slept at the house at Ochtertyre. Before that Lady Augusta 'for the most part dined with her husband and family but afterwards very seldom dined out of her own room' and 'had also been in the use of supping with the family before Mr Harrup settled at Crieff as above but afterwards supped in her own appartment'. During that time Harrup would 'leave the Pursuer and the Company in the dining room immediately after supper, go by a back stair to the defenders bedroom where the defender then was and remain there by themselves till the usual time of the bell being rung for Candles to go to Bed'. After coming down the back stair Harrup would return to the dining room. Patrick McRosly, the butler (who had been at Ochtertyre since 1782) 'very much disliked Mr Harrups using that back passage which no other Gentleman ever took and his going into the Defenders Bedroom without Chapping'. When the bell was rung Sir William always went to bed, and McRosly thought that was a signal for Harrup to return to Lady Augusta's bedchamber.

Barbara Moir (aged twenty), had been governess to the Murray daughters for two years. She often heard Lady Augusta 'speak in praise of Mr Harrups person and address'. On one such occasion when Barbara remarked that in her opinion 'Mr Harrup was rather a forward man', Lady Augusta 'was very angry with the deponent for making the observation'. Barbara saw Mr Harrup in Lady Augusta's bedroom while she was in bed and had seen him enter the room without knocking. He would say that he had been with Lady Augusta 'in her Bedroom giving her medicines which were necessary for her situation'.

Kathrine McIntosh (aged thirty-six, unmarried), who had been housekeeper for the past fourteen years, remarked that Lady Augusta 'seemed particularly anxious that every thing should be right and neat about Mr Harrups room when he slept there all night. Lady Augusta

> was not in the use of going into the room in which any other Gentleman was to sleep excepting the first night that each Gentleman was to sleep there when she would look in to see if there was a good fire, but that she went into Mr Harrups room every night that he was to sleep there and generally carried with her into the room a Bottle of Lavender drops and some sugar together with a Glass.

She seemed 'anxious that the servants should pay Mr Harrup particular respect and said to the deponent that he was a Gentleman outright and ought to be treated as such'. Sometimes Lady Augusta 'gave out Mr Harrups Linen along with the Pursuers and her own to be washed, which was a mark of attention that she never paid to any other stranger nor even to her own sons and daughters'.

The housekeeper had many more observations to impart, including the fact that Lady Augusta 'always seemed pleased and happy when Mr Harrup came into her Bed Chamber.' It is not surprising that 'the familiarity between the Defender and Mr Harrup was a subject of observation to all the servants about the family', but it clearly took some time before they believed 'that there was a guilty Connection between them' Apart from 'the Circumstances above mentioned the suspicions were excited by Mr Harrup's being in the defenders Bedroom so very late at night . . . and also by the defenders attention to Mr Harrup which continued to increase as long as the latter visited in the family, while the attention to the Pursuer seemed gradually to diminish'. Other servants concurred.

In this case there was no need for anyone to inform the husband, for on 26 September the guilty couple were caught in the act – or at any rate, in a compromising enough position for there to be no doubt in the matter. None of the witnesses to the exposure testified, so we have only tantalising hints about what happened. Barbara Moir heard the noise but was unwilling 'for motives of delicacy' to name the person who told her next morning what had happened. The commissaries reminded her of 'her obligation as a witness in this Cause which freed her from any Imputation of Indelicacy or otherwise which could arise from a strict and literal discharge of her duty as a witness,' and she then said 'it was Miss Murray the Pursuers Eldest daughter who informed the deponent that the noise arose from Mr Harrup being found in the Defenders Bed Chamber later than was thought proper', a very delicate way of putting it.

Kathrine Stalker, the wetnurse, was 'alarmed by a knocking at the door of the defenders Bed Chamber and she came out of her room to see what was the matter'. Mr Murray, the eldest son, 'who was at the door advised the deponent to go to Bed which she accordingly did . . . Afterwards she heard the defender in her Bed

Chamber Cry out several times No! No!'. Kathrine said that Lady Augusta 'kept her bed all next day and sent for the deponent and the Child about dinner time . . . the defender was then weeping very bitterly and said to the deponent she would never be thought of more'. Kathrine accompanied Lady Augusta to England, and deponed that 'before the defender left the house of Ochtertyre . . . she said to the deponent that she could not think of staying any longer at Ochtertyre on account of her being a disgrace to her daughters'.

A puzzling aspect of the story is that Sir William must have known long before September that his wife was unfaithful to him. One of the servants deponed that Sir William and Lady Augusta slept in separate storeys of the house from autumn 1790, yet in October 1791 when he brought the action 'she was lately delivered' of another child, whom she took with her when she went to England. A descendant writing a family history wrote that 'she gave birth to a son of whom Sir William was not the father, and was, in consequence, divorced by him'.[8]

In all of the above cases a wife became hopelessly infatuated with another man and risked everything in a passionate affair. None of them attempted to contest the case; all gracefully retired from the scene. What comes across most forcefully is the intimate connection between servants and their employers in aristocratic and upper gentry households, ranging from the intense curiosity and trouble stirring of the younger members of staff to the deep loyalties of long-serving senior members.

Case Studies 7 and 8 are the stories of two more guilty aristocratic or upper gentry wives.

GUILTY HUSBANDS

One obvious question from the Eglinton case is why, with the Duke of Hamilton as paramour, his Duchess did not divorce him. The answer is that after waiting a few more years – in hopes, perhaps, of a reformation – she did just that.

The case of Her Grace Elizabeth Ann Burrell Duchess of Hamilton and Brandon against Douglas Duke of Hamilton and Brandon was extremely amicable and had clearly been agreed on beforehand. They had been married in 1778, and the libel stated that his adultery began in 1787, without naming the 'Lady or Woman' with whom he was then guilty. The case was founded on another affair, carried on over the months preceding the summons in November 1793. His mistress was 'Mrs Eisten the actress', and he brought her to Hamilton and took her along to Arran where they could be seen together by all the servants. Her Grace, having left Hamilton a year earlier, had no trouble obtaining her divorce. She remarried, but not until 1800, so that could not have been the motive for bringing the divorce action.[9]

A greater contrast to such an amicable arrangement could not be imagined than the case of Dame Marianne Campbell against Sir William Cunningham Fairlie of Robertland (married in 1790).[10] The case went on for five years, and in fact a previous action of his against her had started two years earlier. In view of the endless delaying tactics and legal technicalities, only a brief summary can be attempted here. When her action was brought against him in November 1811, alleging adultery with Ann Smith alias Ann Gordon since 1805, Sir William claimed that if the fact were true it was impossible that his wife should not have known about an affair that had allegedly gone on for so many years. However, if she had known then she would certainly have raised a counter process when he raised his action against her. (In that action he proved her adultery, but she pleaded *remissio injuriae*; the commissaries repelled the defence, but she appealed to the Court of Session which upheld it, so the case was dismissed.[11]) What she said was that he was 'in the practice of removing' her 'from one place of residence to another; and he only occasionally came and lived with' her.

Part of the difficulty in proving her case was indeed the peripatetic existence he lived. (When she tried to obtain a commission to have witnesses examined in Cumberland, he objected and said that it would be cheaper to bring them to Edinburgh; subsequently he ended up landed with the costs of bringing witnesses all the way from London.) In August 1812 Sir William started a counter process against his wife, which was conjoined to hers against him and added to the inordinate amount of time which the case lasted. In May 1816 the commissaries found Sir William's adultery with 'a person bearing the name of Gordon or Smith' sufficiently proven to grant Lady Cunningham Fairlie a divorce, while finding 'the proof adduced by the said Sir William Cunningham Fairlie in the action at his instance did not amount to sufficient legal evidence of the truth of his allegations of Lady Cunningham Fairlie's guilt of adultery', so his libel was not proven, and 'the said Lady Cunningham Fairlie was assoilzied'. This also meant that Sir William had to pay the whole of the expenses of £625.13s.4d – and, as an indication of the kind of bitter pettiness that characterised the case, she asked for £2.16s.8d on top of that for 'additional expences which the objector by his litigious conduct had caused the Respondent to incur since the latter of these accounts was audited'. The commissaries ordered him to pay this amount as well.

There were, of course, other guilty husbands amongst the aristocracy and upper gentry, but, on the whole, such men were far likelier to choose prostitutes or servant maids as sexual partners, and those cases appear in Chapter 8. But before looking at them (and after the case studies of more guilty wives) we turn to divorce amongst the lower gentry.

NOTES

All CC references are in the Scottish Record Office.
1. cc8/5/14.
2. cc8/5/17.
3. cc8/5/19.
4. cc8/5/19. *Scots Peerage* vol.III, 459–60.

5. Ibid. The Countess remarried in 1794. Their daughter, Mary, married Lord Montgomery in 1803; the second daughter, Susanna, died suddenly at the age of eighteen.
6. cc8/5/20.
7. Ibid; National Library of Scotland (NLS) MS 21117. Patrick Keith Murray, 'The Family Book of the Murrays of Ochtertyre', 1904. According to this source, Lady Augusta 'was born whilst her father was expecting execution for his share in the Jacobite rising of 1745, and carried to her death a birthmark in the shape of a red axe round her neck. She habitually wore a necklet of velvet to cover this blemish.'
8. Ibid. He got the date of the birth and marriage wrong by a year, but there is no reason to doubt the rest. In 1810 Sir William's son, Sir Patrick Murray, listed this last son, William, as the eighth child and noted that he had gone to the East Indies as an infantry cadet. NLS MS21116. The 1904 book stated that 'William died unmarried in Bengal on 28th June 1831. He was a Captain in the Bengal Establishment and served with considerable distinction.'
9. cc8/5/21. *Scots Peerage*, vol.IX, 393–4. Her second husband was Henry Marquis of Exeter.
10. cc8/5/35. The case takes up 700 pages of the volume in minuscule handwriting; I make no claims to have read it all.
11. The papers do not appear to have survived for that case, but the result was summed up in the case being considered. He apparently went on to appeal to the Lords, clearly without success.

SCOTT VS HAY – AN ELOPEMENT AND A CHASE

Lady Mary Hay, daughter of the Earl of Errol, was only sixteen when she married Major-General John Scott of Balcomie in November 1770; his age may be inferred from his rank and also from the fact that he died in 1775. The divorce action was brought in October 1771, and concluded in December of that year, so it was a short-lived marriage. We get no insight into the relationship between husband and wife, or between wife and lover, in this case, but for dramatic action it can hardly be surpassed.

Lady Mary's lover, Captain James Sutherland of Duffus, was a guest at Balcomie (in Fife) that October. They were very discreet, and none of the servants suspected anything. On the night in question Lady Mary told her husband that she had some letters to write and would be going to bed late, so to avoid disturbing him she would sleep with one of the ladies staying in the house (a common practice of the time). Instead of doing so, at about one in the morning she eloped with Captain Sutherland 'in an open chaise belonging to the Pursuer'.

Rebecca Grant, her waiting woman, who knew her well, having served her since three years before her marriage, had 'no reason to suspect' that Lady Mary 'had any intention of leaving the house having seen nothing in her Conduct nor appearance any way particular or mysterious'. Even the next morning when she drew aside the curtains of the bed and found that Lady Mary was not there she 'supposed she had got up before and dressed herself'. After examining the clothes left behind she was able to describe what Lady Mary was wearing when she went off: 'an Irish muslin Gown stript and figured with colours made in the fashion of a Polinese a french nightcape a white silk cloak and bonnet'. Lady Mary 'carried with her besides the dress she had put on, two Gowns, five shirts, three nightcaps and three pairs of stockings, three suits of laces and one suit of muslins with a number of laced handkerchiefs, and only one pair of blue slippers which she had on'.

Captain Sutherland naturally took his own servant with him, and the man described what his master wore: 'a white Cloath frock with yellow mettall buttons, a white or stript washing waistcoat the deponent did not remember which, white breeches and white thread stockings being the dress he had wore the preceeding day, and when he came to Leith he had on a gold laced hat with a cockade'. En route to the ferry at Kinghorn the chaise overturned; no one was hurt, but 'the Captain got his stockings very much dirtied and wet . . . and when he came to Leith, he on that account desired the deponent to bring him a pair of coloured silk stockings from his portmanteau which he put on.' He also asked his servant 'to bring from said portmanteau a pair of his own white silk stockings for Lady Mary which the deponent accordingly did'.

The fleeing couple feared pursuit, and apart from a two-hour stopover at Durham, they did not spend more than a few minutes at any of the stages on their journey south. However, when they reached Barnet, the last stage before London, they reckoned they were safe, and decided to spend the night at the Red Lion Inn there, supping on 'Mutton Chops'. They underestimated the Major-General. Although it was nine in the morning before he learned of the elopement, which gave the couple more than eight hours' start on him, he immediately set out after them, pausing in Edinburgh just long enough to ask two friends to accompany him and his two servants. They travelled day and night, 'and did not go to bed', reaching the Red Lion Inn at about three in the morning.

The guilty party did have intercourse that night, for the Captain's servant packed up his things afterwards and observed that 'there were two dirty shirts and one clean, and the deponent took notice that there was red stains or marks upon the forelap of one of the said dirty shirts'; Captain Sutherland, he said, was in good health and had no 'disorder'. Rebecca Grant was called back to be interrogated 'whether she knew that Lady Mary had her periodical disorder the two days before she left Balcomie'. Rebecca deponed that she had 'and thought she was tied up on that account when her Ladyship left Balcomie at the time mentioned'. The intimate knowledge a maid-servant had of her mistress is graphically illustrated here, and we may note that a menstrual period did not inhibit a couple from having intercourse.

When Scott and his party arrived they made the 'waiter of the inn' knock on the door. (According to James Hardie, writer in Edinburgh, one of the gentlemen who accompanied Scott, the 'waiter appeared to be in great terror and the deponent remembered it required some threats to make him knock at the door'.) 'Captain Sutherland 'called out "who's there" and the waiter having answered "the chaise is ready" the Captain came to the door in his shirt, opened it and looked out' – but when he saw the Major-General and his party he 'immediately shut the door again and fastened it in the inside'. The servants got a poker and forced the door open, while the Captain leapt out of the window, 'without anything upon him but his shirt and nightcap'. The Captain's servant had been ordered to stay in bed, but he heard the men talking of breaking the door down and then 'a confused noise of people calling out and speaking ensued, so that he could not hear what passed, But he distinguished the defender's voice screaming and calling aloud not to shoot her.' From what passed the servant 'expected every minute to hear pistols fired, apprehending that the Pursuer would shoot Captain Sutherland'.

Hardie deponed that when they entered the room they saw that one of the windows was 'thrown up'. Lady Mary was lying in bed and 'seemed to be in great distress and was weeping and frequently called out for God's sake to have mercy and pity upon her and not to shoot her and take her life, upon which the Pursuer and the rest of the Company assured her, she needed be under no apprehensions of that sort, for that no harm should be done to her'. Hardie particularly remembered hearing her say to her husband, ' "will you forgive me?" To which he answered "That was all over, but that she needed be under no apprehension for her life" '. Hardie also enquired about Captain Sutherland and 'was informed by some of the postilions who were standing without that a gentleman in his shirt had made his Escape from the above mentioned open window of the room . . . by a Balcony to the back part of the house'. Hardie 'then desired one of them to go in quest of him, and to throw a Cloak about him till such time as he should get his Cloathes', but he was told that the 'Gentleman had leaped from the window and had attempted to get into the fields immediately opposite to the house, but being stopped by a hedge, had taken the road to Highgate, and had struck into the fields on the right.'

Scott and his companions went to London to bring Lady Mary's uncle to Barnet, leaving the servants behind with her. Her conversations with two of them are revealing – keeping in mind that she was only seventeen. She asked Captain Sutherland's servant 'If he knew what was become of his Master and said she was afraid he would catch his death by cold, having gone out of the room with nothing on but his shirt,' and she asked him 'if his said Master had been hurt by his fall'. He 'told her Ladyship he did not know where his Master was for that he could not be found and that he had heard he had got a fall from the chair or bench upon which he had dropped in throwing himself from the window, after which he had tumbled from the foot path into the high road, But he did not know whether he was hurt or not'. Lady Mary was 'then in great distress and crying, she did not care what became of her . . . so as they did not kill Captain Sutherland in case they caught him'.

Lady Mary also asked the servant 'what was to be done with him, and the deponent answered that the General had told him no harm was to be done to him, but he was to come to Balcomie as one of his servants'. Presumably the General was acting in a paternalistic manner by offering the stranded servant a secure future, though it also chimes in with the overall picture of a strong, decisive, controlling personality. Lady Mary then enquired 'if he knew what was to be done to her and he answered he did not know But that he supposed she was to be carried to the North.' She 'said she hoped they would not do it and asked him whether they could force her to go in case she did not choose it, To which the deponent replied he really could not inform her Ladyship'.

Mary herself, in spite of her youth, was no passive doll (the secrecy and planning needed for the elopement is already evidence of that). At this stage she sent for Andrew Jack, one of her husband's servants, and asked him if he could help her get away. He said that he could not, and tried to 'disswade her from any attempt which he was apprehensive she might make to get away in the generals absence and observed, as he had been informed she had but little money, and that must soon be run out, That she could not expect to meet with Captain Sutherland, and as she had affronted her family by the steps she had already taken, her going off again would make it still worse.' Lady Mary again begged him 'to assist her to escape, and taking out her purse held it towards him as if offering it'. He 'told her Ladyship he would neither have any hand in her escape, nor allow any person to assist her in it, and she having said she thought he would have been the last person who would have turned against her, the deponent immediately withdrew.'

Lady Mary's uncle took her back to Scotland, and it appears that she did not remarry after the divorce.

At about nine o'clock that night Captain Sutherland crept back to the inn, 'on foot, without any other Cloaths on than his shirt and night Cap, almost starved with Cold, and Scratched in a terrible manner'. He asked whether everyone was gone, and the waiter told him that they had left some time ago. He remained at the inn until the following Wednesday, where he was attended by a local doctor, and told the waiter that when he got out into the fields 'he saw some hay stacks at a distance, that he got up to the top of one of them, which he unthatched and lay there hid till night, in his shirt and night cap only having no other Clothes During his absence, and that at night he returned the back way to the said Inn, on seeing a light there'. The master of the inn deponed that Captain Sutherland then went into lodgings in Finchley for about a fortnight, 'after which the deponent went with the said Captain James Sutherland to Dover, where he saw him Embark on board a vessel, and sail towards Calais in France'. (Why the master of an inn should have accompanied the Captain is not explained.)

For the sake of his pride and 'honour', Major-General John Scott went to all that trouble to pursue a wife he would instantly divorce.

cc8/5/12

ELGIN VS ELGIN – COLD MARBLES AND WARM PASSIONS

Thomas, Earl of Elgin and Kincardine, married Mary Hamilton Nisbet, heiress to estates in East Lothian and elsewhere, in 1799, when she was twenty-one and he was twelve years older. Elgin's biographer, Sydney Checkland, described her as having 'dark hair and eyes, a longish nose . . . and an attractive mouth'. Her 'lively face' was apparently 'matched by a shapely figure, both of which had appealed to the young men of Edinburgh, where her social life had been based'. Although considered cold and reserved by some, Elgin was a handsome man, and it was apparently a love match. Mary became pregnant four months after the wedding. Before his marriage Elgin had been appointed ambassador to Turkey and soon after it the couple set off for Constantinople.[1]

Mary bore her husband three children in the first three years of her marriage, but there are indications of strain, due perhaps to living in such an alien environment. Elgin became very ill, though the contemporary descriptions of his symptoms are so vague as to make it impossible to know what he actually suffered from. He dosed himself heavily with mercury, which suggests a venereal disease, but there is no other evidence for this, and his doctors later said the mercury had been 'unnecessarily' consumed and he should stop. During the years in Constantinople his nose was being eaten away by an ulcer, an unappealing sight for a young wife.[2]

The family visited Athens more than once, and it was during those years that Lord Elgin amassed his collection of marbles and other antiquities. In January 1803, during the Peace of Amiens, the family started their homeward journey. In Malta Elgin decided that they should travel back overland, though the children were sent by sea. There were rumours that hostilities between Britain and France would resume, but Elgin thought that whatever happened his ambassadorial status would protect him. He was mistaken. On 23 May, when the Elgins were in Paris, all British citizens between the ages of nine and sixty were seized. Elgin was the most important of them, and in fact he was held in France until July 1806.

Another British subject seized in May 1803 was Robert Fergusson of Raith the younger, heir to an estate in Fife and an acquaintance of Lord Elgin's (they were the same age), who had taken advantage of the Peace to visit the Continent. The Elgins stayed first in Barèges and then in Pau. In November Mary went back to Paris to work for her husband's release. Fergusson, who had become a confidant, was still there and helped her to plan moves in the attempt to get Elgin freed. He also fell in love with her, and, in the words of Elgin's biographer, 'laid amorous siege' to her. Mary was far from indifferent, but she was pregnant at this time. Her son William was born in March 1804, and she apparently subsumed her feelings for Fergusson (who was released and allowed to return to Scotland) in her new baby, 'suckling him herself, a very unusual action for a woman of her class'. Just over a year later, in May 1805, when Elgin was back in Paris with her, William died, and Mary was devastated. The body was embalmed and sent back to Scotland, with Fergusson standing in for the family at the funeral.[3] (Much later she wrote to him, 'it was you that placed that Adored Angel there. He is happier far than us . . . There is something combined with that Infant, I cannot account for, but I feel as if he was our own)'.

Sexual relations with her husband continued, and within a month of William's death Mary was pregnant again. Elgin decided that she should return to Britain. She was able to get the necessary passport, and went to her parents' house in London. There she would have been 'safe from Fergusson' (as Checkland put it), but obviously she did not want to be safe from him, because instead of staying there she took a small house in Baker Street, where Fergusson was a daily visitor. (Checkland wrote that it did not take Fergusson 'long to exploit the opportunity', which fails to acknowledge Mary's active sexuality.) As he was still assisting her in her attempts to obtain Elgin's release no suspicion seems to have been attached to his visits by outsiders. She had intercourse with Fergusson during her pregnancy, and after the birth of her fifth child, Lucy, in January 1806. At that time she wrote to Elgin that she would never resume marital relations with him; he assumed this 'to be the short-term consequence of childbirth'.[4]

In July 1806 Elgin was back home, but the reunion was not a happy one, for Mary 'maintained her ban on intercourse', while Elgin refused to live with her on a platonic basis. In September he opened a letter which was mistakenly amongst his own post and found that it was from Fergusson to Mary, 'with profuse declarations of love'. Mary then confessed that they had been lovers; Elgin was still willing to be reconciled, but only on the basis of full intercourse, which Mary could not accept. Elgin therefore decided to divorce her. He did so both in England and Scotland. Under the complicated procedures of English law he first had to bring an action of criminal conversation against Fergusson, which took place in December 1807 when Elgin demanded £20,000 in damages and obtained £10,000. The proceedings, in which Elgin's counsel depicted Mary as a saint and Fergusson as a vile seducer ('his manners were soft and alluring; he had been accustomed to study all the weakness of the female heart, and the methods of taking advantage of them; and was well practised in the arts which render gallantry successful') were printed in a pamphlet for the delectation of the public.[5]

Soon after that the necessary Act of Parliament was passed, but because both parties were domiciled and held estates in Scotland Elgin had also brought a divorce action before the Commissary Court, in April 1807. Although uncontested in the English courts, in the Scottish court the case was bitterly fought, presumably because (in theory at least) Elgin would get everything from her estate that would have been his had she died.

There were two main forms of evidence – that of servants, and that of Fergusson's letters – and the striking feature of the case is their juxtaposition. Ann Crerar (aged 22), who had been chambermaid at Fortune and Blackwells Hotel in Edinburgh, deponed that the morning after Mr Fergusson arrived she saw that his bed had not been slept in, 'that she went into Lady Elgins bed room that morning, and . . . from the appearance of the bed she was satisfied that two people had slept in it. That she was convinced of this from the appearance both of the pillows and the sheets. That the pillows had the mark of two people having lain on them, and the sheets were marked in the same manner as if a man and his wife had slept together'. Ann 'told John Fraser the waiter that two people had slept in Lady Elgins bed the night before and asked him if Lord Elgin had slept there'. He told her that he had not, 'and asked her what made her think Lord Elgin had been there', so she told him 'what she had observed on the bed, when he desired her to hold her tongue as she might get into a scrape Lady Elgin's servants being in the house.' Mary Ruper, a servant at Broomhall, said that the housekeeper, Mrs Gosling, 'was called Porter by the men servants in consequence of her letting Mr Fergusson out and in, and that he rung the area bell in place of rapping at the door as other gentlemen did'. On one occasion the maid 'mentioned to Mrs Gosling that the Dog had dirtied a green silk cushion which was on the Sopha when Mrs Gosling said it was not the Dog and shook her head, and this happened one morning after Mr Fergusson had been there the night before and on this occasion Mrs Gosling added it was not the dog but that rogue Mr Fergusson'. She added that all the servants thought that 'there was an improper connection between Mr Fergusson and Lady Elgin.'

Thomas Willey once entered the drawing room without knocking at midday, and saw Lady Elgin lying on the sofa, and 'both Lady Elgin and Mr Fergusson laid hold of a shawl and in great confusion threw it over her Ladyship's legs.' He could not see 'exactly whether her Ladyships legs were uncovered or not, before the shawl was thrown over them', but 'Mr Fergusson and Lady Elgin discovered great confusion when the witness came into the room and particularly her Ladyship whose face was much flushed'. Fergusson 'got up and walked toward the fire with his back towards the deponent and turning round his head said "It's only Thomas" . . . From the manner Mr Fergusson walked to the fire keeping his back to the witness he could not see any part of him in front nor could tell whether his breeches were buttoned or unbuttoned.' When Lady Elgin said to Charles Duff, who had found the house in London for her, 'O! Duff, I am quite miserable', and he asked her what the matter was, she said that if Lord Elgin and her parents plagued her she would go off with Fergusson. Duff said to her, 'God forbid I should ever see that day, as you would be looked upon as no better than a girl of the Town if you go off with Fergusson.'

All this seems thoroughly sordid, but then we turn to the letters. (How a letter from Mary to Fergusson, and no less than four from him to her, came into the hands of Elgin is never explained.)

'Mary', wrote Fergusson on 10 December, 'I can boast of loving you with a passion never felt before; for with all the violence of our feelings which may be found perhaps in others never never was there at the same time such a perfect complete union in our souls. How every feeling, every wish, every thought is alike. Yes, my own beloved Mary, we were made for one another . . . Oh, Mary in my arms, with the friend you love and live in, what may we not do and say – all is then affection and love, every feeling opens. All is concentrated in the total mass of tender feelings which animate us.' In another letter he wrote: 'most adored of beings, whatever our sufferings yet may be we shall for ever, and long already we have enjoyed that delight, that happiness, which only hearts united like ours can feel, in the blessed certainty of loving and adoring one another, in the perfect, total conviction, that to one another we now eternally belong.' And in another: 'Never, never was love true and sure like ours. More and more we love and adore one another – and at last free from all fetters we shall enjoy the most perfect bliss this world can bestow . . . oh God, God we cannot live away from one another.' The exalted nature of such sentiments provides a striking contrast to the way in which the relationship was viewed from outside!

Admittedly, the letters also contained many unpleasant allusions to her husband: 'with him so disgusting to you in every respect, are you to allow, what then becomes gross allusions, vulgar conversation? No! – they are too offensive – they encroach on forbidden ground – and must be treated as such.' Or: 'how horribly the idea of his presence poisons and destroys every feeling of giving way to our dreams of bliss. Oh do you not feel it, Mary? Does not his disgusting presence destroy every Comfort? Oh God how endure it much longer?' And so on . . . (In the crim. con. case this was naturally seized on as proof that it was Fergusson who had caused Mary to be disgusted with her husband, but he could hardly have played on something that did not already exist.)

Lord Elgin obtained his divorce in March 1808. He was embittered by it, but in 1810 he remarried, apparently happily. Fergusson's name appeared in the decreet, so under Scottish law he and Mary should not have been allowed to marry. Nevertheless, they did so. In the 1813–14 case of St Aubyn against O'Bryen a lawyer wrote: 'The only restriction by the Law of Scotland as to marriage in regard to either party after obtaining the divorce is that the Parties guilty of the Adultery cannot marry each other altho' even this is doubted for Lady Elgin has married the man on account of whom she was divorced by her husband and I have heard some of our most eminent Lawyers say that notwithstanding if there were Children of that marriage they would succeed to the large Estates of their Father Mr Fergusson of Raith altho' these Estates are most strictly entailed in favors of Heirs male'.[6] In the event, the question was never put to the test, for they did not have any children.

cc8/5/29

1. Sydney Checkland, *The Elgins, 1766–1917 – A Tale of Aristocrats, Proconsuls and their Wives* (Aberdeen 1988), 28–9.
2. Ibid., 55, 65. Dr Graham Sutton advises me that the ulcer does suggest syphilis, but as Mary was not infected and had healthy pregnancies, it seems that that was not what he had.
3. Ibid., 61–3.
4. Ibid., 63–4.
5. Ibid., 70; *The Trial of R. Fergusson, Esq for Crim. Con. with the Rt. Hon. Lady Elgin* (London 1807), 38.
6. cc8/5/33.

CHAPTER 7

GENTRY DIVORCES

The couples featured in this chapter – the lower gentry and professionals – did not live the lavish lifestyles of those in the last, but nor did they have a struggle for existence as did some in later chapters. In theory, they had complete freedom in their choice of marriage partners, but in practice they were expected to marry within their own 'rank' in society, and, as we will see in the first section of this chapter, disparities in rank and fortune could result in some very unhappy marriages. Of course, equality of rank was no guarantee of marital bliss, and the second section features two examples of unhappy marriages where the discovery of adultery enabled a wife to rid herself of an odious husband. The third section turns from the relationship between husband and wife to the relationship between guilty partner and lover; the fourth looks at wives who regretted their adultery; and the fifth concludes the chapter with couples who were already living apart at the time the divorce action was initiated.

DISPARITIES

In the 1730s Alexander Monro, the first in a line of eminent Edinburgh professors of anatomy, wrote a lengthy essay on 'female conduct' for his daughter, Margaret. He belonged to the liberal intelligentsia of the period, believing in women being well-educated, providing his daughter with enough money to live independently of her relatives, promising not to force or persuade her into a marriage to which she was averse, and stressing the importance of loving the man she eventually married. But he also warned her in no uncertain terms of the dangers of an unequal match. A woman who married a man of great rank and fortune 'has a great chance of being a Wretch in the midst of Pageantry. For as soon as the fit of Fondness is satiated he is ashamed among all his equals of producing a Wife whom he is conscious they pay only a forced civility to, and whom he is afraid they will affront.' And women should also 'be on their Guard against any chance of being engaged with Men of too small Fortunes', so much so that 'if a Lady once discovers either fondness in such a Man towards her, or is sensible that she esteems him an agreeable Companion, it is prudence in her to shun meeting him frequently in Company'. For to marry such a man 'causes her to be slighted and neglected by her Relations and Acquaintances, and if Poverty is her Lot, Domestick jars and Uneasiness generally succeed, these joined make compleat Misery'.[1]

A classic case of a marriage of unequals – lasting from 1751 until the divorce in 1781 – was that of Margaret Agnew of Lochnaw (Baronet) and John Agnew.[2] Her husband had been a menial servant in her father's house, 'and she being young and inexperienced he ingratiated himself into her favours and she was prevailed upon to give him her hand in Lawfull wedlock'. Her friends found a suitable post for him in the excise office, first as an ordinary officer, and then as supervisor, and if he had behaved himself properly 'he would have been still further promoted but by his own bad Conduct he was turned out of his office'.

She thought that the help she and her friends had given him, 'and the many marks of affection' she showed him, 'tho' far her inferior in point of Birth and even fortune', would have made him affectionate and tender, but instead 'it had a quite contrary effect for he turned out a perfect tyrant to her', beating and abusing her. In order to rid herself of him, though she 'had only an annuity of Thirty pounds sterling to support her', she agreed to pay him ten pounds a year out of that, and had done so for the previous eight years. On top of that 'she was prevailed upon to accept several bills for debts contracted by him in order to keep him from Imprisonment which debt she was obliged to pay out of the smallest remainder of her annuity aforesaid by which she was often reduced to great misery and want.' Finding proof of her husband's adultery must have come as a relief rather than a shock, enabling Margaret to rid herself of him and the financial burden she had borne.[3] (But, as we shall see Chapter in 14, she had disastrous judgment, for she promptly married another abuser and was subsequently back in the Commissary Court seeking a legal separation.)

At first glance Christian Dalgleish, daughter of the deceased John Dalgleish of West Grange, and James Kerr of East Grange (Culross parish) appear to be of the same social standing, but in the course of this 1771 case a different picture emerged.[4] According to her (and not denied by him) he 'was well known in the Country to have been originally a herd Boy and the son of a poor labouring man in a neighbouring village', who acquired enough wealth in the West Indies to buy a neighbouring estate. What we have here is old versus new money.

Because Kerr had acknowledged his paternity of a bastard child, which he was maintaining, he could not deny adultery and therefore attempted by way of defence to blacken her character. He had purchased his estate in 1764 and had very little acquaintance with Christian or her father while he had a wife alive, but after that he 'was frequently solicited to make a visit. In autumn 1767 he went and was importuned to return, and

> after dinner the pursuers father and mother having retired, a little dalliance
> ensued betwixt the pursuer and defender which without the smallest resistance
> on her part was carried on to a height that is more proper to imagine than to

mention; However suffice it to say that a Conquest was made of the pursuer on not the most arduous terms The defender for a considerable time after this continued his correspondence with the pursuer and she having Fallen with Child an action of declarator of marriage was then brought against him in which the defender to save the pursuers honour acknowledged her as his wife and in this manner the marriage was constituted.

He added that 'the marriage upon the part of the pursuer and her friends was brought about with the selfish view that the Defender would disinherit his Children of the former marriages and secure his Estate of East Grange in favour of the pursuers Children. But when this could not be brought about then every opportunity was taken to distress the defender.' After that she deserted him entirely, and refused to return, 'so that whatever improper connections the Defender . . . had with another woman the pursuer herself had [been] in a great measure the occasion of it by willfully refusing to live and cohabite with the defender as his wife'.

Without disputing the basic facts, Christian's version of the story was very different. In October 1767, after his first wife's death, Kerr had asked her to marry him and the marriage was to be celebrated in August or September 1768 when he finished winding up his affairs in the West Indies. Her parents admitted him as a suitor and 'never entertained the smallest Idea of any thing disrespectful or dishonourable being offered by a Person who was advanced in Years had been twice married and seemed to behave as a Gentleman But in this they were much mistaken for Mr Kerr under the most solemn promises of marrying the respondent against the time appointed prevailed with the Respondent to Yield to his Embraces whereby she became pregnant'. She had to tell her parents, but Kerr refused to marry her 'unless her father (who had four sons) would give the pursuer a sum equall to the half of his Fortune a proposall which Mr Dalgleish could by no means hearken to and therefore after making more reasonable offers to Mr Kerr and these being rejected a process of declarator of marriage was raised', which concentrated his mind so that he did acknowledge himself married to her.

After this beginning it is not surprising that the brief marriage was not a happy one. After her father's death her family made every effort to persuade her husband to provide her with a liferent and settle a sum of money on her issue, as it was generally believed that he had willed his entire estate to his three daughters of the former marriages, but 'he absolutely refused to make any settlement upon the Respondent and the Issue of their marriage and Mr Dalgleish being dead her husband's cruel usage made her life so intolerable that she was glad to take refuge and reside with her mother at West Grange'. This was not the end of the story, for 'she was prevailed upon by the promisings and cajoallings of her husband and by the persuasion of some of her friends from a motive not to be a burden to them to go and live with him at his house at East Grange'. But that did not last long, as his only motive was to get her to sign a fraudulent contract of separation, and ultimately she ended up – with her child, and pregnant with another – back at her mother's. This is another case where one must conclude that evidence of adultery must have come as a relief, rather than a shock, because it made a divorce (and advantageous financial settlement) possible.

More of such cases – where there was no disparity of rank – appear in the next section.

UNHAPPY MARRIAGES

An early case, in the period when divorce actions were few and far between, particularly by wives, was that between Katharine Gellatley and Captain James Hamilton of Reidhouse. They married in 1706; he left her for another woman in August 1715, and she brought her divorce action in September of that year. She alleged that he maltreated her 'by beating her violently on her face and breast with his fist and threatening to stab her with his drawn sword', at the same time carrying on an 'intrigue'.[5]

Reidhouse could not deny his adultery but contested the case on the dubious premise that Katherine had not been a dutiful wife; when he returned from Flanders he found that instead of going to Scotland as he had ordered her to do she had followed him to England, 'and there continued to expose him to his nearest relations, as she had done before in every garrison in Flanders', 'particularly in the publick playhouse in the foot of the Cannongate in the view of all the spectators, which behaviour the petitioner was so ashamed of, that he was forced to go out of the playhouse, thinking by that means to bring her to a calmer temper', so that 'his deserting her Company at last, proceeded rather from necessity than choice.' She replied that when he left her behind 'in a strange Countrey without any support for life, she was necessitat to follow him over to London, partly to preserve her from starving, and partly to keep her husband from committing such abominable and unaccountable acts and deeds as he had formerly been guilty of, which at present the Lady forbears to name.' As for the occasion he mentioned, he 'might indeed be ashamed to mention the playhouse, he knows his Amours and carriage there in a corner with his Miss in his Ladies sight. It was not fitt nor would the Ladies modesty allow her to tell it, and how Reidhouse beat her in that womans presence untill she vomited blood next morning'. Her version of events proved to be the true one, and she was granted her divorce.

Over a century later the mystery in the 1829 case of Mrs Jane Craig against Andrew Thomson, merchant in Glasgow, is how she put up with him for nearly thirty years.[6] She bore him twelve children, of whom ten were alive at the time of the divorce action. Thomson did not deny that he kept a mistress, nor that he had had sexual relations with various other women, but he insisted that his wife knew all about them. She denied knowing anything:

It is true that for some time before, the Pursuer could not help feeling chagrin and disquiet at the Defenders conduct, as it was marked by a total disregard of propriety – by very unseemly violence of temper – by his utter neglect of his children, as well as of the Pursuer and by his appearing ill at ease when alone with his family, and frequently absenting himself from them from the morning until late at night.

She went on to say that his 'unnatural conduct' toward his family was particularly evident 'on an occasion when it was his duty to shew them more than usual kindness and attention'. She was alluding to the fact that in March 1828 she 'underwent a surgical operation for Cancer in the Breast, which was followed by long and severe illness; and on that occasion, his unfeeling indifference and neglect of the Pursuer and his children was exceedingly marked and revolting.' After that she 'never on any occasion whatever admitted the Defender to the privileges of a Husband by having any sexual intercourse with him.' But at that time she 'adopted this conduct merely to mark her sense of the unnatural, undutiful and cruel treatment to which she and her family were subjected, and without her being in the knowledge of her husband's infidelity.' She said that she was only told of his adulteries at the beginning of September when at Largs with her younger children. His first visit after that took place on the 20th of the same month, when 'he admitted the truth of the accusation, and begged that the Pursuer would forgive him. Most firmly and decidedly did she answer, that she never would, and requested that he would never again visit her, or injure his family by his presence'.

More light is thrown on Thomson's character by a letter he wrote to his eldest son the month after the divorce action was raised, complaining of the treatment he was receiving, and of the hypocrisy, 'for there is not one of them but has been aware of my conduct for years'. He thought his conduct very reasonable: 'Marriage is intended for the gratification of the sexes, and if a husband is refused that, either from temper, caprice, ill health, or absence, what will he do? Just as I did. For nine months before the operation, I could have no connection, for had she been got with child, the swelling on the breast would have increased with the size of the foetus.' (Her procurator abstained 'from commenting upon the abominable sentiments conveyed in this letter'.) Two months later, 'With the view probably of inducing his wife to relinquish the proceedings which she is taking against him,' Thomson was 'insisting upon taking away from her society her four youngest children [aged thirteen, eleven, six and five], and keeping them in his own house; and as he finds that she will not voluntarily part with them, he has intimated his intention to remove them by force and violence.'

Did she really know anything about her husband's affairs before September 1828? Because Thomson pleaded *remissio injuriae*, and Jane had cohabited with him for so long after his adulterous activities began, the commissaries gave her an extraordinarily lengthy grilling on the subject and finally concluded that she was indeed ignorant of them. Her brother apparently remonstrated with Andrew on various occasions, while Mr Scott of Greenock, who married their eldest daughter in January 1826, also 'spoke to the defender in regard to his infidelity to the Pursuer', but it was perfectly feasible that male family members should know about his affairs without telling his wife; they would have considered that they were 'protecting' her and the marriage. A wife was supposed to hear no evil, see no evil, and speak no evil, so whatever she might have suspected she would not have wanted to know more. The breaking point was clearly his treatment of her at the time she had her mastectomy; after that she did want to know. And as she was fortunate enough to live in Scotland, she was able to obtain her freedom from him (and, as the innocent party, to keep her children).

ILLICIT RELATIONS

We have not so far seen many situations where a wife's adultery was carried on under the nose of the husband, but it certainly was in the 1777 case of John Cuming (described as late merchant in Glasgow now writer and messenger in Edinburgh), against Isabell Campbell (daughter of John Campbell of Hay).[7] Her lover was another Edinburgh 'writer', John Hall, and various servants deponed about his daytime visits, retreats into the bedroom, and 'toying and kissing together'. One servant, Grizell Winter (aged eighteen), 'had been desired by the Defender to keep secret their meetings and not to Divulge what she saw passing betwixt them, and told her that if she discovered any thing Mr Hall would take her life'. Grizell also said that 'sometimes when Mr Hall was supping in the pursuer's house he used to open the outer door and drive it to again with a noise, after which he went into the closet of said room and there remained all night'. There was no attempt to keep the affair from the servants, though plenty of threats if they revealed anything. Dorothea Crawfurd asked Mrs Cuming 'how Mr Hall and her came to keep so often company together the defender answered that she was married to him'. Mrs Cuming demanded that Dorothea 'keep those things a secret from the pursuer, and threatned her by saying that Mr Hall would not care to kill the first person who spoke of it'. Dorothea also remembered 'Mr Hall and the Defender agreeing to make an elopement together in March last and the deponent was employed to carry their baggage to a chaise in St John Street . . . Mr Hall then told the defender that he could not go away with her, as his Father would be sorry to part with him'. Dorothea had to lug all the baggage back again.

However, after that false start they did elope in August. Marion McTaggart, who had been Hall's servant, 'was sent with their baggage to the Chaise . . . some time before this Mr Hall told the deponent that he intended to leave the country and asked her to go along with him'. Marion understood that he was to take Mrs Cuming along with him as he had told her that 'Mrs Cuming and he had been married together.' This 'marriage' obviously had no legal grounds, but once they were gone Cuming – a shadowy figure – had no trouble in obtaining his divorce.

In the 1799 case of Alexander Mackinnon Esquire against Mrs Mary Emelia Mackinnon (daughter of Charles Mackinnon of Mackinnon) the couple had been married in 1792 and soon afterwards went to Naples, where she bore him two children.[8] In June 1796 with his consent she returned to Scotland with the children, 'in order to reside there with her relations untill he should find it convenient to come home to his family which he then expected might be soon'. She stayed with her mother in Edinburgh until January 1797, 'during which period' – in the words of the libel – 'she was seduced and led astray by Charles Pickford a lieutenant in the Royal Navy'. They went away together to London, and she had a child by him while her husband was still in Italy.

At the time of Mary's pregnancy a London witness (Sarah Corbert) was told by her that she

> had incurred the displeasure of her relations but the Dowager Mrs Mackinnon [her grandmother] had often written to her intreating her to leave Mr Pickford and she would retire with her to some remote part of Great Britain secluded from society but Mrs Mackinnon had always rejected the offers saying she was married to Mr Pickford had a Child by him and never would leave him and the Deponent never heard till lately that Mr Mackinnon (who she admitted had been her husband but was dead as she said) was alive and in this Country.

The dowager Mrs Mackinnon also arranged lodgings in London for her grand-daughter, at the house of Peter Lentzenick, where the dowager herself always lodged. After Lentzenick realised that Mary was not married to Mr Pickford, she 'being far advanced in her pregnancy the deponent could not find it in his heart to turn them out of doors knowing as no succour could be procured from any where, that they must starve or do worse things, and Mrs Mackinnon would not have remained with them without Mr Pickford'. Lentzenick wrote to the dowager, reminding her of her promise 'that what he did for her [Grand]Daughter He would not be a loser by', and 'begged now for her assistance as it was impossible for him to support her [grand]daughter longer'.

However, the Dowager Mrs Mackinnon refused to help unless Mary left Mr Pickford, which she would not do. Lentzenick's wife felt 'very uneasy that persons of such a description should live in her house', but the Lentzenicks were too kindhearted to turn them out, though Lentzenick begged them to raise some money 'upon the expectation of Mr Pickfords Legacy and leave his house as soon as possible.' The couple left that house, and nothing is known of what became of them.

Another elopement occurred in the 1806 case of Magill Darley, controller of the customs at Campbeltown, against Amelia Price Macneal.[9] They were married in 1794 and had two children. William Muir, her lover, was a clerk in the custom house and lodged in Darley's house for a year before she was delivered of another child. Immediately after that Amelia eloped with Muir, 'carrying with her all her cloaths and sundry articles of plate linens etc belonging to the Pursuer also the foresaid youngest child'. They went to the Isle of Man where they lived together.

The couple were visited in Douglas by witnesses who saw one child running about as well as a new-born infant. They showed Neil Buchanan, shipmaster, 'a Contract or paper which they said they had entered into two years before their elopement from Campbeltown purporting to the best of the deponents remembrance that they were to live together as husband and wife during life and that all they had was to belong to the longest liven and she told the deponent that their names were signed to the said Contract or paper by their blood.' (Amelia also told Buchanan that she and her husband had not slept together for two years before the elopement.) Mary McLean who had been a servant in the Campbeltown household, said that Darley was often away 'for days together on visits to Gentleman in the Country', and that 'upon these occasions the Defender and the said William Muir kept company together almost continually and appeared inseparable.' Amelia wrote a bitter letter to her husband before she left (from which it seems that she was motivated as much by dislike of her husband as by passion):

> Sir as you have made so many frequent attempts of turning me out and even desiring me to leave your house these several months bygone together with your abusing my fathers friends . . . from whom you have had your living these several years and indeed got your future support if you can keep it I now in order to save you any farther trouble must declare that I have voluntarily quit you and your house for ever, but had you given me a peaceable quiet life should have staid . . . With respect to the children you have but two in life which you are in duty bound to provide for; and as to Hector he I must confess has a father whose name I am not now at liberty to mention but will when necessary and in that case you or your family can have no claim upon him nor or at any future period . . . The reason of my taking with me your two Greavy spoon and four salt Cellars is but a small trifle in indemnifying payment for my fathers silver Tankard with many other pieces of plate in like value.

In the 1815 case of Henry Moncrieff, Writer to the Signet, against Charlotte Erskine Rollo, the eloping couple were pursued.[10] Charlotte's lover was Charles Stewart, a clerk in the county tax office of Edinburgh. On the Monday night before she went off she told a friend staying at the house, Miss Caroline Goodsir (aged twenty), that 'she had promised to go off with Mr Stewart upon which the Deponent said "O Charlotte I am sure I don't hear right you could not surely be guilty of that" '. A few months earlier Stewart had informed an acquaintance of his, Patrick Cameron, writer in Edinburgh, (aged twenty-one), that 'he had an Intrigue with a married Lady and he read extracts from several letters which he told the Deponent he had received from the Lady but did not mention her name to the Deponent'. Cameron 'remarked to Mr Stewart that he would bring himself into a scrape as he would be obliged to carry her away with him when he went abroad (which the Deponent understood he was to do) to which Mr Stewart said that he had no intention of that'. The chambermaid in the Tower Inn, Hawick, remembered telling her mistress of the arrival of the eloping couple, 'and asked what room she would get ready and that her mistress asked her if they were Genteel looking people and the Deponent having answered that they were her mistress desired her to make ready the best Bedroom in the house'.

For the pursuit, help was asked of Captain Ninian Lowis, who was informed by Mr Hugh Rollo, Charlotte's brother, that she had left her husband on the preceding Monday. They heard that she had gone to Hull, and followed. When they arrived Charlotte and her lover 'seemed to be in the greatest possible state of agitation and fell down upon their knees clinging round the Deponent and uttering many incoherent exclamations the Gentleman particularly begging the Deponent not to separate them'. He and her brother 'said all they possibly could to prevail upon her to accompany them back to Scotland but could not prevail upon her till next day'.

In the above cases the gentry wives who sinned did so because they had fallen in love with another man. A complete contrast is provided by the case of William Wotherspoon Esquire, accountant in Edinburgh, against Elizabeth Young. When Wotherspoon brought his action in December 1817 he did not even know her lover's name, though he was 'of genteel appearance and of middeling stature'. Subsequently he discovered that the man was Robert Armstrong, 'a student at present either attending the University or acting as a Tutor in a respectable family in this City'. Armstrong was in fact a student of Divinity (aged twenty-eight), who met Elizabeth at St George's Church 'during divine service' and walked her home. She told him that 'she was going next forenoon to some place near Seafield Baths'; Armstrong asked her 'if she would allow him the honour of escorting her', and he 'understood that he would have that liberty'. He met her in Princes Street the next morning, accompanied her to Seafield, and then up to the ruins of St Anthony's Chapel in Holyrood Park (at that time called the King's Park). What neither realised was that they were followed all the way. Wotherspoon, aware of his wife's propensity to pick up young men, had employed someone to watch her movements. When he saw them enter the ruins, William Archibald found a vantage point higher up, and 'saw the Lady lying upon the ground on her back and the gentleman with his breeches down above her and from the appearance of their bodies he has no doubt whatever that they were in the act of copulation'. Wotherspoon had no difficulty in obtaining his divorce.[11]

REGRETS

Charles Gordon of Wardhouse and Katharine Mercer were married in December 1781, and she bore him seven children, of whom six were alive at the time of the divorce action in 1796.[12] However, a servant said that after Katharine had her last child in October 1794 she did not sleep with her husband again, and the servant 'often heard the Defender tell the pursuer that she would not live with him as his wife'. Another servant deponed that Wardhouse and his wife never slept together during the five months she served them and that 'she has heard the Defender say that she did not chuse to live with the pursuer as his wife, and has known her refuse him admittance when he knocked at her door.' It is possible that it was her passion for another man that was the cause, but this was never stated. Her lover was Lieutenant-Colonel John Woodford, and she became pregnant with his child. The midwife deponed that 'in answer to some questions put by the Deponent about her husband, the defender said with a Sigh that the Child was not her husbands but that of another person whose wife was still alive.'

Katharine wrote the following letter in August 1796:

> My much injured husband I cannot leave my fathers house without assuring you that I feel the deepest remorse for the errors in my past conduct and that I am now determined with the blessing of God to lead such a life of innocence and contrition as make me hope for the pardon of Heaven for your pardon and for that of my parents I acknowledge you have all treated me with most unmerited kindness I now beg leave to recommend our dear Children to your utmost care and affection, They never injured mortal may they be blessed and happy.

And his mother-in-law wrote:

> My Dear Son Your unhappy Wife has now left us and we are all in a state of inexpressible misery – God grant that her penitence may be as lasting as it is at present unequivocally sincere – The letter she dispatched to you yesterday will give you some idea of the state of her mind I am sure it was written from the heart – your Daughters have witnessed her remorse and deep Contrition but no language can do justice to it and I shall not attempt to describe it She is now on her way to Glasgow where she is to be under the protection of some very respectable friends whose names must be concealed upon account of the nature of the task they undertake but you I am sure can guess who I mean Mrs Burke accompanies the unhappy creature to Glasgow and will remain with her during her stay there Your Dear Girls enter into all your feelings and are a great comfort to us in our present unhappy state.

The sadness is palpable, but unfortunately we are given no hint of what caused the incompatibility between husband and wife, or of the passion which she presumably felt for her lover, or why the affair ended. We do not even know what happened to her illegitimate child. Only the sad after effects of the affair, and end of the marriage, survive in the record.

Another sad case is that of Dr Andrew Ure, physician in Glasgow, against

Catherine Monteath in 1819.[13] Her lover was Granville Sharp Pattison, surgeon in Glasgow, by whom she became pregnant. She was forced to leave her home and three children by her husband and wrote the following to her lover, then in Paris:

> with a mind overwhelmed with grief and a Breaking heart, I again sit down to address you, it is to me a task of the most painful kind, but my forlorn and destitute situation calls loudly for you to come and give me relief Oh Granville will nothing awaken your feelings or compassion towards me, must I die here in misery and want without one consoling word from you, the Author of all my misfortunes . . . it has separated me from one of the best and most indulgent husbands and from my Dear Dear Children what do you think my Sufferings must have been upon such an awful occasion.

She was living in 'obscure lodgings', hiding from her friends, concealing her situation:

> I have now no Claim upon my husband, that is now over and what am I to do, am I to be allowed to Starve here to death and not a Creature to look to me, and allow me to ask you what is to become of the innocent offspring that may be looked for in a short time, I am now five months and a half gone with child to you. I therefore request that you will instantly write to me and say what provision you are to make for the Child and me, by return of Post I will expect to hear from you I must have relief in some way or other and if you neglect this, I will instantly write to your Sister, and lay the whole before her . . . you need not Suppose you can escape from this, your frequent visits were taken notice of by the Servants at my house.

Presumably Pattison did make provision for her, but Mary Parker, an old friend, who stayed with her the night she gave birth, asked her 'what was to be done with the child – She answered that it was intended to be giving out to nurse but she did not know how to part with it'.[14]

Catherine was not the only gentlewoman to be let down by a lover after the truth emerged. Another example is the case of Captain William Dunlop against Frances Elizabeth Humber (1818–20).[15] The adultery, with James Stewart, lieutenant in the Royal Navy, took place in Gibraltar in 1817. Arthur Gallagher, a servant, 'often brought notes from Captain Dunlop on guard to Mrs Dunlop and she would read them with Mr Stewart and laugh and tear them and say God help the poor old fool he knows but little about it'. The servant 'heard her say she would rather have one joint of Mr Stewarts little finger than the whole of his [her husband's] Body and I told her it was a shame to think so little of the Captain who thought so much of her.' When the truth came out (January 1818) Frances wrote to her husband: 'you abused me, treated me dreadfully and hardened my heart. Your kindness to me these two days has effected what hardship never would, Oh when you said you believed me innocent you almost broke my heart . . . let me beseech you not to prosecute with too much rigour the man on whom all my dependence hangs he is guilty but he is not a rascal he is to be pitied he is young and led away as I was'.

A few months later (September 1818), Frances was writing in a very different vein, to her husband's agent: 'I have to assure Captain Dunlop that I am now totally convinced of the truth of his assertion that Mr Stewart is a villain I also now see my crime in its proper light and I as sincerely repent it as it is possible for a woman to do, in consequence of this I have broken off all Correspondence with Mr Stewart'. She continued,

> I so thoroughly despise Mr Stewart that were I divorced tomorrow and he with the largest fortune to offer me his hand I do solemnly assure you I would if I had a Competency to live on reject it with Contempt – I have therefore to beg you will lay this before Captain Dunlop and say that if he will consent to stop the proceedings for a divorce and allow me thirty Pounds a year to Assist in my Support . . . and pledge himself no further to expose me I will be contented to remain in retirement and peace with my mother.

If he did not agree, 'I shall be compelled (tho much against my inclination) to have recourse to the man I despise beg of him then Sir to save me from Infamy and be assured of my virtuous intentions'.

On 28 November she begged her husband to reconsider his decision to proceed with the divorce:

> Think to what a dreadful condition I shall be reduced, hurled from Respectability to disgrace shunned by my own sex and insulted by the men without shame. My Mother will not then dare to support me even were it in her power but she should incur the Anger of her father. Without a friend without money without character where shall I find refuge where shall I wander, what is to become of me even virtuous industry will be denied me since who will employ an unknown an unfriendless [sic] being without character or recommendation . . . Name any way in which I shall atone for past offences or name any sacrifice be it never so great and I will make it if you will still let me remain your wife do not divorce me and I will do any thing you please I conjure you I implore you not to proceed in this divorce if not for my sake for that of my Mother my Sister my Child for that of your eternal Salvation.

Captain Dunlop proceeded to get his divorce.

LIVING SEPARATELY

The above cases follow a classic pattern of a wife deceiving her husband with a lover, and the husband, immediately after discovering the affair, commencing a divorce action. But even amongst the gentry there are many cases where the couple were living apart for many years before one spouse sued for divorce.

James Dalrymple of Grangefield was married to Susanna Cunningham in 1772.[16] They cohabited until November 1777 and had three children, after which they voluntarily separated, and she went on the stage. Placing actors and actresses in a particular class or rank is almost impossible and would have been equally problematic at the time. As outsiders they lived by their own rules, and Susanna therefore did not 'lower' herself but rather stepped outside the conventional ranks of society.

In 1778 she took up with Henry Mills, 'comedian' (i.e. actor) and lived with him as his wife in Newcastle and elsewhere in England, taking his name, and bearing him three children, baptised under the name Mills. After he died in 1784 she 'came to Edinburgh with the Company of Comedians and then and there formed a Connection with James Bland Comedian and they lived and Cohabited together in Edinburgh'. In May 1785 she joined the company of Mr Sutherland at Forres 'and at first wanted to put up her name as Mrs Bland but on Mr Sutherland Expressing his suspicion Mr Bland would not authorize this, she desired to appear under the name of Mrs Campbell under which name she appeared and acted for four or five weeks'.

After that Susanna 'formed a Connection with Mr Tingey a Comedian in the Company under the direction of the said Mr Sutherland and took the name of Mrs Tingey appeared as the wife of the said Mr Tingey and lived with him as husband and wife In which Character she . . . continued with said Company of Comedians under the direction of Mr Sutherland for several months performing as a Player at the Towns of Elgin Banff Keith Huntly and other places'. They continued to live together, and then in August 1787 they 'went to Peterhead and had a Company of Players of their own, but that breaking up they afterwards went to the Town of Banff and kept a public house there still keeping the name of Mr and Mrs Tingey'. In December 1789 she attempted to rejoin Mr Sutherland's company at Dumfries, 'but Mr Sutherland having declined to employ her she and Mr Tingey then went and joined the Company of Comedians of a Mr Johnston then playing at Hexham in England where she and Mr Tingey remain living as formerly as husband and wife'. Grangefield only brought his divorce action in 1790, and it is fascinating that he was able to provide such a detailed account of her life over the twelve-year period since their separation.[17]

Some members of the lower gentry even went through a second marriage ceremony.[18] Bigamy was a criminal offence, but there is only one mention of criminal action being take against a gentleman bigamist. This was William Storry, surgeon, who married Ann Shaw (daughter of an Esquire) in 1807. Ann alleged adultery from 1815, with the wife of a baker or victual dealer in Airdrie. After that he 'settled in Annan . . . where giving himself out as a single unmarried man he contracted another marriage with Martha Graham then residing at Lockerby . . . And on the ground of which he stood sometime imprisoned in the Jail of Dumfries and was criminally indicted at the instance of his Majesty's Advocate on the charge of Bigamy'. Ann only brought her divorce action in 1824, at which time Storry was again cohabiting with Martha.[19]

We have seen in this chapter on gentry divorces everything from classical betrayal and remorse to separate lives and serial monogamy, where the assumption must be that the spouse bringing a divorce action after many years apart had met someone else they wished to marry. One might surmise that this class, who did not have the resources and assurance of the aristocracy and upper gentry, but who possessed property and valued respectability, would have been the one that most feared divorce, and also would have borne the heaviest costs. We did see one case where terror of disgrace was paramount, but we have also seen gentlemen – and gentlewomen – living separate lives with a new partner without benefit of marriage. The misery of some marriages featured earlier in the chapter contrasts with the passion felt for lovers, and with the insouciance of those who had escaped a joyless marriage and shrugged a shoulder at society's strictures.

NOTES

All CC references are in the Scottish Record Office.

1. Alexander Monro, Essay on Female Conduct in the form of letters to his daughter, c.1738, NLS.MS.6658. Copy by his daughter, Margaret 1739, MS.6659. I am grateful to Rosalind Mitchison for this reference. Monro was only married in 1725, so Margaret could not have been older than twelve when he wrote his essay for her.
2. cc8/5/16.
3. He brought a defence of remissio injuriae on the basis of some affectionate letters (concerning their children and grandchildren) which she had written him as late as 1780. Her procurator argued that they simply revealed that 'she was totally ignorant of the many adulterous and lewd practices which has now come to her knowledge but then totally unknown to her'. He then claimed that she cohabited with him in the full knowledge of the bastard child's birth; the commissaries interrogated her under oath, and on her denial repelled the defence.
4. cc8/5/12.
5. cc8/5/2.
6. cc8/6/168. The inclusion of a Glasgow merchant amongst 'gentry' might seem problematic, but it is clear from the lifestyle described and family connections that they were 'genteel'.
7. cc8/5/15.
8. cc8/5/25.
9. cc8/5/29.
10. cc8/5/34.
11. cc8/5/36.
12. cc8/5/23.
13. cc8/5/37.
14. The case was initially uncontested, but after the commissaries granted the divorce, defence lawyers suddenly appeared and declared that the case had been conducted without the knowledge of the defender, putting forward various defences and attempting to obtain money for aliment and expences. Ure stated that this was all the work of Pattison, and that Catherine had been taken away and could not be found. The commissaries ordered Catherine to appear in court to be examined. Instead she signed an affidavit declaring: 'I was some time ago induced at the solicitation of Mr Burn acting as agent for Mr Granville

Sharp Pattison to sign a mandate . . . authorising opposition to be made in my name to a Decree of Divorce obtained against me . . . I was induced to do so under assurances that it was for my Interest in the way of obtaining an aliment and permission to see my children at pleasure But I now find that I have been deceived and I accordingly hereby recall every mandate I may have granted authorising you to present a Petition in my name opposing the Divorce obtained by my Husband or for aliment to myself or my Child or for a sum to defray expences'.

15. cc8/5/38.
16. cc8/5/20.
17. The libel added on top of the usual clause about declaring the defender as dead that John and Mary Mills, her two children by the deceased Henry Mills, 'ought to be found and declared Bastards'.
18. One example is John Sproul, who married Jean Miller in December 1769, and subsequently, when practising as a physician in Dublin, married a Miss Basket there and acknowledged her as his lawful wife. Jean discovered this in 1774 but waited until 1782 before raising a divorce action and did not receive her divorce until 1785. cc8/6/45. Another example is Captain Simon Baillie of the First Regiment of European Infantry in the service of the East India Company, who married Mrs Janet Alison in May 1788. In July 1789, on board a ship bound for India, he claimed to be single (he admitted his previous marriage but said that his first wife had 'died of rapid decline') and married another woman; Janet brought her divorce action in 1791, by which time the other woman was dead. cc8/5/20.
19. cc8/6/144.

DEUCHAR VS McLAINE – THE DIVORCE LAWYER AND HIS OWN WIFE

From 1721 onwards the name of one lawyer, Andrew Deuchar, dominates Commissary Court divorce actions. The irony of such a man bringing a divorce action against his own wife must have been relished by many, not least because her lover was his own former apprentice, at the time of the litigation a practising lawyer (also a married man), Mungo Herdman.

Helen McLaine, his wife, was the granddaughter of a former bishop of Argyll. She was married to Deuchar in April 1717 and was said to have borne 'several' children, but there was apparently only one surviving when the divorce action was brought at the end of January 1728, though she had miscarried the previous month ('and had such a violent flooding that the whole bed cloaths and feather bed were wett with the blood').

The adultery was first committed on 1 January 1728, though there had been a long lead-up to it. In December, 'appearing some what pensive', and being asked by 'a gentlewoman' (18-year-old Katharine Kirkpatrick) 'why she was so', she answered that 'she behoved to tell her she was in Love, and desired her to Guess with whom it was, and she having told her that she Could not Guess,' Helen said 'she had been in Love five years with Mungo Herdman That it was come to such a height she could conceall it no Longer'. On 2 January she told Mrs Betty Campbell that 'it was not out of Lust But out of Love that she Yielded to Mungo Herdman', and that 'she had strugled for five years betwixt Love and honour and Love had gott the better at Last'. But before getting sentimental over such a long fought-against passion we should note that earlier there had been some scandal about Helen's behaviour with another man, Campbell of Kinpunt, brother to Betty Campbell who plays a prominent part in the story, and on 2 January, when Helen told her she had lain with Herdman the night before she added that she had 'designed that favour' for Betty's 'eldest brother but he had missed it'. There was conflicting evidence about Helen's propensity for drink, but one witness said he had seen her 'disordered in her reason', and she comes across as a silly, neurotic woman, perhaps with not enough to occupy her.

Mrs Betty Campbell was an unmarried girl of 18 (the 'Mistress' simply indicates her gentility) who was staying in the house at the time. Great efforts were made by Helen's lawyer to stop her testifying, on the grounds that she had 'maliciously been the former and foamenter of this unlucky rupture'. She was certainly two-faced, being Helen's confidant, and later even her go-between, but calling all the servants to listen at the door to a conversation between her and Helen. One of the servants (Mary Forbes) deponed that 'when Mrs Campbell called them ben to the door of the chamber she said that it was proper they should hear what the defender was saying about her being with child to Mungo Herdman and that the deponent and the other servants refused twice or thrice to goe but at Length they went'. They heard Helen say that she was with child to Mungo, had been guilty with him on 1 January, and 'that if the child was a boy, was to be named Mungo, and if a Lass after the said Mungo's good mother, and that Mungo should hold up the child to be baptized'.

There are other references to this: on one occasion Helen 'clapped her hand upon her Belly saying, it was there that keeped up her heart, for she was with child to her Dear Mr Herdman'. Now, this was all happening within a fortnight or so of the first time she had intercourse with him (and not that long after her miscarriage), so it seems very unlikely. It is surely significant that when she told Betty on 2 January about having had intercourse with Herdman for the first time the night before she also said that 'if she should have a child by it, she would Love that Child better than any ever she had had', for within a week or two she had convinced herself that she was indeed pregnant.

Before going on to the discovery and what happened after that, can we get any hint of the relationship between Helen and Mungo? One of those who overheard the conversation between Helen and Betty was Roger Oswald, Deuchar's 17-year-old apprentice, at which time he also heard her 'singing a baudy song, and after she was done singing, heard her say that Mungo Herdman had sung the same to her when in Bed together'. To the best of Roger's memory, 'the Import of the Song was That if a man and wife were in bed togither and he should Lay his hand upon the wifes privitys and asked what it was, and she answering that it was a pin cushion, he should make the return that he had a pin to put into it'. Helen told Betty that on one occasion when a servant tried, unsuccessfully, to get into the room to deliver a message she and Mungo 'were engadged to such a height of passion and in such a situation that they could not have moved tho' her husband had come in upon them'. All of which – in spite of Helen's declarations that it was love, not lust that motivated her – suggests a very earthy, physical relationship.

Andrew received the first hint of the adultery (from Betty Campbell) on 6 January, and when he went into his wife's bedroom he found her in bed, with Herdman 'sitting on her bed side in a familiar way and manner'. Deuchar, understandably, 'stormed and appeared highly displeased'. When Deuchar asked Herdman 'if such Behaviour was Decent and Becoming', the latter 'arose and satt down upon a chair in the room seeming to be in great confusion', and when Deuchar 'having said furder in a passionat manner, how come it that (as he was informed) he had been in that room Locked up with his wife, and what possible excuse could there be for such a thing, which was altogither unaccountable Especially In him who by his education and practise with the pursuer while his servant knew the Import of such behaviour and what it concluded He the said Mungo Herdman answered That he could not excuse it But pretended there was nothing ill done or meant'. The two men then retired to another room and when Deuchar asked Herdman if Helen 'had showen any Lascivious Inclination towards him', he answered that 'she had exprest indeed great friendship for him, But all virtuous and had Desired him to kiss her, which he did'. Being asked 'if he got any complements from her he acknowledged that he had got a Diamond ring which had been her mothers'. Deuchar took it from him and expressed his anger. But he did not know that the pair had had intercourse, and he did all he could to save the marriage.

The next day a friend of the family, Alexander Monro, professor of anatomy (who, we noted in the last chapter, subsequently wrote an essay on 'female conduct' for his daughter), was called to the house to chide Helen for her 'imprudent' behaviour, and she solemnly promised never to see Herdman again. Deuchar wrote to him to say that he felt himself greatly injured, and a mutual friend expostulated with Herdman 'in presence of his wife'. However, the adulterous couple found means of communicating, and on the tenth of the month Helen 'pretending to go and visit a certain family of unquestionable good character, went first to the Dwelling house of three young gentlewomen in Hendersons Land,' where neither she nor Herdman 'had ever been before . . . on pretence of visiting, and soon after the said Herdman coming in also there, and calling for her they both went into a room wherein was a Bed and stayed there by themselves the door of the room being Locked or shutt upon them for the space of halfe an hour and upwards'. (Beatrix Blair, one of the gentlewomen, said she had 'intertained no bad thoughts' about what they were up to in the other room, 'but disapproved of her conduct in useing such freedome in a house wherein she was an absolute stranger and never being there before'.) The next day Helen told her husband that 'she wanted to pay a visit to a certain old gentlewoman of unquestionable good character', and being allowed to do so, she left the house at three in the afternoon, went straight to Herdman, and stayed with him until eleven that night. Herdman then had 'the Impudence and boldness to come alongst with and convoy her to her house only a few minutes before the pursuers incomeing'. Helen asked a servant 'what she thought her master would have done or said had he seen Herdman come home she answered no doubt if he had seen him he would have killed him.'

Deuchar went to see Professor Monro again, saying that he had more information about his wife's behaviour, and that he 'was now so fully perswaded of the Truth of their criminall deallings That nothing could give the Least satisfaction to his mind unless Herdman and the Defender would in the most solemn manner make oath . . . That Herdman and she never had had carnall deallings'. Helen expressed herself 'well satisfied to take any oath and in any manner that could be proposed to her, to free herself of any Imputation of the guilt laid to her Charge'. The minister was called for, and Helen renewed her vow. At no time did she confess carnal dealing 'but on the contrary in the most solemn manner and strongest Imprecations denied any such guilt.' As for her promise not to see Herdman again, she told Betty Campbell, who was acting as go-between, that she 'could not' keep it. Within days Helen wrote her lover an 'amorous Letter' and sent it with a verbal message asking him to meet her, to which he responded (in writing) that as her husband 'would be on the watch they therefore behooved to forbear meeting togither for two or three days.' The letter must have been intercepted, for immediately after that Deuchar initiated divorce proceedings.

Did Helen really believe that she could continue to deceive her husband? She told Katharine Kirkpatrick that 'she had acknowledged in presence of Mr Monro Surgeon Mr Blair Minister and the pursuer her being with Child to Mungo Herdman and that it was conserted amongst them she . . . should go to the country to be delivered of the said child, and upon her return, if she reformed her Life the pursuer was to forgive her and to entertain her as his wife.' At that point she seemed penitent, but subsequently she said to Betty Campbell that her husband 'and she was to part, That she was Glade of it for she would have a separat aliment and the Keeping of her Child, and would have better opportunity of meeting with Mungo Herdman and Live as happy as the day is Long, whereas she had formerly Lived with the pursuer as in hell'.

In other words, what she expected was that a legal separation would be agreed, and she would be able to have her cake and eat it. What she evidently did *not* expect – very stupidly, considering what her husband spent his time doing – was that Deuchar would sue for a full divorce, thereby depriving her of status, money, and probably child as well. But perhaps it is not quite as surprising as it seems, because this was the 1720s when *very* few divorce actions were brought. Significantly, Betty Campbell deponed that when Helen came back from Herdman's house after having promised she would not see him again, Deuchar said that his wife 'was as double as the Divel and worse than the Lady Edderline' – a reference to one of the most notorious early divorce cases.

Helen's lawyer (Archibald Tod) fought hard for her. He found witnesses to testify to Betty Campbell's malice against his client and even claimed that in the conversation between Helen and Betty overheard by the servants Betty was imitating Helen's voice! But he could not win, for though no one had seen the guilty couple in a compromising position, there was a mass of circumstantial evidence (including the sound of a bed 'jigging' when the two of them were locked in her bedroom together). The case ran from January 1728 until May 1730 (with an additional supplication after that date which was refused by the commissaries) and takes up about 300 pages in the volume.

There was no suggestion by any of the witnesses, even on Helen's side, that Deuchar treated her badly in any way, and his unwillingness to believe the worst of her bears this out. She, on the other hand, had already tried to seduce another man, and admitted that Herdman would not have attempted to take advantage of her if she had not encouraged him. Betty Campbell was a nasty piece of work, but Andrew

Deuchar was unlikely to have remained in ignorance of his wife's infidelity even without her conniving presence.

Did Andrew Deuchar sometimes remember his own traumatic divorce case when he acted as procurator for others? He remained the dominant figure in the Commissary Court for nearly three decades after that, his last case being as late as 1758.

cc8/5/3. Andrew Deuchar's name does not appear as a member of the Faculty of Advocates or as a Writer to the Signet, and it has not been possible to discover anything more about him.

CHAPTER 8

ADULTERY WITH A SOCIAL INFERIOR

Nowhere is the double standard more glaring than it is across the social divide. An upper-class husband who impregnated servant maids could expect mild disapproval; an upper-class wife who slept with a lower-class man caused outrage. Even so, the range of possible relationships was, for either sex, far greater than one might imagine. We might try to categorise them as gentlemen with mistresses or servants, gentlemen with whores, and ladies with lower-class men. But the first two categories cannot be strictly demarcated, not only because gentlemen who slept with their servant maids often visited bawdy houses as well, but also because the ranks of prostitutes who made a full-time living out of sex were swelled by 'part-timers' who supplemented the living they made as servants, mantua makers or whatever, by offering sex for payment on the side. And, in any case, a more meaningful distinction emerges between the men who took advantage of every woman they could lay their hands on (such men usually had sex with both servant maids and whores), and those who committed adultery with only one woman, who happened to be of a lower rank in society. We begin with cases of this kind, then go on to exploitative men, and finally to upper-class women.

STABLE RELATIONSHIPS

Unusual witnesses in the case of Ann Coutts against Ingram Ball, late Captain Lieutenant in the Seventh Regiment of Dragoons (1784) were the keeper of Newcastle Prison, his wife, family and servants. Ball was prisoner there for a few months and had a woman with him whom he called Mrs Ball, but who was subsequently found to be called Peggy Giles, and who bore a child during that time. As he was a gentleman he 'was not kept prisoner in the common gaol but in Mr Harles house'. When rumours reached Mrs Harle that he was a married man, he told her that he had 'had an unhappy connexion with a Lady in Scotland but that he had never lawfully married her'. When he was carried to London by habeas corpus, Peggy and the infant accompanied him. Anthony Perrot, attorney at law in Newcastle, who accompanied them on the journey south, heard a maid servant at the inn in Durham say, after hearing a waiter call for Mrs Ball, the maid servant, 'that's Peggy Giles not a

Mrs Ball what don't you think I know Peggy Giles'. Perrot added that 'the said Ingram Ball has every appearance of a Gentleman of Fashion and Education but that the said Peggy Giles is a vulgar illiterate and Low bred woman from which circumstances the deponent never did believe that Mr Ball and she were husband and wife'.[1]

Similarly, in the 1830 case of Mary Stuart Courtenay against George Johnston, Ensign in the British army, a lodging house keeper in Edinburgh deponed that Johnston took lodgings for himself and a woman whom he called his wife, and the witness believed them to be a married couple. But 'while they were living with the deponent the manner of the lady appeared so different from what she had heard of the real Mrs Johnstone, the one being remarkable for the Correctness of her behaviour and this lady the reverse – the deponent's suspicions were excited', and she discovered that 'this lady was not the person for whom she gave herself out.'[2]

A stable relationship across a very wide social divide (the man was a baronet and Lord-Lieutenant of Ross-shire) is seen in the 1796 case of Mrs Cochrane Chalmers against Sir Hector Mackenzie of Gairloch. They had married in 1778, when Sir Hector was only twenty, but separated in 1787. While Lady Mackenzie was at Gairloch Jean Urquhart was a chambermaid, but after that she became housekeeper. She bore Sir Hector five children, and witnesses declared that 'after Lady Mackenzie had left the house, Jean Urquhart sat at the head of Sir Hectors table and acted as Mistress of the family', and that 'the Children were kept up in the family like the Children of a Gentleman.' Jean would never have been accepted by 'society', and obviously the children would have been illegitimate (but well provided for), yet this was clearly a happy, stable relationship. By the time Lady Mackenzie raised the divorce action Jean was dead. Sir Hector married another woman of his own class the same year, so clearly it was raised at his request.[3]

In the 1801 case of Mrs Ann Ramsay against Matthew Baillie Esquire of Cairnbrae, Margaret Miller, a servant, bore her master three daughters, all maintained by him in Edinburgh unknown to his wife. When Margaret first became his mistress she left her employment at their house in Hamilton and went to the house at Cairnbrae where the family was not then residing. Thomas Green, a fellow servant, did not see her for some time after she left Hamilton, 'but having occasion to go upon a message to Cairnbrae he saw her there – That the Deponent asked her what she was doing there, and she gave no answer but fell a laughing'.[4]

A sad case is that of Mrs Mary Kennedy, in Dumfries-shire, against Captain George Manual, married in 1793.[5] In 1809 Elizabeth Smith, a servant in their house, became pregnant by him. She left under pretence of going into the service of a lady in England but instead the Captain, 'under the fictitious name of Mr Jones', took lodgings for her in Carlisle where she went 'and resided and passed under the name of Mrs Jones'. She had her child in April 1810, and the Captain visited her regularly both before and afterwards. John Lemon, reed maker in Carlisle, in whose house the Captain had taken lodgings, said that the gentleman had told him he was an 'officer in the Commissary department of the army, and could only come to Carlisle occasionally and by leave but would be coming and going while she staid in the deponent's lodgings.' But gradually a rumour began to spread that Elizabeth was not really his wife. He 'and Mrs Lemon his wife were unwilling to believe it as her behaviour had made a very favourable impression upon them, but being himself an overseer of the poor and learning additional circumstances which made him suspect the report might be true he felt it to be his duty to ascertain the fact'. He therefore wrote a letter to Mr Jones care of Mr Kerr, writer in Dumfries, and learned the truth. When (about a month later) Elizabeth was delivered of a daughter, and 'the child was about to be christened', Lemon 'remonstrated with her upon the impropriety of using a fictitious name, and told her it was the practice in the case of illegitimate children to give up the mother's name for the baptism, and she accordingly then first told the deponent that her true name was Elizabeth Smith'. Captain Manual wrote the following letter to Mrs Manual's agent:

My Dear Sir, I mean not to make any defence whatever in this most unfortunate and wretched business . . . neither do I mean that my once dearly beloved Mary shall be in the least or in any manner whatever molested or troubled all I want is that the remainder of her days may be satisfactory in every respect to herself – as to my self I care not what becomes of me: I am ruined and miserable, I have got leave to go to London to see if I can get any of my old India friends to do something for me, I wish I could get out again to India.

Presumably it was the scandal that 'ruined' him. The poor man clearly cared for both women. Mary obtained her divorce in 1812. There is no indication of what happened to Elizabeth.

EXPLOITATION

A very different pattern of behaviour emerges from our second group of upper–class men. In an early (1730) case, Isobell Anderson declared that her husband, Walter Welsh of Lochquharet, 'was heard oftener than once acknowledge that he had made use of and had carnall dealling with one Elizabeth Jack his own servant woman', and also with 'Elizabeth Walkinshaw then his servant woman . . . that at one certain occasion he had had adoe with the said Elizabeth Walkinshaw five severall times'. Another time, 'when the pursuer had found them in bed together and expostulate with them for such unlawfull conversation, they both of them fell upon her and beat and abused her most unmercifully which obleiged her to call for some persons to her relief'. Her husband also 'basely and familiarly conversed with one Isobell Good-fellow then his servant woman'. When that woman was 'challenged for her said criminall conversation and asked how long the defender and she had dealt in that adulterous manner she fell aweeping and said that she had ruined herself soul and body for that the defender had made use of her at his pleasure since the first Sabbath of January and owned that she was at that time thirteen weeks gone with child'. Lochquharet contested the case and brought a counter-process of adultery against his wife, but he was unable to prove this, and there was ample evidence of his brutality and adultery.[6]

In the 1772 case of Mrs Anne Sinclair of Brabster against Robert Sutherland of Langwall, the pursuer named: 1. Anna Millar, servant at Brabster, pregnant early in 1768 and sent away, at the defender's expense, to have her child in Edinburgh; 2. Margaret Millar, chambermaid (in 1769), which he confessed to the minister at Latheron 'and redeemed himself from Church Censure by paying a Fine to the poor for said offence'; 3. Marshel Shearer, an out servant, in 1770 and 1771, and 'she bore a child to him at Langwall of which he acknowledged himself to have been the father'; 4. Ann Monro, housekeeper at Langwall, who bore his child in November 1771 and was again pregnant in 1772; 5. Nelly Adams 'who came home a house-keeper at Langwall when the said Ann Monro was lying in of the first child', and 6. Ann Raffold, out-servant, at the end of 1771 or beginning of 1772.[7]

It is clear that the marriage was unhappy, and there are hints that Anne might actually have preferred Sutherland to sleep with the servant maids than to sleep with her. The one relationship that shocked her when she discovered it was the one with Ann Monro. She told Benjamin Greenfield, sheriff officer in Dunbeath, that 'tho she entertained suspicions of her husbands guilt with other women, she little suspected That Ann Monro would have been the person to use her so, or words to that purpose, and that the reason for her not suspecting Ann Monro was, that she had shown particular Regard to her, and that she had been brought up about her mothers family from her infancy'.

At the beginning of this chapter it was mentioned that the line between prostitutes and servants was not clear cut. This can clearly be demonstrated by the 1802 case of Mrs Georgina Lindesay against Lieutenant Frederick Carmichael.[8] Married in 1794, they had lived separately since 1796, and she was able to prove his adultery with a number of different women. A great favourite of his was 'Baby Forsyth', who often met him in a house of assignation in Falkland. For example, a widow deponed that she 'was sent by Anne Findlay to desire Baby Forsyth to come there, and that Baby Forsyth afterwards told the deponent it was to meet the defender . . . Deponed that after his marriage the deponent has seen the defender in Ann Findlays house complain to Ann Findlay of bringing Margaret Honeyman to him and the deponent supposes he was angry, as he wanted Baby Forsyth to be brought to him'. Ann Findlay herself testified to his 'fondness' for that woman, and said that 'Baby Forsyth made no secret of the connection, and the deponent believes that it subsisted for sometime before as after the defenders marriage,' adding that she knew 'perfectly well that Baby Forsyth got money from the Defender on the occasions above mentioned'.

Baby Forsyth was at one time a servant to the pursuer and defender 'but was turned away before the term', which does not occasion much surprise. But when *Barbara* Forsyth herself appeared as a witness, she was described as servant to a writer (i.e. lawyer) in Anstruther. It is therefore clear that she earned her living as a servant and merely supplemented her income with some prostitution on the side (perhaps solely with Lieutenant Carmichael). And in fact, she, along with Mrs Carmichael, was infected with venereal disease by him.

But, of course, there were the professionals as well. The general openness about sex which characterised the age certainly manifests itself in the way that acknowledged prostitutes appeared as witnesses in divorce cases. And, as we shall see, it was also a way for them to make a bit of extra money.

John Spens and Ann Adamson in Perth had been married in 1753 and had six sons and two daughters.[9] She alleged adultery (with prostitutes in Edinburgh) from 1771, when he first contracted venereal disease, but her case was based on what had occurred the month before she brought her action in December 1775. Louis Farquharson, 'running stationer', deponed that when Spens arrived from Perth (with another man, James Spence) he

asked him if he the deponent could carry them to a house where they would get a dram and a Lassie, That accordingly the deponent carried them to the house of one Grant in Roxburgh Closs, where they got a Bowl of punch and some oysters, That after the punch and oysters were brought the deponent went some other messages, and upon his return got two or three glasses of punch, when he observed Mr Spens from Perth in naked bed with a girl . . . Depones that the deponent took the woman who was in bed with Mr Spens from Perth to be a whore, and deponed that Grants house in Roxburghs closs is habite and repute a bawdy house.

An interesting sidelight is thrown by a witness's remark that Spens had gone to an agent in Edinburgh, 'and upon telling the agent of his being in Mrs Grants house along with a girl there in bed, the Agent said it would be unnecessary to defend in any action that might be brought against him on that account, as the fact would be proven and the defence would only tend to lead him the defender into expences'.

In the 1778 case of Dame Eglantine Maxwell against Sir Thomas Wallace Dunlop of Craigie, adultery was alleged with Janet Stein and Nancy Beagle in houses of bad fame. Sir Thomas also tried to rape a 16-year-old servant girl in the house. Janet Stein, aged nineteen, deponed that 'she saw Mary Stewart in tears with her cloaths almost torn off her – That next day Mary Stewart told the deponent That Sir Thomas Wallace had offered her a guinea if she would lye with him, but that she had refused it.' Janet also stated that 'after Mary Stewart had left the room, the deponent continued sometime in the room and Sir Thomas Wallace then had carnal dealings with the deponent . . . and being further examined Deponed that after she the deponent came out of the room from the defender, he gave her eight shillings with directions to give three of it to Mrs Jack her Mistress.' Janet Innes confirmed that he 'called into a private room in which there was a bed a little girl whose name is Mary Stewart, That a little after the said Mary Stewart came out of the room with her cloaths torn off her, and crying and said that Sir Thomas Wallace had used her badly and she would not stay in his company'. And Mary herself said that he 'dragged her into a bedroom and endeavoured to lay her down upon the bed, that the Deponent struggled and made her escape, and had her cloaths almost torn off her.'[10]

A more typical case was that of Mrs Jean Thomson against Lieutenant Kenneth Mckenzie younger of Red Castle, Ross-shire, in 1780.[11] They had been married in 1767 and had six children. Ann Forrester deponed that Mckenzie came to her house

with some other Gentlemen on the night before the last review of the Twenty fifth regiment then lying at Edinburgh . . . That the defender staid all night in the deponents house and slept with a Girl from Aberdeen called Jean Davidson, who is staying in the deponents house at present and is a Girl of pleasure That the Deponent received half a Guinea from the defender out of which she retained half a Crown to herself for his Lodging and gave a shilling to his Barber at his desire and paid the remaining seven shillings to the said Jean Davidson.

A second girl, Mary McGregor (aged seventeen), testified that he had slept with her several times during the previous two or three months. Another witness, Margaret Campbell (aged twenty), was in that house on one of those nights and

went into the room where the defender was in bed to get some tea cups for breakfast that the defender on seeing the deponent come into the Room pulled the bed Cloaths over his head upon which the deponent said to him that he need not endeavour to conceal himself for she knew him very well upon which the defender uncovered his face and said that he thought the deponent would not have known him as she had not seen him since she had seen him dressed in the highland dress.

Margaret herself had sex with him a few nights later. Mary Mckenzie from Inverness was brought by him to yet another house, and he returned there subsequently, asking for 'the highland Girl'. Alexander Cameron, running stationer in Edinburgh, confirmed that the three houses named by witnesses were 'reputed houses of pleasure and that the deponent has often gone with Gentlemen to these houses at night.' There was also evidence of Mckenzie's having contracted venereal disease.

A revealing comment was made by one of the prostitutes who witnessed against Lieutenant-General Henry Fletcher of Salton in the 1781 action by his wife (Mrs Mary Crawford) against him. She had been told 'That if she would be a witness in this Cause against General Fletcher she would be handsomely rewarded when it was over by Mrs Fletcher'. This was not a case of bribery, since it was perfectly allowable to pay expenses for someone's trouble in appearing as a witness for them, but it helps to explain why these women were so ready to come forward.[12]

Another case where prostitutes appeared was that of Mrs Maria Stewart against Richard Legrand Esquire of Bonington (1781–2). Mary Fairlie alias Mrs Young deponed that Legrand often came to her house

and upon these occasions he was always very Drunk and supported by a chairman That he used to ask for Miss Margaret Chalmers who lived first with Mrs Moore in Peebles Wynd and afterwards had a house of her own and that she does not recollect of Miss Chalmers ever being with the defender in her house because the deponent always made an excuse and told him that she was not at home and she never sent for Miss Chalmers and her reason for not sending for Miss Chalmers was because she had Girls of her own in her house that the Girls who then lodged with the deponent were Miss Anderson and Miss Hutchison that she has often left the Defender in the room with these Girls sometimes both and some times only one were in the room.

Mrs Young's testimony also confirms that sex paid better than reputable trades. One night, she said, a woman came to the house to deliver some yarn, and Legrand 'borrowed a Crown from the deponent' (one cannot help admiring the cheek of this!), 'and carried this woman into a separate bed room and after the Defender had gone out of the house the woman showed the deponent the five shillings which she said she had received from the Defender and added that she would spin to the deponent every week if she could earn as much when she came with her work'.[13]

It accords entirely with the ethos of the period, as explored in the Introduction, that the heyday of cases involving bawdy houses and prostitutes should have been the late 1770s and 1780s. This is not to argue that such houses ceased to function after that, but the rise of evangelicalism meant there was no longer the same openness about their existence, so that it might have been far harder to find evidence of a husband's philandering in them.[14]

There was always a darker side to the trade. The 1801 case of Georgina Lindesay against Lieutenant Frederick Carmichael was featured earlier when his affair with 'Baby' Forsyth was discussed. Apart from his relationship with such 'part-timers', he also kept a mistress whose name was concealed, and visited bawdy houses. One morning William Boyd, a Writer to the Signet in his thirties, was taken by him to a house in Falkland which looked like an ordinary ale house. But when they were inside 'the defender touzled and used freedoms with both the women who kept it and her daughter who was a very young girl.' The Lieutenant then 'drew the girl into a room or at least out of the deponents sight, after which there was a great noise, and screaming, at which the mother pretended to be angry, but the deponent did not think she was as she laughed and the deponent had reason to believe, from what the defender afterwards told him, that he had carnal dealings with the girl, but which the deponent could hardly believe on account of the girl's age'. He added that Carmichael 'was kissing the girl at the time he drew her away, and that the girl made a noise and struggled as girls in that situation often do . . . Deponed that from what the deponent saw in the house, the deponent had no doubt that at least the mother was willing to grant favours to any Gentleman who would ask them of her.' Boyd's distaste for the whole situation is very evident.[15]

In the 1813 case of Janet Crawfurd against Lieutenant Standish Fottinham Lowery, a fellow soldier declared that he had often seen Lowery 'in company in Lisbon with women of loose conduct in such houses as those women resort to', but when asked 'if in these houses he ever knew the Defender have carnal connection with any of these women', he replied sarcastically, ' "No I never did it is not usual for them to have company in these cases".'[16] But that was not necessarily true, as evidenced by the 1820 case of Margaret Balcanqual against Andrew Monach of Mount Helen, residing in Glasgow. William Maltman (a married man in his thirties) went with Monach to a house in the Saltmarket of Glasgow. After drinking for a while Maltman went to bed with one of the girls, 'whose Christian name is Mary but whose other name he does not know':

> Depones that there was a candle burning in this Room and he saw Andrew Monach and another of the Girls whose name was McSwane or McSwaine as the Deponent thinks strip off their Cloaths and go into another bed which was also in that Room Depones that they were in naked Bed to their shirts and he saw the bed moving in which the Defender and this other Girl lay and heard Sounds as if they were in carnal copulation several times Depones that in particular he heard the girl who was in bed with Monach say to him when as the Deponent thought he was going to repeat the Connection with her 'hoot you have had it twice already'.[17]

But now it is time to leave 'gentlemen', who could easily commit adultery with those of a lower social class, and look at 'ladies' who did the same.

UPPER-CLASS WOMEN AND LOWER-CLASS MEN

The 'one sexual relationship that was totally outside the bounds of the moral order in eighteenth-century England was adultery between an upper-class woman and a lower-class male, especially a mere domestic servant', wrote Lawrence Stone; 'Such a liaison represented the gravest of social inversions, as well as a breach of the theoretical bond of fidelity between servant and master.'[18] His comments would also hold true of Scotland, but nevertheless liaisons of that nature did occur, and in this section we look at some of them.

In a 1719 case, when Agnes Kennedy, wife of Andrew Craufurd of Craufurdstone, eloped with her lover, she tried to pass herself off as a common woman.[19] He was Simeon Bardou, a Frenchman and soldier in a regiment of dragoons. (In order to meet him secretly she would disguise herself 'by putting a Dragoons Cloack about her and a hatt on her head and her hair hanging down like a man'.) When the fleeing couple were caught Simeon was allowed to go free if he wrote a full confession. In it he described their first meeting, and that afterwards she asked him to come to her and 'She professed great love and kindness to me and spoke very much to the prejudice of her husband'. Some days later she came to him in Mistress Smith's house,

> no body being in the room but she and I, she . . . Imbraced me in her arms and took my hand and putt it on her naked belly and told me that she could give me no plainer demonstration of her love than that she would allow me all the freedom I could desire If time and opportunity would allow, and opportunity allowing att that time by the absence of Jean Smith all the evening, I was prevailed upon to have carnal dealings with her.

Later, Jean Smith told Simeon that 'the Lady Craufurdston was married to her husband against her will and pitied her condition'.

The affair lasted for about ten weeks. Then, she 'fell upon my neck a crying and told me she was the most miserable woman in the world if I did not help her away for all friends had got word of it, and if her husband did she would certainly be turned out of doors And if I did not carry her off, she would stick or poisone her self and then her ghost would haunt me, To prevent which after a great deall of Intreaty, I did promise to carry her off.' The next morning she gave Bardou 'some things to carry off for her out of Craufurdston her husbands house' (in fact, she ransacked the house) and told him to come for her the next day. They rode from Ayr to Kilmarnock where they looked for lodgings. A 21-year-old servant deponed that on the night in question he met the Lady coming up the street, and she asked him

> where she might have Lodging, and the Deponent haveing said Madam if your Ladyship pleases, ye may goe to Andrew Dicks or Mrs Monets, to which she answered she would not goe to any of these houses and said that the Deponent was mistaken in calling her Madam, for she was a Dragoons wife To which the Deponent answered, O Madam when did Crawfordstone take on to be a Dragoon To which the Defender Replyed that she was not Crawfordstons wife but was a Dragoons wife.[20]

Lady Crawfurdstone was also recognised by Mary Galt, a neighbour of Jean Templeton's in Kilmarnock, with whom they eventually lodged; she 'advised the Land Lady to give her a pair of clean sheets to ly on, For she was not used to Ly without sheets when at home'.

It was Agnes's brother, rather than her husband, who came after and found her. The town officer, who took him to the house, deponed that 'the said Quintin Kennedy ran heastily to the bed side, and said to the woman lying in it, O Nanny Kennedy has thou changed the bed of an honest Gentleman Crawfurdstoun thy husband, and come to such a nesty bed as thou art lying in, how shamefully has thou disgraced thy husband and kindred and relations with severall other expostulations of this kind, And she fell a crying and weeping'. But when he asked her 'Will you not go back to your oun house in Aire, she answered, that she would rather go any where to be drouned before that she would go back to Aire.'

Stone noted that a wife's infidelity with a servant 'involved the risk that a great estate might pass to a child of lower-class paternity'.[21] One such Scottish case was that of Dougald Campbell of Ederline (Argyllshire) against Jean Lamond in 1727, where the man involved was John Mcfarlane, a servant, whose parents looked after the child until it died.[22] The case was bitterly contested, and her lawyer argued that it 'might have been begott by the husband, and have been born either Ten days after the nine moneths or in the seventh moneth without any Considerable Deviation from the ordinary rules', and that Ederline had forced the parents of the servant whom he mistakenly believed to be his wife's lover to look after it on pain of death. But there were too many witnesses (most of them objected to, of course) to her adultery for this to hold up.

For example, there was Duncan McIntyre, a servant who was in the brewhouse and saw Jean and Macfarlane enter and go

> to a straw bed upon the Floor which was the Dairy maids bed, that the said Mcfarlane and the defender kissed one another and Mcfarlane laid the defender doun above the foresaid bed and the defender made no strugle, and that Mcfarlane took up the Defenders Cloaths almost to her breast and that he unbuttoned his own breetches and that he lay on her naked belly, and that he made motions as is usuall betwixt man and woman in the act of carnall copulation.

McIntyre, in common with many other witnesses, did not speak English; the interpreter was Archibald Campbell, advocate.

The couple were anything but discreet, as they were seen in the act at various different times and places. More striking evidence of the nature of the relationship came from another servant, John Black. On one occasion, he deponed, Mcfarlane was going to see his father, and 'upon his goeing away the defender threw her selfe down upon the Floor in the Hall and fell acrying and Greeting [weeping]'. Mcfarlane, 'hearing the defender greet came back again to the house, and upon meeting with the defender said O! Jean, Jean you'll shame both yourselfe and me'. He then went outside again, but 'the defender followed after him calling on him with a voice betwixt shriking and greeting', and he eventually he came back inside with her, and they bolted the door after them. (Black also deponed that Macfarlane told him he was the father of Jean's child.)

Again we have a violent infatuation, in this case lasting several months and witnessed by a number of servants. Jean certainly did not want to lose her position; the case was viciously fought. But at the time of the affair she was oblivious to everyone and everything but her lover. It was not only she who suffered, for Macfarlane was forced to flee the country.

The protagonists in the next case were also Highlanders. Malcolm Macleod of Raasay married Mary Mackenzie (daughter of the late Alexander Mackenzie of Applecross) in 1713.[23] At the time the divorce action was brought in 1734 she had borne him seven children, of whom five were still alive. The adultery was with John Bethune, a servant, and she was pregnant by him when the action was brought. It was uncontested. Raasay had been unwell throughout 1733 – as one servant put it, he was 'sickly and indisposed keept a separate bed and was dealling with Druggs and plaisters' – so there was no way she could have passed the child off as her husband's. Some attempt was made at concealment, but again servants witnessed them in the very act. (The interpreter this time was Alexander Mackenzie, writer.) When Euphan Mackintosh took a pail of milk to the cellar and opened the door, she saw 'the Defender standing with her back to a large Chest and her Cloaths up above her midle and up to the slott of her breast and did see the said John Bethun with his britches down amongst his feet, standing closs to the Defender betwixt her thighs makeing motion with his body to hers'. Another servant testified that on one occasion when Raasay was entertaining company and sent him to fetch Bethune to wait at table, he discovered Mary in bed 'and the said John Bethun with his Britches down lying above her and betwixt her thighs makeing great motions upon her'. (He told Raasay that he had been unable to find Bethune, pretended to go outside looking, then came back and got him.)

Another observation of Lawrence Stone's was that 'domestic servants shared both the double sexual standard and the highly deferential norms of behaviour suitable to each rank, even if in practice their daily duties threw them into the most intimate relationship with their superiors.'[24] We can see this, and the servants' resentment that one of them should behave in unacceptable ways to the lady of the household, in the 1740 case of Francis Carruthers of Dormont against Margaret Maxwell, daughter to the deceased Sir Alexander Maxwell of Monreith.[25] Once again the adultery was with a servant, James Bell.

The case was strongly contested. Margaret argued that while her 'conduct had not been altogether so circumspect and observant as she wished it had been', this was only because of 'the low sphere of life she had been obliged to act since she became the pursuers wife, beneath her Birth and education'. She had the charge of all the provisions, had to superintend the grinding of meal, make up the accounts with the servants of seasonal labourers etc. etc., so that 'the low part of life she was obliged to act, led her to be more conversant with all the servants, and encouraged them to be more familiar with her than was suitable to her birth and Rank'. Furthermore, 'the Defender from her Infancy upwards was alwise noted for the most timerous fearfull disposition in the world scarce durst sitt in a Room by herself upon full Day light, much less to go to bed in a Room by herself'.

Dormont's procurator laid on the sarcasm: 'Because she was to take care of her Husbands provisions, was she therefore to Robb him of his honour. Because she was oblidged to count with her servants, was she therefore to lye with them, and Because she was of a timerous Disposition, was she therefore to take in a fellow to the bed with her to keep her from being frighted?'.

This was yet another case where a woman, totally absorbed in a lover, was unaware of how indiscreet she was being. During the harvest Grissell Steel often saw her mistress and James Bell 'sit down together by the stoucks, and eat together while the shearers were hard by'. Agnes Bell, another servant, 'observed the Defender have a more particular Regard towards Bell than towards any other of the servants, For she had knowen him severall times get a potinger of tea from her in her own bed chamber, had seen him dine and sup with her severall times'. By peeping through a hole in the kitchen door Agnes had once seen them kissing, but more significantly 'she had observed Bell when speaking to the Defender usually keep his hat on his head, whereas the other servants when they spoke to her, were always uncovered'. David Bell, Dormont's herdsman, deponed that

> the Defender did use James Bell with more familiarity than the deponent had seen her use with the other servants, particularly he had seen her in the harvest time, take Bell from his work, when the shearers were going to Dinner, and make him dine with herself in the Fields upon the harvest Ridge in sight of the shearers, and particularly in the hay harvest last, the Defender sitting among the hay, part of the hay fell upon her which James Bell was forking up to the Ruck, That the said Bell carefully gathered the said hay together, Layeing it upon every side of the Defender, covering up her body save her head with it, and then he fell down upon his knees and kissed the Defender.

The herdsman also made the point that all the other servants removed their hats when speaking to her, but he had several times 'seen Bell and the Defender in a conversation together for a considerable space Bell never moving his hat from his head all the while, nor did the Deponent think he gave the Defender that Reverence he ought to had done'. Yet another servant, Janet Ferguson, did not think that 'Bell carried towards the Defender with that Respect That a servant ought to do, Having observed him frequently talk to the Defender with his hat on, Deponed that she thought that Bell was a Rude forward fellow, and That he usurped too much over the servants and that he used as much freedom in his conversations with the Defender when out of Dormonts sight while he was at home as when he was abroad.'[26]

The 1772 case of John Hamilton of Redhall against Mrs Isabella Stirling, (daughter of Sir Henry Stirling of Ardoch) has similarities with the others but we are now in the era of 'sensibility'.[27] Isabella and her lover, Duncan Macfarlane, even exchanged love letters; one of his concluded, 'For God's sake take care of yourself and may the almighty remain with you and be your comforter in all your distress, which my dearest of Women is the sincerest wish of your affectionate Lover till death'. When Margaret Smith, cook maid, aged twenty-nine, entered service there Macfarlane had already been there for six months. He 'did not wear livery but served at the table and took care of two horses belonging to this pursuer'; 'he also cleaned the silver plate and kept the Key of the Pantry and Cellar'. Margaret 'was not above ten days in the family when she observed indecent behaviour betwixt this Defender and said Duncan Macfarlane, and saw her the said Defender in her own Kitchen put her hands about the said Duncan Macfarlane's neck and kiss him, calling him at the same time her dear Jewel'. There were other causes of resentment, for Macfarlane told her that 'he had got five cotton waistcoats in a present from the defender, That the deponent saw these waistcoats and they were lined with linnen, part of a web which the defender had got for making shirts for the children'. And one day 'the defender also brought down a pair of worsted stockings which she said she had made a present of to Macfarlane, and desired this deponent to wash them'. When Macfarlane left, Margaret 'heard the defender crying and weeping . . . complaining much that the pursuer had parted with one of the best servants in Scotland'. Isabella continued sending him presents and letters – and it was after intercepting one of those letters that Redhall instigated divorce proceedings.

Lack of discretion was something that Isabella shared with previous wives in this section, for she would go to the room that Macfarlane shared with the ploughman, Robert Burns, and have sex with him there. (Burns at first thought that it was one of the women servants creeping into Macfarlane's bed.) But the ploughman shrank from telling his master, 'because he was afraid that the pursuer would not believe him, and be angry with him.' It fell to one Hugh Cameron, journeyman watchmaker, who was staying at the house and heard what the servants were saying and who 'thought it his duty to inform Mr Hamilton of what he had seen and heard'.

Jean Robertson, aged fifty-seven, who looked after the children and never saw any indecencies between Isabella and Macfarlane, heard Isabella 'once say, that Macfarlane was very like a Gentleman and very like a certain Lord's son' – a very revealing comment, showing her need to elevate him (no dragoon's wife she!) in this period of 'sensibility'.

One gets little inkling of the husbands' feelings in any of the above cases, but the departure and deception of his wife, Sarah Ann, were a real shock to Robert Barclay Allardice of Ury in 1792.[28] Sarah was the only child and heiress to James Allardice of that Ilk; she married Robert in 1776 and bore him eight children, of whom seven were alive. In 1788 he was elected MP for Kincardineshire, and they lived in London while parliament was in session, returning to Ury during the recess. At the last recess Ann was indisposed and did not accompany her husband to Scotland. A few days after he returned to London he came back to his lodgings from the House of Commons at about ten at night, and after his wife had spent some time with him 'she rung the Bell and desired the woman servant to bring a Candle to show her to Bed which was done and she went out of said Room'. Soon after that she returned to it and took up her Cloak and Muff and when at the door of the room she turned round and wished the said Robert Barclay Allardice Pursuer Good Night, this she had been accustomed to when she retired to her Bedroom'.

However, 'instead of going to her Bedroom', she went 'to the outer door and went away in a Coach which she had previously ordered to be in readiness for that purpose'. Robert, when he heard the sound of the coach, 'went down stairs and on enquiry at the woman servant was informed, that the . . . Defender had gone away in the said Coach'. He rushed out of the house, 'and in the hurry without taking his hat, to endeavour if he could overtake the Coach but which he was not able to do the Night being dark and raining and the Coach by driving fast having soon got beyond Notice'. And that was the last he saw of her.

His wife had been consorting with John Nudd, a footman and servant in the family, and their affair was 'at first carried on in a private and concealed manner'. But after Robert went to Scotland 'Nudd lived almost constantly in the Family breakfasted, dined supped and slept' with her, 'and were even so publick as to take their Breakfast in Bed together on many different occasions'. At least one of the servants, John Lamb, had felt strongly about the relationship and about three weeks after Nudd started sleeping in the house Lamb 'taxed him with the Impropriety of his Conduct towards Mrs Barclay . . . and the said John Nudd did not pretend or affect to deny and the deponent particularly said that if Mr Barclay came to the knowledge of it or Catched him in the house or with Mrs Barclay he would blow his Brains out or run him thro' the Body whereupon Nudd said that he believed he would'. Nevertheless, 'Nudd slept in the house the same night and with Mrs Barclay as the Deponent has reason to believe altho' he had promised that he would not'. Lamb also 'spoke to Mrs Barclay of the Impropriety of her Conduct with this Man . . . and the Deponent said she was injuring her husband and ruining her family That Mrs Barclay said it was no business of the Deponents, she knew what she was about and was doing no Injury to Mr Barclay and that there was no harm in it'.

About ten days after his wife's departure Robert had a writ served on Nudd by the sheriff officers. Lamb was there to witness:

Nudd was then putting on some of his Cloaths . . . Mrs Barclay who was in the Bed seemed frightned and asked 'are they going to take Mr Nudd' and the Deponent saying that they were not about any such thing but only wanted to see them in Bed together whereupon Nudd said if that was the case he had no objection, put off his cloaths and went into Bed again That he then called up the Sheriff officers and on their coming into the room the Deponent said 'Gentlemen there is Mrs Barclay and John Nudd' That the sheriff officer delivered a writ to Nudd reaching over Mrs Barclay in Bed Nudd said it was very well whereupon the Officers making an apology retired.

As to why Sarah had made such a precipitant departure, according to Mary Rock (a servant who knew all about the affair), Sarah believed that her husband had guessed 'of her Connection with Nudd and that he would have Lawyers there to Morrow and therefore that her best way was to go off'. In reality Robert had no suspicion at all. After spending half the night searching for his wife he was told about the affair by Lamb and then said that 'he would search for her no more and had he known as much before he would not have gone after her'. Mary Rock said that 'she never heard Mrs Barclay Complain of any Ill usage received from her husband, but she said she had taken a liking to Nudd from the first day he came into the house'.

Indeed, she bore Nudd two sons and then they married in England in August 1795. She lived in Norfolk until her death in 1833.[29] This is a rare example of an upper-class woman defying the barriers to have a lifelong relationship with a man in a lower social class.

The phenomenon of upper-class women committing adultery with lower-class men virtually disappears by the beginning of the nineteenth century, and the odd exceptions do not follow the same pattern. We have seen in earlier chapters the effects of alcohol, and in the 1816 case of Dugald Gilchrist of Opisdale against Catherine Rose (daughter of a lieutenant in the East India Company) abuse of drink reduced an upper-class wife (married in 1800), and mother of several children, to a prostitute. Amongst the witnesses was Colin McKenzie, a jeweller who, when asked by Catherine to go to bed with her 'said he was afraid to do so lest she was diseased having been with so many men lately', but 'the defender urged Colin McKenzie to go to bed with her saying that he would meet with no harm from her in doing so.' Her landlady deponed that 'whenever the Deponent went from home the Defender was visited by young men whom she took that opportunity of admitting and the Deponent was sure at her return to find a young man with the Defender sometimes one and sometimes another'.[30]

Otherwise, in the later period the 'upper-class' women committing adultery with lower-class men were those who had risen from a modest background to marry into a higher social grouping. One example was Eliza Allen, married to Major-General Keith Macalister of Loup and Torrisdale in 1814, with a divorce action brought in 1818. Her adultery was with Charles Candy, a shopman or clerk in a warehouse in London. Eliza had been the Major-General's mistress, left behind in London when he went up to his newly-acquired estate in Argyll. At that time (1814) he 'had a violent paralytic attack, and during his illness the Defender came from London without any invitation on his part, and took up her residence in the neighbourhood; and at last the Pursuer was induced to sanction their connection by a regular marriage'. At the end of 1815 he went back to London 'chiefly with the view of having the command of the best medical advice, and there he was detained by his continued illness until the period when he discovered the Defenders guilt in November 1817. – Upon making the discovery his first step was to dismiss her from his house and the next to commence legal measures for procuring a divorce.'[31]

The absence by the end of our period of the kinds of cases discussed earlier in this section suggests that the distance between gentry and servants had become greater and the taboo in sexual relations all but absolute. But, whether in stable or exploitative relationships, *gentlemen* continued to enjoy sex with lower-class women.

NOTES

All cc references are in the Scottish Record Office.

1. cc8/5/17.
2. cc8/6/166.
3. cc8/5/23; *Complete Baronetage 1665–1707* (Exeter, 1904).
4. cc8/5/26.
5. cc8/5/32.
6. cc8/5/4.
7. cc8/5/14.
8. cc8/5/27.
9. cc8/5/15.
10. Sir Thomas Wallace Dunlop's second wife also attempted to divorce him, but she married him in England, where they spent all of their married life, so he contested the court's jurisdiction and had the case thrown out. See Chapter 11.
11. cc8/5/16.
12. Ibid.
13. Ibid. The witness added that 'she has seen the defender Toying and Laughing with Miss Hutchison and Miss Anderson and taking them upon his knee but never observed him kissing them and has often seen him put his hands in their bosom That when he came to the house of the deponent as above mentioned he commonly called for Drink and he is at present her Debtor both for Borrowed money and for entertainment that the drink was sometimes wine and some times Cherry Brandy'.
14. One later case which was similar to the above was that of Ann Selby Lady Ashburton against Ranald George Macdonald Esq. of Clanranald in 1829. Elizabeth Thomson, one of the women named, deponed that she resided in the house of a Mrs Hume in Rose Street, and that 'men and women were in the practise of meeting there for sexual intercourse'. She also deponed that the defender 'was well known in the house and Mrs Hume used sometimes to call him "Clan" and sometimes Macdonald'. cc8/6/163.
15. cc8/5/27.
16. cc8/5/35.
17. cc8/5/39.
18. Lawrence Stone, *Broken Lives – Separation and Divorce in England 1660–1857* (Oxford 1993), 243.
19. cc8/5/2.
20. cc8/6/7.
21. Stone, *Broken Lives*, 243.
22. cc8/5/3.
23. cc8/5/4.
24. Stone, *Broken Lives*, 243.
25. cc8/5/7.

26. Francis Carruthers of Dormont denied the paternity of his wife's daughter, Elisabeth, born in May 1741. Elisabeth married in 1758 and died in 1768, 'leaving a son and daughter whose claims to the estate gave rise to a lawsuit which lasted for 14 years and formed the basis of the plot of "Guy Mannering", as was admitted by Sir Walter Scott in a letter to Lady Abercorn.' *Burke's Landed Gentry*.
27. cc8/5/13.
28. cc8/5/21.
29. SRO.GD49/529/2.
30. cc8/5/35.
31. cc8/6/138 and 139. This was a bitterly contested case. The Major-General died immediately after the commissaries granted the divorce; Eliza appealed against the decision, and the legal battle continued between her and the pursuer's trustees, as the financial implications were great. The case only ended in 1823 with her death.

NICOLSON VS PORTERFIELD – THE LADY AND THE LAD

This case set the precedent of the paramour as witness and is a classic of its kind: the infatuation of a 'lady' for a young servant in a country-house setting, with servants watching every move. And, as the couple were never seen in the act, there is the added interest of seeing how the defence lawyer tried to clear his client.

Margaret Porterfield, daughter of Boyd Porterfield Esquire of Porterfield, had married Houston Stewart Nicolson Esquire of Carnock in 1765, only three and a half years before she committed adultery, and had already borne him two children. The youngest was not yet weaned during the crucial period, but was being suckled by another woman because Margaret's breasts were sore (implying, rather surprisingly, that she would otherwise have breastfed her own child). The couple visited Sir William Maxwell of Springkell and Lady Maxwell (Mr Nicolson's sister) in Dumfries-shire during the summer of 1768, and Margaret stayed there without her husband from August until November.

The young overseer, William Graham, was the son of a tenant of Sir William's and was popular in the locality. Katharine Johnston, spouse of John Little, mason, who lived about half a mile from the house of Springkell had known him 'since he was a Boy', remembering him at the house 'first a Liveryman, then a Butler and afterwards a grieve about the Family of Springkell.' In fact, both sides tried to keep his name out of the case, but the commissaries demanded the name of the paramour, and though appealed all the way to the House of Lords, this demand was upheld.

Margaret had been aware of Graham before this visit, for she told Nelly Hetherington, the servant who acted as her maid at Springkell, that 'she had seen Graham wearing Livery at Sir Williams marriage and remarked how well he looked in it'. Had he been a member of her own class, then much of her behaviour with him would not have been remarked upon. On a Sunday, when the corns 'were cutt down but not fully taken in', at about 11 o'clock in the morning Katharine Johnston's four-year-old daughter 'told her there was Mr Graham walking with a Bra Lady'. Katharine 'went and stood in the Threshold of the Door and observed William Graham walking within a few yards of the Door with a Lady in Black and which Lady had a Book in her right hand and had her left hand leaning upon Grahams arm or holding by his arm'. Recognising her as Mrs Porterfield she 'was surprised to see

William Graham and such a Lady together walking in such a manner'. Soon after Margaret's arrival, Nelly Laing, a nursery maid, observed her 'talking familiarly with said Graham that is more familiarly than in the Deponents apprehension a Lady should talk to a servant'. The butler, John Reid, first observed a 'familiarity' about a fortnight or three weeks after Margaret came to the house, when he saw them 'conversing and laughing together'. He was told by John Little, Sir William's 'fowler', that when he was standing by the side of a canal near the house one day, Margaret 'threatned to throw a Terrier which was bye into the Canal upon which Graham said if she did he would throw her in too', which was quite enough for Little to suspect that there was 'something more' between them than he wished to say. A servant simply did not speak to a lady in such a way.

The prosecution averred: 'This Graham who is remarkably well looked soon attracted the Eyes of the Defender. That she made the first advance to him the Inferiority of his station leaves no room to doubt.' And, indeed, much of the evidence supports this claim. For example, Jean Crawford, who was suckling Margaret's child, had often heard Margaret 'express Her regard for William Graham by smiling on him and Clapping his Cheek and saying there was not such a bonny lad in all the house'. She added that 'no person could observe' them 'ten minutes together But they must think there was more betwixt them than what ought to have been'. Nelly Hetherington described an occasion when Graham had a pain in his side, and Margaret applied a warm flannel to it, 'and at the same time that she Clapped his Cheek she said who would not take care of so bonny a Lad'.

On one occasion Graham received a letter from the woman whom the servants had all considered to be his 'sweetheart'. Margaret asked the maid to take it from his pocket while he was asleep and bring it to her (if she were to do it herself 'the rustling of her silk Gown might awaken him'). In the letter Graham was asked to come to Moffat on the following Sunday, but after reading it Margaret said to the maid that 'he should go no such way for she would stop him that he might stay at home and walk with her on said Sunday'. Nelly recalled Margaret once entering Graham's room while he was not there, 'and observing some of the Cloaths particularly vestments and Breeches hanging on a pin', Margaret said to her maid that if she 'liked any body well she would think nothing of kissing their cloaths when absent'. Nelly had replied that 'she would be very sorry to kiss any Bodys Cloaths', but 'by a side look' she saw her mistress 'take hold of said Cloaths and put them to her Cheek'.

Infatuation, walking and laughing together, and even the occasional kiss, were source for gossip, but not sufficient evidence against Margaret. However, she frequently went up to Graham's room on the garret floor, and they would lock the door. A chambermaid, Agnes Rowlandson, once saw this happen, 'having first heard her coming up stair and the rustling of her silk Gown . . . upon hearing the rustling had put her head out at the door of Miss Hendersons Room to observe who it was as no Lady lay in the Garrett story excepting Miss Henderson who was not then in her Room'. Graham entered the room a little later and closed the door, and Agnes 'thought it was very odd' that they 'should be in the room together with the Door shut upon them and had likeways heard that their behaviour before had not been very decent she therefore had the Curiosity upon hearing the door shut to go and try whether it was locked and accordingly she directly went and having tried Thrice by lifting the sneck to open the door of Grahams Room she found it would not do from which she concluded that the Door was locked and the key was not on the outside'. She immediately 'went down to the Nursery which is on the flatt immediately below where she found Nelly Hetherington and Nelly Laing both nursery maids', and said to them, 'Lasses you are here But there is a woman locked up with Graham in his own Room'. She did not name the woman 'as the story betwixt her and William Graham was not then quite Publick in the house', but clearly they all knew about it, for 'the maids fell a laughing'. She then went downstairs to the laundry where she found the laundry maid and dairy maid and 'repeated the very same words to these two' and they also laughed. Not everyone was amused. Magnus Swanston, Mr Nicolson's own servant, was 'in a passion and threatned to acquaint his master with what happened', but Agnes 'disswaded him from it in case some mischief should have happened'.

The servants by now knew what was going on but did not know what to do. However, there was another gentlewoman staying there at the time, the above-mentioned Miss Henderson, and they turned to her. The Defence tried hard to stop Katherine Henderson, a first cousin of Sir William's, from testifying, on the grounds of her near relationship, and because she had been present when Sir William interviewed the servants. The pursuer stated that 'as the witness has herself no Interest in this matter and has purged herself of malice and ill will against the Defender her rank and Character places her above suspicion of giving false evidence'. All witnesses might, in theory, be equal, but the weight of evidence by a woman of rank was clearly feared. The objections against her were nonsensical and were not sustained.

Katherine had hardly needed the servants to raise her suspicions. On one occasion Margaret told Graham to take a pen knife from Katherine which she had given her and which the latter had refused to return. Katherine was highly indignant and said, 'whatever Liberties Mrs Nicolson you may allow Graham with you I will not allow him any with me'. Later that evening she said to Margaret (in Graham's presence), 'Mrs Nicolson I do not understand this behaviour of yours with Graham', to which Margaret replied 'Houston is much obliged to you for taking such care of his wifes Virtue', and Katherine answered, 'I had much need as you do not seem to take care of yourself'. She had said this – she told the court – 'laughing and in a Jocular way and Mrs Nicolson was also speaking in a Jocular way', but only 'to prevent her taking [it] amiss', for Katherine had meant it seriously. She was in a tricky position.

After Mr Nicolson returned in November, Margaret 'appeared melancholy and confused and very different from what she had ever been'. She simply could not stay away from Graham. For three nights the servants kept a watch, and finally, after some of the maids told Katherine that Magnus Swanston, Mr Nicolson's servant, had sworn he would inform his master the next time they 'were locked in together', she 'was apprehensive that this might produce fatal consequences and she therefore thought it her duty to inform Sir William Maxwell of what she had learned among the servants'. She told him 'of their having been watched by Magnus and some other servants the third Night after the pursuer had returned to Springkell and of their having been watched by the Chambermaid the second Night after Mr Nicolson's return.' Sir William said he did not believe it but asked her 'if ever she had known them locked up together', and Katherine told him that she had, and that she had also known Margaret 'frequenting his Bed Chamber'.

Sir William told his wife, and Lady Maxwell said to Katherine that night that Margaret 'was frolicksome and might be guilty of some imprudences But that she could not believe her to be guilty or Criminal'. There were some things in Margaret's conduct 'which she did not approve of', but when she had raised the subject Margaret took it 'so hot that she avoided doing it again as it brought on a disagreeable altercation'. Lady Maxwell said she would only believe it if she found them locked up together. That very night – the fourth after Mr Nicolson's return – she did so. She did *not*, however, tell Houston Nicolson of this. The couple were only staying a few days longer, and when Lady Maxwell sought Katherine Henderson's advice, Katherine said that 'it was a very delicate matter', but she thought that Margaret, if guilty, would behave similarly elsewhere, 'and that it would be much better that she were discovered in any other place than Springkell'.

So Houston Stewart Nicolson went home in blissful ignorance, and might have remained in that state if his wife had not again become pregnant, and if another visit to Springkell had not been suggested. Lady Maxwell told her father (who was also Houston's father), Sir Michael, why she was reluctant to have them, and Sir Michael informed his son that 'the Information he had received had determined him to make his Settlements in such manner as to exclude the Child of which Mrs Nicolson had lately been delivered', as he believed the child was 'spurious'. Apparently he told his son of his wife's adultery 'when off his guard and rather more from accident than by design'. But the mischief was done, and though it was now more than a year since it had happened, the divorce action was raised in December 1769. (The child died of smallpox during the course of the process.)

How could her lawyer defend her? First, he produced a series of letters written by Lady Maxwell to Margaret in the intervening period, arguing that she would not have written such friendly letters, discussing family trivia, if she had really believed that her sister-in-law was an adulteress. But since Lady Maxwell had made a conscious decision to keep her discovery from her brother, that did not go very far. He then tried to discredit Nelly Hetherington as a witness, asking if the dress she was wearing had been given to her 'by Lady Maxwell as a compliment to her the witness and whether she ever had so fine a dress before'. Nicolson's lawyer objected to this line of questioning; apart from the fact that Lady Maxwell was not a party in the cause, 'supposing Lady Maxwell knowing her servant maid was to appear in this Court before respectful Judges and the Defenders learned Council and agents and so many other persons, had thought it proper she should appear in a better dress than she usually wore in the Country . . . it would not signify in the smallest degree unless the Defender will qualify her objections with an offer to prove that she received these from her Lady as a Bribe to give evidence in this Cause'. However, the commissaries did allow the question to be put, and the reply throws an interesting light on a maidservant's perks. She got an old gown from Lady Maxwell every year, she said, 'in consideration that the deponent and another maid dress her by turns she having no particular maid to attend her tho the deponent was hired for a different purpose viz To keep Sir William's oldest son and if she did not get part of my Ladys Cloaths she would think herself entitled to higher wages'. Nelly added that when she received the gown 'she had no Conversation with Lady Maxwell relative to this cause'.

The main tactic of the Defence was to keep the most crucial witnesses, such as Katherine Henderson, from testifying. 'Lauchens a negro slave belonging to Sir William Maxwell', clearly had vital information to import, for he was strongly objected to, on the grounds that he was not a Christian, and because he was a slave. The prosecution said that Lauchens had applied to several clergymen to be baptised and would be able to swear he believed in God. As for his status, there was 'no proper slavery known in the Country a servitude for Life is known but no slavery'. The whole question of a slave's freedom when he stepped on British soil was at that time before the Court of Session. He was to be examined 'upon the articles of his Faith' before a decision was made, but in fact, his testimony proved unnecessary once the battle over the right to cite William Graham as a witness was won. Since Graham had confessed his guilt to Sir William and others, there was simply no legal impediment to his appearance in court.

His testimony was straightforward: 'This Deponent had Carnal dealings or copulation with the Defender early in the morning of the Twenty first or Twenty Second of October 1768 in the Bed Room of the house of Springkell in which the Defender usually lay at that time . . . the Defender had sometime before desired the Deponent to waken her that morning . . . at different times after this the Defender desired this Deponent to waken her at Six O'Clock in the morning which he accordingly did and that generally upon these occasions he the Deponent had carnal copulation with the Defender tho not every day'.

There was still the testimony of Lady Maxwell to come. On the night of 12 November 'when Miss Henderson told her of the Defenders being locked in with Graham (which she did in a whisper being then in the Nursery) The deponent answered it was impossible To which Miss Henderson replied go up and see'. Lady Maxwell 'left the Nursery and went up to the Garrett story in which Grahams room is', and 'being desirous to observe any person that should come out of the Graham room she went into the Room in the Garrett story immediately opposite the Door of it . . . walking upon her tip Toes in order to make as little noise as possible.' She saw William Graham come out of the room and went straight into it herself and in the dark made out a woman sitting on the side of the bed. 'Good God Mrs Nicolson', she exclaimed, and Margaret 'answered in a Low voice what ails you Lady Maxwell', to which she replied, 'you may think there is nothing in this I think there is a good deal'. She 'immediately went down stairs and into the first room she found open which was the nursery and finding herself trembling sat down there'. A little while later she went into her own room where she found Margaret, who again 'said to her what ails you Lady Maxwell what's the matter with you'. Lady Maxwell answered, 'did I not find you locked up with a man or with a footman'. 'Yes', said Margaret, brazening it out, 'and what of that'.

The divorce process took more than a year and a half, but in August 1771 Houston Stewart Nicolson obtained his divorce. It was revealed in the course of the action that Margaret had misbehaved with another young man (of her own rank) before her infatuation with Graham, so clearly she had a roving eye and a strong sexual appetite. What happened afterwards to her husband or children is not known, but in her blind passion she swept up a young man who, when he was dismissed, was seen 'crying and much affected at leaving the Family'.

cc8/5/12

FRASER VS ABERNETHY – SCATTERING HIS SEED

Records of kirk sessions (parish courts) in the eighteenth century contain many cases of a young woman pregnant with an illegitimate child who, instead of naming the true father, claimed to have been impregnated by a man who had left the parish or was dead or untraceable. Sessions always assumed in such cases that the father was a member of the gentry class who was willing to pay for the upkeep of the child but totally unwilling to stand in front of the congregation to undergo public humiliation (a necessary part of the process of redemption for every sinner in the eyes of the Church). Sessions rarely managed to learn the true name of the child's father,[1] but here it all came out in the divorce court.

Amelia Fraser, niece to one of the senators of the College of Justice, and closely related to Lord Strichen, brought her divorce action against her husband, William Abernethy of Crimonmogate (Aberdeenshire), in November 1773. They had been married as long ago as 1749, and she had borne him ten children, of whom nine were still alive.

The first evidence to be produced were extracts from Kemnay kirk session records. In March 1759 Jean Matthew, a servant of Abernethy's, had refused to name the father of the child she was pregnant with. In July 1760 she had named one Frederick Skinner, who had left the country. She was not believed, and the session had made every effort to get at the truth, but without success and eventually she was allowed to make her public appearances in order to be absolved of the sin. Other extracts concerned another woman, Ann Beattie, who had been a servant in the house of Crimonmogate and was suspected to have been with child. She absconded in 1764 and when she returned with a young child in 1766 she named James Murray, a young unmarried man who had gone to England, as father. She was not believed either. The names of many more women emerged in the course of the process, but those two were key witnesses because they themselves appeared before the court.

Jean Matthew was thirty-six and still unmarried when she appeared. She was not obliged to name herself but, in the accepted terminology, she stated that she entered the service of the pursuer and defender in 1758, and 'it consisted with her knowledge, that he did ly with and had carnal dealings with a woman whom she knew not to be the pursuer . . . that the said woman did bring furth a male child, of which the

Defender was the father'. Abernethy had paid the expenses of the birth and the fine imposed on her by the kirk session. She added that 'the said woman obtained her absolution from the Minister without having given up the Defender as the father of the child, having then told that one Frederick Skinner then abroad was the father of the Child, and that she did this at the desire of Mr Abernethy the Defender, But that thereafter the said woman confessed the truth to Andrew Clark Schoolmaster at the kirk of Slains when the child was sent for his Education, and told that Mr Abernethy the Defender was really the father of this child'. Not only that, but Abernethy 'desired to have said child bred to the sea, had told the mother that unless she consented to that, she should have no more money'. Ann Beattie, who was now aged thirty, told a similar story. She had received money for the maintenance of her daughter until the previous year and had told the parents of the man she had falsely named that Abernethy was the real father.

The next witness, Margaret Henderson, had been spouse to a male servant of Abernethy's, knew of those two women bearing children to him, and had been told by two others, Elizabeth Steven and Jean Auld, that they too had borne his children. Margaret had got money from Abernethy for Jean Auld, who had gone to London. She also mentioned a further eight women with whom he was alleged to have been guilty, having heard the reports at various times, two of them 'so late as last year'. Alexander Jack, who had been a servant at Crimonmogate ten years earlier, deponed that one night he 'having gone into the Defenders bed room to take away his shoes to clean, found one of the servant maids in bed with the Defender, whose voice he well knew tho' he did not see her, and heard her say to the Defender "O lett me away now that you have got your will of me"'. (She was Isobel Forbes.) He added that 'there was a very common report in the Country that the Defender had criminal conversation with several young women both within and without the house of Crimonmogate', and Jack 'believed that the report was well founded'. A more puzzling witness was David Simpson, who had been Abernethy's gardener. He said that when Jean Auld was with child 'as was the Custom of the Country the Defender was reported to be the father of it.' He explained the phrase as meaning that when the laird was a bachelor any child borne by a servant maid in his house was said to be his, but added that 'it was not usual when the Laird was married to mention him as the father of any Bastard child begot in his family.'

A glimpse into the nature of the marriage comes from another witness, an elder of Longmay kirk session, who said that Amelia had come to him once complaining of her husband's treatment of her, not that he beat her but he 'intimidated' her. Abernethy's lawyer, in an attempt to discredit her, asked 'whether or not it was the Report and general understanding of the country That the pursuer was a soft simple woman, who knew nothing or little of the Management of Country affairs and was a bad oeconomist in her family and inattentive to her children, who had been better taken care of since she left the family than before?'. The elder answered that 'by common report the pursuer was reckoned a simple woman in the management of country affairs, by which he meant the business of a farmer's wife both with respect to his country affairs and management of his house and the care of her children, tho' at the same time it was also said by others that Mr Abernethy entirely directed every thing about his family himself, and that the pursuer was not at liberty to exert herself in any of these capacities'. So we have a bully and lecher of a husband, and a woman thoroughly under his thumb.

In view of the weight of evidence against him, Abernethy could not deny his adultery, so he fought the case on the defence of reconciliation, insisting that his wife had told others that she knew of his adultery before she left him, that she had subsequently slept with him one night in 1772, and that she had sent him many affectionate letters. He insisted that she would admit this if she were questioned under oath in court, and when the commissaries refused to allow this he appealed to the Court of Session. 'His wanting to have me examined in publick court proceeds from no other motive than thinking my simplicity and weakness occasioned partly by his own usage could not undergo the trial', commented Amelia.

The Court of Session upheld the commissaries' decision, but allowed a series of questions to be put to her in writing regarding the allegation that she had known about his adulteries. She replied: 'a short time before I last left his house, I recollect to have asked Mr Lundie the minister and Mr Charles Wemyss if they knew of my husbands amours with bad women – who told me to the best of my remembrance there were such reports going, but Mr Wemyss entreated me to give no faith to such reports, at the same time putting me in mind of my husbands peculiar temper and frolicks'. She admitted that she sometimes went through his pockets (in hopes of finding some money, because he never gave her enough) and that she once found a letter from Jean Matthew 'giving an account so far as I remember of her son being a pretty boy and that she would not be excommunicate for all the lands of Crimonmoggat and that she was willing to give up any person he pleased as the father of her child'. Amelia had been 'very uneasy upon receiving it, and did tax him thereanent, upon which he flew in a passion and swore he would prosecute her for lying on him – the serious manner he did deny it, and hearing the Minister had absolved her, upon giving up another man as father of the child, made me really imagine it might be a lye on him.'

As for the other essential aspect in the defence of reconciliation, she was 'very angry to hear that Mr Abernethy or his doers insinuates a forgiveness on my part – He never asked it of me, nor had I any opportunity or certainty to know he needed it, and now when I do know, I never will forgive him on that head however simple he takes me to be.' And the letters she had written him 'which he makes such a handle of was partly occasioned by my destitute situation for want of cloaths and other necessaries, which my Mother was unable to give me as the maintainance of me distrest her'. The commissaries repelled the defence of reconciliation and attempted to grant the divorce, whereupon Abernethy's lawyer came up with an accusation of adultery committed by her.

This was instantly rebuffed as 'not only untrue, but impossible, for he fixes the time and place of the supposed guilt to be the month of July 1766 in his own Garden of Newhall in the County of Aberdeen, when the fact is that the Respondent left his house, and came to Edinburgh with her uncle Captain Campbell as far back as January 1765' – and there were letters to prove it. Moreover: 'If the Defender has been unlucky as to time and place, he has been sufficiently prudent as to the person with whom her supposed guilt was committed, for he makes choice of a dead man, who will not contradict him, and as to the list of witnesses given in, he no doubt considers them all to be very trusty persons, who will make no scruple to annihilate time and space in order to serve him, tho' he does not fully explain, whether he means to establish by the oaths of these witnesses, that she was in Aberdeenshire, and in the embraces of his deceast friend, John Urquhart, at the time that all her friends imagined they daily saw and conversed with her in her mothers house at Edinburgh, or whether It was only her Ghost they saw in the Garden'. So Abernethy got nowhere with that line.

It was evident, said Amelia's procurator, that Abernethy's plan was 'to tire or starve her out of it if possible, especially now that he thinks she has lost her chief support by the death of Lord Strichen'. First he had denied guilt, then when she had convicted him 'with near a dozen and half of different females' ('in spite of his conveying material witnesses out of the way'), he gave a contrary defence, that of reconciliation, and when that was overruled and his bill of advocation was refused he made this absurd counter-charge. Abernethy appealed to the Court of Session, but his bill was refused. Three more petitions to the commissaries followed, all of them refused, before Amelia was granted her divorce on 12 April 1776.

As we saw in the last chapter, William Abernethy was far from unique in impregnating a number of servant maids, but one wonders how many unknown descendants he has.

cc8/5/14

1. See Leah Leneman and Rosalind Mitchison, *Sin in the City – Scotland 1660–1780* (Edinburgh, forthcoming), c.7.

CHAPTER 9

'COMMON' DIVORCES – PART 1

With over 600 cases to choose from, it is obvious that there will be a wide disparity of circumstances, but as divorce actions below the gentry level represent the majority of cases they are the most typical and illustrative of the period and subject. Because of the emphasis placed on being able to read the Bible, a substantial proportion of Scots were literate in this era, though more men than women. However, while participants' own words are once again used as much as possible, one soon realises that with humbler and less articulate clients more of those words were shaped by their lawyers.

The subject of 'common' divorces is divided into six sections, three in this chapter and three in the next. Although not all who came before the Commissary Court were bitter – as has already been seen, many divorce actions were brought long after the event – those who *were* conveyed the most detail about the relationship, and the first section looks at unhappy marriages. The second section moves from the relationship between the married couple to the relationship between the guilty party and paramour. The third part examines attitudes toward adulterers, for, unlike sinners of higher classes, 'common' adulterers might incur direct action on the part of their community.

UNHAPPY MARRIAGES

The marriage of Robert Harries, 'hair merchant' in Portsburgh (Edinburgh), and Christian Mackie comes across as the partnership of a weak man and an aggressive woman who needed someone to stand up to her.[1] Married in autumn 1726, he alleged that she was guilty of adultery from spring 1728, and he brought his action in October 1730. On one occasion he came home to find her with her lover, who

Did come to the back of the chair whereon the defender was sitting and pulled the chair with her sitting on it back upon his body and then clasped his hands upon her breasts and belly kissed her and used a great deall of other unseemly behaviour against which the pursuer being enraged and changing color which the man perceiving said to the pursuer Are you jealous Damne me if you be not welcome to play with my wife or have carnall deallings with her before my Eyes and that he would not be offended or displeased with it, and that while he had a groat in the world the said Christian Macky should have the halfe of it, and with which Lewd treatment the said Christian Mackie seemed to be noways Displeased.

When Harries insisted that 'she behoved either to give over keeping the said man's company' or part with her husband, she 'swore and imprecat That God might Damne her if she would not raither part' with her husband than with her lover.

However, after she told her lover that her husband had forbade her to see him, they agreed that she would promise to be a dutiful wife and not to see him, so she swore a solemn oath to that effect while at the same time continuing to meet him. She told several people that 'the forsaid man was the beautifullest man she ever saw and that she had more Love from [sic] him than for the pursuer her husband, and that the pursuer was not to be compared to him, and several times wished that the first news she should have of her husband might be that he was dead Drowned or broke his neck that she might have her full Liberty to enjoy the said beautifull man'. And during that time she attacked her husband, 'Beat him tore his flesh and cloaths Threatned to wring or wash her hands in his hearts blood and rive the Thraple out of him, Imprecat that God might Damne him and his concerns called him Rogue Rascall Villain and severall other ill names, and also had purloined destroyed and squandered and put away his effects means and substance and by these her vile actions reduced him to great Extreamitys.'

Was she really as bad as that? Pursuers and defenders were all too likely to try and blacken one another's character, and in this case Christian went to the kirk session, telling them that her husband was pursuing a divorce against her and asking for a certificate of her good character. The elders and deacons of her district reported back a week later that 'her Character was fair and blameless'.[2] However, the session's detective work was not very thorough, for when Christian had been a servant to Lady Campbell at Stirling, other servants had seen her having sex with a dragoon, and told their mistress who, after locking her up for a few days and calling her 'a whore and Truker and severall other bad names . . . payed her her wages and turned her out of the house'.

Witnesses also described fights between husband and wife. John Johnston, merchant, had heard Christian say that she would burn her husband's house, and said that Harries gave her no provocation, and that he told the witness that 'he had suffered more from his wife than the deponent could endure from his own.' Harries obtained his divorce in October 1731.

Peter Williamson had been married to Jean Wilson for seventeen years when he brought his action against her in November 1788; they had had nine children, of whom four were still alive.[3] Peter was a printer and master of a penny post office, as well as the publisher of the annual Edinburgh Directory. Jean was a mantua maker, 'profits arising from which far exceed any thing the pursuer can earn either from his penny post office or the publication of his directory'. In fact, he applied for the benefit of the poor's roll and was granted it. When Jean argued that his circumstances did not warrant this, he answered:

> His spouse not contented with the irreparable injury she had done him, had added those of frequent and repeated abstractions from his income. This was only lately discovered owing to a quarrel amongst his men when to his astonishment he learned that Mrs Williamson had been mean enough to enter into a combination with them whereby she was enabled to appropriate for her own private purpose little short of three fourths of the whole profits of the penny post.

This was a rare case in which the children were a bone of contention between the couple. Peter was bitter because his wife 'by her arts enticed away the children from him.' In spite of being so much less well off than Jean, 'he always wished to have his children with him and will cheerfully receive them if the Defender would allow them to come to his house and take up their future residence there.' He added that she and her father 'carried off privately every thing that was valuable and left not sufficient to pay the rent'. Not only that, but Jean and her father had 'set up a penny post in opposition to the Respondents so that she has the profits of it in addition to those of her business as a mantua maker.'

Peter had no difficulty in proving that she had had intercourse with several different men, and he gained his freedom from her in March 1789. In spite of lasting for so many years, this marriage was clearly on the rocks quite apart from her infidelity. Jean's own skills already gave her a measure of financial independence; by dishonest means, and with the backing of her father, she accrued even more and therefore had no financial motive to stay with a husband she despised.

In contested cases the parties produced conflicting versions of their marriage. A good example of this can be seen in the case of Cecilia Smith, who brought her action against John White in August 1801.[4] His version was that in 1780 he became clerk and shopkeeper to Thomas Waugh, grocer on the shore of Leith. Waugh died bankrupt two years later, so his widow, 'then not a very young woman was left in a very destitute situation burdened with six Infant Children The youngest of whom only two months old'. Subsequently White and Cecilia set up business together as grocers in Leith, a business 'burdened with the support of the pursuers six Infant Children which the Defender never once objected to – on the contrary he strained every nerve for their behoof'. The business partnership was fixed for three years and after that time White had intended to leave, but Cecilia 'soon fell upon a method of making the co partnership a little more strong – She was then above thirty six years of age and the Defender a Boy scarcely twenty, so that the difference of age may easily account for the Defenders folly in forming such a connection. Long before their actual marriage she had been exceedingly familiar and ingratiated herself with the Defender', and finally her 'superior address' got the better of him 'and he was induced to marry her', and he had brought up and supported all her children.

But according to Cecilia, White had never been clerk to Waugh but just a lowly assistant. After her husband's death she was far from destitute: she had £120 cash paid to her by her husband's creditors, her father gave her £100, and her mother advanced her a further £40, while her husband's creditors also gave her £150 worth of furniture. She could have supported her children had it not been that 'her unfortunate connection with the defender caused every friend and acquaintance which Mr Waugh or she had [to] desert her, and almost so heartily to despise her on this account, that they would not speak to her when they met.' She admitted that White '(who is neither so young nor so unexperienced as he pretends) induced the pursuer first to enter into a Copartnery with him, and next to marry him, and the folly of both connections she has since most amply suffered for.' He was 'brought from a state of absolute want to the possession of a good business by the pursuers means alone'. And he had done nothing at all for her children.

He for his part claimed that they had lived together happily 'till very lately that by the advice of some people who pretend to be her friends she deserted the respondents house without assigning the smallest reason or even hinting in the most remote degree that she was displeased at him and intended leaving the house'. *She*, on the other hand, claimed that 'so far from living in any kind of friendship together the whole neighbourhood can vouch that they have frequently been obliged to rescue the petitioner from the Respondent to prevent actual murder'. As a string of prostitutes came forward to depone about White's carnal connection with them, many of whom had been physically threatened by him if they testified against him, the commissaries had little doubt about whose story to believe.

Robert Herdman, in his 1823 action, claimed that twelve years earlier he, 'then very Young was enticed into an illicit connection with Mary Torrance then in his father's service as a worker in the Bleachfield'.[5] She became pregnant and went to live at her mother's where he used to visit her, and some time after that they acknowledged themselves married to one another in the presence of witnesses. She told the same story, except that it was he who 'gained her affections and, sometime afterwards under a promise of marriage, he prevailed with her to submit to his embraces, the consequence of which was, that she became pregnant and was delivered of a Son.' After the birth of a second child he 'intended to deny the marriage, as if it had never existed, and followed up his intention of doing so, by suddenly leaving Scotland, without making any provision for the maintenance or support of his wife and children. He left them in fact totally destitute, without food or money to purchase it; and but for the Defender's mother, who received them into her house, they must eventually have either starved, or been thrown on the Parish.'

In his version of events he denied that his intercourse with her had been under promise of marriage. While she was staying with her mother her brother had sent for him and they met in a public house in Canongate. 'He then and there by threats and other means . . . was concussed to write a Note acknowledging the Defender as his wife'. But during the ensuing period, when she was pregnant with their second child, 'having seen her frequently intoxicated and other circumstances, he felt so disgusted with her conduct that in order to avoid her he went to England; during his absence she continued to be supplied by his directions with the necessaries for her maintenance', by means of his brother, Dr Herdman. Herdman admitted that he had been living 'principally either in England or Ireland for the purpose of being at a distance from her and out of the reach of the bad language with which she at all times assailed him when she had it in her power.' But he insisted that he had continued to send her maintenance via his brother until he learned of her adultery. He eventually managed to prove this and obtained his divorce.

If Herdman's father owned the bleachfield in which Mary had worked, this suggests a disparity of social status, which seems even likelier from the fact that his brother was 'Dr' Herdman. In Chapter 7 we saw that disparities between social status was one of the causes of unhappy marriages among the gentry. This is harder to measure between humbler parties, particularly as young people routinely went into service with families of their own social status. Basically, the last case and the next two contain the classic scenario of master sleeping with servant and subsequently claiming to have been conned into an irregular marriage. And in all of those cases the accounts of the marriage in the legal documents come across as greatly influenced by lawyers' shaping of the circumstances to influence the commissaries.

Robert Sempill, brewer at Castlebarns, said that Jean Mann 'entered home to the pursuers house as a servant maid and continued therein for about Two years During which time the Complainer Robert Sempill having most unwarily used too near Familiarities with her she had art and address enough to prevail upon him the Complainer to marry her at least to live and converse with her as her husband'. In the course of rancorous exchanges of insults (including accusations on both sides of attempted murder), he declared that she had borne him two children before there was any talk of marrying, but then she threatened to prosecute him for marriage on the grounds of a promise in writing – which he claimed was a forgery – and as he was just starting in business and could not afford a legal process, he agreed to have her as his wife. She bore him seven more children before he brought his divorce action in 1774, but it was clearly a *very* unhappy marriage (of which more below).[6]

James Somerville, son of a tenant farmer in Berwickshire, whose case against May or Marion Shiells was brought in 1791,[7] declared that in 1786 'the Respondent had the misfortune to conceive an affection for the Petitioner then one of his Fathers servants and without consulting any of his friends he run off to Edinburgh where they were Clandestinely married. At that time such was the regard the Respondent had for the Petitioner that he had determined to take himself to some line of business and he would have suffered any hardship and willingly have embraced all the odium and disrespect of his friends attending a low Marriage rather than that she should have suffered in the smallest degree.' However, he had not been long married to her before he discovered that 'he had been grossly deceived and he found many Circumstances attending the Petitioners Conduct which left him no room to doubt of her Infidelity – of these however he had not at that time proof, but they made such an impression on his mind as rendered residence in this Country almost intolerable to him – Soon after his Marriage he had been debarred his Fathers Family on account of his Misbehaviour and being bred to no business he was laid under the necessity of trying his fortune in the West Indies'. His father gave him £100 'in full of his Legitim', and he set off for Jamaica. While he was away she bore a child to another man, which formed the basis of his divorce action.

In this case there clearly *was* a recognisable social disparity between the two. David Gray, a merchant in Edinburgh, was married to a relation of Somerville's. In May 1786 a woman came to his house and asked if he knew anything of Somerville's being in town, which he did not. The woman then said that she had expected to find him there and was disappointed not to have done so. Gray asked her 'what concern she had with James Somerville and what reason she had to be so much concerned at his not having come to Town, the woman then said she was his wife'. Gray 'was very much surprised to hear her say so and immediately exclaimed "You his wife, you do not seem to be at all his equal in point of station nor look like a woman he would take for his wife" To which she answered "It is true indeed that all his relations slight me but I am as good as any of them."'

Some hours later Somerville himself arrived and Gray 'said, "O James what have you been doing you have given a great alarm to your Friends for a woman has been here who calls herself your wife" To which James announced that he had been in Town since the day before and that the woman was really his wife'. Subsequently James Laidlaw, writer to the signet, another relation, came to Gray's house and said to Somerville, '"O James this is a sad affair but are you really married" to which he answered "Yes Mr Laidlaw I am Married",' and he showed Laidlaw the marriage lines which satisfied him that James really was married.

Disparity in social status is one theme, but by far the most persistent theme in unhappy marriages amongst lower-class couples was alcohol and associated anti-social behaviour. Marion Lochhead wrote that the eighteenth century in Scotland was one of hard drinking, and that 'drunkenness in itself was not held a sin, though the teak-headed were admired and envied'.[8] However, this was undoubtedly less true for women than for men, and whereas the occasional bought of drunkenness might have been overlooked, constant inebriation was another matter. In the case of Robert Sempill against Jean Mann, introduced above, he declared that she

> gave herself up to a course of drinking which grew upon her from year to year In so much that she was drunk almost every day and in this situation made great noise and disturbance in the complainers house and neighbourhood would frequently leave her house and stay out till one or two in the morning and

sometimes whole nights making great noise and disturbance when she came home and refused to give the complainer any satisfaction where she had been and she also embezzled and put away his goods and effects to a very considerable extent.[9]

Katharine MacCleish, who had been their servant, bore this out, declaring that Jean was 'generally drunk every day and she used also sometimes to call for drink in the night time That on these occasions she used to speak nonsense and to abuse the pursuer and this Deponent and the others in the family and used to curse and swear and used sometimes to reel and fall down and the Deponent has also seen her vomit'. Furthermore, she knew that Jean would 'very often sell privately without the pursuers knowledge quantities of malt to distillers That she has known the Defender often entice the pursuers servants to give her the money they had received for barm and also she used to entice the Bakers who came for the Barm to give her the money for the same'. And she also sold her body.

'If there ever was a worthless woman upon earth the defender is one', said Robert Cummins, carver and gilder in Edinburgh, of his wife, Jean Anderson in 1794. She was defending herself by claiming that he was the one who came home drunk and beat her, but he averred that 'the whole Neighbourhood, where she and he resided can instruct that for years past, when he came to his own door, he seldom got admittance, she being either out of the house or within it drunk, and incapable of opening the door, or if she was within the rule was almost uniform, that she was attended by a Troop of Bauds and Vagabonds'. He added that 'since he turned her to his door her mother has also been obliged to turn her to her door, for her shameful conduct, and she at the moment is living as an open prostitute, being one night in one Bawdy house and sometimes in another at times sleeping with one man and at others with two – Such is the behaviour of this woman who is a disgrace to her sex'. As some of his witnesses deponed to having had intercourse with her (and to her frequent drunkenness), he was able to prove his case.'[10]

In 1807 William Baillie, tailor in Edinburgh, declared that his wife, Ann White 'several years ago addicted herself to dram drinking.[11] The pursuer used every means in his power to reclaim her from this vicious habit – he had her boarded in various parts of the Country and with her own relations but nothing would reclaim her. She stole from his house every article she could lay her hands on and disposed of it for whiskey and had nearly ruined him both in health and circumstances.' He may have been relieved to discover that on the nights she spent away from the house she was committing adultery, so that he was able to win his freedom from her. The same could be said of Matthew Newlands and Agnes Brownlee in 1822. They had been married for seventeen years, most of them happily, but over the past few years she had

given herself up to a state of drinking ardent spirits to such excess that the Pursuer (who till Whitsunday last was in business as a Rope-maker and kept a shop) has repeatedly been under the necessity of shutting up his shop in the forenoon. This occurred repeatedly even upon Market days. On these occasions the language of the Defender towards the Pursuer was so abusive, and her conduct toward him so scurrilous and outrageous, that to prevent an exposure to his respectable Customers from the Country, who were in the habit of dealing with him, he shut his shop, altho it was only on Market days they could call for him.

He had taken lodgings for her in the country, but after her return she was worse than ever, and 'on account of her rioting and drinking, she was frequently taken into custody by the Police Officers . . . The consequence of this mode of life naturally was, that the Defender fell into the kindred vice'. Once he knew of her adultery he sued for divorce.[12]

In all of those cases, and a number of others as well, it was a *woman*'s addiction to alcohol that was held responsible for causing the breakdown of the marriage. Although the wives in such cases tended to accuse their husbands of the same vice, few of them made it stick. To some extent this was just a feature of the double standard, i.e. that behaviour accepted as normal in a man was unacceptable, and unusual, in a woman. Also, a husband was unlikely to need to pilfer his wife's goods, let alone sell his body, to procure alcohol. And heavy drinking was more likely to render a man incapable of intercourse, whereas women, when released by alcohol from the constraints of decorum, tended to find their way to public houses, and whether from lust, devilment, or simply as a way of earning more money, often ended up having sex with other men, thereby giving their husbands the grounds to get rid of them. The divorce records skew the picture in showing so many drunken wives, though this is counter-balanced in the later chapters on separation cases, since drunken men were all too likely to abuse their wives.

However, it is time to leave unhappy marriages – for a while, anyway – and look at some relationships between husband or wife and lover.

EXTRA-MARITAL RELATIONSHIPS

Chapter 8 dealt with gentlemen who frequented bawdy houses or impregnated their servant maids. 'Common' adulterous men who seduced either their own or other men's maids were not crossing a social divide; indeed, more than one of them persuaded the women that they were unmarried and eligible. And rising disposable incomes at the end of the eighteenth century made it possible for men of humble status to emulate their social superiors by supporting bastard children and by paying for sex.

Margaret Muirhead, wife of William Reid, late manufacturer in Glasgow, then journeyman weaver in Kilmarnock, brought a divorce action against him in 1810.

Janet Macpherson, whose husband had been absent with his regiment for several years, met Reid in June 1809 'upon the occasion of her soliciting work from the Defender at his warehouse in Glasgow for the deponent's daughter Mary Macdonald who was then between fourteen and fifteen years of age.' At that time 'a criminal connection took place between the defender and the deponent, the consequence of which was that she became pregnant and was delivered of a female child to the Defender'. Subsequently her daughter, Mary, who was 'employed by him in winding yarn and had occasion to be frequently in his warehouse' was also seduced by him. And another woman, Margaret Baird, thirty-three, who kept a public house in Glasgow, declared that Reid frequented her house, declaring his name to be Mr Douglas, an unmarried man; 'and that the purpose of his attentions to the deponent were in the view of courtship for marriage she having been a widow for six years and a half bye past.' She had 'believed these professions of the defender for sometime, but having learned about Candlemass 1810 that he was a married man she immediately turned him out of her house, and although he returned once or twice she refused him admittance; and has had nothing to do with him whatever since.'[13]

In the 1813 case of Isabella Morton against John Borland, farmer in Ayrshire, she accused him of adultery from a few months of their marriage in 1805, and named five different women, 'all in the County of Ayr and in consequence no less than five or six Children had been brought into the World by these women of which the said John Borland acknowledged himself Father and paid for their aliment and upbringing'. One of those women, Mary Watt, declared that when she met Borland on a Kilmarnock market day in 1808, he passed himself off to her as John Craig from Kirkhill, an unmarried man. 'That the Deponent from the solicitations of the Defender and under promise of marriage yielded to his embraces', and about Whitsunday 1809 found herself pregnant. At about that time a friend advised her of Borland's true identity, and that 'he was a married man and great Blackguard, and she advised the Deponent to keep no farther company with him'. At least Borland acknowledged himself father and paid maintenance charges without protest. One of the other women, Mary Cameron, Borland's own servant, had had to petition the local justice of the peace court against him for maintenance of her bastard child.[14]

A wife committing adultery with a servant man was less usual, though not unknown. Unlike the situations described in the last chapter, the social status of the parties was not dissimilar. In an 1821 case Jean Russell was seen in bed with William Gray, a servant of her husband, John Wilson, miller in Lanarkshire. When questioned by her husband 'she acknowledged that she had carnal connexion with the said William Gray and added "that although she were killed for it she would still continue to love him".' Wilson had turned him out of his service but Gray came back several times after that and took Jean 'several times out with him about the fields and the last time that she went out with him she rose from her naked bed when he the said William Gray was chased away by the pursuers servants'. (Gray was reputed to be 'the father of several bastard children'.)[15]

In the last chapter we looked at both men and women who crossed the social divide to commit adultery with social inferiors. But lower-class women could cross the social divide by committing adultery with social *superiors*. John Bonthorn, mason, brought his uncontested action against Margaret Waddell (daughter of labourer in Kirkcaldy), in 1811. Mrs Betty Allan testified that Margaret had lodged in her house and was delivered of a child there, without naming the father:

Depones that a genteel looking man whose name the Deponent does not know was in the practice of visiting the Defender while she resided in the Deponent's house. That this man generally came there about nine or ten o'Clock at night and the deponent has heard him sometimes in the defender's room the following morning . . . Depones that this man visited the Defender several times after her delivery and she has told the deponent that she got money from this man and the Deponent herself understood that she the Defender was chiefly supported by him.

Others deponed likewise, and the divorce was granted.[16]

A sad case was that of Alexander Wedell, cart and plough wright in the Canongate, against Mary Banks, in 1812. At the time he courted her he was working as a journeyman for his brother while she was a servant. 'It was his misfortune to form a strong and honourable attachment towards the defender'. She agreed to marry him, but his brother advised him to make enquiries 'as to the previous Character of the Defender before concluding the marriage'. At Mary's suggestion he contacted Mr William Hamilton, Writer to the Signet, in whose service she had been for some years. 'The Pursuer accordingly waited upon Mr Hamilton and received from him a most satisfactory character of his intended spouse – So much indeed was Mr Hamilton interested in the matter that he himself wrote a letter for the Pursuer to procure the marriage lines from the session clerk and the parties were in consequence married'. What he did not realise was that William Hamilton was her lover. Soon after the marriage she disappeared, and he was unable to find her. A year later 'by mere accident he was informed that a young woman answering the description of the Defender had been recently delivered of a male child'. He 'obtained sufficient information to convince him that an adulterous correspondence had subsisted betwixt her and Mr Hamilton for a considerable period back' and immediately raised a divorce action.[17]

We have now seen some of the relationships between adulterers and their lovers – but how were they regarded by others?

REACTIONS

In 1829, William Colquhoun, hatter in Glasgow, declared that his wife, Mary Anne McCully (daughter of a lacemaker in Dumbarton) had left him a few months after their marriage in 1816 to live with Joseph Dixon, provost of Dumbarton, 'in the character of his kept mistress'.[18] One of the witnesses, James Aitken, glass blower, deponed that 'some short time after the marriage the Defender was taken into keeping by Mr Dixon and went to reside at a Cottage belonging to him – the provost had a house in town for himself.' The witness knew she had four children to him as two of them had been nursed by the deponent's wife, and 'they were called Jacob Dixon and John Dixon'. He added that he had 'had some hesitation in allowing his wife to nurse the last one which was sent but he agreed to it upon the provost coming into the Glasshouse and asking it as a favor that he would allow his wife to nurse "his boy" '. This suggests a certain amount of disapproval, though not too deep seated.

In 1782 Jean Nasmith in Paisley was accused by her husband, James Hattrick, of adultery with several men, including Robert Hodgart.[19] One witness, an 18-year-old silk winder, deponed that 'both before and since the Pursuer left his wife she has heard the Pursuers eldest Daughter remonstrate with her mother upon the impropriety of her conduct with Hodgart to which the defender answered it was no wonder that other People took freedom in speaking of her when her own daughter did so.' The daughter also 'used to take measures to disturb the meetings of the defender and Hodgart'. Many folk 'spoke of the defender in the Country for allowing Hodgart to take such libertys with her' – which leads to the subject of community action.

In a 1776 case, Henrietta Smith, wife of George Beaton, journeyman printer in Aberdeen, was accused of adultery with William Burr, wool comber, and others.[20] A 60-year-old neighbour, Jean Mowat, said that Henrietta 'behaved in so indecent a manner that the deponent never saw any woman behave like her – and upon the deponents reproving her she flew into a passion and for the most part she was drunk'. Jean's 30-year-old daughter, Margaret, slept in a room adjoining Henrietta's, 'only separated from hers by a single deal partition'. She 'often heard uncommon and indecent noises in the defenders room when she and Burr were therein with the door locked upon them and the conversations which she heard passing between the defender and Burr and the other men who came to her was so indecent that the deponent must be forgiven not to repeat it as no woman having any regard to decency can repeat it.'

Another witness, Elizabeth Sime, deponed that one day while she was 'employed in bleaching cloths at the Den burn of Aberdeen' she saw Henrietta

> running down the Den burn brae in company with three men and followed by a Mob of boys – that one of the said three men was a tall man and she knew him to be an wool comber by his dress and smell and from the reports the deponent had formerly heard she immediately conjectured that the said man was Burr before mentioned – That he the said man took hold of the said Henrietta Smith by the arm and ordered her to go with him which she did followed by the huzzas of the Boys – That it is customary in Aberdeen for the Boys to follow any woman in that manner who is under the publick character of being a whore.

It may have been the same occasion when another witness, William Glass, 'saw the said William Burr running up the Lochside of Aberdeen followed by the said Henrietta Smith and a Concourse of people.'[21]

In this case we can also discover what became of her later. She eloped with Burr in 1771. In June 1774 another Aberdeen woolcomber encountered Burr in Darlington: 'the people who wrought with Burr asked the deponent if he knew William Burr's wife and upon his answering that he did and that she was a woman about fifty years of age They said, "Then it is true as people said the woman whom he had here with him is not his wife her name was Henny Smith"'. They told him that the couple had cohabited as husband and wife for some time. The following day the witness was in Durham and saw Henrietta in a public house; 'when she was gone the Deponents companions told him that William Burr had turned off the foresaid woman at Darlington . . . and since that time she had turned out a common whore in the city of Durham'.

Strong action was taken in East Lothian in the 1794 case of George Allan, shoemaker, against Janet Blair.[22] Her adultery with Robert Guild, corn dealer 'became so public in the village of Tranent, that the Inhabitants of said village rose upon the said Janet Blair and publicly exposed and afronted her by what is termed "riding the stang with her thru the streets"'. (The 'stang' was a rough pole or tree trunk on which an offender against local conventions was mounted and carried about in public.[23])

Archibald Rodger, apprentice and journeyman to Allan, had been watching Guild sneak into the house when Allan was away, and one day he put his ear to a keyhole and heard sounds of kissing and the creaking of a chair. He burst into the room, and Janet got up immediately while 'Guild fell backwards toward the fire place'. Guild 'was pulling down the fore part of his Shirt and was putting his privy parts into his breeches . . . the witness upon seeing this said "You Villain What have you been doing?" That Guild at first only laughed and then made this answer "I have been doing nothing at all" That the Defender was silent That the witness was so Shocked at what he had seen and the behaviour of Guild that he left the room immediately'. Rodger also recalled that 'at one time a number of the inhabitants assembled and proceeded to the house of John Guild Wright in Tranent where they seized the Defender and threatned to duck her as an adulteress but her Brother seeing this rescued her from them and carried her into a Change house at Tranent'.

In the 1782 case of Elizabeth Sommerville against William Sommerville, sometime skinner, the father of the woman with whom William committed adultery could not find a constable to assist him to enter the house where his daughter and William were shut up, but when he returned to the house 'he found a great mobb assembled' which broke open the door with a stone. In a case of 1813 Elizabeth Westwood, wife of David Gilmour, flesher in Glasgow, had been guilty of adultery with John Muirhead, head journeyman flesher. James MacAlpine, a widower in his fifties, was one of the witnesses who saw them in bed together in a house in his neighbourhood. About half an hour after he left the house he saw Elizabeth and her sister and Muirhead, 'but Muirhead came out by the back door and the two women by the front door as a mob was then gathering at the house having heard of what had happened and were threatening to punish the Defender and Muirhead for their conduct which the Deponent himself interceded with them not to do but leave the law to its own course'.[24]

A rather extraordinary case (in 1822) was that of William Miller, type founder in Newington, against Margaret Duff, whom he accused of adultery with a number of different men. The couple had been married for nearly thirty years, and her procurator protested that not a breath of scandal had sullied her reputation during all that time; yet now 'the Defender was most injuriously accused of infidelity to the marriage bed, and the action was not founded upon a predilection for any one individual but is of that grossly sensual nature as to implicate no fewer than four different persons as her paramours. Now it must be allowed that this was a most unaccountable transition from virtue to vice, and fully as sudden as it was unaccountable.' Miller answered: 'It was true that the defender was not a young woman and the pursuer sincerely hoped and trusted that in her earlier and best days the defender was incapable of the degrading conduct mentioned in the libel. She unfortunately suffered herself to be seduced into the gross, and on the part of the female sex, the very disgusting vice of intoxication.' He had gone to England on business and when he returned he found that his wife had 'rendered his house as infamous as the most notorious house of bad fame . . . crowds of people assembled about the outer gate when they knew that the defenders associates were with her and when these gallants left the house the mob frequently pursued and cast stones at them.' His allegation was proven by witnesses, and he got his divorce.[25]

In the above cases of mob action the adultery was blatant. What about situations where a man or woman left their spouse to cohabit with another partner? There were no large anonymous hotels to go to, so the evidence of lodging house keepers features regularly in divorce cases. In the case of Sommerville against Sommerville mentioned above, the defender was not only guilty with the woman whose father was so incensed. Adam Smith, merchant in Stockbridge, in whose house William lodged, described one morning when William came 'down stairs accompanied by a woman who had the appearance of a Common Strumpet and whom the deponent believed to be such that the defender acknowledged that he brought this woman from the end of the new bridge and that he sleept with her all night upon which the deponent observed to the defender that if he brought such cattle to his room he would not give him the use of his room any longer'.[26]

In the 1775 case of John Carmichael, servant, against Elspeth Largue, a maidservant in the house where Elspeth lodged deponed that 'having observed to Mrs Whitelaw the defender's Landlady that the defender's character seemed a little suspicious as she was not in service and did not appear as a Lady Mrs Whitelaw desired the deponent to enquire about her situation and way of life, That the deponent having accordingly questioned the defender about this Matter, she told the deponent in answer that Gentlemen took care of her . . . That Mrs Whitelaw having discovered the defenders reall character she turned her out of her house'. In the 1792 case of Tarbet against Tarbet, Thomas Comb deponed that the defender lodged in his house at Bruntsfield Links with a woman whom he 'represented to the deponent to be his wife'; 'the deponent upon discovery that George Tarbet and the said woman were not husband and wife would not suffer them to continue longer in his house'. William Henry Malcolm of the Commissariat Department attached to the British Forces lately serving in Spain and France, brought his action against Agnes Crawford in 1814 for adultery with Sergeant James Bruce. The landlady and fellows lodgers testified that Agnes spent the night in Bruce's room, though when the landlady discovered that Agnes 'was not really Bruce's wife she would not allow them to remain in her house any longer'. In the same year the landlady of a house where Thomas McCliesh, printer in Edinburgh and husband of Christian Isabella Tod, cohabited with Ann Thom deponed that 'one night they had a serious quarrel with each other and upon that occasion the Deponent came to understand that they were not married persons, whereupon she dismissed them from her house'.[27]

In Edinburgh there were known 'bad' houses, where men knew they could bring prostitutes or mistresses.[28] In all of the above cases the landladies were clearly determined that their own lodgings should not be characterised as such but remain 'respectable'. However, that does not mean that disapproval of a married individual cohabiting with someone other than their spouse was universal during our period, for, as we will see in the next chapter, many did so for years before the divorce action was raised.

NOTES

All CC references are in the Scottish Record Office.
1. cc8/5/3.
2. Edinburgh St Cuthbert's kirk session minutes 25 March and 10 April 1731, SRO.
3. cc8/5/19.
4. cc8/5/26.
5. cc8/6/142.
6. cc8/5/14.
7. cc8/5/21.
8. Marion Lochhead, *The Scots Household in the 18th century* (Edinburgh, 1948), 49–50.
9. cc8/5/14.
10. cc8/5/23.
11. cc8/5/29.
12. cc8/6/133.
13. cc8/5/31.
14. cc8/5/33.
15. cc8/5/40.
16. cc8/5/31.

17. cc8/6/96.
18. cc8/6/163.
19. cc8/5/8.
20. cc8/5/15.
21. Glass added that 'Burr run into a Closs and was followed by the said Henrietta Smith who was staggering and seemingly very drunk – that someone in the Mob said they had heard the said Henrietta say to Burr "You shall play with me this night when I am willing – as you have caused me do it with you when unwilling" ', and that Burr's character was that of being addicted to drinking and women.'
22. cc8/5/22.
23. For a description of 'riding the stang', see John R. Gillis, *For Better, For Worse – British Marriages 1600 to the Present* (Oxford 1985), 80, 131.
24. cc8/5/16; cc8/5/33.
25. cc8/5/41. He was away from 17 May to 2 July. 'During that time the defender and her visitors consumed no less than twenty gallons of whiskey twenty four dozen of Porter and a considerable quantity of wine.'
26. cc8/5/16. Another witness deponed that Somerville acknowledged 'that he had brought the prostitute from the Newbridge and that as it was a cold night that he had chosen her as the fattest among several women and had had carnal knowledge with her both on that night and also on several other occasions'.
27. cc8/6/33; cc8/5/20; cc8/5/33.
28. See my article, ' "Bad Housekeeping" in Eighteenth-Century Edinburgh', *Scottish Local History* (vol.33, 1995).

ESPY VS DEVEREUX – PAIN AND PASSION

William Espy, merchant in Edinburgh, brought his divorce action against Ann Devereux in July 1771. They had been married in 1756; there were no children. Her adultery was said to have begun in summer 1766 with 'a certain man who then often visited her under a pretence of his having something to say to her he being a priest and of the Roman Catholick perswasion of which the said Defender herself is. She and the said man were often seen in her own bed chamber and other rooms locked up together in very suspicious and unseemly Circumstances and on occasions they went to Leith together in the stage coach under cloud of night having taken out the whole Tickets so as to prevent any persons being in the Coach but themselves in order that thereby they might carry on their criminal correspondence' – which has to be one of the most startling allegations in any libel.

The priest was subsequently named as Peter Fraser, but he was by now abroad, and therefore – alas – features no further in this case, which was based on the second allegation in the libel: that from summer 1770, 'she pretending to be sick dismissed the ordinary Physician and applied to a young man a Student of Physick and he under pretence of giving such advice frequently came to the Pursuers house . . . and having been discovered in very unseemly and unbecoming postures the Pursuer did thereupon discharge the said young man his house on which occasion the said Ann Devereux deserted the Pursuers house and family and went to Rooms that were provided for her by the said young man'. The young man was Robert Barclay, and though they were found in bed together, the case was vigorously defended.

Ann's first petition claimed that her 'life from the time of her unfortunate Marriage with William Espy had been one continued scene of distress', and that she had been forced to leave him. She also petitioned for money, claiming that her husband was worth about a thousand pounds and that it was all due to her: 'Mr Espies business was to distill Brandy but he never distilled a Gallon or was worth a shilling sterling till the petitioner not only discovered the method but pursued the Manufacture with the utmost Care and attention.'

Naturally Espy provided his own 'history of this defender': 'Her extravagance and dissipation, and at last her criminality in the most gross and abandoned terms, during which time he could with Justice have appealed to the world, and particularly to the persons with whom they were connected, that he was a faithfull Industrious and affectionate husband, and if he had a fault it was in being too indulgent to this defender, by supporting her in a way more than he could afford, and which she basely took the advantage of, In introducing her Gallants into his own family, and there violating her husbands bed by repeated acts of Infidelity.' He denied that she had made him rich. 'It was only a few years ago, that the Pursuer began business without any stock, by a very hard labour he had been Just able to support his family, and so far was the defender from assisting him, that during the most of that time she pretended to be sick and thereby had her Gallants introduced to her.'

Before going on to the events immediately preceding and following the divorce action, there are a few other circumstances we can discover about the marriage from witnesses' depositions. For one thing, it appears that Ann really was ill (though the nature of her illness is never made clear), for Isabell White, a widow, attended her as a sick nurse (she subsequently stood in for some weeks for a servant who had left them, and therefore was around during the crucial period of the marriage break-up). Mrs White insisted that William always behaved to Ann 'as an affectionate husband,' and thought that Ann did not behave to her husband 'with a proper degree of love or affection . . . very often chiding' him 'and giving him bad names'. Was there some disparity of social status? Ann was described simply as daughter to Philip Devereux at Carrick, with no further designation, but Mrs White, 'deponed that one day Mrs Espy being on the recovery and pretty well, she had dressed to go out and sit for her picture,' but she then 'fell a crying, and said she had once sat for her picture before, and then had Ladys and gentlemen to attend her, but now she had no more attendance with her than If she was a Beggar That she wept bitterly, wrung her hands and threw herself upon the bed'. Unfortunately, there is nothing more than this cryptic statement to go on.

Mrs White also deponed that 'after Mrs Espy recovered from the above illness, she would not allow the pursuer to sleep with her, but got one Mrs Mordaunt to sleep with her for sometime', and she also heard Ann say (when talking about not sleeping with her husband) 'The Devil a one of his Yellow Pelt shall ever lye beside me'. Mrs White knew that William 'desired to sleep with the defender and that she refused to allow him,' adding that William had often told her to let him know whatever his wife wanted 'and she should have it,' and never grudged Ann 'any thing.' On the Sunday night before the couple separated, 'being to go out in a chair with said Mrs Mordaunt, she told the deponent she would curse the Pursuer to his face as she went out, That they endeavoured to disswade her, but in going along the passage, said defender cursed the Pursuer then in the kitchen the whole way she went into the chair, upon which the pursuer said "hold your tongue you Impudent strumpet." '

Mrs Mordaunt was another witness to this unhappy marriage. (Ann's lawyer tried to stop her from repeating what Ann had told her under oath of secrecy, but she insisted that she felt bound by the oath she swore in court to tell the whole truth, and did not feel bound by a private oath.) She deponed that after swearing her to secrecy,

Ann had 'said she never considered herself as married to Mr Espy for tho' he had swore seven times upon the holy bible to her, she had never swore to him'. She added that she had heard Ann say that she wished her husband 'would die, or that he would hang himself which she said, he had sometimes threatened to do'. Mrs Mordaunt also said that 'she never heard the pursuer refuse the defender any of the necessaries or conveniencies of life, and she never knew said defender without money in her pocket . . . That she observed the Pursuer appeared very much grieved during the defenders illness, and the deponent verily believed he was so, but the defender said it was all hypocrisy.'

Then Robert Barclay entered the picture. Ann had a physician, Dr Gardner, who visited her; presumably he brought Barclay with him as his student, for when she was nearly recovered she told the doctor that she did not need him any longer – but Barclay continued to visit. One of the things she confided to Mrs Mordaunt was that she loved Barclay and was determined to marry him. It is not clear whether they actually had intercourse at that stage; neither Mrs White nor Mrs Mordaunt believed they had, though both had seen physical affection between them. Before Mrs Mordaunt left the house William made her 'swear upon the bible, if she knew of any carnal dealings betwixt Barclay and the defender, and the deponent swore she did not, but believing the defender to be virtuous endeavoured to perswade the pursuer that she was so.' Mrs White 'did not suspect that the defender and Barclay had any Criminal conversation within the Pursuers house, because she thought her a woman above it, and the deponent at first imagined that the defenders familiarity with Barclay might proceed from his being her Countryman, tho' at last, from what she observed she really thought that the defender had a greater regard for Mr Barclay than for her husband, but she could not say that she harboured a criminal thought of them'. However, she 'oftener than once entreated the defender to dismiss said Barclay the house, and said it would be better for him to pay for a Surgeon than have him for nothing, and rain displeasure between her husband and her'.

William Espy was extremely jealous (with good reason). On the day Ann was crying because she did not have ladies and gentlemen attending her, Mr Barclay went up to her, and lay beside her with his arms around her. Mrs White 'went down stairs immediately being under some apprehension that there might be blood shed if Mr Espy had then come into the room, having heard him some days before tell a story how Julian [sic] Caesar, or some Emperor had killed his Empress for Imprudence, for walking in a Garden with a Nobleman or some such thing,' Finally, on the day before they separated, Mrs White declared, Barclay came to the house and told William he would see how Ann was: 'That Barclay was not above three minutes gone when the pursuer got up and run upstairs, and the deponent hearing the defender screaming violently, went out of the kitchen and catched the defender in her arms, thinking to get her into one of the Rooms, That the defender tossing the deponent from her, run out of the house, and the deponent having followed her to the Closs she turned about and said "has he killed Mr Barclay?" '. Mrs White went to see, and William, 'turning to the deponent said "You old deceitful Bitch, you have been privy to all their doings".'

Ann fled first to a Mrs Dorrett's house and then moved to Mrs Graham's. The defence lawyer did his best to stop Mrs Dorrett appearing as a witness, but he was unsuccessful, and she declared that William once told her that if she could show him his wife in bed with Barclay he would give her £10 and that she had told him she never would take money for that, 'for that if she was called upon as a witness she would alwise tell the truth'. She deponed that she had several times seen Ann and Barclay in bed together and that when she removed the sheets from the bed where they had lain 'she observed those sheets stained with such marks as were the natural consequence of a man and woman having copulated there together', adding that 'whenever Mr Barclay slept in the house with the defender they had a pair of pistolls in the Room with them which she was told were loaded . . . That the reason she gave for this precaution was least they should be surprized by Mr Espy from whom she was in terror of her life'.

It is not clear why Ann left Mrs Dorrett's for Mrs Graham's, but the intriguing thing is that she once again enlisted another woman (Mrs Graham's daughter, Margaret) to help her in her romantic intrigue. The witness to this was Grizel Milne, 16-year-old servant to John Mackintosh, writer, and his wife, who lodged in the same house. Grizel 'observed that Mr Barclay never came to see the defender but when Mrs Grahame the Landlady was abroad, she further took notice that if Miss Graham happened to be in the Defenders room when Mr Barclay came to visit said defender she Miss Graham used to come and go between the kitchen and said room till about an hour before Mr Barclay went away, and she has also observed that about the time Mrs Graham was expected home said Miss Grahame used to go to the outter door, and if she saw her mother coming she used to go into the defenders Bedchamber as the deponent conjectured to inform Mrs Espy that her Mother was coming home'; on one occasion she 'heard said Miss Graham upon going from the outter door into the defenders Bedchamber say "Mrs Espy there is Mamma."'

Finally there was the day of the discovery. It was a Sunday morning in summer and Grizel 'was alarmed by Mrs Espys screaming out from the adjoining one and before she got to the door, she heard Miss Graham calling murder from the kitchen, That when she came to the door of said room, she saw Mr Espy and three men with him, one of them appeared to be lame, another blind of an eye and a third whom she saw here today along with the blind one was then standing before Mr Barclay whose back was to the kitchen door, That she observed said Mr Barclays' Breeches open and he was endeavouring to put them up with his hands'. Naturally the Defence tried to stop the three men, all cadies who had been 'hyred on purpose to be witnesses for the Pursuer in the Cause', because they had received money for this. William's lawyer called this objection 'altogether Rediculous and absurd', as indeed it was.

One of the three died before he could appear, but Andrew Little, 'running stationer', aged fifty, deponed that last September Miller asked him to attend a gentleman, along with Fraser, and that they met up with William who 'told the deponent and the rest, that he had taken a room for his wife at the Sciennes on account of her health, and that he had credible Information, that there was a man then in bed with her and desired the deponent, and the persons abovementioned, to go along with him to catch them. That the deponent asked what authority the pursuer had, for going to said room, and he answered that he had his Lawyers advice, upon which they agreed to go along with him.' When they came 'to said room door, the deponent saw said pursuer turn the handle of the lock thereof as if to open the door, which appeared to the deponent to be shut, that having done so, he turned to the Company and said Gentlemen You see I must break it open, upon which he took from his pocket a Coopers adze with which he drove a hole in the door and the adze went thro' into the Room That the deponent then looking thro' said hole saw a woman come out of a bed in the room in her shirt, and thereafter the deponent saw a young man open said door and make immediately at the pursuer, whom he forced up to a kitchen door in said trance; That the deponent upon this seized said young man and clapping a pistol to his Breast desired him to be quiet. That as soon as said young man opened the door the above mentioned woman gave the deponent a blow upon the collar bone with the foresaid adze which she had thrown among the company . . . That the deponent observed said young man when he came out of the room had his breeches unbuttoned and a little down from his breech and while the deponent was holding him by the Collar he took notice that said young man Buttoned his Breeches. That after this, the pursuer clapping his hands upon said young mans shoulder said to him "I have nothing to say to you, you go about your business this is all I wanted".' Alexander Fraser corroborated the story.

There was one final witness, Samuel Evans, 'student of physick', who deponed that 'Robert Barclay did several times acknowledge to this deponent that he had had carnal dealings at different times with the defender'. On the Sunday of the discovery 'He Barclay came into the deponents room in Edinburgh, and having shut the door, said it was all over with him and that he was undone; and the deponent having asked him what he meant, He said the Pursuer had surprised him and the Defender that morning, and the deponent having asked if the pursuer had found them in bed to-gether, He answered no, But that he had just had carnal dealing with her and that they were lying aside one another upon the bed'. After that Barclay 'told the deponent that he was advised by several of his friends . . . to leave this country on account of said discovery and the deponent did also advise Barclay to the same purpose'. Before he did so, the deponent was sent for Ann 'who appeared to be much distressed and in tears. That the Defender then told the deponent that it was absolutely necessary Barclay should leave this Country, for if he was catched, she the Defender would be ruined, and bid the deponent tell Barclay so'. He had since received several letters from Barclay, 'some of which contained messages to be delivered by the deponent to the defender, But which he the deponent never did deliver'. He wanted nothing more to do with their affair and had refused to see Ann again; she sent him so many messages that he 'was at last obliged to refuse admittance to the Cadie'. It was believed Barclay was in Ireland, 'of which he was a native'.

The most surprising thing about this case is that it was contested at all, and not just because the evidence of adultery was so clear. There is no hint of any remnants of affection by Ann for her husband, nor could there have been any real hope, under the circumstances, that he would ever have lived with her again as husband. Basically, she had burned her bridges behind her, but it seems she did not accept this but thought she could escape being 'ruined' if Barclay was no longer around either to witness against her or to be challenged by her husband. (Though from his attitude at the time of the discovery it is clear that by this time William Espy's jealous rage was directed solely toward his wife.) She must have been a woman of charm and beauty, not only by the effect she had on her husband and lover but also on the various women who assisted her in her affair, even those who felt that her husband was hard done by.

cc8/5/13

CHAPTER 10

'COMMON' DIVORCES – PART 2

This chapter concentrates on couples who were already living apart when the divorce action was brought. The first section looks at husbands and wives who eloped with their lovers; the second looks at couples who had agreed on a formal separation some time before the divorce; and the third looks at bigamous second marriages. There was rarely a reason for anyone suing for divorce to explain why he or she did so; when this occurred after some years apart the likeliest motive was a desire to remarry after someone new appeared on the scene.

ELOPEMENTS

In an early elopement case (1726) Alexander Herbertson, wright and looking-glass maker in Glasgow, left his wife, Marion Steuart, and fled to Ireland with Jean Brodie, a servant.[1] Robert Miller, a fellow wright, had heard Herbertson 'say severall times That he could not Live Longer in Glasgow, and therefore would go to Ireland to Live and take alongst with him Jean Brodie whom he would marry after he went there . . . and the defender farder said he would get a warrand from the Bishops Court in Ireland for to marry her'. Miller, having 'expostulat' with Herbertson 'why he would go to Ireland with the said woman, he answered that he was obliged to do it, because he was under promises to her, and that she had an affection to him, and she was of ane agreeable temper'. Before Jean left she said goodbye to Elizabeth Aitkin (aged eighteen), a fellow servant, 'and said weeping' that Elizabeth 'would never see her again'. The next day Jean's father told Elizabeth that his daughter had gone off with Herbertson 'and that it was the report of the Town of Glasgow that they were gone off togither to Ireland.' Herbertson had advised Robert Mcbraw, looking-glass maker in Glasgow, that he was going to Ireland with Jean Brodie, and when Mcbraw 'Expostulate with him why he took a woman with him when he might gett severall women there where he was goeing', Herbertson 'answered that he was obliged to do it, and sooner than he designed because the said Jean Brodie forced him to it, and that he designed to marry the said Jean Brody in Ireland'.

This is a rare occasion when we can get an idea of the appearance of someone in a divorce case, for witnesses who saw the couple in the course of their journey to Ireland described Jean as 'a black stroping woman Tollerable well favoured' ('black' meant black-haired). The frequency of travel between the west of Scotland and northern Ireland, in an era when travelling by sea could be much easier than by land, is evidenced by the fact that several witnesses saw the couple in Belfast. Alexander Rankine, maltman, had dined with Herbertson, and he saw Jean Brodie: 'during Time of Dinner the defender Intertained her as his wife Giving her the Compellations of my dear, and the deponent looked upon her as such'. He had 'heard in Belfast from severall persons that the defender and the woman are habite and repute spouses, and that they Dwell togither as such'. But because he knew better he 'Expostulate with the defender as to his present way of Living not being as he apprehended in Gods way, and advised him to return to the pursuer his Lawfull wife To which the defender made Little and no answer.' Mary Gray, a 48-year-old widow, also saw Herbertson with Jean who told her she was four months gone with child. And Herbertson said that 'he was Troubled with the Bishops Court which obliged him to conceall Jean Brody'. Mary carried a letter to Jean from her father:

and observed when Jean read the Letter she weeped, the deponent did not hear the Contents she having read it softly to her selfe, but was told by David Brody when she gott the Letter from him, That he had wrote to his Daughter that she was all this while Lying in Adultery, and bid the Deponent also tell her so, and that if she would Leave the defender, and come to any place in Scotland, her father would come to her, Deponed that having asked Jean Brody where and by whom she was married, she said she was married at Douchadee by a priest.

There was plenty of ambivalence there about the supposed marriage in Ireland. And no one had anything to say about Marion Steuart, Herbertson's wife, who obtained her divorce from him.

An odd case is that of Archibald Mcarthur, chapman traveller formerly in Langholm, against Rebecca Clappertoun, in 1733.[2] Rebecca had fled to England with another chapman traveller, John Hownam, with whom she was cohabiting. While they were still in Scotland, Rebecca's brother and other relations caught up with them. Her brother 'chided the said Hownam for running away' with Mcarthur's wife. Hownam answered that she was not Mcarthur's wife 'but his own wife for that he had bought her from the pursuer'. Wife-sales have been recorded in England,[3] but not previously in Scotland. (Admittedly, there is no other evidence that this actually occurred.)

In a 1771 case, Dunbar McConnel, wife of Samuel Paterson (a shopkeeper in Wigton), had run off in August 1768 with William Hunter, another travelling chapman, who took with him money and effects.[4] They were traced to Edinburgh by Hunter's brother James, who had been his partner and who took back some of the goods and gear. William promised to return with the rest of the money but did not keep his promise, so James 'caused Publish them in the newspapers and offered a reward to any person that would secure them'. This made it unsafe for them to remain in Scotland, so they went to London and then to Boston, Massachusetts. James Hunter declared that when he found his brother in Edinburgh he 'expostulated' with him about eloping with Dunbar, 'which he acknowledged and said at first That as she had gone off with him he could not now leave her'. After James 'represented to him the Consequences of this affair and particularly the distress that it would occasion to their mother the said William Hunter seemed very penitent, and promised to return and leave the Defender.' However, at a second meeting William 'appeared hardened'. The evidence in this case also included a number of letters, the first of which was written by Dunbar to James, begging him not to put an advertisement in the papers:

> I assure you Sir I depend upon your Goodness so far as to hope you will not Endeavour to part us seeing how far matters are gone and its impossible for any thing but death ever to separate us – we are very Sensible Sir That this is contrary both to the Laws of God and man but the like has been done before and we hope for forgiveness of that God which we have offended – and why would you be so cruel as to part us when you see we Love each other so well surely your heart has never been sensible of this fatal passion else you would have had more compassion upon us.[5]

The later letters were from Boston and then New York, where the couple had established themselves. This is another case where we have a description (from the advertisements) of the parties: Hunter was described as aged twenty-six, 5 foot 8 inches, 'wore his own hair of a light brown Colour tyed with a Black Ribbon'. Dunbar was 'a Genteel thin woman with Red hair and remarkably pretty'. Once again, it is worth noting that none of the efforts to bring back the defender were made by her spouse, who appears a shadowy figure in the evidence.

Helen Crawford also eloped because she was in love with another man, in 1816. Her husband was John Stobbo, master of a brigantine at Irvine, while her lover was David Dickie, upholsterer in Kilmarnock. Helen wrote to her husband after he raised the divorce action (the spelling has been left untouched):

> I have been informed by my freands that the publick wishes to make me a common woman but belive me I never have bean guilty of that horad crime but with Dickie O Sur I wronged you by marrying you for when I gave you my hand my heart was Dickies I was his by promeses . . . I know that I was to blame why did I encorege him but he came round me with flattery and the promeses that I made to him but O do not beleve that I ever encoureged any other man . . . after Dickie had libertys with me I never could think to stop and to decive you the best of men you deservd one more worthy but I hope you will be more fortunat in your next caise.[6]

In the 1786 case of Alexander Drummond, weaver in Kinross, against Janet Playfair, it appears to have been more a desire to escape her husband than overwhelming passion for her lover, Donald Maclaren, a 'reduced sergeant', aged forty, that prompted her to flee. Robert White, glover in Edinburgh, had known Janet from her infancy. In response to a letter from her mother, he went to enquire for her and saw her with Maclaren. White 'asked her what made her leave her husband she said she had been badly used by him and would rather Jump into the Sea than return to him'. Drummond wanted to see his wife 'face to face', so White brought them together, when they 'both turned into a passion and the deponent cannot recollect what passed betwixt them.'[7]

The above is just a sample of cases where a spouse eloped with a lover. But many marriages had ceased to function long before a divorce action was brought.

LIVING SEPARATELY

Cases of cruelty where wives brought actions of separation are featured in later chapters, but an example of such a marriage in which the husband also committed adultery is that of Rachel Forbes against John Sharp, late tenant in Monktonhall in 1773. She alleged that he 'had frequently beat and Insulted her and even threatned her Life on account of which Barbarous treatment the pursuer was for her own safety oblidged to leave her house But the said Defender had also been Guilty at various times and places of Committing adultery'. The case was undefended, and she petitioned for a commissioner to take her oath of calumny in Canterbury, where she had fled for fear of her life. A glimpse of Sharp's character was provided by Christian Bain, aged twenty-two, who had been their servant from Christmas 1772. During the time of her service he made 'several attempts in order to have carnal dealings' with her and 'did at last prevail' – and also managed to infect her with venereal disease. And 'while in the pursuers service she had seen the Defender several times use the pursuer very badly and beat her'. Others confirmed Sharp's ill treatment of Rachel and of his adulterous activities, and Rachel gained her divorce (and expenses).[8]

Stewart Bell Cruickshanks married Alexander Barclay, junior weaver in Linlith-gow, in 1769.[9] Ten years later a contract of separation was drawn up, which began:

> That the said Alexander Barclay the defender from respect of Business whereby his Family and children have been on sundry occasions left unprovided for joined with maletreatment and personal abuse upon the body of the said Stewart Bell Cruickshanks Pursuer his wife that in so much as in the month of January then Last she was for preservation of her life and support and maintainance of four infant children obliged to leave her husband and his house and take shelter under the protection of a relation upon whose charity and benevolence they have been all hitherto supported.

Presumably Stewart subsequently met someone else she hoped to marry, for in 1783 she brought a divorce action against him. Witnesses declared that Barclay was 'much given to drunkenness and never was dutifull to his family since the time of his marriage', and also that he 'has been much addicted to Gallantry'.

Many couples lived separately for a number of years without cruelty being alleged. An example was the case of William Brown, flaxdresser in Milnathort, against Katherine Farquhar or Forfar (1780). They had been married in 1763 and had one child. She had left him in 1766 and had been guilty of adultery with David Keane, in Cupar Fife. In June 1772 she had a child, and Keane acknowledged to Cupar kirk session that he was the father. In January 1775 she had another child, which she claimed was her husband's, but Brown had not been around for years. David Keane (a married day labourer, aged thirty) confessed to having had carnal connection with her around 1772, saying that 'he never knew that Katharine Farquhar was a married woman untill after the first time she was with Child . . . she always passing herself for an unmarried woman previous to that period.'[10]

John Blair, late labourer in Kilbirnie parish now resident in Beith, married Jean Stirret in 1760.[11] He brought his divorce action in 1782, but the marriage had actually collapsed within days, when he discovered that she was pregnant, though he had not had intercourse with her beforehand. She was called to appear before Kilbirnie kirk session and admitted that Hugh Orr, a sailor, was the father of her child, which Orr acknowledged. Blair had nothing to do with his wife after that, and a few years later he went to Antigua, and did not raise his divorce action until he returned to Scotland. In the meantime, Jean had had another child, which was maintained by its father, John Reid.

It was noted at the beginning of this chapter that the likeliest explanation for raising a divorce action was the desire for a second marriage, but a different motive appears in the case of Alexander Ponton, servant to distillers in Edinburgh, against Jean Tweedie.[12] They married in February 1786 and separated in November 1788; subsequently she sued him for aliment, to which he responded with a divorce action. He readily admitted that 'if the Defender had remained in retirement he never would have thought of bringing her conduct under Judicial Investigation But as she very Improperly Endeavoured after defiling the marriage bed and living separately for some time to impose herself upon the Pursuer or to obtain an aliment, he found himself called upon to bring the present action in order to obtain redress.' When, in the course of the action, she petitioned for money for aliment, he answered that because of her conduct he had been 'driven to the direful necessity of taking his only Child from under her Charge and displenishing his house which she indeed had in a great measure pillaged and Conscious of the Impropriety of her Conduct she submitted to the separation not only from the Respondent but also from the only Child without reluctance and in place of reforming gave herself up to a general course of lewdness and dissipation.' He brought proof and obtained his divorce in 1791.

A particularly interesting case is that of Elizabeth Stewart against David Forgie.

They were married in Newcastle in 1754, then lived in Berwick, and came to Edinburgh. From about 1766 he 'followed a course of Beating and Maltreating her in a most Cruel and barbarous manner.' She brought an action of separation and aliment in 1773 on the poor's roll and was successful. In 1784 she brought a divorce action (again on the poor's roll), naming four different women who had borne his children.[13] Rather surprisingly, he vigorously contested the case. 'The Defender when a very young man not exceeding 15 or 16 years of age, was married to this pursuer then a woman of 30,' he stated, and 'for some time after their marriage the parties lived and cohabited as man and wife':

> But whether from the great difference in their age, or from the pursuers being instigated by the Bad Council and advice of her relations on her coming to Edinburgh, the defender cannot say, But from one cause or other, joined to a natural hasty passionate and perverse Disposition, the defender about 14 years after their marriage found it impossible for him to remain longer in family with the pursuer; not only did she refuse to pay him any kind of respect as her husband and refused to admit him to her bed or to perform the Conjugal duties of Husband and wife; But the pursuer did also allow her passion to Brake [sic] furth into great rage, and fury against the Defender, and being aided by two of her near relations that staid in the house, the defender was soon overpowered and drove from his house into the streets where he was left to seek for shelter as he best could.

About a year later 'the parties agreed mutually to separate from each other' and with the assistance of friends drew up a certificate. But instead of adhering to the conditions of the agreement she, 'in great opulence', instigated a process of separation and aliment against him which he, as a poor journeyman tailor, could not defend, nor was he ever able to afford the £8 per annum he was supposed to pay, 'In consequence whereof he was no less than six different times thrown into prison, from whence he was only liberated by his obtaining the Benefit of the Act of Grace.'

He claimed that her refusal to live with him 'did not intirely proceed so much from her resentment against the Defender, as from her affections having taken a different Course, and Centered upon one William Mchardy a soldier late in 25 Regt of foot, who in the month of October last she accepted of as an Husband, and who has lived and cohabited with her as such'. As for her accusations, 'the fact is that being unjustly accused by these women, and the matter brought to trial before the magistrates of Edinburgh in actions for aliment of their Children the defender was assoilzied [absolved] from these prosecutions, so that these accusations are intirely groundless'. However, as Elizabeth produced three women who swore that he had had carnal dealings with them, she won her case. She, of course, denied marrying Mchardy, though it seems likely they were cohabiting in the expectation of marriage after she obtained her divorce. (If she really was thirty when she married, she must have been over sixty at this time.)

In 1798 William Wilson, smith in Edinburgh, brought an action against Christian Gemmel or Gamble, whom he had married in 1785. In 1793 they had gone to live in Dundee where she 'gave herself up to the baneful vice of drunkenness, kept loose and disorderly company embezled the Complainers goods and carried her improper behaviour to such a length that the Complainer found it impossible to live with her and accordingly they parted with mutual consent'. In July 1795 he came to live in Edinburgh, where she was also living, and 'understood that in place of seeing the errors of her ways she not only had been in the practice of keeping Company and drinking with soldiers and frequenting houses of bad fame' but for at least the past three years had also been guilty of adultery. The action was contested, but he was able to prove his case.[14]

Also in 1798, Christian Thomson, daughter of a minister at Dailey, Ayrshire, brought her action against William Hay, 'sometime farmer', now merchant or grocer in Glasgow. They were married in August 1794, and in 1797 they moved to Glasgow, bringing with them the surviving child of twins. She was apparently very unhappy there, for she went back to her father's in Ayrshire, decamping 'one night about one o'clock in the morning, on account as she said to the Deponent of her not being able to live comfortably with the Defender'. His association with prostitutes was proven in the course of the action.[15]

How did women who left their husbands manage if they did not have a parental home to return to, or a new partner to cohabit with? In the previous chapter we looked at the case of Isabella Morton against John Borland, who fathered five or six bastards on different women. As they were married in 1805, and she alleged adultery from that same year but did not bring her action until 1813, the commissaries wanted to know when she had first come to know of her husband's infidelities, and whether she had ever cohabited with him subsequently. She declared that she came to know of at least one of them at the beginning of 1808 and immediately left him. Ninian Jameson, 62-year-old wright in Darvel, deponed that after leaving her husband Isabella lived with her mother for about a year, then went into service for two or three years; after that she resided with her uncle for about six months, and was now a servant to the deponent, 'and during all that period to the best of the Deponents knowledge she has not cohabited with the Defender'.[16]

Another couple who had separated some years before a divorce action was brought were David Smith, tailor in Edinburgh, and Sophia McLean. They were married in January 1805 and had several children, but 'while living in a house in Rose Street the dispositions and temper of the said Sophia McLean or Smith became so troublesome and vexatious to the pursuer and her family that he was compelled to enter by her desire into a contract of mutual separation'. They had lived separately since May 1818 and he paid her the allowance stipulated in the contract. He brought his case in November 1822, alleging adultery from 1821, with William McLaughlan or Anderson, weaver, late in Edinburgh now in Paisley, where she cohabited with him as his wife, 'representing to her neighbours and associates that her husband the pursuer was dead and the Children she had bore to him during their marriage were living with his relations in Edinburgh from whom she received a yearly allowance for her maintenance which had been provided to her by her deceased husband'. The case was uncontested.[17]

As we have seen, a number of individuals subsequently divorced by their spouses had already been cohabiting with other partners for some time, but none of those so far discussed went through a second marriage ceremony. However, from the 1690s onwards, when the Episcopal church was replaced by a Presbyterian establishment and unemployed ministers flocked to Edinburgh, irregular marriage, with no questions asked, was readily available in the city. Many couples took advantage of the option; in South Leith there were decades in the second half of the eighteenth century when irregular marriages outnumbered regular ones.[18]

BIGAMY

Marrying for a second time while a first spouse was still alive started early in our period. John Anderson, a servant, was married to Janet Young in 1693; they had two children but she left him in 1699. Some time later she began cohabiting with another man, whom she actually married in 1707. Anderson brought his divorce action in 1709. Janet did not appear, but in her confession to Tolbooth kirk session she declared that she and Anderson parted about eleven years earlier 'upon the account of poverty that they were not able to keep house together'. She also said that she had 'thought the said John Anderson her first husband was dead'. Anderson declared that he had seen her since that time at her father's house in Dysart, 'And that he did give her some money and desired her to stay with her father for some time untill he was in a better condition to take up house in order to Cohabite with her', but that was five or six years earlier, so it is possible that she really did think he was dead.[19]

In a 1738 case Alexander Stewart was unusual in being a Highlander. (Neither pursuer nor witnesses spoke English; their interpreter was Robert McIntosh, writer in Edinburgh.) Stewart and Anna Reid, from Foss in Perthshire, had been married for about seventeen years, but she had left him four years earlier. Her new man was James Campbell, a soldier in one of the Independent Companies, who 'pretended to be sick when the Company marched from Foss and stayed behind'. Anna went with him first to Inverness, then to Edinburgh, where they married and bought a still, and finally to Dunfermline where they were looked on 'as man and wife' and 'carried on a trade of Distilling aquavitae and brewing.' Anna was not in any doubt that her first husband was still alive; indeed, she and Campbell hurriedly left Dunfermline 'upon her receiving the summonds of Divorce'.[20]

In the case of James Gowans, journeyman wright in Edinburgh, against Mary White, they had been married in 1731 but split up within a year.[21] In 1740 she told a neighbour that 'she was courted for marriage by George Gibb shoemaker in Caltoun, and that as her husband Gowans had parted from her, she showed some Inclination to the Deponent to accept of the proposall'. Some time after that the neighbour saw Mary and George in the house, as well as 'one of the Name of McClaren who called himself a Minister, which McClaren the Deponent did see and hear Celebrate a Marriage betwixt the Defender and this Gibb.' James got his divorce in April 1741, but that is not the end of the story, for Mary and George were hauled before South Leith kirk session in December of that year. They confessed their irregular marriage, and Mary declared that she had not known whether her first husband was alive or dead but that since remarrying she had received a citation to the Commissary Court. They were forbidden by the presbytery to continue cohabiting but when they were told this George said that 'she will not go from him', and Mary said 'He may as well take away her Life as put her away'; and they continued living together. In May the sentence of greater excommunication was pronounced against them. (This barred them from communion or having a child baptised, though it had no civil consequences.)[22]

Donald McNair, residing in Rosemarkie, Ross-shire, was married to Isobel Forbes in Edinburgh in March 1766. In 1779 she 'entered into a second marriage with George Murdoch porter in Leith with whom she has lived there at bed and board for these eight years last by past and she owns and acknowledges him as her husband although formerly married to the pursuer and she has borne several children to him as the Complainer is informed.' McNair brought his uncontested action in 1789 and obtained his divorce.[23]

Margaret Fergusson apparently could not make up her mind whom she preferred as her husband.[24] She was married to John Cairns, a fellow servant, in February 1769 but within months was guilty of adultery with another fellow servant, James Surrel. They went to Edinburgh together, were married by a minister in the Canongate, cohabited for some weeks in Edinburgh, and then went off to London, where they were living at the time the divorce action was brought in 1777. The landlady of the house where the fleeing couple stayed deponed that a lad in green clothes had rented a room from her and showed her the marriage certificate. But then Cairns had come along, and the landlady deponed:

> That the pursuer put his arm about the defenders neck and called her 'Peggy my dear' – That he desired the deponent to go for a dram and insisted on the defenders taking a bit of bread before she tasted the dram, That the pursuer said that the child the Defender was with was his, That the lad with the green cloaths said he could say nothing with regard to the child till he saw whether it answered to the time of his marriage with the Defender That the defender said she would not stay with the pursuer whether the lad with the green cloaths kept it or not.

Andrew Wilson, merchant in Edinburgh, deponed that about five or six years ago the defender told the deponent she was married to two men who were servants in the same house with her and that one of them was a livery servant, That the two men were likewise sometimes in the Deponents shop and told the deponent that they were both married to her – That one time when they happened to be in the shop . . . they fell a disputing who should have her, That the deponent said he thought it a foolish dispute, and said she was not much worth having, Deponed that the deponent was sent for to a house in the pleasants [Pleasance], and upon his coming into the room the Defender Margaret Fergusson was in bed but immediately got up, and that she had nothing upon her but her shirt and petticoat, That the Livery man was in the room at this time, That the Defender appeared to the deponent to be like one out of her reason as being concerned for what she had done and that the Livery man likewise seemed to be very sorry at seeing her in that situation – That the defender acknowledged to the deponent that she was with child, but the Deponent does not remember which of the men she said was the father – but that the Livery man said he would not take with the child unless it came to his time. That to the best of the deponents remembrance the other man was either the gardener or the gardener's son and that he seemed to think the child was his and was fond to have the Defender as his wife.

But after she left Scotland Cairns wanted his freedom to remarry.

In the case of Robert Bennet, farm servant in Newbattle parish, against Margaret Cleland, the minister at Newbattle, the Reverend James Brown, deponed that about the end of 1803 or beginning of 1804 the couple had appeared before the kirk session declaring that they had been married irregularly in June or July in the Canongate of Edinburgh 'and produced lines of their marriage and requested the Session to confirm their marriage'. They were rebuked and fined, their marriage was confirmed, and they cohabited. Some time later Margaret 'came on Sunday to the Session, accompanied by a man of the name of George Mill who was then a Servant to Mr Bruce a Farmer at Bryam in the parish – and to the astonishment of the Session the Defender said that she had lately married the said George Mill as she liked him better than the Pursuer and wished the Session to confirm her second marriage with the said George Mill.' Needless to say, the session did no such thing, forbidding her to cohabit with Mill. But, 'notwithstanding thereof the Defender and George Mill lived and cohabited together at Bryams and the Deponent is informed that they are still living together somewhere in the South Country.' Bennet got his divorce in 1806.[25]

The above cases are of interest in showing that it was not only men who remarried in the full knowledge that they had a spouse still living, but consciously bigamous wives were not typical. Amongst bigamists found in urban kirk session records, out of 21 husbands 18 knew full well that their first wives were alive, whereas out of 18 wives, only six were aware of this, the remainder having been deserted with no way of finding out what had happened to their husbands.[26]

Male bigamists naturally turn up in the Commissary Court records as well. Thomas Borthwick, a sailor, married Annabella Mckenzie (daughter of a goldsmith in Inverness) in autumn 1740. They had a child, but in 1745 Borthwick married Anne Rodgers in Kent. In 1748 he was in Scotland, and Annabella with their child and Thomas's father visited him on board and stayed the night. Anne somehow came to hear of this and wrote to Borthwick's father, asking him for the truth of the matter, 'That I may know whither I have a husband or not, for if he has a Wife with you she is his Wife and not me, which I am very sorry for her Misfortune to have such a Roge'. Borthwick wrote to Anne that the woman who had visited him had borne his bastard child and given out that she was married to him (and had only stayed the night on board ship because 'It blowed very hard'!). But the game was up, and Anne testified before a commissioner in Gravesend, producing copies of the marriage certificate, Borthwick's letters to her, and his will in which he left everything to his 'Loving Wife Ann Borthwick'.[27] So Thomas Borthwick ended up with neither wife.

Ann Borthwick was not the only woman to be conned into thinking she was marrying a single man (Chapter 13 will have yet more examples). In the 1788 case of Menny Katharine Stewart against William Chapman, Jean Hutton deponed that in August 1787 the defender 'paid his addresses to and proposed marriage to the deponent, and prevailed with her to marry him'. Afterwards Chapman begged Jean 'to give him a sight of the marriage lines and vowed solemnly to return them to her again, but after getting them he twisted them into his hands and then put them into his mouth and the deponent never received them back again from him.' After the marriage was consummated they went to Edinburgh, and Chapman 'said to the deponent that he was going to see a sister and he hoped she would not take it amiss his leaving her that the deponent then learned for the first time from a young man . . . that the defender was married to the woman whom he went to see and whom he called his sister.'[28]

So far we have seen no indication of any 'common' bigamists being referred to criminal justice, but John McDonald, tailor in Perth, who married Grace Blair in 1804 and Barbara Leslie in 1814, was 'served with an Indictment to stand trial before the Circuit Court of Justiciary to be held at Inverness for the Crime of Bigamy'. He was found guilty and sentenced to six months' Imprisonment in the Perth jail. On his release he went right back to Barbara ('in defiance of law') and was still cohabiting with her when Grace brought her action in December 1816. Possible criminal proceedings are mentioned in another case in the same year, that of Allan Angus, garrison schoolmaster at Edinburgh Castle, against Mary Jamieson. They were married in 1810, but in 1816, having 'represented herself as a widow', she was married a second time to Alexander Anderson, mason in Edinburgh, now a private in the 79th regiment. He was ordered to France with a detachment of his regiment, and she embarked with him 'as his lawful wife'. The commissaries appointed 'a copy of the proof of proceedings in this case to be transmitted to the Lord Advocate in order that his Lordship may have an opportunity of Judging whether any Criminal prosecution on the ground of Bigamy should be instituted against the Defender.'[29]

Inevitably, the war years brought about a rise in bigamy. Wives who were left alone for years found consolation in the arms of another, while husbands serving far from home started new families. James Campbell married Helen McEwan in 1803, when he was a private in the Perthshire Militia, and they had a child. In 1808 he enlisted in the Royal Staff Corps and went to the Continent with the army, which was the last that Helen saw of him. In 1814 he married the widow of a soldier in the corps at Bordeaux and brought her back to England with him, and they cohabited at Hythe up to the time that Helen brought her divorce action in 1819. Witnesses who had known both parties in Perthshire expressed disgust at Campbell's behaviour. One such witness deponed that he had 'challenged the Defender for living with this woman knowing that he was already married to the Pursuer but the Defender made light of it and swore "Damn it it did not signify it was not in Scotland".'[30]

Lawrence Stone wrote: 'One gets the strong impression that the number of bigamists in early modern England must have been quite large.'[31] That impression is borne out for Scotland by the evidence in the Commissary Court. And, of course, a marriage ceremony was not necessary in Scotland, so many people were 'habit and repute' man and wife, without realising that their partner had a previous spouse still alive. A common situation must have been the one brought out in the 1827 case of Jane Henley against her husband, Joseph Walker (a servant). A lawyer testified that Walker had 'for some years lived with a woman not the Pursuer in his house in Glasgow, and that the said woman goes by his name and that the Defender has several children by her who pass by his name also'. A year earlier Jane had applied to him for aliment from her husband, and the witness had obtained some money for her, Walker admitting that she was his wife. The witness added that 'the Defender was living with the said female openly and allowing her to take his name previous to the period when the Pursuer applied to the Deponent upon the subject of aliment as deponed to, and the Deponent was surprised at the application being made to him as till then he had considered the woman the Defender lived with to be his wife.'[32]

NOTES

All CC references are in the Scottish Record Office.
1. cc8/5/3.
2. cc8/5/4.
3. Lawrence Stone, *Road to Divorce – England 1530–1987* (Oxford 1992), 143–8.
4. cc8/5/12.
5. It is clear from some of the letters that Dunbar left a child behind, and that it was her parents, not her husband, who was looking after it.
6. cc8/5/36.
7. cc8/5/18.
8. cc8/5/14.
9. cc8/5/17.

10. cc8/5/16.
11. cc8/5/17.
12. cc8/5/20.
13. cc8/6/47. The separation case is in cc8/5/14.
14. cc8/5/24.
15. Ibid.
16. cc8/5/33.
17. cc8/5/41. She was not 'kept' by her lover, for witnesses deponed that 'they worked together in Mr Sims Manufactory', making silk shawls.
18. See Rosalind Mitchison and Leah Leneman, *Sexuality and Social Control – Scotland 1660–1780* (Oxford, 1989), c.4, Leah Leneman and Rosalind Mitchison, 'Clandestine Marriage in the Scottish Cities 1660–1780', *Journal of Social History* (vol.26, no.4, 1993), 845–61, and Leah Leneman and Rosalind Mitchison, *Sin in the City – Scotland 1660–1780* (Edinburgh, forthcoming), c.8.
19. cc8/5/1.
20. cc8/5/4.
21. cc8/5/7.
22. South Leith kirk session minutes 17 December 1741 – 20 May 1742, SRO. After obtaining his divorce James asked the session to be proclaimed for marriage with another woman; he was told that he had to produce the extract of the decreet before this could be allowed; he did so and was proclaimed with Margaret Wilson.
23. cc8/5/19.
24. cc8/5/15.
25. cc8/5/29/2.
26. Leneman and Mitchison, 'Clandestine Marriage in the Scottish Cities', 849.
27. cc8/5/9.
28. cc8/5/19.
29. cc8/5/25; cc8/6/112.
30. cc8/5/37.
31. Lawrence Stone, *Road to Divorce – England 1530–1987* (Oxford 1992), 142.
32. cc8/5/36.

CHAPTER 11

ENGLISH MARRIAGE AND SCOTTISH DIVORCE

The couples featured in earlier chapters were mostly born in Scotland, married there, and resided there. A few had married in England, on the Continent, or in America, but as they were natives of Scotland the commissaries had no problem in granting them divorces. However, toward the end of the eighteenth century some English women realised that while their own law did not allow them to divorce,[1] if their husbands spent at least forty days in Scotland, they could bring an action before the commissaries. After all, a man and woman could not marry irregularly in England after 1753, yet if they crossed the border to marry irregularly in Gretna Green their marriage would be recognised in England, so why not cross the border to dissolve the marriage as well?

Unlike previous chapters, where only a sample of any one type of case could be presented, this one tells the story of all those English couples. The focus of the cases is a legal one: the question of jurisdiction, and the differing viewpoints of the Commissary Court and the Court of Session.[2]

THE EARLY CASES: DOMICILE EQUALS JURISDICTION

The first person to seek such a divorce was Dame Elizabeth Brunsdon against Sir Thomas Wallace Dunlop in 1789, but she was not successful. Although both were born in Scotland, they had been married in London and neither had a residence or domicile in Scotland at the time of the action. When she was allowed to bring proof of her allegations, Sir Thomas appealed to the Court of Session on the grounds that the commissaries had no jurisdiction over an English marriage. His appeal was initially refused, but after a second petition the superior court directed the commissaries to dismiss the action.[3]

In the case of Mary Pirie against Andrew Lunan in 1794, the decision went the other way. Mary was the daughter of a writer (lawyer) in Aberdeen where she had married Lunan in 1778. They initially lived in Edinburgh and had two children, and in 1782 went to London where they had two more children. But in 1787, 'under a false pretence of being a Batchelor', Lunan bigamously married another woman and had lived with her ever since. When the commissaries dismissed the process as incompetent, Mary argued that although she continued to reside in London, yet 'after being thus openly and entirely deserted by her husband, her natural and proper residence is in the house of her father at Aberdeen'. Moreover: 'So far as the petitioner knows this is the first instance in which it has been found that natives of Scotland, contracting a marriage in this Country and residing in it afterwards for years can thereafter be exempted from the Jurisdiction of the law of Scotland respecting marriage.' This was very different from the Wallace case since here they married and lived together some years in Scotland. Although the commissaries refused the petition, and a second petition as well, after appeal the Court of Session instructed the commissaries to hear the case, and a divorce was granted.[4]

In 1798 although Esther Lambay had married George Hewit in 1753 in Cumberland, she had no difficulty in persuading the commissaries of their jurisdiction in the case, because they had resided in Glasgow for many years before he left her in 1774 to live with another woman in England. Furthermore, not only had he recently returned to live in Glasgow, 'he lately brought an action of adherence before this Court against his wife, which is at present in dependence'. So his plea of non-jurisdiction was plainly absurd.[5]

The next case was unusual in having a male pursuer. Lieutenant-Colonel John French was Scottish, his wife, Henrietta Pilcher was English, and the marriage had taken place at Gretna Green.[6] When French raised the action, Henrietta was not in Scotland, and the summons was served on her in London in November 1798. She did not contest it, but the commissaries decided they had no jurisdiction in the case and dismissed it. French petitioned on the grounds that the marriage was contracted in Scotland, where the couple had cohabited for some time, and that he was a Scotsman born and had intended that their permanent residence would be in Scotland. He added that if the commissaries' decision was not overturned, Henrietta could not be divorced here, 'and in England where she resides, the action of Divorce, as a consequence of conjugal infidelity, is unknown', except by private act of parliament, which 'not one man out of a thousand' could afford. Thus a Scottish wife 'may be guilty of the grossest infidelity, and yet evade punishment, and obtain [sic] her Status as a married woman, by merely stepping across the Tweed.'

But as Henrietta had not been cited in Scotland, 'nor is in any shape amendable to the Courts of this Country,' the commissaries refused the petition. The Court of Session, remitting the case back after appeal, remarked that Henrietta should have been cited at the usual places (market cross at Edinburgh, pier and shore at Leith) 'and at the house of her husband'. However, the Lunan case had set a precedent, so they instructed that the action be heard. In September 1800 the divorce was granted.

The case of Elizabeth Ann Wyche against Charles Burrel Blount was different in that both were English, had married at Gretna Green and never lived in Scotland, though in this case the summons was personally served on Blount as his regiment was in Musselburgh at the time. Again, the case was not contested, but the commissaries decided that as Blount had no true domicile in Scotland they had no jurisdiction. However, as he had been in Scotland for more than forty days, the Court of Session found he had established a legal domicile, and the commissaries were therefore instructed to proceed with the action, which resulted in a divorce in July 1801.[7]

The lack of a domicile had caused a case to fail in the preceding month. Maria Morcomb, an Englishwoman, had married John Law Macclelland, a Scot, in Plymouth, and as they had lived in England ever since, he denied the jurisdiction of the court. The commissaries agreed, as (on appeal) did the Court of Session, and the case was dismissed in June 1801. In the case of Lindsay against Tovey, the pursuer was a Scot, the defender an Englishwoman who contested the case on the grounds of jurisdiction; the commissaries found they *did* have jurisdiction, but the case went not only to the Court of Session but to the House of Lords. However, Lindsay died before a final decision, thereby frustrating the commissaries of a precedent in a rare contested case.[8]

Lord Paget, an Englishman, had been married to the Right Honourable Lady Caroline Elizabeth Villiers (daughter of the Earl of Jersey) in 1795 and by the time the divorce process was initiated in June 1810 she had borne him eight children.[9] They had lived together happily until she

> lay in of her last child and although during her Confinement on that occasion his Lordship paid her the kindest affectionate attentions yet from that period his love and affection for her as a wife seem to have been entirely estranged. While his Lordship lived in the same house sat at the same table and frequented the same Company with his wife he treated her person with the coldest indifference and neglect withholding all Connubial intercourse with her and constantly sleeping in a different room from her.

Lord Paget had, in fact, fallen in love with another woman, Lady Charlotte Wellesley, wife of the younger brother of Lord Arthur Wellesley (future Duke of Wellington). In November 1808 Lord Paget went off to fight in Spain, but on his return he and Lady Charlotte took up where they had left off, and in March 1809 they eloped. Lady Charlotte's husband sued Lord Paget for damages and divorced his wife by private act of parliament. During this period Caroline, Lady Paget, had formed an attachment to the Duke of Argyll, and therefore a divorce was as appealing to her as it was to her husband. This could not be had in England, so Lord Paget came to Scotland with Lady Charlotte, where they stayed together at a hotel in Edinburgh and then in Perthshire. If Lady Charlotte had been named she could not have married Lord Paget under Scottish law, so it would have been convenient for him to be found in bed with someone else, but she 'positively refus'd letting Lord Paget domiciliate with any other woman', so it was arranged that chambermaids and other witnesses would depone that they had no idea of the identity of the woman whom they saw in bed with Lord Paget. This may even have been true, for it was said that Lady Charlotte 'eat, drank and slept in a black veil'. Within a few weeks of the divorce Lord Paget married Lady Charlotte (and they subsequently became the Marquess and Marchioness of Anglesey), and Caroline married the Duke of Argyll. 'At the end of 1811 Lady Bessborough wrote: "Lord Paget's children are all in town in their way from Inveraray to Beaudesert; they talk with filial tenderness of Mama Argyll and Mama Paget: Vive La Liberté!".'[10]

Three English pursuers (Margaret Wilcox against Richard Parry, Elizabeth Aldous against Henry Alden, and Mary Rogers against Charles Burton Wyatt) obtained divorces without difficulty in 1811, before a series of hotly debated cases came along.[11]

COMMISSARIES' UNWILLINGNESS

Elizabeth Utterton, from Cheshunt, Hertfordshire had been married to Frederick Teush Esquire in England, in 1790. By 1800 he had three children by his mistress, and Elizabeth unsuccessfully petitioned the House of Lords for a divorce. In 1811 Teush came to Scotland with his mistress, and in June Elizabeth raised a divorce action against him.[12] The commissaries were unaware of her previous attempt at a divorce, but his defences were so intangible that they suspected collusion. Since the couple had married and cohabited in England, and from the evidence given there was no reason to think that Teush had established any kind of permanent residence in Scotland, the commissaries dismissed the case on the grounds of lack of jurisdiction.

The case was appealed to the Court of Session, which ordered the commissaries to proceed with it. Lord Meadowbank provided an explanation. 'If the law refused to apply its rules to the relations of husband and wife, parent and child, master and servant, among foreigners in this country,' he argued, 'Scotland could not be deemed a civilised country, as thereby it would permit a numerous description of persons to traverse it, and violate, with utter impunity, all the obligations on which their principal comforts of domestic life depend.' As for fears of collusion

> The purpose of the foreigner in choosing Scotland as the scene for the violation of his marriage vows, cannot disable the innocent party from claiming that redress which the law of Scotland affords for such a wrong. Such party having neither suggested the measure, nor furnished the means or perpetration nor refrained from using means to prevent it, may surely, with a pure and good conscience, claim the redress afforded by law, though more ample than that afforded by the law of his own country, and of course more desired.

The divorce was granted in October.

Lady Hillary's action against Sir William Hillary was brought at the same time, in

May 1811. Sir William was living with another woman in the precincts of Holyrood-house, a sanctuary where debtors could not be pursued for their debts, and had been there for five months. He entered defences, and after the commissaries expressed doubt about their jurisdiction in the case, his procurator argued vigorously that because the marriage was contracted under English law it could not be ended in Scotland. So this case, at least, does not appear to have been in any way collusive. Nevertheless, the commissaries dismissed it, a decision reversed by the Court of Session. But before hearing the case the commissaries ordered both parties to 'state in mutual memorials what is the Law of England as applicable to the case and whether the decision of it ought to be regulated by the Law of England or the Law of Scotland.'

This was an astonishing request, for as Lady Hillary's procurator put it, 'as parties in a Scottish Court, and assisted exclusively with the advice of Scottish Counsel and agents they have great doubt if they can state the Law of England correctly upon any subject':

> But the difficulty is greatly increased from the circumstance that the Memorialists are required to state what the Law of England is as applicable to the present case; for they humbly Conceive the Law of England never was applied to a Case the same as this nor can be applied to it, and never could have it in Contemplation . . . The only possible answer that can be given is that there is no provision in the Law of England for such a case, or in other words that the Law of Scotland must decide it.

The divorce was granted in January 1812.[13]

Frances Hewitt, who brought her action against James Webber Esquire, of Southampton, in August 1811, was given a thorough grilling when she swore her oath of calumny:

> Interrogated Depones that the deponent's husband never intimated to her in any way his intention of Coming to this Country before he left England. That since he came here the deponent has had no communication with him whatever respecting the present action. That her husband never at any time or in any way gave the deponent to understand that he wished her to institute the present process.

The commissaries suspended the action until the judgment of the Court of Session was known on the two earlier cases, then heard the proof and granted the divorce, in January 1812.[14]

In spite of these judgments the commissaries still insisted on a statement about why it was believed the commissaries had jurisdiction in the case of Lucy Ann Long against Thomas Bayley Howell Esquire, married in England. Her procurator argued from 'the general principle that every person owes obedience to the laws of the Country in which he is domiciled'. Howell said he had come to Scotland over a year ago, 'in prosecution of a plan, in which he is engaged of an extensive publication connected with the history of this Country.' So, while he might remain in Scotland for some years, he might also choose to return to England at any time, and thus he argued against the commissaries' jurisdiction. Since the commissaries were so vehemently opposed to any hint of collusion, it seems likely that these arguments were presented simply in order to avoid any suspicion of such a thing. In any case the divorce was granted in March 1812.[15]

The above cases were all of wives divorcing husbands, something they would not have been able to do in England. James White Esquire, of Southampton, came to reside in Edinburgh some months before bringing a divorce action against his wife, Esther Hester, in November 1811. Strangely enough, Esther was also residing in Edinburgh, but White swore that since coming to the country he had 'had no communication whatever with her and has not even seen her excepting meeting her occasionally on the Streets when he did not speak to her.' He added that 'the defender at no time nor in any way whatever ever gave the deponent to understand that she wished him to institute the present action'. It seems likely that when White learned that his wife was in Edinburgh he came himself in order to take advantage of the simpler and cheaper divorce laws, without his wife being any party to it. In view of the earlier decisions, the commissaries allowed the case to proceed and granted a divorce, in March 1812.[16]

The commissaries were particularly suspicious of collusion in the case of Ann Sugden against William Martin Lolly, a distiller from Liverpool, raised in December 1811, because he had brought his wife along with him and then took a prostitute back to the inn where they were staying. (Ann alleged that he had been guilty of adultery in Liverpool for many years, but she founded her case on the adultery committed in Scotland.) Ann, when questioned, claimed that she had not known her husband was coming any further north than Carlisle, but there he 'said to her that as Edinburgh was a fine place he would take her along with him to see it', and that she had gone with him in the hopes of a reconciliation after years of bad treatment from him. The proof revealed 'such circumstances of undisguised profligacy in the conduct of the defender, as led the Court to suspect that there might have been connivance on the part of the pursuer.' They therefore summoned both parties back to court for a judicial examination. Lolly declared that 'nothing could be farther from his intention than to give her an opportunity of divorcing him', and his wife swore 'That she is certain from every circumstance that nothing could be farther from her husbands intention than that she should become acquainted with his guilt', and that 'the defender has endeavoured to persuade her to give up this action since it was raised, and has offered her terms to do so which she has absolutely refused.' Under the circumstances, the court had no option but to grant the divorce.[17]

This had an unfortunate sequel for Lolly, for after returning to England he married another woman, was arrested and sentenced to transportation for seven years for bigamy. He appealed against the sentence, but the twelve judges of England unanimously agreed that no foreign court could dissolve a marriage made in England by an Englishman, and therefore found him guilty and upheld the sentence. Lolly spent some months in the hulks awaiting transportation, before 'common sense prevailed, and he was pardoned by the Home Office and released'.[18]

Until this happened, it appeared that the precedents set would guarantee an easy passage for future English couples wishing to divorce in Scotland. But after that English decision the commissaries demanded more, rather than less, legal arguments about their jurisdiction from English couples. But still they came.

DEFERENCE TO ENGLISH JUDGES

Catharine Pollock, married in England, brought her case against Russell Manners in October 1812.[19] As he had been concealing his name while living with another woman in Edinburgh the commissaries had no concerns over collusion, and after allowing her a proof they found the adultery proven. But at that point the decision by the twelve judges of England was made known, and the commissaries decided they needed statements on both sides regarding the effect which this rule of English law should have on the decisions of this court. There was no longer a solicitor acting for Manners, so the court appointed the solicitor for the poor to present his side of it. Catherine's lawyer could not see 'that the opinion of English Judges in their own proper Courts, not in appeal against Scotch Judgments before the house of Lords, ought to have any influence at all upon points in the law of Scotland. They knew nothing of the law of Scotland nor did not pretend to know anything of it'. The judges in the Lolly case had not denied that the Scottish court had acted according to law:

> Indeed it would appear that the prosecutor in his argument was drawn to the necessity of maintaining that the parties might remain married in England while their marriage was legally dissolved in Scotland; a proposition certainly strange enough and totally inconsistent with any sound or rational principle But it was absolutely necessary in that Case; because it was not and could not be denied that there was a legal Divorce according to the laws of Scotland.

As for the question of an English marriage being indissoluble in England:

> It might be thought that a particular deference was due to the law of England though it would hardly be decent to express it, and in fact it could not be expressed without a surrender of the independence of the Scotch nation. In abstract law no greater deference was due to the law of England than that which was due to the laws of other civilized Countries.

The commissaries found that as the adultery had been committed in Scotland, where the defender had been resident, and that he had been personally cited and appeared, it was competent for them to judge the case. As 'adultery committed in Scotland was a legal ground of Divorce without distinction as to the Country where or form in which the Marriage was celebrated', whatever the views of the law of England, they could grant a divorce – and did so, in April 1813.

The commissaries also demanded statements from both sides in the case of Marianne Humfray against Thomas Newte Esquire (married in Wales), brought before them in December 1812.[20] Her procurator argued that it was one thing to warn couples what might happen if they tried to remarry in England but quite another to refuse them justice in this court:

What Scotch Lawyer could have guessed that the English Judges from peculiar views of their own municipal system would have formed the opinions mentioned in the Interlocutor upon points of International law It would have excited no greater surprise if they had resolved that no marriage contracted in a Foreign Country should be valid without an act of Parliament and in particular that the whole of the Scotch nation were illegitimate in England.

He also referred to the nineteenth article in the Treaty of Union, which guaranteed the perpetuity of the Scottish legal system, 'from which it seemed to be at least extremely doubtful, whether the decision in the case of Lolly was a correct decision'.

The commissaries eventually decided that they should hear the case, but then a complication arose. Letters were written to one of the commissaries by a man called Rice, alleging that the parties had agreed on the divorce, and that Mrs Newte would receive £250 or £300 a year in consequence, 'and warning the Commissaries against deciding in so fraudulent a Case'. The receipt and content of the letters was not revealed until later, but when Marianne swore her oath of calumny she was subjected to intense questioning: had their separation been by agreement (no), where had she lived since then, how had she received money for maintenance, how much did she get from her husband, etc. etc. When asked who had given her the idea of divorcing she said it was her father, Sir Jere Humfray, and that when she had heard of her husband's adulteries in Scotland she had told her father, who made enquiries.

At this point the zealous procurator fiscal of the court, who had been enjoined 'by every means in his power to endeavour to detect any collusive agreements among parties in Process of Divorce', requested that Marianne's father, who was in Edinburgh, be cited to undergo a judicial examination. Her procurator strenuously objected. At the time the process was started Thomas had deserted Marianne for nearly two years, a year of which had been spent in Scotland: 'There was surely nothing in this which could warrant a suspicion that the Defender was one of those birds of passage who took up an occasional residence in aid of a collusive purpose'.

There was therefore no reason to suspect such a thing and no precedent for citing her father. Nevertheless, the commissaries appointed Sir Jere Humfray to appear in court, whereupon Marianne appealed to the Court of Session. That court not only instructed the commissaries to allow the proof to proceed, they also instructed that 'no farther investigation with regard to the supposed Collusion shall take place', and found the procurator fiscal liable for 'the whole expences incurred upon the point in dispute'. After the proof, a divorce was granted, in September 1814.

Collusion was also strongly suspected in the case of Jane Arundel St Aubyn against Captain Charles O'Bryen, raised in February 1813.[21] After overcoming the first hurdle of demonstrating Scottish jurisdiction over an English couple married in Devon – easier now that the Newte case could be cited as precedent – Jane also had to undergo a rigorous interrogation when she swore her oath of calumny. Asked how she came to know of his adultery in Scotland she declared that she learned by accident of his being in Scotland, and that she 'had at one time thoughts of obtaining a Divorce from him in England but being advised that she could obtain a more complete Divorce in Scotland the Deponent wished to know and made enquiries if there were grounds for such a Divorce against him in this Country'. After this the proof was allowed to proceed – until one of the witnesses dropped a bombshell.

Isabella Milligan, who kept a bawdy house, was a witness for Jane, but in the course of questioning by the judge examinator she declared that O'Bryen had told her that he and his wife lived unhappily together, and they 'at last come to an understanding betwixt one another that he was to come to Scotland and that both parties had come here to obtain a Divorce.' The judge examinator stopped the questioning and called in the other commissaries, whereupon the witness expanded on her original remark. Captain O'Bryen, she said, had suspected that his wife was guilty of adultery with an officer and found some correspondence which bore this out. His wife and her friends did not dispute the charge against her – according to Isabella – but 'it had been proposed by them that he Captain O'Bryen should come down to Scotland to enable her to obtain a Divorce and that this measure was agreed upon between him and his wife's friends'. He subsequently told her of his wife's arrival in Scotland and where she was lodging. Isabella added that 'Captain O'Bryen told the Deponent that after his wife had obtained the Divorce she was to marry this young Officer.'

Jane's agent – Donald MacLean, Writer to the Signet – was then summoned to court. He said that O'Bryen told him 'he had come merely for pleasure and to pass a little time', though he had also said that 'he supposed his wife would raise an Action of Divorce here and that he understood she had formerly intended to do so in England.' This was before the divorce summons was issued, and after receiving it O'Bryen had called at his house and

seemed to be in a state of irritation at receiving the Summons and perhaps heated with liquor as this interview took place after dinner and he then expressed himself warmly against Mrs O'Bryen saying he had detected her in improper correspondence with a young Officer a friend of his although the Declarant silenced him and refused to hear more of such communications the statement made such an impression on the Declarant that he had thoughts of refusing to act longer as the Pursuers Agent.

However, when Jane came to Edinburgh she convinced him that Captain O'Bryen had forged letters to the officer in her name and then pretended to find them in her drawer. MacLean therefore did not believe there had been any communication between pursuer or defender, or any agreement or understanding between them, and he was satisfied that Captain O'Bryen 'latterly wished the Divorce should be obtained but all times he expressed in the strongest terms that there was no kind of collusion betwixt him and Mrs O'Bryen or betwixt him and any of her Friends.'

The commissaries wanted to examine McLean further, but the pursuer's procurator strenuously objected that no agent should be examined on confidential information imparted by his client. On appeal the Court of Session found, as in the Newte case, that the commissaries had overstepped themselves, and instructed them to proceed with the case. The commissaries awaited the Court of Session's judgment on the case of Gordon against Pye – discussed below – but after that (December 1814) they granted the divorce. However, in their decreet they bemoaned the fact that the defender appeared to have taken up residence in Scotland 'with the view of founding this Action which he likewise allowed to proceed in absence', described the steps they had taken, finding that 'although in the opinion of the Court there were strong presumptions of collusion in this case yet the actual existence of it had not been established and the Court was precluded from all further investigation in regard to it'.

James Fergusson, one of the commissaries, commented in the wake of this: 'The objection of collusion, unless when evidence shall arise from the oath of the pursuer, may be considered as thus laid to rest; and perhaps it was vain to expect that any effectual obstacle could be opposed to fraudulent devices against the English law, in cases of divorce, by judicial inquiry upon this head.'[22]

THE COMMISSARIES' LAST STAND

One might have thought that enough precedents had by now been set to ensure that when Mary Margaret Gordon, of Somerset, brought her case against Allen Hampton Pye Esquire in July 1813, she would easily have won her divorce, but no such thing. As they married and lived in England, the commissaries dismissed the case, which was then appealed to the Court of Session. The commissaries, of course, had never believed that they should grant divorces to such couples, and this case offered them another opportunity to make a stand. As Commissary Gordon put it, 'This is one of those Divorce Cases betwixt English parties of which we have had so many within the last three years.' He had disagreed with the decisions of the Court of Session (knowing that his opinion was shared by the twelve judges of England) and was pleased that the point was again brought under consideration. He, and the other commissaries, all provided a host of arguments for their opinion, which then formed part of the process which the Court of Session considered. The problem, as they saw it, was that only two defenders (Sir Thomas Wallace, whose case was dismissed, and Major Eccles Lindsay, who died after his case was appealed to the House of Lords but before a decision was pronounced) had genuinely defended their cases, the rest having shown 'no disinclination to be divorced, and would even seem privately to have connived with the pursuers.' Hence the court itself had been forced to seek for the arguments on the other side.

The first point was whether a temporary domicile was sufficient to establish the court's jurisdiction in the dissolving of a marriage. But the fundamental issue was whether it was the *lex loci contractus* rather than the *lex domicilii* that should determine the question. An English contract 'must be tried by reference to the law of the country where the contract had its origin'; in England a marriage was held to be indissoluble, therefore it was not competent for a Scottish court to dissolve it. But the Court of Session disagreed, because 'By marrying in England, parties do not become bound to reside forever in England, or to treat one another in every other country where they may reside according to the provision of the law of England.' The duties and powers of marriage, and redress of wrongs, belonged to the law of country where they eventually resided. ('Would a husband in this country be permitted to keep his wife in an iron cage, or beat her with rods of the thickness of a Judge's finger, because he had married her in England, where it is said this may be done?') The proof was heard, and Mrs Gordon was granted her divorce in August 1815. But even this was not seen as setting a cast-iron precedent.[23]

Three cases followed in quick succession and were considered together.[24] The unusual feature of the case of Mary Butler against The Honourable Frederick Augustus Forbes was that the couple were Irish, had married at Port Patrick in Scotland, and then returned to Ireland where they lived until Forbes came to Edinburgh and committed adultery. (Ireland came under English law at the time; their marriage at Port Patrick was the equivalent of a Gretna Green marriage.) The case of Thomas Stirling Edmonstone Esquire against Annabella Lockhart differed because both parties were Scots who had married in England only because his regiment was stationed there, and the case was strongly defended by Mrs Edmonstone. However, the couple eventually came to an extrajudicial agreement so a final decision was not made by the court. The case of Jane Duntze against Philip Stimpson Levett was similar to others we have already seen. He came from England to Scotland with another woman and lived at inns and furnished lodgings until cited for divorce in October 1813. Mrs Levett made no attempt to show 'that he had any home, establishment, or concerns of business in this country . . . Unless it were to be supposed that he wished to give the pursuer an opportunity of dissolving their marriage by this action, no further indication of his reasons for coming to Scotland, and continuing here, could be any where found in the record of the cause.' The commissaries therefore concluded that he, in common with Forbes, had no genuine domicile in Scotland and dismissed the cases.

The cases were appealed to the Court of Session and came back with instructions that the pursuers be allowed to prove the defenders' domicile in Scotland. This was missing the commissaries' point: what they wanted was proof that the defenders *really* had changed their domicile, i.e. that they planned to make their homes permanently in Scotland, for then there would be no quibble over granting them divorces according to the law of Scotland. But what they got was simply more proof of what they already knew, that the defenders had spent enough time in the country to establish a legal domicile. The commissaries therefore came up with a new idea. Although divorce *a vinculo matrimonii* was not available in England, separation *a mensa et thoro* certainly was, so, adultery having been proven, they offered the pursuers a judicial separation, which was compatible with the law of the country where they had contracted their marriage. This clearly seemed like a brilliant idea to them, but not to couples who had spent a great deal of time and money to obtain something that was not available in their own country. Both cases were appealed to the Court of Session, which as usual reversed the decision, so that both received their divorces.

The commissaries made their final stand in the case of Lucy Kibblewhite against Daniel Rowland Esquire. When she brought her case in October 1814 she stated that they had always lived in England, that her husband had told her that he was going to the Lake District with a man servant and a male companion and she 'entertained no apprehension that the Defender meant to act improperly.' But he had gone on to Edinburgh and wrote to another woman who took the next mail coach up to join him. Lucy, after hearing of this, came up to Edinburgh and raised her action. 'In the meanwhile the Defender finding himself pursued into Scotland and made the subject of prosecution there departed to England.' The commissaries did not believe that he had a real domicile in Scotland, so they absolved him. They offered Lucy the chance of a separation *a mensa et thoro* instead of a divorce, which she refused.[25]

The case was not fundamentally different from those for which the Court of Session had already reversed their decisions, but this seemed to them to be the 'extreme point' that such cases could be taken to:

If Mrs Rowland, who appeared never to have visited Scotland in her life, and who certainly never cohabited with her husband in this country, nor had a domicil here, is entitled to a decree of the Consistorial Court of this country, dissolving her English marriage, because he had committed adultery, and has resided for a few weeks at this place, during which her summons was served upon him; then, beyond all doubt, such a decision not only must invite, as by open proclamation, all other spouses of every nation, who wish to obtain divorce *a vinculo* by judicial sentence, and cannot accomplish that object under the rule of their law, to resort to this jurisdiction, but also must have the effect of a regulating precedent to compel this court, in future, to entertain all their actions of divorce indiscriminately.[26]

Lucy appealed to the Court of Session, and that court instructed the commissaries to hear the case. A divorce was granted in May 1817, and the Commissary Court accepted that a far-reaching precedent had been set. When James Fergusson wrote a book in that year, discussing all of the above cases, with the arguments and conclusions, he anticipated with dread a rush of English couples coming to Scotland for their divorces. What happened in reality?

In April 1818 Elizabeth Cole, of Huntingdon, brought a case against her husband who was committing adultery in Holyroodhouse. 'In conformity to the principle of Decision pronounced by this Court in obedience to the instructions of the Superior Court in the recent case of Kibblewhite against Rolland', the commissaries allowed the case to proceed (though they refused to allow the pursuer to swear her oath in London but insisted on her coming to Edinburgh). A divorce was granted in October. In September of the same year Charity Chute, residing in London, brought an action against her husband, Major Robert Torrens. Again, the commissaries abided by the precedent and allowed the action to proceed, though this one took somewhat longer because Charity claimed not to know the name of the woman who was with her husband, and the commissaries made her swear under oath that she had made every effort to find out. The divorce was granted in May 1819. In May 1819 Major Henry Hickman, who had been married in Sicily to Elizabeth O'Brien, brought proof that she was cohabiting with a surgeon in Edinburgh, and obtained his divorce a month later. In 1820 Lord Erskine withdrew his case against Lady Erskine after his wife denied the jurisdiction of the Commissary Court; but, of course, he was able to bring his action before an English court, though it would have cost him much more. The next case was not until April 1823, when Eliza Foster Richardson, of London, brought her case against Samuel Beagley who had been cohabiting with another woman at hotels in Edinburgh for about three months. Once again, the name could not be ascertained. The divorce was granted in August. In the case of Frances Burrel against Thomas Gould in 1826 the commissaries initially refused to grant a commission to examine witnesses regarding the marriage in London, but after she appealed on the grounds that they thereby made it impossible for her to receive justice, they relented, and the divorce went ahead.[27]

And that was all: up to 1830 no other English couples sought divorces in Scotland. Nor is there any reason to believe that they did so in any significant numbers in the decades that followed. During the debates that preceded the passing of the Matrimonial Causes Act of 1857, Caroline Norton pointed out the anomalies between the laws of the different parts of Britain: 'they are all the subjects of one

Queen; the English ladies whom no amount of ill-usage can divorce, and the Scotch ladies who can divorce so easily. Nay, *in the same family* different persons find themselves under different laws.' Mrs Norton was herself 'united to one member of a family in which there are five marriages; in two of which (being Scotch marriages), the right of divorce would be equal – while three (being English marriages) could only be dissolved in favour of the husband, and by Act of Parliament.'[28] The possibility of dissolving an English marriage in Scotland seems no longer to have been entertained as a possibility.

The reason must have been the awful warning of poor Lolly. If the main reason for divorcing was to remarry, and English law considered the second marriage as bigamous then it was a pointless exercise unless they were prepared to exile themselves to Scotland. Fergusson commented that prior to that decision Scottish couples who had married in England and divorced in Scotland remarried under English law with no ill consequences. And, in fact, Fergusson's comment was disingenuous, for after his Scottish divorce Lord Paget married Lady Charlotte Wellesley, 'first in Scotland, and then, after finding some difficulty in persuading an English clergyman to perform the ceremony, in England'.[29] This was a *cause celèbre* at the time, but no one brought it up when Lolly was so harshly treated. There was clearly one rule for the nobility, and another for everyone else, but after such a draconian decision by the English judges, few would have dared risk it again, and so the option was closed. English wives would have to wait until 1923 before they could obtain a divorce on the grounds of simple adultery on the part of their husbands, as Scottish women had been able to do since 1560.

·NOTES

All CC references are in the Scottish Record Office.
1. A wife in England could obtain a divorce only if she had grounds of incest or bigamy on top of adultery, and none succeeded before the nineteenth century. Allen Horstman, *Victorian Divorce* (London and Sydney 1985), 4.
2. Much of the material in this chapter previously appeared in 'English Marriages and Scottish Divorces in the Early Nineteenth Century', *Journal of Legal History*, vol.17, no.3 (Dec 1996), 225–43.
3. James Fergusson, *Reports of some Recent Decisions by The Consistorial Court of Scotland, in Actions of Divorce* (Edinburgh, 1817), 259–60. The process papers for this case do not appear to have survived; as the case was so frequently cited later, no doubt some lawyer borrowed and never returned them.
4. cc8/5/23. This case is mentioned in Fergusson, *Reports*, 260–2.
5. cc8/5/24.
6. cc8/5/25; Fergusson,*Reports*, 264–5. The paramour in this case was a son of a key figure of the Enlightenment, Principal William Robertson.
7. cc8/5/25; Fergusson, *Reports*, 262.
8. Fergusson, *Reports*, 264–5. Process papers do not appear to have survived for either of those cases.
9. cc8/5/31.

10. Marquis of Anglesey, *One-Leg – The Life and Letters of Henry William Paget 1768–1854* (London, 1961), 89–111.
11. cc8/5/31; Fergusson, Reports, 267–8.
12. Horstman, *Victorian Divorce*, 22–3; cc8/5/31; Fergusson, *Reports*, 23–67.
13. cc8/5/32.
14. Ibid.; Fergusson, *Reports*, 269.
15. cc8/5/32. Fergusson does not mention this case.
16. Ibid.; Fergusson, *Reports*, 269.
17. cc8/5/32; Fergusson, *Reports*, 272. In the extracted decreet the name is spelt 'Lolley', but I have adhered to the spelling used in all subsequent references to the case.
18. Lawrence Stone, *Road to Divorce – England 1530–1987* (Oxford 1992), 358–9.
19. cc8/5/33.
20. Ibid.
21. Ibid.
22. Fergusson, *Reports*, 374.
23. cc8/6/101; Fergusson, *Reports*, 277–362.
24. Fergusson, *Reports*, 68–225 (and appendices); cc8/5/36. The date of the summons in the case of Butler against Forbes was March 1814 and for Duntze against Levett October 1814. The divorces were not granted until March 1817, so it was a long haul.
25. cc8/5/36.
26. Fergusson, *Reports*, 231–6.
27. cc8/5/36; cc8/5/37; cc8/6/122; cc8/5/41; cc8/6/151. In January 1819 Elizabeth Ogilvy brought an action against John Maitland Esq, who was residing in Bath, but not only were both parties born in Scotland, he still owned an estate in Fife, so this case was not comparable. cc8/5/37.
28. Caroline Norton, *A Letter to the Queen on Lord Chancellor Cranworth's Marriage and Divorce Bill* (London 1855), 24. I am grateful to Caroline Jackson-Houlston for this reference.
29. Fergusson, *Reports*, 18–19; Anglesey, *One-Leg*, 110.

CHAPTER 12

DESERTION AND ADHERENCE

As noted at the start of this book, those who wished a divorce on the grounds of desertion had to go through a legal pantomime. First the pursuer had to bring a process of adherence; after obtaining that decreet, and the errant spouse not returning, he or she had to go to a civil court to have the spouse declared a rebel and 'put to the horn'; thereafter a petition would have to be presented to the presbytery asking that it excommunicate the deserter, a request that was expected to be formally refused. Only then could the action for divorce be raised. This final action was something of a formality, and such actions rarely produce much evidence about the marriage or reasons for deserting, as those issues were dealt with in the initial adherence case. So it is upon the adherence cases that this chapter will largely focus.

THE EARLY PERIOD

Some of the early cases are a puzzle. The first one in the registers is that of Thomas Symmers, flesher in Edinburgh, against Jean Boyd. They were married in 1684, and she deserted him two and a half years later; she refused his appeals to return and left Scotland. It is difficult to see what point his decreet for adherence in 1694 had, since he did not sue for divorce (it was a further sixty-two years before anyone with a decreet for adherence went on to sue for divorce). In the second case, in the same year, that of Elisabeth Heriot against Alexander Tennent, it was proven that he had deserted her eight years earlier. The commissaries awarded her an aliment, but Tennent was out of the kingdom, and it is not known whether she was able to get it from his estate.[1]

The third case reveals a more obvious motive. In 1693 Margaret Seaton, daughter of a skipper in Leith, went 'from Edinburgh to London about her merchandizeing affairs', and stayed with Edward Callendar, her uncle, a merchant there. In October she married his son, her cousin. They stayed in England for a while after that, then she 'upon her own credit provided herself of such Merchant goods as she used to trade with in Scotland', and they returned to Edinburgh where she bore his child. After eight months, 'he pretending business abroad', deserted her and went to

Holland. The problem was that as a married woman she could not longer carry on the business in her own right. Together with her uncle and aunt she travelled to Holland, where she begged her husband to grant her a 'factorie', 'or otherwayes that he would return home and manadge his own and her affairs himself, which he altogether refused to do'. Margaret had 'to return home to Scotland for preservation of her own Credit, her Trade and Commerce being all upon her own faith and Trust.' The decreet of adherence from the commissary court (in 1696) could not have had any force in Holland, but presumably in some way it enabled her to carry on trading without her husband.[2]

Some early adherence processes were brought by husbands to force wives whom they had maltreated to return to them. For example, Lady Jeane Keith, who married George, Lord Bamff, in 1669, left him in 1685 because of his abuse. She had brought an action before the Scottish Privy Council, proving that she 'Can not safely Nor honourably According to her Qualitie Cohabite with The said Lord Bamff And that she ought to have ane aliment of him', and was awarded that aliment. But in 1686 Lord Bamff argued in the Commissary Court that the Privy Council decreet was not relevant since it ordained an aliment only while she was forced to lived separately, and he now admitted being at fault and promised to behave better in future. As he was 'willing to cohabit with his Lady peaceablie' the commissaries granted him his decreet of adherence, though they ordered him to find caution for his future behaviour to her (the equivalent of being bound over to keep the peace).[3]

George, Duke of Gordon, was married to Elizabeth, daughter of the Duke of Norfolk, in 1676. She left him in 1694, and he brought an adherence suit against her in 1696. In reply she claimed that she 'hath all wayes bein loath to make any publict complaint of the evill treatment and hardship she hath receaved it being better to suffer her misfortoun silently, And tho few have ever been so calme and patient to Indure such Indignities and contempt' as she had received from him, 'yet she choised raither to withdraw than complain'. She continued to hope that someday her husband would 'receave her With that love and affection that is agreeable to their conjugall vowes . . . As the dutie of a Wife is weell known on the one hand that she ought to cohabit and adhere so it is not admitted to a husband to tyranize'. She alleged that he gave her almost no money and stinted her of clothing and necessities; she did not have the choice of her own servants, and those he appointed were encouraged to disregard her orders and treat her with insolence. After further allegations on both sides the commissaries found that her grounds were 'not relevant to justifie ane willful and contumacious separatione and divergence'. But by this time she had taken refuge in a convent in Flanders, and in 1707 she obtained a decreet of separation from the Privy Council.[4]

Even in this early period the commissaries did not *always* take the husband's part. In 1696 Mr Patrick Reid, preacher of the gospel, brought an adherence case against Elisabeth Ogilvie, whom he had married in 1687, alleging that when he left Edinburgh in July 1695 and took a house in the country she refused to come and live with him. But it was only after Elisabeth obtained a decreet for aliment from the Privy Council on the grounds of his maltreatment of her, that he brought the adherence case against her.[5] His lawyer argued that the Privy Council decreet was irrelevant as it was for aliment only, was not meant to separate them, and was not for all time, so that now that he had forgiven her and asked her to come back she should have to do so. The commissaries found that 'a Decreet of Aliment dureing separation does not take off the obligation to adhear', but allowed her to bring proof of his treatment of her. Her procurator said that 'his reall design and Intention, is not only to frustrat her of the benefite of the said Aliment, but to render her life most miserable for the future, by starving her quyte to death, besides his barbarous usage and maletreatment of her otherwayes, and so to make her gray hairs go down to the grave in sorrow.'

Amongst the things she offered to prove were his refusing to provide her with sufficient meal or money, his banishing her from the house without any just cause, and his 'most barbarous and unchristian speech, and contemptible expressions of her, viz, That he had no more satisfaction by her, than of ane stock or ane rock, or Cat or Dog'. Furthermore, all possible means had been taken by ministers of the Church, and others, to reconcile them, without success. Reid denied all this, though with regard to the alleged unchristian speech, he argued that if 'those expressions had been uttered, yet that cannot be sustained to be a ground of separation . . . [as] upon provocations many things may fall out betwixt man and wife, such as rash words, which immediately they repent.' However, after hearing Elisabeth's witnesses, the commissaries found 'the Pursuer's maletreatment, unsuitable and undecent deportment, and expressions towards the Defender proven, And particularly, That he did not allow the Defender ane competent aliment and Intertainment, nor to eat with himself whilst she remained in family with him, And that at last he thrust her out of his house and refused to receive her again, untill she obtained ane Decreet of Aliment befor the privy Councill'. They therefore absolved her, thereby effectively granting her a legal separation. In later periods, after the abolition of the Scottish Privy Council, husbands sometimes brought unsuccessful counter-processes for adherence against wives who had brought actions for separation against them.[6]

THE MIDDLE PERIOD

The first divorce action on the grounds of desertion was raised in 1756, but in 1769 Robert Innes's lawyer was seemingly not aware of the various steps that had to be followed, as his initial process was for divorce, not adherence. The commissaries dismissed the case for not following the procedures outlined by the Act of James VI, in particular he had 'neglected to insist for or to recover a decreet of adherence against the defender his wife which is a preliminary step required by the said act and the practice of this Court previous to the obtaining a divorce'. The following month

(January 1770) Innes raised an action for adherence. His wife, Margaret Watson, contested the case, claiming that she had 'emitted a declaration' stating that 'she was willing to adhere to her husband provided he would find caution to maintain her and her children or that she was willing to live with her children separately provided her husband gave her a certain allowance weekly to support them but on no other terms was she willing to adhere to him'. But Innes was able to prove that she wilfully deserted him, for in December 1768 he taken out a legal 'Instrument of Protest' against her, 'at which time she Expressly refused to return home without giving any reason for this her conduct'. The commissaries granted his decreet of adherence. Margaret appealed, claiming that he had only brought the action in order to get a divorce, but her appeal was rejected. Curiously, Innes does not appear to have initiated another divorce action; perhaps he had had enough of lawyers (and lawyers' fees) by then.[7]

The 1771 divorce case of Jean Chaplin against William Jamieson, barber, went through all the preliminary phases before hitting a snag at the very end in the form of a letter from the minister at Kinnell.[8] The minister had attested to the marriage several months earlier in expectation of this divorce action, but as it now appeared 'she has been married to another man prior to her seeking the divorce and that she was with child to that man of which she is now delivered', the minister judged it 'impracticable to let the Divorce out'. Jean's lawyer strongly objected to a third party interfering in this action and told her story: in 1761 Jamieson 'had the address to impose on the whole Town of Montrose by giving out that a large succession had opened to him by the death of a friend in the south Country and the better to Carry on this deceit he forged Letters from a man of business in Edinburgh informing that his service as heir to this imaginary friend had been expeded [sic] before the macer of the Court of Session and wishing him Joy of his large fortune.' As a result 'he got most extensive Credit from the merchants in Montrose for fine Cloaths and all at once became a very fine Gentleman in so much that he visited the best families in the Town of Montrose and was entertained there and in the neighbourhood upon the supposition that he was what he really pretended.'

During this time he courted Jean, and they were married, but a week or two after that 'Jamieson conscious of his Guilt and dreading a discovery thought proper to make his Elopement', and his wife 'heard that he had gone for England where he changed his name forged a Bill and had been tried and transported'. Thus was she 'rendered a laughing stock to the whole Country and reduced to a miserable and unhappy situation . . . and she was at last Obligded to retire to Arbroath where by her own Industry as a mantua maker she has ever since Earned a livelyhood.' About a year ago a man in Arbroath proposed marriage to her, and she agreed, but as there was no certainty of Jamieson's death it was judged proper to procure a divorce. She denied having remarried before the divorce, but her lawyer argued that this was in any case irrelevant. Even if Jamieson were to appear personally and offer to prove that Jean had been guilty of bigamy and adultery, 'this would not operate a relevant defence against the divorce upon the head of willfull desertion these two offences being separate and distinct from each other'.

The commissaries were not convinced, but the next thing that happened in this singular case was the discovery that the so-called 'minister's letter' was a forgery. The commissaries nevertheless insisted on her proving that the allegations in it were false; however, after an appeal to the Court of Session they were instructed to 'entirely disregard the Letter as a manifest forgery' and 'proceed in the usual form when there was no appearance for the Defender'. Jean was granted her divorce in June 1772.

The absurd procedure which required the pursuer to petition the presbytery to excommunicate the spouse who deserted, but which the presbytery was expected formally to refuse to do, caused problems in two cases. In 1772 David Reid, inspector general of his Majesty's Customs in Scotland, petitioned Edinburgh presbytery after obtaining a decreet of adherence against his wife, but instead of the standard refusal, the presbytery 'postponed and delayed to do the same under colour of entering into a process of enquiry or review of the merits of the Case'. Reid would not 'acquiesce in any such process' and raised his divorce action. The commissaries were not happy about this and demanded that he 'again require the presbytery to admonish the Defender to adhere and in case of obstinacy to excommunicate her In terms of Law'. His lawyers could not understand such a ruling

> unless the Court have adopted the notion of some of the Presbytery (for it is not the notion of all) that no regard is due by them to the Decreet of adherence of this Court nor to the law upon which it is founded nor to the Diligence of Law consequent upon such a Decreet, but that the Presbytery have a Jurisdiction of rehearing and rejudging the Case or in other words that they are not to act executively but Judicially.

Reid was granted his divorce in May 1773.[9] But the requirement for the formal presbytery refusal continued for all subsequent cases.

The other case in which this caused problems did not occur until fifty years had passed, but for the sake of coherence it is discussed here (by coincidence, in this case the *defender's* name was David Reid).[10] Agnes Nimmo, in Linlithgow parish, obtained a decreet of adherence in 1828. Reid had left her and the children, 'and went from place to place without a fixed residence, or taking up any other House of his own', never returning to her though she continued to live in the house where he had left her. About four years after he left she raised an action of adherence, though she took her time about following through the next steps in hopes that her action might have brought him to his senses. He did not return, so her only option was to 'rid herself of him altogether by following out the procedure she had taken, to the effect of obtaining a divorce on the head of wilful desertion, so that she might be able to do something for herself and her children, without any risk of the interference of him or of those to whom he might be indebted with her exertions for their support.'

She applied to the presbytery in the usual way, but Linlithgow presbytery 'not being accustomed to such applications,' instead of refusing the petition, 'as is customary', appointed the minister of Linlithgow to speak to Reid and report. Reid apparently expressed himself willing to receive Agnes back, claiming that she had always refused to return to him. The presbytery refused to proceed further, and when the case came before the commissaries it was dismissed, 'In respect it appears from the Extract Minutes of the Presbytery produced, that the Defender is willing to receive the Pursuer to live with him'. This was nonsense, as she had continued to live in the same house, 'the door of which *was always open for his reception*, while he was going from place to place *without any settled residence* whatever, *or any House* to which the Complainer could go to him'. The commissaries refused her petition to reconsider their decision, but after an appeal to the Court of Session she was granted her divorce, so the presbytery's unwarranted interference merely delayed things.

The above cases have been interesting primarily from a legal history viewpoint, but we can look at one final case in this middle period where there is more human interest. In 1786 Elizabeth Lockhart first raised an action of separation, not adherence, against her husband James Maltman, druggist in Edinburgh.[11] She declared that he had beaten her and finally thrown her out of the house. Maltman denied being married to her: she had been his servant, and one night, he said, she 'made such advances, that the defender was naturally led to familiarities, which he never would have thought of', and which resulted in the birth of a daughter. He continued to refuse to marry her, he declared, even after the birth of a second daughter, although she pretended to everyone that she was married to him. She made life so unpleasant for him, he said, that he agreed to live separately from her and to pay her two shillings a week.

Elizabeth's response was that they had lived happily enough together 'till his Incontinency with a servant maid who bore a child to him, proved the occasion of almost daily insults to the Pursuer both from her husband and her Servant'. She therefore 'resolved to make trial how she could live in a state of separation from her husband, upon the scanty allowance of two shillings per week of aliment, the Result of which trial has been that she can by no means support herself on so small an allowance, and as the terms were imposed on her by the severity of her Husbands temper she is not bound to abide by them.'

There was plenty of proof that they were married. For one thing, argued her lawyer, Maltman had described her 'throwing knives and Forks at him while at diet with him – The Pursuer believes there may be similar Quarrels in other Families, and some jocular folks would hold these Quarrels alone as sufficient and undoubted Evidence of Man and Wife'. But apart from his bedding with her, and procreating the children, there was also evidence in writing of his acknowledgment of her as his lawful wife when the children were baptised. The commissaries were convinced of the marriage, but at this point Elizabeth realised that as 'no person lived in the house with her husband and her while they were in Family together, it might be very difficult for her in these circumstances to bring such proof of the maltreatment as the law required', so she withdrew her action for separation and raised a new one for adherence.

Maltman's lawyer argued that 'a process of separation and aliment, and a process of adherence, at the instance of the same pursuer and against the same defender, is such an absurdity, and carries such a contradiction in the face of it, that it is believed the like has been seldom heard of'. This would have been true if adherence cases were raised to force the return of an absent spouse, but by this time it was normally either a prelude for divorce or a means of obtaining aliment from a husband who was living separately. In this instance 'the chief article of ill usage complained of being that she was turned out of the house by the Defender and no allowance made for her maintenance etc. she has been advised to bring this process of Adherence'. She was able to bring witnesses who heard Maltman order her out of the house, and who heard Elizabeth say 'that her leaving the defenders house was much against her Inclination'. The decreet for adherence was granted.[12]

THE LATER PERIOD

The adherence case of James Sturrock, weaver in Carseburn, Angus, against Elizabeth Crab was not contested, but in 1805, when he had completed all of the procedures and raised an action of divorce for desertion against her, she fought it, claiming that when the adherence case was raised 'she was not only ignorant of the meaning of the Summons served upon her, but was unable to raise money to pay any person to attend to her interest.'[13] She went on to allege that he had forced her to leave the house soon after the marriage, and that afterward he had no fixed residence where she could have returned to cohabit with him, until he 'formed an illicit connection' with another woman who bore his child, and it was because he wanted to marry that woman that he had initiated the divorce process. She was 'satisfied that the Commissaries will not incline to permit a Divorce like the present to go on, when it is evident that the sole purpose of bringing the action is to enable the pursuer to marry a woman with whom he has during his marriage with the Defender been guilty of adultery – a connection which the law has been very anxious to guard against'.

Sturrock's version of events was very different. When Elizabeth agreed to marry him in 1796 he had not realised that she had already 'formed a connection' with another young man. Nor was he told that on the very eve of the marriage she had declared that she could not bear to hear his, Sturrock's, name, 'and made an attempt to run off so as to avoid the intended marriage but she was forcibly detained from running away.' Sturrock soon discovered her feelings: 'Such was her dislike to him that she actually slept beside him with part of her apparel on her body.' Though he did everything in his power to please her, she left him just four months after the marriage, 'carried off the bed on which they slept,' damned him 'and said she would go with them to whom she liked better.'

Three years later he met her returning from church and asked her to join him: 'She passed him without returning any answer, but after being a little way off, she stopped and turned to him Damned or called him a bugar why did he speak to her'. He declared that he had always had a fixed residence, and as for his 'alleged connection with another', that matter was 'not before the Court, and if it be true could form no Defence nine years after the Defender had forsaken him and deserted his society, and poured on him every species of unmerited abuse.'

Elizabeth countered that Sturrock had known of her earlier attachment before the marriage, and the fact that she had married him should have satisfied him 'of her preference of him'. But the marriage had got off to a very bad start, and he had turned her out of the house four months later. Now he lived in open adultery, a 'fact well known to the whole neighbourhood', which made it impossible for her to adhere to him, though she still offered to return. Sturrock's lawyer argued that an offer to return was not admissible at this stage in the proceedings, otherwise she could come back to him for a few weeks only, then again desert him and thus 'lay him under the necessity of renovating the whole process after the lapse of other four years', and could do the same again and again. After further petitions, the commissaries allowed Sturrock to swear his oath of calumny and then 'Found the Defences however relevant in the process of adherence now incompetent after Decreet of Adherence has gone out.' As Sturrock had 'taken the steps required by the Act James Sixth' they granted the divorce.

The remainder of cases discussed in this section were contested adherence cases, and the issue was generally money. For example, in the 1806 case of Jean Shaw against Thomas Herd, servant to Lord Kellie, the couple had lived separately for fourteen years, and she 'having in vain applied to him for a proper and decent aliment he refuses to make her any allowance.'[14] He claimed, in defence, that he was perfectly happy to adhere to her, that with the help of his master he had had all their children educated, and that she was in a better financial condition than he was. If she wished him to adhere 'she must come to him. His services in the noble family who have so long entertained him cannot be dispensed with, and if he leaves that Service he knows not where to find another.' She replied that from his 'residence being in the house of his master and from his having no furniture house or home where to lodge his wife and family, that the willingness held out by him to adhere to and entertain his wife is altogether affected.'

But the commissaries demanded that she 'state her objections (if she any has) to the offer on the part of the Defender to cohabit with her . . . and her reasons for such objections', and she replied that her summons was originally meant to be for aliment only, and adherence was added by her lawyer, since because of her husband's 'former bad usage and behaviour to her' he knew that she 'never could consent to live again with him', so 'he in order to put a good face on his plea professed the utmost willingness to adhere to her and to entertain her as his wife if she would come to him'. If this was so, responded his procurator, then she should have raised an action for separation and aliment, and brought proof of maltreatment. This was a process for adherence, and the defender had 'declared his willingness to adhere, and for that purpose invited the pursuer to come to him and fulfil her duty as his wife. He cannot be bound to leave his service and go to her.' However, the commissaries found her entitled to an aliment of £5. 5s. a year until he cohabited with her again. He petitioned against this on the grounds that he could not leave his service to go to her, and it was a wife's duty to follow her husband. But the commissaries, 'In respect it was admitted by the Defender that he never had any suitable house or residence for the pursuer and their family to reside with him in', refused his petition.

The marriage of 18-year-old Margaret Rae and 50-year-old John Aitken in December 1813 was an obvious mismatch. Six months later Margaret went to her father's house to give them both time for reflection, but though she was pregnant at the time Aitken refused to have her back and instead sent her a draft contract of separation, granting her an aliment of £50 per annum. The marriage contract had stipulated £120 per annum plus £500 for furnishing a house, so in December 1814 she raised an action against him, demanding the aliment stipulated in the marriage contract if he refused to adhere to her.[15]

Aitken responded bitterly: 'from the day of his unhappy marriage with her untill the day of their separation her conduct was such as to disappoint entirely the expectations of domestic comfort in her society which he had formed . . . The misconduct was all on her side, and as such a kind as not to admit of even the supposition of her being again under the same roof with him.' When he had signed the marriage contract it was in expectation of domestic happiness, but his wife 'instead of contributing to his domestic comfort was to him the source of incessant misery The Contract of marriage therefore had no concern with the present state of things.'

Margaret's procurator called the defences 'preposterous and absurd'. She was his wife, was his equal in rank, and had borne his son. No proof had been offered of 'the violation of the domestic or conjugal duties', indeed there was no mention even of what those duties were which she had apparently disregarded. The lawyer also produced the following letter which Margaret had written to him:

From the very *commencement* of my most unfortunate marriage, Mr Aitken rendered his house extremely uncomfortable to me; – he found fault with everything I did complained of extravagance when every thing was done in the most *economical* manner. I had a number of most respectable acquaintances both in Edinburgh and Leith who were willing on my account to pay Mr Aitken every attention and who of course called upon me on my first going there and as was customary on such occasions to offer wine and ale; This was counted extravagance. I also received our friends in the dining room, the breakfast parlour being too small, and there being a fire in the two rooms was also much complained of . . . Mr Aitken had lived so long a batchelor and contracted so many peculiar habits, that he ought to have remained as he was, and not have come to destroy the peace of any young woman, and made so many promises which he never intended to fulfill. I was led to expect very different treatment from what I received. There never was any thing like his *narrowness.* He grumbled at every thing that was got into the house, even the very coals and many other things too trifling to mention. He gave me a book of house expences in which I marked down every *penny* I laid out but he did not approve of the way in which I kept it and therefore gave it to the servant a circumstance which very few women would have put up with. In short, I never did any thing that gave him the smallest satisfaction; he is a man that no person will *ever* please.

This all appears horribly convincing, though hardly calculated to further endear her to him, and indeed when the commissaries ordered him to state if he was willing to receive her back, he declared that the abuses which she had 'thrown out' against him in court would of themselves 'be almost sufficient cause for his refusing to permit her ever to enter his house again'.

He went on to describe her misconduct. She would strike him, spit at him, and 'apply to him the most opprobrious epithets'. She neglected household affairs, and furthermore 'her behaviour towards certain men different from her husband was such as to attract public attention, and excite scandal.' These 'particulars were mentioned merely because when a husband was obliged to inform a Court of Law that he could not receive his wife into his house he owed it both to himself and public decorum to give his reasons.' Her lawyer replied that the only relevant point in that 'extra-ordinary' paper was that he refused to receive her back as his wife. The commissaries awarded her the decreet of adherence, and after many objections by Aitken, granted her the aliment which she had asked for, in accordance with the provisions of the marriage contract.

A more traditional type of desertion appeared in the case of Margaret Scott against John Craig in 1819.[16] They were married in Tranent in 1804 and had one child when he enlisted with the Durham regiment of militia, 'and left her altogether unprovided for and to shift for herself and their child as she best could'. Eleven years later (eighteen months before bringing the action) she discovered by accident that 'he had settled in Business as a Baker in Auchtermuchty in Fifeshire'. She immediately went to him 'and insisted on her rights as his wife, but he refused to receive her into his house'. By engaging a lawyer she managed to get £20 out of him, but that was not enough to pay her debts, so she again applied to him, and he offered her £6 a year aliment. She considered this insufficient to his circumstances and her needs, and asked the court to award her £15 a year.

In his defences Craig first tried to blacken his wife's character by claiming that he had married her in a public house while he was drunk, and that his enlisting as a soldier was because she led an 'abandoned' life, and furthermore, six pounds a year was all he could afford. She disputed his version of events: they had known each other a long time before the marriage, which was 'deliberately agreed on and regularly gone about'. They cohabited for two years before he deserted her, 'and even when the Regiment was disbanded he did not return to Tranent but having drawn up with another woman he secretly went to Auchtermuchty in Fife and there commenced business as a Baker in which he has been very successful'. The commissaries granted her a decreet of adherence and awarded her £10 a year.

Margaret was lucky; there must have been thousands of men who failed to return to their wives after the war years but whose whereabouts were never discovered.

ALIMENT ONLY

In view of the manifest hypocrisy of bringing an adherence case against a spouse with whom one had no desire to cohabit, the obvious question is why, if the parties were already living separately and the wife merely wanted to force her husband to pay aliment, she could not bring a straightforward action for that purpose. Some did so before other courts, but had this been a successful option there would have been no need for the adherence cases described above. A handful of wives tried it before the Commissary Court, but the successes were mostly those with unusual circumstances.

For example, the case of Jean Aitken against James Sibbald in 1772 was actually brought by Jean's brother, John, surgeon in Edinburgh, on the grounds that Jean's mind was 'disordered', and her husband had neglected, maltreated and finally deserted her. When the action was raised it was believed that Sibbald had gone off to America, and after hearing all the evidence the commissaries found it proven that 'the pursuer tho in a most miserable situation and by her State of mind altogether incapable of providing for herself has been for a considerable time past neglected and abandoned by this defender her husband, and that he had now at last left the country without any intention so far as appears of returning to her.' And they awarded her an aliment. At this point Sibbald suddenly turned up, having gone no further than the north of England, and reclaimed his wife. The case dragged on until October 1775, by which time Sibbald had again deserted his wife – and left her pregnant – and the original decreet for aliment became final.[17]

Another unusual case was that of Grizel Donaldson against Dr Robert Blair of Merchiston, Regius Professor of Astronomy at Edinburgh University.[18] She alleged that for many years he 'treated her with the greatest disrespect and the most studied neglect, and to such a degree as to deprive her of all domestic comfort' until finally, in December 1821, he deserted her entirely, 'without making the smallest provision for her maintenance and support', so that since then she 'had been dependent on the kind benevolence of her Sister'. When the case came to court in spring 1822 Blair appeared, denying that he had deserted his wife 'or had the most distant intention of doing so'. He had gone to his property near Berwick to sort out his finances and to supervise farming operations, he said, 'and it was also necessary for him to go to the

North of England to take charge during the Christmas vacation, of his son who was boarded with a clergyman in the neighbourhood of Durham.' His wife had been left with unlimited credit, he alleged.

Grizel's lawyer denied that Blair gave his wife 'any credit whatever on leaving Edinburgh'. It 'seemed a strange reason to account for absence and total silence from Christmas to *Midsummer* to say that the defender went "to take charge of his son during the Christmas vacation."' And his 'farming operations were upon such a small scale that it was idle to pretend that they required his presence.' But even if either of those statements had been true, 'would they justify continued absence and total silence upon the part of the defender for five months and the inhumanity of leaving his wife during that period without the means of subsistence?' On his return in May he had removed his wife from their house and placed her in a miserable house with virtually no furniture; he 'had never once slept in the house, but slept it was believed at the Waterloo Hotel, although he saw Mrs Blair generally once a day He seldom however spoke to her, and he did not even treat her with ordinary respect or delicacy.' Nor had he given her any money.

At this point in the proceedings Blair's procurator was in difficulties because Blair had suddenly gone back to Berwickshire 'on urgent business', without leaving any instructions with his law agents. His lawyer still did his best, claiming that 'there were only two grounds on which the Pursuer was entitled to Aliment viz maltreatment or desertion'. The first was not alleged, and as for the second she was living in his house at this time. However, the fact was that he had again disappeared, without leaving her any money, and her procurator suggested that 'the conduct of the defender Doctor Blair had been so extraordinary capricious and unreasonable that . . . he ought to be called upon to undergo a judicial examination respecting the facts and circumstances of the case and his treatment of Mrs Blair.' The commissaries agreed, but as Blair never did appear, his wife was granted the aliment she had asked for.

Between those two dates was a straightforward but unsuccessful case of a wife who wanted money from her husband without having to pretend to want to live with him. Alexander McDougal, a Lieutenant in the Royal Navy, was married to Colvil Kennedy in 1814, but was called to join his ship a few weeks after that. Since his return she had often asked him to support her, but he refused, and in 1816 she raised a process against him. McDougal's lawyer argued that the process was incompetent, as it 'contains no conclusion but for aliment only.' McDougal stated that on the day he returned from sea he went to see his wife, who lived with her mother, 'but contrary to his expectation, he . . . was ordered to be gone' and told by his wife that she was determined 'to have nothing to do with him.' She admitted to the court that he had come to her mother's house on his return, 'but he behaved in such an unbecoming manner that the Pursuer was glad to get him out of the house.' The commissaries dismissed the action as incompetent.[19] In this instance, one's sympathies are with the husband.

The case of Ann Shaw against Lieutenant-Colonel Shaw, in 1823, suggests that an action for aliment might become more acceptable during the nineteenth century.[20] They married in India, where she was born, in 1808. After returning to Glasgow he deserted her and forcibly removed their two sons from her care. According to his defences, she had far more money settled on her than he did, and he claimed that when he left her ('because his life was rendered wretched in the extreme by her ungovernable temper') she was well provided for, having 'lying in the branch of the Bank of Scotland at Glasgow £560 sterling in her own name, and at her own credit, and disposal'. In spite of this she had 'dismantled' his house and sold the silver.

According to her lawyer, after Shaw left her penniless he laid an interdict on her money in the bank, so that she was reduced to 'selling some articles of plate which she had hitherto been accustomed to use as luxuries, to defray the absolute wants of the establishment'. Ah, but, said Blair's procurator, producing evidence to prove his point, she had sold the silver plate and gold coins on 9, 11, and 14 November 1822, yet the interdict was not in place in the bank until 3 December. Her lawyer responded with the true facts of a wife's situation at that time:

> What is it to the purpose when the Interdict was laid on? It is sufficiently clear that no Interdict was necessary to place the fund beyond the reach of the Respondent. The Respondent was a married woman and consequently the Fund tho' remitted in her name was just as much under the administration of her Husband, as any other part of the goods in communion, – No Bank would have paid the sum upon her sole order or indeed upon any order but that of her husband, particularly after he had left her society.

Even if the commissaries decided that her aliment should be limited to the interest of her own property, 'there must be a judgement finding her entitled to aliment, because without it, she has no means of appropriating to herself any part of the goods in communion'. The commissaries came to the same conclusion and granted a decreet for aliment.

After such a catalogue of unhappy marriages, one might well ask if in the later period a husband or wife ever raised an adherence suit not out of a desire for a divorce or aliment but because he or she genuinely wanted a spouse back. In general the answer is no, but the rare exception forms Case Study 13.

NOTES

All cc references are in the Scottish Record Office.
1. cc8/5/1.
2. Ibid.
3. cc8/6/2.
4. cc8/6/3. In spite of the commissaries' ruling, there is no decreet of adherence amongst the papers, but in any case some papers must have been lost, for the final documents are dated

May 1697, yet a legal commentator quotes a decision of June 1697 in which the commissaries found that as there had been no physical violence she had no right to a separate aliment on that ground, though as the Duke had committed adultery she was entitled to sue for aliment under that head, but that the Court of Session altered this judgment. James Fergusson, *Treatise on the Present State of the Consistorial Law in Scotland* (Edinburgh 1829), 190–1. The information about her retirement to a convent in Flanders and later separation comes from *The Scots Peerage*, vol.4, 550. As there are no process papers for any separation cases in the Commissary Court before 1714 I assume that this must have been obtained from the Privy Council in its last year of existence, though I am unable to confirm this as the index of Privy Council minutes does not extend to that date.

5. cc8/5/1.
6. Examples are Baillie vs Murray et contra, 1714, cc8/5/2, and Cairnagy vs Murray et contra, 1728, cc8/5/3.
7. cc8/6/26; cc8/5/12.
8. cc8/5/13.
9. Ibid.
10. cc8/6/164.
11. cc8/6/47.
12. cc8/6/48. There was further dispute over the amount of aliment Maltman should pay her, and a sum was never fixed.
13. cc8/5/29/1.
14. cc8/5/29/2.
15. cc8/5/34.
16. cc8/6/120.
17. cc8/5/14.
18. cc8/5/41.
19. cc8/6/109.
20. cc8/6/149.

MacGREGOR VS COLLIER –
THE ROMANTIC FOOLS

Spens Stuart Collier, the daughter of a barrack master in Glasgow, was only nineteen when she married Major Duncan MacGregor, a widower of forty, in December 1819. They went to the West Indies where, she alleged, he had 'a brain fever', since which time he had 'been constantly subject to fits of peevishness, jealousy, and occasionally frantic passion'. Back in Scotland, in October 1825 they were staying in Portobello, where they were joined by Margaret Collier, a sister of Spens's, and the couple quarrelled. According to Margaret the Major 'appeared to be discontented with every thing about him, with the place, with the table, and every thing else'. Spens 'begged of him to be more contented and to be satisfied and remain in one place, and she would be so too'. Margaret thought that they seemed 'very unhappy together'. In the course of their quarrels, the Major told Spens that if she was not happy where she was she should go back to her relatives; Margaret urged her sister to do so. And she did.

The Major brought his adherence suit against his wife a year after this, in November 1826. Spens's father appeared as a witness, declaring that he had tried to persuade his daughter to return to her husband, but 'she has always remained firm in refusing to return, and still persists'. Margaret told the story of the quarrel to the court and said that she and her other sisters agreed in thinking that Spens should not return to him. Up to this point the case had been uncontested. However, though Spens still refused to return to him, her lawyer argued that MacGregor was barred by his own conduct 'from insisting in a process, and obtaining a decree of adherence against the Defender, with a view to a divorce, at his instance.' This statement was founded on a series of letters written by the Major between December 1825 and the raising of the adherence action in November 1826.

In the first one he wrote: 'I was deceived, an unfortunate union cannot be dissolved in less than four years, unless by proven infidelity on either side, you must still continue to go by my name, longer than I am likely to live . . . I will candidly state that finding I could not otherwise forget you, I had resolved if our union could have been dissolved soon, to try and do so in the arms of *another* woman, and had really in view, *one* to whom I was much attached, ere I saw you, and though your good sisters cannot credit it, the attachment was returned. She is *almost* as *young* and fully as good looking as yourself, and I believe would never have deserted me either in prosperity or adversity, sickness or sorrow, but that is now hopeless, and in the grave alone can I forget how happy I was with you.' He went on to write that he had never intended to leave her destitute and had settled a sum of money on her.

Spens clearly sent a letter refusing even to see her husband again, for in February he wrote: 'To say, I do not feel grieved and disappointed, at your letter of yesterdays date, would be base hypocrisy – I do feel both in a very great degree – and every shadow of hope of our re-union being now vanished, and our unhappy marriage *virtually* dissolved, would it not be better for both parties that the same was completely so? . . . I feel assured in my own heart, that were you with me only 24 hours, all would be well, but that I find is hopeless . . . you are the victim of a *rash* step, for which *I was greatly* to blame, and you wish to preserve the appearance of *consistency* in adhering to it. I am sorry for your declining the *interview* I so much wished, and you yourself will yet feel equally so – it has completely marred my kindly intentions towards you, as you will ere long find'.

He still thought a divorce was the best solution and suggested colluding in one by means of yet another woman. 'All my failings through life have been from a too great fondness for bewitching women,' he wrote, 'which disposition was hereditary to me – I now deservedly suffer for it, but to *you*, I made a faithful husband, in thought, word, and deed, since the day we were united.' The suggestion of a divorce was clearly anathema to Captain Collier, Spens's father, for he refused to enter into any further correspondence with the Major, who wrote plaintively to Spens, 'when I proposed the scheme of a Divorce, I certainly thought it would be eagerly grasped at both by yourself and friends . . . Your Father labours under a mistake in imagining that I have any wish to marry again . . . The Lady alluded to by me . . . was to enable *you* to lay some foundation before the competent tribunal . . . for a Divorce – which, I really concluded *you* and your friends were particularly desirous of effecting . . . Your friends, and yourself, must be fully aware, that *mental agony* and the deepest distress, occasioned by your cruel and unwarrantable desertion of a husband, fond of you to distraction, occasioned my ever thinking of this *mode of relief*'.

He went on: 'That I sincerely and truly love you, is apparent to every one, and that I would sacrifice the world's wealth, had I it, to procure a reconciliation I solemnly assert . . . How happy we were always away from the influence of your friends, you will not I think deny, and your even often saying it was not your wish to settle very near them – O that I had gone with you far away this time two years, this would not have occurred'.

In March the Major did write to her father again, stating that rumours having reached him about his wife's conduct, 'no wise affecting her moral character, though otherwise sufficiently disreputable to a married woman', he was 'resolved to take that notice of it, instantly, which a high minded husband, feeling his honor ought to do.' In other words, he was proposing to take part in a duel. He continued: 'In case of an accident, which I certainly anticipate, and indeed now desire, there will be found a memorandum in the shape of a will . . . I wish my body to be taken out of the House at Tay-bridge, and carried by my own kinsmen, who I wish to be numerous, clad in the Highland garb, with pipes, and having all sprigs of fir in their bonnets. I know I am beloved, and numbers will attend – let them be regaled after the funeral, in the old true Highland fashion.'

There is no indication that the duel took place, and in his next letter he wrote to her that his feelings had changed: 'The contemptuous indifference with which you viewed yesterday morning my appearance on the Parade; to peril my life on your account, occasioned by your unbecoming levity of conduct . . . has produced this alteration of my sentiments – I have too long followed an unfeeling heartless woman, possessing, however, many valuable and agreeable qualities; and have been much to blame in considering so long your relations as *Principals*, in our separation, though some of them, I know, have acted a damnable part . . . I wish really to say nothing ill natured, for I am firmly persuaded, had you married a man you were much in love with, you would have made a better wife, than is to be found in thousands of women. You have made me miserable and I think yourself cannot on reflection feel happy – All my fame and prospects have been blasted, since our connection, but I acquit you of all blame.'

The Major then sailed to Canada, and in May he wrote to his wife from Montreal: 'Your curiosity, if no other motive, must be interested in knowing whether you are a *wife* or a *widow* . . . Our marriage has certainly turned out as unfortunate, as it was imprudent in the first instance, in justice to myself however, I must say, in the most solemn manner, that I had no more intention of asking you in marriage, on the ill fated day I walked with you in the Green, than I had of leaping into the Clyde; I knew well . . . the manifest imprudence of marrying a young woman, *greatly too young*, for me, who had not a shilling, my *asking* therefore, and your sudden *consenting* appears to me now like a dream . . . I do most truly sorrow for being the cause of unhappiness to you, though never intended, you will allow, and I would have felt it the more, were it not for the total want of feeling you uniformly displayed towards me, what I repeatedly heard of your flirtations, though I believe and hope, for your own sake, entirely innocent ones, and your expressing yourself in your last letter, to be *perfectly* happy and *comfortable*, these were your very expressions, that letter hurt me more, and did you more dis-service in my estimation than any thing you had previously done, because it was a calm deliberate insult – I can therefore have no great wish for a reconciliation, though I will never give your friends the advantage (which they would readily, I know, take) of saying, I shall not be at all times ready to receive you, while you have a right to be called my wife. Your return, unless God was graciously pleased to give us a *Bond of union*, I mean children, would always be accompanied with *doubt*, and even with *dread*, of what your *dislike* to me, and perhaps attachment to another, might induce you to attempt.'

Up to now we have no notion of how Spens herself was reacting to all this, since all we have heard of her has been filtered through her sister, lawyer and husband. But when the case was back in court the Major produced a letter she wrote to him in May

1827: 'I now throw myself on your Mercy, in full confidence that you will not betray me to any-one, I have long thought of doing it, but was afraid to venture to ask you for fear that you would refuse and expose me to my friends, for if they knew that I had given you the least hint that I wished to return to you, I would appear bad indeed in their eyes, as I almost promised not to do anything till I heard what the court said, but Oh! Major, if you only knew how miserable I have been about it for this some time back you would not refuse my request, ever since I received the letter you wrote to me from Strathardle, I wished to return'.

On a previous occasion 'you came all the way from St Andrews to carry me off because you got a letter advising you to do so, therefore I think and trust that when you get one from me asking and begging of you to do it again, that you will not refuse . . . what I now implore of you is, to come exactly as you did before only *by no means send any message* beforehand for that would spoil it all, if you will be at the door with the noddy a few minutes *after nine* as I think the window curtains will be down then, any night after you get this, I will always be on the look-out, and tell the person that comes to the door to say that *my old servant* wishes to *speak* to me . . . Now, Major, if you will do this and keep it a profound secret, I will _promise_ to do all that lies *in my power* to regain your good opinion, a friend told me when I was in Edinburgh that he was sure we would be very happy were we together again. Do not write to me or any person. I am sure you will come, I don't know when I may get this sent off, as I never go out alone. I will direct [it] to you at Edinburgh as I don't know where you may be, but where ever you are I am sure you will put off no time. Oh! MacGregor I fear that when my friends hear that I have consented to stay with you, that it will make a complete quarrel, which I am grieved to think of . . . If my poor father thought that I was capable of doing this, it would put him mad. Do not let the people who comes with you know that I ken anything about it.'

This letter reached him on the evening of the 24 May, 'and without losing an instant he set out on horseback travelling for 20 miles through the night to Perth, which he reached in time to meet the Glasgow Coach, and arrived in Glasgow a distance of 90 miles within 24 hours of the receipt of the letter.' In the meantime, however, Spens confessed to her sisters that she had written to her husband, and they convinced her to 'change her resolution,' so when he arrived at the gates of Glasgow barracks a second letter was put in his hands, in which she wrote: 'I no sooner sent off that rediculous and madlike letter, than I regretted having done so . . . as I am certain our living together again would be absolute misery, for we could never put confidence in each other'. MacGregor immediately 'sat down and wrote an affectionate letter to his wife urging her to break through the trammels in which she appeared to be involved and to fly to his arms for protection, promising in the most solemn manner to bury in eternal oblivion every cause of discord, and never more by word or deed to reflect on their late differences.'

'Evil counsel', he told the court, 'have unhappily overcome the unbiassed dictates of her own heart', and he had been told that she again refused to return to him. He believed that only a decreet of adherence from the commissaries would 'have the effect of recalling the Defender and her relations to a proper sense of their duty and interest'. He emphasised: '*The pursuer seeks adherence not divorce*, and should the Defender even at the eleventh hour return to her duty the Pursuer again promises in the most solemn manner to receive her with the utmost kindness and affection and to bury all past differences in utter oblivion'. The commissaries granted the decreet, and there is no subsequent divorce in the records, so one may assume that as they were so evidently well-suited to one another, their marriage was, if not happy, at any rate never boring.

cc8/6/154

CHAPTER 13

NULLITY

Before the Reformation (and after it in countries which remained Catholic), an action for annulment – usually on the spurious grounds of some kind of distant incestuous connection – was the best hope of getting out of an unhappy marriage, but in our period it was a rarity, producing only twenty-eight cases, of which ten were unsuccessful. However, those cases – some of which were brought by third parties concerned with inheritance – provide insights into untenable marriages not available elsewhere. A curious aspect of Scottish legal practice is that the pursuer could ask either for a simple decreet of nullity, which stated that the marriage had never legally existed, or he or she could add to that a decreet of divorce.[1] The logic of a divorce from a spouse to whom one was never legally married is nowhere explained. The main grounds for an action of nullity of marriage were impotence, bigamy, and the 'forbidden degrees', but we shall also see others.

IMPOTENCE

There was a cluster of cases in the early years of our period. The first one, Mareen Miller in Cardross parish, against John Reid, was in 1690.[2] The couple had been married for sixteen years, and he had always been impotent; one can only assume that the action was brought because Mareen had met another man whom she hoped to marry. The commissaries were ready to pronounce judgment very quickly, but as processes of this kind occurred so seldom, Reid's lawyer asked them to inspect their past records and adopt 'the ancient forme of proceeding in like Cases'. This seems an odd request, but the commissaries duly examined the records and established the form. The pursuer had to swear the oath of calumny, 'that she has just reason to pursue the proces, not out of levity, collusion or particular design to be freed of this particular husband, but really upon the grounds mentioned in the Lybell'.

Mareen declared that she had been about sixteen years of age when they married and that she cohabited and bedded with her husband for some considerable time, but 'he never had carnal dealing with her, nor was never in an posture for it to her knowledge, nor was he ever betwixt her leggs, nor had any erection or standing in his privy members', so that finally she left him and went back to her father's house. She added that 'dureing her abode and bedding with him she did frequently kiss and imbrace him and did all that in modesty she could to allure him to the dutie of ane husband but in vain'. Reid testified that 'his wife was sufficiently observeing and affectionat to him, frequently kissed and imbraced him And did never hinder him to put his hands to any part of her body that might allure him.' Before his marriage 'he thought he had been capable for a woman as another man, But that neither since or before he had ever carnal dealing with the pursuer or any other woman And that finding he was unfitt for the duties of marriage, he was willing and desireous that his wife should go home to her father and leave him'. Witnesses declared that he was reputed to be incapable, and the commissaries granted Mareen her freedom.

The next decreet was granted three years later, in June 1693, to a higher-ranking couple, Sophia Drummond, daughter of Sir William Drummond of Hathornden, and John Murray of Cringlety.[3] In this case too the couple had been married for a long time (fifteen years) before the action was brought. It was stated that he had had always been impotent, was aged about forty but 'has no beard, and the hair about the genitals is thin and downy, his voice is shrill like a woman's or rather ane Eunuch's.' Also, 'In his scrotum he has somewhat like stones which is flat, soft as Wool, and insensible of pain and without any kernel whereby he never has nor can have erectio penis, and so is incapable of coition.' He had acknowledged his 'infirmity' and declared that had he been aware of it he would never have married, and that as he was incapable of begetting children, if his wife bore any they would not be his and should not succeed to the estate. Murray was cited in order to have an inspection carried out; his understandable failure to appear was taken to be a confession, and after the testimony of doctors was heard the commissaries found it proven that he 'has no testicles but that his Ball cod is soft as wool', and declared the marriage null and void.

The next two decreets were both granted in November 1693, and both were to Gaelic-speaking couples in Argyll, one in Glencoe parish, the other in Lochgoilhead. This must surely be more than coincidence, but just how it came about there is no way of knowing. The case of Janet Mcmaluack against Archbald Mcglashan contains some quite extraordinary evidence. Not long after the marriage in 1686 he left her 'upon the account of a Report spread abroad in the Country, That ane or other of them were impotent'. Their relatives therefore decided to make a 'Tryall'. They put them in bed together and stationed a relative at either end. Mcglashan lay on top of her

> And after his making some faint simulat motions, the Complainer was by the said two friends inquired if or not the Defender was any wayes virill or active, or had any erection or ejaculation by these pretended faint motions, whereunto the Complainer Answered, that he was neither virill, potent or active, and had no ejaculation nor erection at all, yea not so much virility or strength as to enter the secret of her body, Which being then by the Defender faintly tho

impudently denied, the freinds forsaid for a further tryall of the matter, put down their hands betwixt their two bodies, by which they fand that what the Complainer had formerly declared, was manifestly true of the Defender, And further fand he had no erection nor appearance thereof Which being by the saids freinds so clearly found and discovered, and publickly Declared by them in presence of diverse famous witnesses then present the Defender rose from his Bed and having put on his Cloaths withdrew himself from the Complainer, and ever since has had no society or Converse with her, knowing himself not capable thereof.

Mcglashan declared in court that he had tried to have carnal dealing with his wife but never achieved an erection; he had never known any woman either before or since the marriage. Acknowledging his 'infirmity', he 'earnestly desired to be freed from the Bonds of marriage betwixt him and the Pursuer, and Deponed there was no Collusion betwixt the Pursuer and him for that effect.'[4]

In the other Argyll case, Janet Nickalm alias McGillairint against Patrick McGlass, 'he being visited and his secret parts being handled by his honest neighbours known to have skill in such matters, they found him nowayes qualified to perform that duty which a husband ought to do to his married wife'. Janet was asked by the court 'if she did use any charm to make the Defender unable', and 'deponed negative'. She declared that he 'never had Carnal dealing with her in any sort', though on their wedding night, and for many weeks after it she

gave him all the incouragement and Invitation to do the samen, by kissing and clapping, Imbraceing, and all other the like inducements, and by prostrating herself upon her back, and having her leggs spread, and Imbraceing him in her arms . . . notwithstanding of all the forsaids Inducements & provocations used by the Deponent to the Defender to Incite him to have had Carnal Copulation with her, yet he never did so much as to feell or take her by the Navell or privie members.[5]

Perhaps the most interesting aspect of this evidence is the light it shines on the acceptable, and indeed expected, behaviour of a married woman in bed.

The final decreet in this cluster, in 1696, was also granted to a Highlander, Isobel Mcintosh in Moy parish, Inverness-shire, against Angus Mcbean, soldier in Inverlochy. Apparently he had never been successful in having carnal knowledge of any woman and was forced into the marriage by his father who was upset about the scandal of his only son's impotence. Afterwards he informed his father that he could not consummate the marriage, left his wife and enlisted as a soldier. The commissaries found it proven that the defender 'hath no instrumentum virilie, but ane soft stock like ane wrat, so altogether Inhabile for coition or generation'.[6]

After that it was over a century before another nullity action on the grounds of impotence was brought, and it failed. In July 1813 Elizabeth Paterson alleged that John Cumming, foreman to manufacturers in Glasgow, whom she had married the previous month, was impotent.[7] His response was that her complaint amounted only to this: 'that in the space of *two* nights he did not use the privileges of a husband.' On the day of the marriage, 'as was usual with those in the station of life of the Pursuer and Defender a great deal of liquor was consumed, and the Defender not being accustomed to such liberal potations was put to bed very much intoxicated', and fell asleep immediately. The following night she said she was unwell and turned her back on him and asked him to leave her alone, which of course he did. She 'continued or pretended to continue indisposed for several days and then communicated to him she had changed her mind and was not disposed to live with him.' They agreed on a voluntary separation, but Elizabeth did not think this sufficient and raised the action for nullity, which he objected to because her allegation 'was altogether untrue . . . he was as perfect in the parts referred to as other men'. He added that 'he was most ready and willing to submit to any inspection the Commissaries might think it proper to order to satisfy of his ability to perform a husbands duty where the Pursuer alleged he was deficient'. The commissaries, 'In respect that actions to annul marriages solemnly and regularly entered into ought not to be instituted or entertained upon slight grounds and in respect it appeared that the Pursuer had instituted this action with a great deal too much precipitation assoilzied the Defender'. She petitioned against the decision, asking that a medical inspection be carried out on him.

What was actually going on here? Cumming told his tale. He was forty, and as a bachelor, 'like others in his situation he had for many years been in the habit of dining at an ordinary where the expence was moderate'. The pursuer, as Mrs Veitch, kept one of those houses. She was between fifty and sixty years of age, twice married and widowed, with seven children. Several years earlier she had begun sending him occasional notes, 'expressing affection for him in the strongest terms'. Once she sent for him to her room and treated him 'with some desultory conversation and gin. The same thing happened almost daily for a fortnight when she told him plainly either to quit the house entirely or to come to it altogether.' He did not respond; she asked him to meet her at a public house, where she insisted on paying for the drinks; the same thing happened again until she 'at last told him that it "*looked daft like*" to meet in that manner at night and desired him to come to her house regularly of an Evening and always to send for her'. They continued to meet regularly, and she 'pressed' him to marry her, which he declined, 'till one evening in Tradeston when having got a glass overmuch with the Pursuer he said "he would go on with it and marry her"'. ('As an additional inducement to do so the Pursuer represented herself as having Four hundred pounds at command and stock equal almost as much and in such circumstances as to be able to make both very comfortable.')

A marriage contract was drawn up, and the marriage took place. After the ceremony 'much mirth and jollity took place . . . and he was laid so low as to be unable to take off his clothes'. The next day she received a letter which he was not allowed to see, and after that 'there was a visible change in her behaviour'. She 'told him her conduct for entering into the marriage had been much censured by her family and friends and therefore she had made up her mind she "would never heat sheets with him as long as she lived" '. He tried to persuade her that this was absurd, 'but having failed to make any impression', he agreed to go back to his old lodgings, and subsequently signed a formal deed of separation. He was perfectly amenable to any physical inspection, as long as she paid the expenses. The commissaries refused, but after an appeal to the Court of Session a surgeon and a physician examined his genitals and reported. They 'found all the parts in a natural state there being no preternatural formation of any kind and . . . could not discover any physical impediment to copulation'. He was absolved, and she had to pay full expenses. Obviously this all arose out of her mortification when her grown children told her off for marrying a younger man with whom she was infatuated, but she must have convinced herself of his impotency (perhaps because he had not attempted any physical intimacy before the marriage) to take her case to the lengths she did.

The early cases had been brought during a period of great openness and frankness about sexuality. As discussed in the introduction to this book, (and revealed particularly in Case Study 5 when the Court of Session fined the litigants for their indelicate language), the rise of the cult of 'sensibility' in the course of the eighteenth century made such frankness increasingly unacceptable. This trend went even further in the period which followed. Patrick Fraser in the second edition (1876) of his treatise on marriage law commented that an action on the grounds of impotence had become very rare, though it had been 'common enough' both before and after the Reformation. He expressed repugnance and thought it should be abolished entirely.[8]

BIGAMY

By far the commonest ground for a nullity suit, totalling fourteen, half of all such suits, was the existence of a prior marriage. The first case was in 1696; the last in 1825. Second marriages subsisted for as short a time as a few days and as long a time as three years. As most individuals who married more than once did so irregularly, proof had to be brought that the first marriage was indeed valid, but few such cases were contested. While the majority of bigamists were men, women were perfectly capable of marrying more than once.

Such a woman was Jean Connelly, and the 1752 action against her was brought by Alexander Fraser of Culduthel, brother and heir to Malcolm, her deceased second husband – or was he her third? Jean was claiming a third of the estate on the grounds that she had married Captain Malcolm Fraser in 1744, and been accepted as his wife by 'the Gentlemen officers in the Regiment and others'. Alexander claimed that at the time she was already married to George Reynolds, who was not only still alive, but appeared in court to give convincing evidence.[9]

Reynolds described how ten days after the funeral of her first husband, John Petrie, in Asthoven, Germany, he courted Jean, the widow, for marriage. They had had to find a Protestant clergyman and were married in the presence of a soldier who spoke 'both high Dutch and French' and acted as interpreter. For the next three weeks they cohabited as husband and wife, and then his detachment was ordered to Flanders. Jean asked him to be allowed 'to come down by water', which he agreed to, 'and left her in the hospitall at Asthoven, where the deceased Captain Malcolm Fraser of Culduthill was then lying sick'. At Ghent George kept expecting his wife, when to his surprise a sergeant came 'and told him that he had bad news to tell, and the deponent saying that he hoped he had not disobliged his officers, he answered he had not, but what he had to tell him was, that his wife had gone along with Captain Fraser as his Miss to Bruges'. George managed to get a furlough to go there and enquire after her, and located the inn where they were staying. When he got there his wife heard his voice and 'fell aweeping'. The Captain's servant tried to stop George from forcing his way into the room, but he managed to do so and found them together. He

said to her My Dear why do you Cry, I never used you ill, and asked the Capt whether he keept her as a servant or a miss, to which he in passion, said, You Rascall how dare you enter my Room, what is that to you, how I keep her, whereupon the deponent got hold of her and dragged her down stairs and carried her to a publick house, where he took from her finger the Ring with which he wed her, That she told the deponent she had got by the Captain a venereal distemper, That the deponent said he wished she might keep it, for that he had done with her, and should have no more communication with her; and the deponent askt her for the Certificat of her marriage with him, which she took out of her pocket, showed it to the deponent and afterwards committed to the flames and burnt it.

After that George sometimes saw her with the Captain, 'but was afraid to speak to her, lest he should disoblige the officers of the Captains acquaintance'. About a year later he heard that they were married, and a short time after that he saw Jean in Bruges and she sent him a message to come and speak to her. He still had a soft spot for her, for when they met he 'said he would take her back again, but she said she was married to the Captain', and begged him 'not to come near her any more for fear of disobliging the Captain and hurting her Character'. George told her that 'she should always be welcome home to him', and she replied that if the Captain died she would come back to him! George asked her 'how could she with a safe conscience say that she was married to the Captain when she was the deponents spouse and her answer was that the whole world was a Cheat and that they were fools that had not a hand in it'.

Similar sentiments may have motivated the two women whose cases follow.

John Leechman, journeyman bookbinder in Edinburgh, was married to Isobel Mair in 1803. After cohabiting for some time in the south side of the city he wanted to find a house in the Cowgate, nearer to his work, at which point Isobel's mother 'advised him against doing so, and said that in the Cowgate, he might hear something that would not be agreeable to him'. She then informed him that his wife had previously been married to another man, John Hamil, 'but added that if he ever returned, means would be fallen upon to get him kept quiet'. Leechman was unwilling to remain married to another man's wife and raised an action for nullity; Isobel fought back. First she claimed that she had never been married to Hamil, then that Leechman, having heard about Hamil before the marriage, established that he was dead. Leechman totally denied this. The commissaries found the first marriage proven and declared the second one null and void.[10]

In November 1807 Robert Moncrieff, of Houton, Orkney, married Elizabeth Ray in Edinburgh; in January 1808 he discovered that 'she was the wife of another man named William Lyle or Leyle presently a Journeyman Boot and Shoemaker in London' and left her.[11] Elizabeth denied this, adding that she had informed Robert 'of the minutest circumstances connected with the history of her past life and the marriage was not gone about in a hasty or irregular form. On the Contrary an antenuptial Marriage Contract was prepared and executed and the marriage was solemnized in facie ecclesia'. She said that he had taken all her property and effects and then turned her out. Robert told a different story: he 'who is now pretty far advanced in years has lived during the greater part of his life upon a small property belonging to him in the parish of Orphir and County of Orkney. It will therefore readily be believed that he is little acquainted with the deceptions and intrigues that are carried on in the Metropolis of this Country.' While visiting Edinburgh he became acquainted with Elizabeth,

> who then kept a tipling house or ordinary in Leith Street – The Defender observing the pursuer to be a good natured simple Country man used every possible means to ingratiate herself into his favour. She was so successful that at last the pursuer consented to marry her. The Defender knowing that the pursuer was possessed of a small property then proposed that a Contract of marriage should be executed betwixt them. This was accordingly done, and in the event of the Defender surviving the pursuer she is secured in an annuity of fifty pounds Sterling and the pursuer obliges himself to grant heritable security for payment of the same.

After the marriage they went to Orkney, and soon after their arrival there he discovered that she

> was a woman of the most depraved manners and vicious habits. This naturally created in his mind a suspicion that owing to simplicity and credulity he had been grossly imposed upon when he consented to accept of the defender as his lawful wife – Conviction soon followed for in a very short time the pursuer by

means of a letter which he found in possession of the Defender dated in August 1807 discovered that at the time the Marriage ceremony was performed . . . she was really and truly the wife of William Lyle or Leyle.

It was not true that he had taken any money or property off her, 'On the contrary, the connection which sometime subsisted betwixt the parties cost the pursuer more money than he is willing should be known.' He proved his case, and the marriage was annulled in July 1811.

However, not all actions for nullity on the grounds of bigamy were successful. Richard Cockburn, wright in Edinburgh, raised his against Florence Munn three months after she raised one of adherence and aliment against him.[12] His defence against her action, and grounds for his against her, was that before marrying him she had been married to a man named Bamburgh or Bamborough, whose child she had borne. Florence said that seventeen years earlier she had borne a bastard child to Bamborough, and had taken his name for the sake of the child; since then Bamborough had married another woman in North Berwick and had a family there. Cockburn claimed that he only learned of the connection two days after their marriage, and when he taxed her with it 'she fairly owned, in the most amazonian stile, that she had lived with another man for years, and that he was still alive – but she added that they were never married, tho' she had born several Children to him.' He then made enquiries and discovered that she and Bamborough had cohabited for years and were acknowledged by everyone as husband and wife.

Cockburn was able to produce a number of witnesses, but though several of them had been told by Florence that Bamborough was her husband, none of them heard Bamborough acknowledge this, and indeed one of them declared that Bamborough had specifically denied being married to her. The session clerk of North Berwick told the court that about fifteen years earlier Bamborough married a woman named Burnet who still lived with him as his wife. Shortly after the marriage Florence had gone to North Berwick and claimed him as her husband. The minister, one or two elders, and the session clerk were sent for to Bamborough's house, and when they got there 'a good deal of altercation took place betwixt Bamborough and the defender in the course of which the defender more than once asserted that Bamborough was her lawful husband' – but 'Bamborough denied that the defender was his wife'. The Kirk accepted his version and sanctioned his marriage to Burnet, and Florence returned to Edinburgh without making any further claim on him. But in January 1801 the commissaries found that as she and Bamborough had 'cohabited together and lived at bed and board as Man and Wife Acknowledged each other as such and were habite and repute such by their Neighbours and Acquaintances', they had to be accounted married persons, and therefore Cockburn was entitled to a decreet nullifying the second marriage.

Florence appealed against the decision and proposed that Bamborough be adduced as a witness. Cockburn strongly objected: Bamborough would have to perjure himself by swearing that he was never married to Florence because if he did not he could be prosecuted for bigamy. The commissaries agreed that he was inadmissible as a witness. Florence appealed to the Court of Session, and in July the higher court found that there was 'no sufficient proof' of the prior marriage, so she was absolved, and was subsequently granted a decreet of adherence, forcing Cockburn to pay her a yearly aliment.

A final point to be considered about bigamy is whether a man or woman who was happy in a marriage and then discovered that their spouse had previously married someone else would necessarily have been keen to dissolve the marriage. Some might have felt so cheated that they felt impelled to do so, but it seems fair to assume that actions for nullity on the grounds of bigamy represent a fraction of bigamous marriages, and were generally raised because the pursuer wanted to get out of an unsatisfactory marriage for other reasons.

MISCELLANEOUS

Marriage within the 'forbidden degrees' probably formed the commonest grounds for annulment before the Reformation but virtually disappeared after it. (The affinity did not have to be by blood but could be brought about by an in-law relationship.) Only two successful cases contain any hint of such grounds, and both were unusual. John Ramsay in Ayrshire married Marion Campbell, who had been his servant for some years, in January 1798, but she refused to go to bed with him that night 'and cried much . . . and repeatedly wished that she had been a thousand miles off from the pursuer'. The next morning she confessed to John's mother that she was with child to his brother, William Ramsay. A few days later she went away with William, bore his child, and had been cohabiting with him in Dumfries ever since.[13] These facts were proven by witnesses, but the commissaries 'before signing any Judgement in so singular a case, ordained the pursuer to appear in Court and answer such Inter-rogatories as might appear pertinent to the issue'. He did so, and they found that

> altho the hands of the parties were joined by Mr William Crawford Minister of Straiton, and the forms of marriage gone through between the parties, still it appears that the Defender had no serious purpose of entering into a marriage with the pursuer, seeing that immediately after the ceremony was performed she declared that she would never be his wife, and that she could not in conscience be bedded with him, she being then pregnant by William Ramsay the pursuers own Brother with whom she had for sometime before maintained a criminal intercourse, and has since lived at bed and board Found That no legal marriage was contracted between the parties.

The decreet of nullity was granted in February 1803.

The other case was also an oddity, though it raised an interesting legal question. After David Kinninmount died, his brother, Alexander, carried on their haberdashery business with David's widow, Isabella Rodger. In 1819 they went to America together, where they were married 'by a Clergyman of the Church of England . . . not having stated to him the relationship in which they stood to each other'. They returned to Scotland in June 1820, were told that marriage to a brother's widow was illegal and invalid, and separated. The defences were put forward not on behalf of Isabella, but on behalf of their child, on the grounds that if the action succeeded he would 'be disowned by both his parents and only remembered as the offspring of a criminal and discreditable connection'.[14]

The main point argued was the validity of the marriage. In the first place, it was not clear if it was unlawful for a man to marry a dead brother's widow in New York, where the marriage had actually taken place. But even if it depended on Scottish law 'Your Lordships have next to consider, whether according to the view taken by modern Lawyers, it is unlawful for a man to marry the Widow of his deceased brother'. Leviticus gave a clear prohibition against adultery with a brother's wife, but that did not imply any intention to prohibit *marriage* between a man and the *widow* of his deceased brother: 'In itself there is nothing against nature in a man marrying his brothers Widow, on the Contrary your Lordships know that by the Jewish Law . . . he is even *enjoined* to do so as a duty . . . In Scotland the question has never been precisely fixed, it is believed by the decision of any Court, at least in modern times'. The pursuer's lawyer replied that the law of America was the same as the law of England, so the marriage would have been unlawful in New York as well, and that it was also invalid under Scottish law. The commissaries accepted this and declared the marriage null and void.

There was one other attempt on the grounds of some kind of incestuous connection. In 1793 James Dickson, butcher in Coldstream, brought an action of nullity against Catherine Heathers and her infant son. Six years earlier Catherine had married Robert Dickson, who was in his eighties, and who, before he died, aged ninety, procreated a child. James was the nephew and, setting aside the claims of the infant son, legal heir to Robert Dickson. Catherine was Robert's grand-niece, and therefore, claimed James, the marriage was invalid. But he failed to produce any witnesses, and she was absolved.[15]

Two nullity cases on the grounds of what we might term mental incapacity were naturally raised by third parties. The first, in 1747, was brought by John Blair of Borgue against Hugh Blair, his brother. Hugh had been deaf and dumb since birth and, according to John, also an idiot. Their mother and Archibald Mitchel, surgeon, attempted to arrange a marriage between him and Mitchel's daughter. The minister refused to authorise such a proclamation as he thought Hugh 'quite incapable of giving consent or of taking on marriage vows', but the parents went ahead with the 'pretended' marriage.[16]

Hugh appeared before the court, and after the commissaries' examination of him it is difficult to imagine that any evidence could have convinced them that he had much comprehension. When they asked him 'Have you got your dinner?', he answered, 'Hugh Blair', and gave the same answer when he was asked his age. When he was asked how many fingers he had, 'at first he made no answer, but his Fingers afterwards being pointed to, he compted the Fingers of each hand twice, without stopping. Being desired to hold up his right hand; he held up the left'. Finally,

> having set before him in writing as follows Answer the following question: what brought you to Edinburgh; in place of giving answer in writing when desired he transcribed verbatim the writing so set before him.

After hearing a great deal of evidence, in March 1748 the commissaries found 'it proven that the defender Hugh Blair, Is, and has been from his youth, a naturall Fool, and void of that degree of Reason and understanding which is necessary to the entering into the marriage contract', and therefore declared 'the pretended marriage betwixt him and Nicolas Mitchell to have been from the beginning and to be in all time coming void and null'. Nicholas, the bride, makes no appearance in this case.

In the 1806 case of Mrs Janet Stewart, spouse of Lieutenant Archibald McDonnell, against her brother, John Stewart of Lassintulich, and Margaret Menzies, the examination had taken place in an earlier legal action. In 1802 a petition had been presented to the Court of Session by John's closest relatives, 'stating that he was so much deranged in his mind as to be incapable of managing his own affairs, and praying that a proper person should be appointed Curator bonis to him, alongside with which petition there were produced Certificates of the said John Stewart's derangement of mind by two medical practitioners upon soul and conscience'. A curator was appointed, and John was put under the care of a surgeon, but in April 1805 'he was inveigled away from the House of the said William Menzies and taken to a place called Coshieville in the said shire of Perth, where, it is pretended, that a marriage was then celebrated between the said John Stewart and Margaret Menzies . . . in consequence of which pretended, clandestine and irregular marriage, the said Margaret Menzies has since assumed the name and styled herself the lawful Wife of the said John Stewart'. The pursuer and her husband initiated an enquiry by the sheriff of Perthshire as to 'whether the said John Stewart was *in compos mentis fatuous* and a natural idiot, so that there was reason to be afraid of his alienating his Estate and Effects moveable and immoveable', and it was found by a jury that since 1802 he had been 'incomposmentis to that degree, as to be incapable of managing his own affairs'. In view of this he was clearly 'utterly incapable of giving his consent to any Contract whatsoever, and more especially he was incapable of taking upon him the matrimonial vows and of giving the consent necessary to the solemn marriage Contract', and the commissaries pronounced the marriage null and void.[17]

One curious case does not really belong in any of the above categories, as it was brought primarily on the grounds of fraud – though in the end it appears that the pursuer was the more dishonest of the two. In 1782 Janet Jamieson, widow of the Reverend Mr Alexander Home, minister of the gospel, claimed that in 1779 Thomas Jaffras or Jaffray courted her at her father's house in Berwickshire, 'under an assumed Character of an opulent and wealthy Farmer and Tenant of the Three Farms of Norham muir or Mount Carmel, Norham and Crookham, all in the north of England paying Rent of some Hundred Pounds per annum'. He prevailed on her to go to Edinburgh with him where she married him, but on the marriage lines 'she observed that Jaffras had therein only designed himself in general terms Farmer of the Parish of Norham' and 'remonstrated that he should have been mentioned as Tenant of one or all of the three Farms'. When he refused, she 'began to entertain suspicions of his being an Imposter and therefore she declared her dissent from what had passed and refused to consummate the marriage'. She subsequently learned that he was 'only in the Station of a Labourer' ('he sometimes had been a Fisher as a Servant upon Tweed at other times works at Farm work thro' the Country in Summer and threshes Corns, and performs other servile work during the Winter about the Borders, sometimes in Scotland and sometimes in England'.) As he 'was guilty of a gross fraud and Imposition towards her And seeing that no Consummation or Carnal Intercourse followed upon the said Celebration of Marriage fraudulently brought about' she asserted that the marriage should be declared null.[18]

He responded that even if it were proven that 'he had assumed an improper designation it could have no effect in the present action, it being an established point that no circumstance such as this can void a marriage'. Nor could simple non-consummation, but in fact though the marriage was never publicly acknowledged, she had cohabited with him as his wife in Northumberland and elsewhere, while continuing to draw a pension as a minister's widow. When that fraud was discovered, the manager of the fund raised a process against her, which was why she was 'endeavouring to get free of the marriage altogether'. The commissaries absolved him. One cannot help feeling that they deserved each other.

NOTES

All CC references are in the Scottish Record Office.
1. Maurice Lothian, *The Law, Practice and Style Peculiar to the Consistorial Actions Transferred to the Court of Session* (Edinburgh 1830), 185. When I first began collecting divorce cases I included those for nullity which included a divorce, but as the grounds for nullity suits were entirely different from those for divorce, I subsequently removed them, so they do not form part of the divorce statistics cited in earlier chapters.
2. cc8/5/1.
3. Ibid.
4. Ibid.
5. Ibid.
6. Ibid.
7. cc8/5/34.

8. Patrick Fraser, *Treatise on the Law of Scotland as applicable to The Personal and Domestic Relations* (2nd edition, Edinburgh 1876), 81.
9. cc8/6/19. The case did not proceed to decreet.
10. cc8/6/81. When he realised that the case was being contested Leechman applied for the benefit of the poor's roll and was admitted. The summons was dated April 1806 and the final decreet (unextracted) April 1807.
11. cc8/5/31.
12. The adherence decreet is in cc8/5/26; the nullity absolvitor is in cc8/6/72 and 73.
13. cc8/5/27. The action was also brought in order to make certain that the bastard child was not considered his.
14. cc8/6/144.
15. cc8/6/60.
16. cc8/5/15.
17. cc8/6/54.
18. cc8/6/42.

CHAPTER 14

SEPARATION – PART 1: PATTERNS OF ABUSE

The first separation case was not raised before the Commissary Court until 1714, but, as we saw in Chapter 12, some abused women who had left their husbands appealed to the Privy Council for a separate aliment. One such action was that of Barbara Cockburn, Lady Saintmairtines, against James Dallas of Saintmairtines in 1704. Although most of the abuse took place in the bedroom where servants could not see what was happening, it culminated in his refusal to call a midwife while Barbara was in labour, and there was enough proof of that for the Lords of Privy Council to grant her a separate aliment.[1] A case like that one – and like some of the early adherence cases in Chapter 12 – reminds us that domestic violence has never been confined to the working classes.

In earlier chapters we witnessed many unhappy marriages, but moving from divorce to separation cases is to enter a different realm, with graphic descriptions of the brutality of husbands against their wives. There are various aspects of these cases worth exploring. In this chapter we begin by looking at different forms of abuse and some of the sources of conflict. In the next chapter we ask how wives could endure such awful treatment, and then at the means they used to escape and the help they received from others. In the third separation chapter we look at how men defended themselves in these cases, why some cases were dismissed or abandoned, and the implications of the financial settlements.

THE REPERTOIRE OF ABUSE

Domestic violence, in the eighteenth century as now, does not begin or end with beatings and punchings, though there are few cases in which those do not occur. A whole range of tactics exists by which husbands control or intimidate their wives, from verbal abuse and threats to starvation and incarceration. Rather than present snatches of evidence from many different cases, we will look in some detail at three cases from completely different periods, and then go on to look at some cases in which no physical abuse took place (unusual in this court, though no doubt closer to the norm in unhappy marriages).

The first is the 1741 case of Margaret Crawford against Samuel Forbes of Knapernie, brought less than three years after their marriage.[2] Her libel began with mental abuse: Forbes would be out drinking with 'debauched company in the neighbouring alehouses', and when he came home if she 'was waiting dinner for him, he would curse her for waiting, he had eat by himself before he had seen her, and he could eat alone when she was gone, and if she happened to had dined after waiting till five or six at night, he would say he saw nothing had been designed for him, and Damn, curse and sink her during the whole time any Meat was getting Ready for him.' When he got home at four or five in the morning and found her in bed he would 'after many horrid Imprecations against her for not Being up before he came either pull away all the cloaths or drag her out'. He had 'for hours together given her abusive language and scandalous names such as Damned Nesty futty Bitch and Cursed vile punny whore, and terrified her with most sinfull and horrid Imprecations, such as God eternally Curse her for a Damned whore and God everlastingly sink and confound her for a Cursed Bitch'. He had 'threatned to thrust the child in her Body out at her Broadside to throw her over a window to beat out her Brains and chased her from Room to Room with such threatnings'. And, as well as all this, 'he had frequently Beat her Barbarously and Cruelly to the evident prejudice of her health and imminent danger of her life'.

On one occasion Forbes kept up his curses and threats from eight until eleven at night, until she 'was like to drop down with fear and grief, her joints trembling and shaking'. The following night he refused to allow her into bed, 'but with curses and threats forced her, when almost her whole cloaths were off to fly out of the house after midnight, and to stand half naked in an open outter closs and Raining Winter Night for half an hour and upwards and until he having gone to his bed she went quietly in again to the house and sleept with her woman [servant]'.

Some months after that he attacked her so ferociously that her 'cloaths were all torn her face cut in three severall places near her eye, her head, Belly and Back all Bruised, and Black and blue, and one of her legs so wounded, that she bore the marks of it a considerable time thereafter, and had not the napkins which were upon her head preserved it, her Brains might had been dashed out and she was not able to rise the next day nor able to walk for a long time afterwards.' Forbes could not restrain himself even in the presence of a visitor, a young gentlewoman, Elizabeth White, who saw him striking his wife on the face 'till the Blood gushed out from her mouth or her nose . . . and ran down upon her cloaths'. Elizabeth tried to stop him and 'was so much surprized at what had passed she was quite Disordered and almost Confounded'. The minister in whose house they lodged testified that one night when Margaret took shelter in his flat she told him that 'she had not been above six weeks married to him, when she was maltreated by him, That he had continued frequently to maltreat her, and that she had hitherto Bore it, but could Bear it no longer'. Finally, she persuaded her husband 'to give her Horses to the Town of Fraserburgh (about six miles Distance) under pretence of paying a Visit there, and then got an opportunity to make her escape for the safety of her life'. Forbes contested the case, but Margaret was granted a separation.

Our second case was raised more than forty years later, in 1787, by Euphan Neilson against her husband John McCrobie, who kept a grocery store.[3] He cursed and swore at her, beat and bruised her, and 'bound her with ropes different times and confined her in a back room,' sometimes for two days at a time, 'without allowing her the smallest subsistence, and if he Condescended to visit her in that Condition his Solicitations were "Damn you, you bitch are you not dead yet".' He then threw her out of the house, raised an action of 'Lawburrows, That she might not give him more trouble', and had her apprehended and incarcerated in the Tolbooth. There she remained from 2 April to 25 May (1781) when she was liberated as a result of an application made by the Keeper of the Tolbooth, as she was pregnant and starving. When she was liberated she went home and begged her husband to 'have some Compassion upon her, and allow her some subsistence', but instead of doing so 'he knocked her down beat and bruised her in a shocking manner to the great effusion of her blood and she even appeared to be without life – When in this Condition he took her in his Arms and threw her to the open street, and sent for a party of the City Guard to Carry her to the Guard house, but when the soldiers came and saw her in the Condition she was in, they refused to interfere', and she 'would have been left to perish in the open street, had not the mob who gathered around her had pity upon her, and broken open the Door' of her husband's house, and made him take her in. Needless to say, her life was no happier after that, and McCrobie 'even fell upon means to get the Complainer confined in Bedlam as being mad, where she remained for near three months when she was liberated upon the report of Mr Alexander Wood Surgeon and the Managers of the Charity work house, that she was sound in her mind'.

Witnesses bore out her tale. Richard Lock, who had been a turnkey at the Tolbooth, went several times to McCrobie asking him to give some sustenance to his wife, but 'he was always answered with harshness'. When Euphan applied to the keeper of the prison for subsistence, 'he answered her in these terms "Woman if you was confined for a crime you would be entitled to aliment but you have a husband and it is your duty to apply to him" . . . and if the prisoners who had very little to spare for themselves, had not given her some scraps to support her life she must have died for want'. A neighbour testified that she once found Euphan 'in her Sons bed and bound very straitly that she begged the deponent to loose her and the deponent then discovered that she had been bound about the hands and shoulders in so strait a Manner that her Wrists were cut with the Cords, that the deponent also perceived upon the face of the pursuer, Marks of recent Violence'. When this witness went into the house McCrobie 'desired her not to loose the pursuer for she was Mad, but the deponent saw not the least Marks of Madness about her'. On another occasion the same neighbour saw him striking his wife 'with such Violence that the blood gushed out of her Mouth and she turned Stupid and appeared to be much Damaged with the blow'. Another neighbour came into the shop at midday one Sunday to buy a pound of Cheese. She found the outer door standing a Jarr which she pushed open and having advanced into the shop she heard some groans issuing from an adjoining room and seemed to come from some person in great distress she then pushed open the door of the appartment within the shop and saw the defender lying above the pursuer and cramming a handkerchief or Towel into her Mouth, That the Deponent then took the defender by the Arm, saying 'John McCrobie I hope you are not going to Murder your Wife upon the Lords day' – Upon which he looked very stupid but said nothing and went into the Shop and weighed out the Cheese.

What the witness 'saw at this time had such an Impression upon her Mind that she had scarcely ability to go out of the shop'. The commissaries granted Euphan a separation in August 1787, though it was June 1788 before the financial settlement was agreed.[4]

The 1809 case of Janet MacIntyre against John Clark, butcher in Edinburgh, was just as horrific.[5] He once beat her so savagely that the neighbours, 'alarmed by her Cries of Murder', came into the house and 'found her in such a deplorable situation' that they sent for a doctor, 'and he having come and commenced administering to her relief the Pursuer oftener than once fainted while under his hands in consequence of loss of blood and the wounds and bruises she had received'. A few weeks after that Clark dragged her out of bed one night and took her to an asylum, 'where she was for a considerable time confined under pretence that she was insane altho' the pursuer was at the time in her perfect and sober senses'. After he relented and took her back he continued to beat her savagely, and shortly before the action was brought he tried to force her into a coach to take her to a private madhouse, when neighbours, alerted by her 'screams and the Cruel treatment she was receiving, interfered and rescued her'. At that point, when she 'saw that she behoved either to submit to confinement as an Insane person or to be deprived of existence she came to the resolution of throwing herself on the Charity of the world, rather than return to her husband's house', and was taken by neighbours to the house of a distant relation where she was sheltering when she raised her legal action.

Clark contested the case, doing his best to blacken her character, agreeing only that he did not want to live with her. Her procurator responded: 'These defences are exactly of the same nature as occur in every case of the kind. The Maltreated injured wife must be held up as the cause of the Husband's bad conduct, and for this purpose faults and vices imputed to her which never existed.' Clark had 'admitted he has so far lost all affection for her, that he cannot live and cherish her, as by his marriage vows he is bound to do, and has consented that your Lordships shall pronounce decree of Separation, so that no question remains, but the extent of the aliment the pursuer is entitled to, for that she is entitled to an aliment, is unquestionable.' The commissaries agreed.

Those cases all contain abuse so great that the woman's life clearly was in danger, and this is true of nearly all successful separation actions. However, at least three separations were granted where there was no physical abuse. The first of these was Mistress Grisell Baillie against Alexander Murray younger of Stenhope, in 1714, and forms Case Study 14. In the 1782 case of Jean Luke against Robert Crawford of Possill,[6] their marriage had become so intolerable by 1778 that they nominated relatives on either side to draw up a contract of separation, agreeing on an aliment to be paid to her, and for Crawford to have the custody of their two sons while she retained the custody of their daughter. After that Jean 'had the flattering prospect of enjoying in future a domestic quiet to which she had for some years preceding been a stranger'. But this peace did not last long, for when she 'wrote enquiring after the health of her two sons who remained with their father', she was advised that her husband 'would not permitt her to correspond with or shew the boys any such mark of her maternal respect. He further peremptorily refused to allow them the satisfaction of seeing her and to compleat the severity of his Treatment he not long afterwards threatned to force away her daughter to his own house and assume the sole custody of her himself.'

She could hardly believe he was serious but soon discovered that he intended to carry out his threats. 'In vain did friends represent to him that such proceedings was a Breach of Compact on his part and that the tendency of it was to embitter the only relish for life now left to the mother of his children He was inflexible', and wrote her a letter revoking the articles of separation.

Following this Crawford withheld her aliment, and raised two legal processes, one before the Court of Session for custody of their daughter and the other for adherence before the Commissary Court. She was puzzled by the latter since in his letter to her revoking the articles of separation he had expressly prohibited her from entering his house, but felt she had no option but to return to him. When she arrived at the house 'he said to her sternly "Madam this is your apartment where you are to eat and sleep you are not to enter any other room in my house nor to have any communication with any person in my family my daughter shall from hence furth be in my custody and under my sole direction and no person whatever shall visit here or see you under my rooff without my express permission".' Since then she had 'passed one solitary night after another in the aforesaid bedroom where she has been and still is in a manner imprisoned by her husband'. None of her relatives, not even her mother, had been allowed to see her; 'Her children have been discharged to visit or even speak to her And tho called home to perform all the duties becoming a dutiful wife to her husband she has been tyrannically debarred from the exercise of any one duty and from the enjoyment of any one privilege belonging to a wife'. Crawford raised typically character-blackening defences, but as he agreed to a separation, the commissaries did not consider it necessary to hear any proof of her libel, and the only point of contention after that was the amount of aliment payable.

Since Jean's life had not been in danger, the commissaries might not have granted her a separation if her husband had not agreed to it; as he had done so, this case did not set a precedent. However, the case of Catherine McClellan against John Fulton of Grangehill, in 1810 – which forms Case Study 15 – did set a precedent. After that date two wives raised separation actions without alleging physical abuse; in both cases they were accused of infidelity by their husbands; neither went all the way to a decreet.

In the case of Christian Cameron against John Macdonald Esquire, raised in 1820, her lawyer argued: 'It may be said indeed that verbal injuries have not the effect of immediately endangering life, but although this may be true, it is clear that the constant repetition of false accusations against a womans virtue, must, if she be truly innocent render her situation altogether intolerable and impair her health.' The case was messy for various reasons – the alleged infidelity had occurred in the West Indies some years earlier, she claimed that he had forced her to leave the house, which he denied, he claimed that she had come back to live with him after leaving him, which she claimed was for a short period only because one of the children was sick, etc. – and it dragged on until April 1823 when two witnesses were heard on her behalf, but there are no further documents after that.[7]

In the above case the motive seems to have been the wish to live separately and be paid an aliment. In the 1824 case of Louisa, Countess of Kintore, against the Right Honourable Anthony Adrian, Earl of Kintore, Lord Falconer of Haulkerton, the husband did not deny having dismissed his wife from the house and refusing to have her back, nor did he refuse to support her 'in a manner suitable to her rank status and dignity'.[8] They agreed that a separation was desirable but differed over 'whether the separation is to be awarded merely because their living together is impossible, and is felt to be so by both of them, or whether it is to be rested upon the specific ground of bad usage on the part of the Husband'. The Countess was using this court to air her grievances and clear her name.

The libel had alleged ill treatment, without specifying what this comprised, but merely stating that her husband had long been 'offering indignities calculated to render her condition at once discreditable and uncomfortable'. His lawyer had some fun with this: 'These words may mean anything; and it is extremely probable that they mean nothing. Some Ladies reckon their situations discreditable and uncomfortable if there be a Ball within a hundred miles which they are not permitted to attend; and some think that they are equally ill used, if they be obliged to discompose themselves by attending any Ball whatever'. She had never alleged any ill treatment before he demanded she leave the house, so this was alleged to be an attempt at character blackening. However, as we shall see later, he was not an easy man to live with.

This was a second marriage for the Earl, but he was still only thirty years of age. When the Countess was about to be delivered of her first child, he went to England ('on account of his health') but arranged for Dr James Hamilton to attend her. Instead, Dr Hamilton's nephew, Dr Alexander Hamilton, who was 'married but was a Young Man', did so, and it was this man whom the Earl claimed was her lover. 'The idea of a Lady of her rank degrading herself by a guilty intimacy with her Accoucheur, could not occur to any Husband,' he said, 'unless it were forced upon him by behaviour so imprudent as to be almost impossible But he did certainly see and hear enough to make him think that she was extremely indiscreet, and that the Doctor exercised a most improper influence over her'. After other incidents which roused the Earl's suspicions he intercepted a letter from the young doctor to his wife which, though very ambiguous in its wording, convinced him of her guilt, after which he immediately wrote to his brother-in-law, stating that he had discovered his wife's guilty secret and would no longer live with her. His reason for wishing a separation, rather than a divorce, he told the court, 'arose from tenderness' toward her.

As the case progressed, the Earl did some backtracking, saying that from the style and content of the letter he believed that his wife had been unfaithful: 'But admitting the inference to be hasty, no human being can entertain a doubt that the Letter at least affords irresistible evidence *of a most improper familiarity* having been established between the Correspondents'. Her lawyer said that his client had been turned out as an adulteress: 'If she is an Adulteress she was most properly turned to the Highway with contempt – If she is not an Adulteress, her Husband had no right to bar his gates against her, *as* an Adulteress. The important question was whether the adultery of a wife was to be taken for granted without legal evidence: 'Suspicion may justify coldness of behaviour or distance of Intercourse; But no suspicion can sanctify the actual charge of Adultery, and ejection from the door, *upon that footing*'.

Apart from the unproven charge of adultery, an example of one of the minor charges and rebuttals provides a flavour of the marriage. One evening while she was entertaining guests, she said, her husband 'on entering the Drawing Room, after dinner accused the Pursuer and her family as a set of "damned Methodists", with other offensive expressions, so as greatly to frighten and agitate the Pursuer'. She left the room in tears but was forced by her husband to return. He responded: 'When the Gentlemen returned to the Drawing Room after Dinner the Ladies were playing or singing horrid Italian Music; and they continued to torture their male Friends with that most tedious of all pastimes'. He had 'got fretted and recollects distinctly that he said something strong in order to put an end to that interminable squalling.' But, though he did not remember the particular words, he positively denied 'that they were worse than what hundreds of good Husbands utter and hundreds of happy Wives submit to, any day in the week. He has no doubt, tho' he does not positively remember the fact, that the Pursuer retired in tears, because she is of a violent and hysterical temperament, and she took occasion to weep and be fluttered at every trifle'.

The commissaries asked both parties for statements reviewing all the evidence, and in September 1824 had them in hand and were considering their decision. However, no decreet was issued; the couple were reconciled, remained married for another ten years, and produced three more children. Happily ever after? Not quite – Louisa divorced him in 1840, four years before his death.[9]

What those cases show is that wives (and their lawyers) now considered it worthwhile bringing separation suits to the Commissary Court where there was no physical abuse, and no life at risk. But both before, during and after this time, many wives were appallingly treated and did, indeed, fear for their lives. Why did their husbands behave in such brutal ways?

JEALOUSY

Jealousy was the basis of the first separation case in the Commissary Court registers – described as Case Study 14 – and it surfaced often enough after that. Within a year of marrying Mary Duncan in December 1722 John Harrower, shipmaster in Perth, was accusing her of planning to commit adultery with a neighbouring surgeon, and beating her on that account. On one occasion seeing her talking with a neighbour 'in a Civill Manner', he beat her 'upon the face to the Effusion of her blood'. One night a few months later he returned from London, and having gone to 'his wifes bed he arose therefrom and sayed that he would not lay in that bed any longer because it smelled of adultery'. When she 'modestly asked him why he sayed so without ground he arose and beat her . . . most severely calling her Damned whore threatned never to be satisfied till he was full of her blood and that he hoped to see her put out of the Town by the hands of the hangman'. Her action was raised in December 1727, and witnesses testified to brutal beatings. A servant often saw him do so, and said that 'he was constantly chyding her accuseing her of adultery and calling her whore and bitch'. The case was contested, but the separation was granted in April 1729.[10]

In a 1791 case Charles Calder had also begun beating his wife, Dorothea Proudfoot, and accusing her of infidelity, within a short time of their marriage in 1783. A doctor, James Latt, moved into the same tenement, and Calder went to see him, saying that 'he had now catched the damned Bitch' and told Dr Latt that his wife 'had got the venereal disease'. But when Dr Latt examined her 'he found she was labouring under the Fluor albus [thrush] a distemper commonly subsequent to the monthly period and quite different from the venereal distemper'. The doctor 'gave her the Medicines used for the Fluor albus only and which have no effect in curing the venereal distemper which entirely removed the Pursuers Complaint in a few days.'[11]

John Tully, in a case of 1827, was also convinced that his wife, Agnes Steel, was unfaithful, and believed this justified his treatment of her. They kept a lodging house, and in November 1826 'a Gentleman of the name of Pritchard, a Performer in the Theatre Royal', came to stay. It was with this man that he alleged she had been guilty; he also claimed that she was habitually drunk. Tully did 'not deny that he may have made use of words and epithets, which in ordinary circumstances, would have been viewed as harsh and unjustifiable, but when these were called forth by the repeated instances of intoxication, and the improper and indelicate intimacy which was exhibited betwixt the Pursuer and Pritchard, not only distressing to the Defender himself, but productive of the worst consequences to his Daughters, it is scarcely possible to think that his conduct could be even blameable.' Katharine Coutts, their 17-year-old servant, was a key witness. One night her mistress came into the kitchen 'in a state of terror and alarm', and Tully followed her and accused her of improper conduct with Pritchard, and of infecting him with venereal disease. Katharine, the witness, 'remonstrated' with Tully for making such an accusation, 'and said that she could not listen to it, whereupon he laid hold of the Deponent by the shoulders to put her out of the house'. Katharine 'was alarmed and screamed out,' and Agnes, her mistress, came to her assistance, so Tully attacked his wife instead, 'who in consequence of his violence fell upon her back on the stone floor'. The servant said that Agnes 'always conducted herself in a proper manner and as a wife ought to do,' and added of her own accord 'that she was particularly circumspect in her conduct in reference to Mr Pritchard'. The separation was granted.[12]

A more unusual case was that of Agnes Christison against John Strachan, a farmer in Aberdeenshire, which began in June 1819, three months after he had forcibly ejected her from the house.[13] At the time she gave birth to a second child, at Whitsunday 1818, he claimed to have 'the strongest possible reason to doubt her fidelity to his bed'. This was a rural area where kirk sessions were still investigating such matters, and the local session investigated the conduct of Agnes and one of the farm servants, James Angus. After the court found them guilty of 'scandalous behaviour' Strachan felt justified in evicting his wife, and he used the kirk session minutes as evidence. Agnes and James had denied 'even any indecent familiarity together', but the servants had other ideas. One said that 'he saw that James Angus and Agnes Christison had a notion of each other and liked each other to outward appearance; that he has seen them walking out together frequently alone.' Another 'thought they paid more attention to one another, than he had seen between an unmarried man and a married woman'. One saw them lying on a bed together but 'never saw any thing that he minds of but what might be called harmless diversion'. Believing that he went to her bed at night, the servants once put sand and another time pins outside her window to see if she was visited, but the results were inconclusive. The kirk session found no proof of adultery, and the charge of 'scandalous behaviour', as Agnes's lawyer pointed out, was 'a different and lesser species of offence cognisable only in the Church Judicatories and unknown in other Courts.'

Agnes's lawyer argued that Strachan had admitted 'the principal fact complained of', i.e. that he had thrown her out of the house and refused to have her back. He also argued that the defences 'establish that there is a manifest hatred existing in the Defenders breast against the Pursuer, proceeding from his Jealous disposition, which of itself would be sufficient ground for this action'. With the utmost irrelevance, Strachan alleged that his wife was inferior in rank to him, but her lawyer insisted that the marriage 'was equal in every thing excepting the difference of the age of the parties, and from that and the Jealous Disposition of the husband, and the habits of an old Bachellor have arisen the wifes Misfortunes'. She averred that she was 'completely innocent and unconscious of Crime or the Intention of Crime, though certainly rather inattentive to the rigid Decorum observable in the more polite and refined Classes of Society in this Country.'

The case subsequently deteriorated into a wrangle over whether her ejection from the house had really been by force, as well as over an incident the following day when she returned to the house and was forcibly prevented from taking her child. She accused him of eating in the kitchen with the servants instead of with her, of allowing her only one servant so that she had to do many of the household chores herself, and of keeping her short of meat and tea; he countered with accusations of extravagance. And so it went on. But in June 1822 the commissaries did find him guilty of abusing and maltreating her and granted the separation.

SOURCES OF CONFLICT

Disagreements over household rights and duties are actually far more common in commissary court separation cases than are displays of sexual jealousy. Roderick Phillips, looking at court cases during the French Revolution, wrote that husbands 'beat their wives on the slightest pretext . . . In one case the immediate cause of the assault was the wife's refusal to fry an egg'.[14] The point that Phillips misses is that this refusal was not merely a 'pretext' for violence; it challenged the husband's absolute authority over his wife. In such marriages a wife could do no right, since the husband manipulated every situation to her detriment.

Two separate issues are covered in this section. The first is when a trivial incident was perceived as challenging a husband's authority and sparked off a violent attack. The second comprises longer-term, or more major, conflicts.

In Chapter 7 we looked at the unhappy marriage and divorce in 1781 of Margaret Agnew, daughter of Sir Andrew Agnew of Lochnaw. Unfortunately, her choice of husbands was just as bad second time round. Within two months of her marriage to Peter Hendry (described as vintner or gardener in the Abbey of Holyroodhouse), he was beating and abusing her in a variety of ways.[15] He once 'pissed in the Complainers face', and 'another time threw a live Cat at the Complainers throat and which fastned on her breasts and hurt her much'. Jean Inglis had been their servant for only eight days, 'as the Disturbance of the family was so great that she could not stay'. She described an occasion when Hendry went to bed, very drunk, while Margaret stayed with Jean in the kitchen. Hendry twice called his wife to come to bed, to which she answered 'that she would come when she was ready'. This was perceived as challenging his authority, for after the second time he came downstairs and Jean 'saw him knock down the pursuer on a Chest in this Kitchen and tear the Cap off her head, and that he beat and bruised her arms and legs with the poker and tongs with which he gave her some several strokes that the pursuer could not be seen for some weeks as her Eyes were swelled and sunk in her head.' After that he dragged her upstairs and beat her some more.[16]

In the 1798 case of Janet Miller against David Hume, marble polisher in Leith, a neighbour testified that she knew Janet 'to be a peaceable good tempered Industrious woman and obliging to her neighbours when she has it in her power to be so', and that Hume was 'much given to drinking and when in that state is capable of any violence'. On one occasion when the neighbour heard Janet crying out murder she ran into their flat and found Hume 'very drunk, holding a table knife in his hand and threatening to murder his wife, alledging as his cause of offence against her that she did not please him in dressing his victuals nor give him diet which he wanted to have'. Similarly, in the 1804 case of Elizabeth Ann Harris against Andrew Ramsay, slater in Edinburgh, Ramsay came home unexpectedly one afternoon after the family had dined. Elizabeth prepared food for her husband 'as expeditiously as possible' but during the time of dinner he appeared to be in very bad humour, and gave her 'a great deal of abuse'. She made the mistake of saying, 'mildly', that 'it was very hard to be so used when she was doing everything in her power to please him, no sooner had she uttered this' than he 'threw the knife which he had in his hand at her, and thereafter got up,' seized her 'by the throat, and furiously knocked her head repeatedly against the wall, gave her some strokes with his fist and then with all his strength dashed her upon the floor'.[17]

Even the sternest advocate of a husband's absolute authority over his wife, and a wife's duty to anticipate a husband's every wish, would admit that such violent responses to trivial challenges to that authority were unacceptable. The cases which follow are different, for they concern allegedly serious grievances.

This was the story told by Thomas Bell of Land in Annandale after his wife, Jean Irvine, raised a separation action against him in 1743:[18] four years earlier, when he was a boy of sixteen, Jean, aged 'towards 30', and her brother persuaded him to leave school and go with them to Carlisle, without the knowledge or consent of his father, telling him they were going there 'to consult the wise man about some cloaths that had been stolen from them', but when they got there they sent for an attorney to draw up a special marriage licence.[19] Bell had had 'no notion at that stage of Life of Marriage' and was shocked 'upon the bare mentioning of it'. But they got him very drunk and eventually found a clergyman who joined them 'together into what now appears a very unhappy Wedlock . . . The Lords Commissaries cannot be much surpris'd if after this the said Thomas Bell being admonish'd by his Friends, and having time to cool, was not extremely fond of a wife who . . . in point of age might have been his Mother, and who had drawn him in to the Marriage by the Means above represented'. In fact, he tried to leave her a few days later, but she brought an action of declarator of marriage and was able to prove the marriage a valid one.

Jean claimed that she was in every way his 'Equal, was a Gentlewoman as good as he could pretend to be, and the marriage could be reckoned no Disparagement to him or any of his Friends', and furthermore 'he had Vow'd the greatest Passion and

Affection for her, and pretended to be greatly Enamoured with her Beauty (as indeed she was generally reckon'd handsome)'. Her lawyer insisted that the disparity of ages between them was only five or six years, but argued that in any case it was of no consequence 'whither the pursuer was Twenty five or thirty years of age, or whither the Defender was seventeen or eighteen at the time of their Marriage, surely the Defenders procurators don't intend to lay it doun as a general Position in our Law, That a Husband may thrash his Wife if she be half a dozen years older than him'.

Witnesses testified to great brutality on his part, and to great forbearance on hers. A visitor once heard him call his wife 'Damned bitch' and vow that he 'would neither Eat or Drink with her untill he was Revenged of her'. Jean must have greatly regretted enticing this young man into marriage. Presumably they came to a private agreement, for there is no decreet amongst the papers.

Another case where the husband felt cheated was that of Alison Darling against Robert Spence, raised in 1745, only nine months after the marriage.[20] His story was that 'haveing been bred from his Infancy a Sailor', and wanting to procure money for his old age, he volunteered to go on 'the Expedition to the South Seas under the Command of Commodore Anson'. On their return from the East Indies his ship was fortunate enough to capture a rich prize, but all he got out of it was a dividend of about £300 'for the Risques he run, hardships he suffered and services he performed in this long and hazardous Voyage, during which he not only resigned his Life frequently, But was so maimed in one of his hands as to render him almost altogether unfitt for prosecuteing his Vocation as a Mariner, the only Imployment he was bred to.' With his small stock he returned home 'with a Designe to carry on some small Trade . . . so as to afford him some quiet and Comfort in his old age.' It was suggested that after his wandering life marriage was 'the most proper step he could take', and Mrs Alison Darling was 'recommended as a very proper Match, being a Minister's Daughter, who had the Benefite of a virtuous and pious Education', and had an additional 'strong Alurement accompanying her To witt a well founded Claim for no Less a sum than £200 sterling.' So he 'after a very short acquaintance, made his addresses, was well received; and, in a few days, Marryed.'

According to their servant, the key witness, they got along reasonably well at first, which chimes in with Spence's story that though his wife almost immediately 'began to assume the port and air of ane Admiral's Lady rather than a poor Maimed Mariner's wife', with extravagant claims on his money, it was only after further investigation that he discovered that her supposed claim to £200 was 'a Mere Bubble', and that by the marriage contract he had pledged to her twice the amount he actually had, so that he foresaw utter ruin ahead. 'It is but naturall to believe' he claimed, 'That a marriage brought about and bottomed upon Such Tricks and Devises as this could not Subsist long without Grudges, Debates and Quarrells, and thus indeed it happened'. His attempts to curb her extravagance led to their first 'misunderstand-ing', he said, adding that he did not 'intend to Justifie intirely the way in which he endeavoured to correct or amend his wife', nor 'Descend into a particular account of her Disloyall or disrespectfull Behaviour to him.'

Spence may well have been cheated, but here are some examples of how he tried to 'correct or amend his wife': on one occasion Spence beat his wife 'upon the back with his fist', and she 'parted with Child [miscarried] next day'. He threatened to burn her eyes out and then 'kicked her with his feet, and he did beat her so severely with his fist upon her nose and mouth so that the blood gushed out, a great quantity of blood at the nose, and the deponent likeways observed her mouth both bruised and blooding And that the skin of her face was likeways hurt and blooding'. Eventually the servant called a neighbour who pulled him off her, and the servant 'Called the Guaird, who came and seized upon the Defender, whom they carried to the Guaird'. At least in this instance the forces of law and order did intervene in domestic violence. His wife was granted a separation and small aliment.

Case Study 16 relates another story of a man justifying his behaviour on the grounds that he was cheated in the marriage contract, but for now we will turn to men who felt undermined because their wives actually supported the family.

USELESS MEN

In the final quarter of the eighteenth century, there was a rise in living standards, which has been attributed less to the expansion of wage rates and employment opportunities for males than for their expansion for women and children.[21] It was at that time that women breadwinners are first recorded in the commissary court. The association between male unemployment and violence towards their wives is well documented for modern times.[22] A major difference is that modern employment is external to the home, and that unemployment often stems from external economic forces. By contrast, the men described in the separation cases were (nominally) employed in and around the home, and their situation directly reflected their own qualities and abilities.[23] These men were not just useless but positively harmful to their wives' industry.

In January 1776 Isobella Hutchison, wife of Alexander Johnston, declared that during the whole of her marriage she

> wrought her own industry, and without any assistance from the said Alexander Johnston her husband, hath not only supported and maintained the family, and even allowed her husband one shilling per diem of pocket money, but acquired as much money as has enabled her to erect a tenement of land in Nicolson Street, of upwards of eighteen pounds sterling of yearly rent, and to furnish the same with valuable furniture part of which subject she lett out furnished.

Johnstone, meanwhile, 'lived an idle and profligate life never working at his business and presently squandering away the money and effects the complainer had acquired'.

Instead of being grateful, or even kind to her, he treated her so badly that she fled from him. Friends and relatives tried to bring about a reconciliation, and they met in a change house, where in the presence of witnesses he 'without any Cause broke out in a rage, Cursed and Swore and acted the part of a Madman Seized the Complainer by the hair of the head, and dragged her up and down the room, kicked beat and abused her to the great effusion of her blood and contusion of her body which rendered her incapable of removing from that house for some days during which time her life was in imminent danger'.[24]

Three years later, in August 1779, Jean Purves raised an action against John Tuck in Coldingham. They had seven children, and he was 'an indolent man and never followed any particular business for the support of his wife and family'. Jean

who had been bred up to an active life by her parents upon marrying the said John Tuck applied herself to merchandizing, making of Meal, attending fairs and markets with Goods and other honest shifts, whereby she has not only ever since her marriage supported the family genteelly, but has even acquired upwards of Nine hundred pounds sterling solely by her own industry without any aid directly or indirectly from the said John Tuck her husband.

She thought he might have been appreciative of her efforts, but instead he would beat, curse, and threaten her, and had been 'vaunting to his Intimates how he had beat and abused her and intended to continue the same usage in future'. Tuck contested the case but died before it was concluded.[25]

In 1788 Mary Callender did not mention in her libel that she was the family breadwinner but described in detail the vicious attacks by her husband, Alexander Anderson, in Edinburgh. It was left to a witness to comment (after confirming Anderson's violence against his wife) that Mary 'sold ale porter and spirits for the support of her family and the deponent has seen people who would not come to the house on account of the mobs and disturbances raised by the defender'. In the case of Dorothea Proudfoot against Charles Calder in 1791, noted earlier in this chapter because of his mistaken belief that she had venereal disease, Calder was described as a 'vintner', but he played little part in running the public house. Indeed, while Dorothea and her sister 'managed the business of the house and settled accompts', Anderson was 'incapable of this by reason of his being frequently Intoxicated'.[26]

The need for a legally binding decreet for separation is illustrated by the 1822 case of Jean Taylor against Walter Finlay in Glasgow.[27] They were married in 1806 and had three children, of whom two survived. He treated her badly, and then in 1808 deserted her and went to England. Jean 'with the assistance of her friends conducted a shop in which she retailed goods and by the profits arising from the sales not only maintained herself and her children but got into circumstances comparatively comfortable'. In September 1814 Finlay turned up and stayed for about three months before disappearing again for about two years. He then stayed with her until August 1820, beating, kicking and throwing furniture at her, so that she often had to flee and seek shelter with neighbours. His leaving her would have been a great relief except that he had contracted heavy debts, 'thereby ruining her in her pecuniary circumstances'. In October 1821 he was back again, and refused to leave, so that she 'being in danger of maltreatment and abuse similar to that which she had previously experienced at his hand and in danger even of her life and therefore afraid to dwell with him has left the house'. She emphasised that since the time of his first desertion he had never contributed anything to her support or the support of the children. Jean was granted her separation.

A final case in this section is that of Euphemia Vallance against George Jeffrey in 1828, where again the man was not just useless but ruinous to the wife's industry.[28] For the previous ten years their butcher's business in Edinburgh had been carried on entirely by Euphemia, supporting the whole family. Jeffery not only maltreated his wife, but was 'also in the frequent practice of insulting and abusing the Customers who come into the Shop, whereby the business is likely to be utterly destroyed'. On two occasions he got some money from her to spend on meat, but instead spent it on drink, came home 'and without the smallest provocation assaulted and struck the Complainer in the face and other parts of the body with his clenched fist, whereby she was unable to attend the Shop for at least a week.' Recently 'a Servant Girl came into the Shop and made some purchases'; Jeffrey 'called her a whore, and said she would get nothing out of his shop.' Euphemia 'endeavoured to pacify her husband, and explained to him that the Girl was a respectable Servant in the Neighbourhood and would pay for what she purchased.' Jeffrey then called his wife 'a bloody whore, an infernal whore, and lifted a knife which was lying on the Counter, and brandished it in his hand, saying that if she gave the Girl any meat he would render her incapable of ever again attending the Shop.' About a week later she was serving a gentleman customer called Lindsay, when 'her Husband pushed her aside, and called her a damned infernal whore'. On 'Mr Lindsay remonstrating with him on the impropriety of his conduct, he seized Mr Lindsay by the collar of the Coat and attempted to strike him'. On both occasions 'the neighbourhood was much disturbed'.

Their servant, Ann Erskine, confirmed that Euphemia supported the family, and that lately customers had stopped coming to the shop because of Jeffrey's behaviour and that Euphemia 'put up with a very great deal of bad usage and was always anxious to conceal it from Customers'. Euphemia did not ask for an aliment when she was granted her separation.

We have seen women who were in a financial situation to live separately from their husbands, and in the next chapter we look at some of the reasons why such women remained in abusive relationships for so long, and the various escape routes which they tried.

NOTES

All cc references are in the Scottish Record Office.

1. SRO.PC.2/28/ff.328–337. I am grateful to the late Peter Vasey for this reference.
2. cc8/5/7.
3. cc8/6/50.
4. The pursuer and several witnesses alleged that McCrobie was guilty of adultery, so this is one of those odd cases where the wife could have sued for divorce but chose to sue for separation. McCrobie made only a halfhearted defence to begin with, but when he realised that he was going to have to pay her a hefty aliment he fought back, trying to blacken her character, and claiming that the last two witnesses 'are Busy Bodies and Gossippers of the Pursuer's and that they in their Paths have misconstrued a great many Circumstances to the Petitioner's disadvantage which they ought not to have done.'
5. cc8/6/88.
6. cc8/5/18.
7. cc8/6/137. An odd light on her motives in leaving him is cast by a letter he produced as evidence. He had written it to her three days after she left him, asking her to return to her family, 'if you can do it without those strange scruples that induced you to quit them. It is surely an unnatural whim to abandon your most interesting five children in the most interesting time of their lives, merely on pretence to avoid the chance of adding any more to them.' Fear of pregnancy is not mentioned in any other case.
8. cc8/6/143.
9. *Scots Peerage*, vol.v, 252.
10. cc8/5/3.
11. cc8/5/20.
12. cc8/6/162.
13. cc8/6/131.
14. Roderick Phillips, 'Women and family breakdown in eighteenth-century France: Rouen 1780–1800', *Social History* (2, 1976), 209.
15. cc8/6/44. In her libel for the separation action in November 1784 Margaret claimed that after her divorce she 'for some years after this lived upon her annuity in the greatest happiness' before marrying a second time. However, the divorce was granted in May 1781, and her second marriage occurred in November of the same year.
16. Jean tried to stop him and 'received some strokes upon her Leg'. After that Hendry again asked his wife to come to bed, and she answered, 'how could she come to bed when he . . . was going to Murder her As he had done his first Wife'. Hendry 'Jumped out of bed in a great passion and looking for his breeches said that he would Cut the tongue out of her head,' but Jean 'concealed the breeches' and he 'went to bed again'. Jean said that Margaret was 'always kind to his children and attentive to his Interest'. The case did not reach a conclusion.
17. cc8/5/24; cc8/5/28.
18. cc8/6/14.
19. This seems like Gretna Green in reverse. Other Border couples did marry irregularly in England – see Rosalind Mitchison and Leah Leneman, *Sexuality and Social Control – Scotland 1660–1780* (Oxford 1989), c.4, but the extent of the practice is not known.
20. cc8/6/15.
21. A. J. S. Gibson and T. C. Smout, *Prices, Food and Wages in Scotland 1550–1780* (Cambridge 1995), 338–9, 353.
22. Jan Pahl, *Private Violence and Public Policy* (London 1985), 43.
23. I owe this point to Graham Sutton.

24. cc8/6/34. Her 'industry' was 'in merchandizing and selling of Lawns Muslines etc'. This case did not proceed beyond the libel, summons and defences.
25. cc8/6/37.
26. cc8/6/50; cc8/5/20.
27. cc8/5/40.
28. cc8/6/155. A similar example of a more than useless man can be found in eighteenth-century Pennsylvania. Margaret McCrea kept a boarding house, and her husband, William, picked fights with her in front of the boarders, on one occasion shouting that he had to eat their leavings; as a result of his behaviour the lodgers left. Merrill D. Smith, *Breaking the Bonds – Marital Discord in Pennsylvania 1730–1830* (New York and London, 1991), 172.

BAILLIE VS MURRAY – THE
GREEN-EYED MONSTER

Grisell Baillie was born in 1692 to George Baillie, receiver-general of Scotland and proprietor of Jerviswood in Lanarkshire and Mellerstain in Berwickshire, and Grisell Hume who, as Lady Grisell Baillie, became well known in the twentieth century after the publication of her remarkable *Household Book*.[1] Alexander Murray was the son and heir of Sir David Murray of Stanhope. The couple were married in August 1710, and Grisell endured over three years of misery until in December 1713 she, along with her parents, raised an action for separation, the first to be heard by the Commissary Court.

This case is unusual because no physical abuse was alleged, and no witnesses appeared. Murray not only contested the case but raised an unsuccessful adherence case against her. The case rested almost entirely on a series of letters which Murray wrote to Grisell's father, the only other evidence being a *Tatler* magazine carrying a story about a jealous husband who had killed his wife, which Murray had given – according to the pursuers as a warning – to Grisell.

Before he married her Murray did not believe he had any hope of doing so, and his passion for her combined with his own lack of self-esteem laid the basis of what followed. 'I take God to witnes I married with a full resolution and inclination to Love and gratitude, yea too much Love,' he wrote, 'Because she was the only thing I Loved She was my God and all my duty to my Neighbour For all thoughts of duty whatever were either banished or forgot, and center'd in her . . . I truly Lov'd her face, thought (and was not deceived) she had sense, was reasonably perswaded she Loved me, was sensible she preferred me to better worthy offers and made me happy, without her all the world would not have satisfied me at the time (I doe really believe) and therefore it was I valued nothing and no body in any manner of comparison to her, I thought if I gott her I had all I wanted . . . I never knew what Jealousie meant further than that there were men who suspected their wives, and as this was my only Notion of it, I never entertained the least fear of it in her, On the contrary, how could I but think her a good woman, who in the midst of so many and better offers, choosed me only for love, and because she had a better opinion of me than I even then was conscious to myself I deserved'. So what went wrong?

In one of his letters to George Baillie, Murray explained that, afraid to approach

Grisell himself, he had asked a mutual acquaintance, Alexander Hamilton, 'to drop as much as he could to my advantage in your family, and particularly to speak to your daughter of my Love for her.' Murray was told by Hamilton that he had done so, but a few days before the marriage Grisell 'told me the contrary, and that she had not so much as seen him in that time', which 'discovered his treachery to me'. So he was already suspicious of his friend, and on the afternoon after the wedding, when there was entertainment and dancing, Hamilton apparently monopolised her attentions: 'it was then I was first seized, and all of a sudden with that intollerable passion that has tortured me in all shapes ever since'. On that day Murray produced a letter which he claimed to have received from an anonymous well-wisher, accusing Grisell of 'Lewdness before her marriage'. In fact he had written it himself, that same day, in a frenzy of jealousy (as a warning, he later said), which was bizarre behaviour. The scene was set for a *very* unhappy marriage.

Hamilton never even visited them (which Murray put forward as yet another suspicious circumstance!), but Murray tried to stop his wife visiting various other friends of whom he entertained suspicions, and she was not the kind of woman to submit tamely to such restrictions on her freedom. As Murray put it in the first letter to her father: 'I have allwayes found that all my Expostulations with her upon this head did but make her worse and widen our breaches, and allwayes in the time ended in a passion on her part or mine, or both our parts, Then I have always found myself allwayes the weaker person, For I shall not call it good nature, when I allwayes out of Decency or tender heartedness have been forced to come and beg pardon For what she nevertheless was as much to blame for her harsh words.' Pouring out his feelings to her father, he continued: 'It is God alone who can work a change either upon her or me, and without his Blessing both she and I must be both miserable in this world . . . none is more sensible than I am of my weakness, and I believe nothing has added more to it than stiffling my foolish thoughts and Jealousies with myself, For whatever has been said . . . I never spoke evil of her, or discovered any thing of this sort to any soul upon earth'.

Grisell had a miserable time, but reading Murray's letters it is impossible not to have sympathy for his appalling mental state. Through jealousy, he wrote, 'I have been rendered altogether incapacitat of a serious and continued thought . . . I either was in greiff, in fury, in revenge, in sullenness or in discontent, and but seldom or very short intervalls I had of indifference and pride, But in all the former as well as in the later passion of indifference, I always had a return of love and doubt and fear that I might be unjust and the cause of all my misfortunes, and my wife Innocent of all I laid to her charge, and this consideration allwayes ended in one of those above mentioned passions, which in their turn tortured me in their several horrid shapes . . . In my fury, for so is the rage of Jealousie I was capable of doing and saying any thing against God or Man, I have said no doubt the worst of things, (But I hardly remember any thing) Blasphemed his name, and in short I have only this comfort that I knew not what I said, for God had left me, and it was his mercy and no vertue in me that took care of me that the violence of this passion never lasted long at a time, Else neither by Constitution of body or mind I could not have bore out with it, and I must have run into as mad actions as I did expressions . . . tho I have often thought within my breast that those whom I suspected with my wife did deserve to be killed, did I find them in the time, Yet as far as I remember I take God to witnes my heart would never allow me such a thought about her, For this alwayes came in my eyes, what would you do if she were dead, and this consideration never failled to calme me altogether from the storme of anger into greiff'.

It is easy to see why Grisell's parents used these letters to form the ground of a separation action. Murray no doubt squirmed as his outpourings were read by lawyers and judges. And he vigorously contested the case. Jealousy, it was argued, 'could give no ground for separation, that being an Incident frailty frequently proceeding from very much affection'. And no physical violence of any kind had been alleged. Her lawyers answered, 'Jealousie was the strongest of all passions, It was strong as death, and was capable of produceing the most violent resolutions and effects'. If 'affection be the cause of Jealousie, which was disputable, Yet that Jealousie destroys and extinguishes affection, and often exposes the life, the fame and the quiet of the party to the outmost hazard.' And 'altho sudden emotions of Jealousie at different times and upon different occasions are frailties incident to many men, and in some measure consistent with affection,' Murray's jealousy had been 'a habite of the mind . . . so strong as for a tract of time to induce a life, which as the defender defines it, Is a hell upon earth'. His behaviour, Grisell's lawyer argued, gave greater cause for a separation than single acts of physical violence, which 'might be the effects of transient passions, of no duration or consequence, But in our caice there is habituall passion which has exceeded all bounds'. Such passion 'caused often disorder more unsupportable than blowes, and renders then the lives of women most miserable, For Jealousie was an evil which exhausted the patience even of the most vertuous seeing it misinterprets the Innocentest actions, The modesty, greif and the Joy of a wife in that unfortunat circumstance gives equall cause of suspicion to a spirit galled with that madness, which converts every thing that might be for its cure to its destruction'.

The case was dragged out with petitions and counter-petitions. Murray asked the commissaries to order his wife to appear in court and swear an oath that she did not believe she could safely cohabit with him. Obviously he did not believe that she would swear such a thing – but she did. The commissaries granted the separation on 5 March 1714.

Utter misery in a marriage was not a ground for separation, and the concept of mental cruelty was not yet formulated at this early date. With no physical violence at all, and the evidence of real danger to her life – which was supposed to be the essential requisite for a separation to be granted – very slight, the ease with which Grisel obtained her decreet seems surprising. The explanation may lie in a comment made many years later in another separation case. In 1748 Ann Montgomery was unable to allege any violence by her husband, George Moir of Leckie, and the above case was cited as a precedent.[2] Moir's lawyer stated that 'the Decree of separation in that Case pronounced has alwayes been lookt upon with an unfavourable Eye as the consequence of strong interest and Influence by the Ladys friends whether Justly or unjustly'.

cc8/5/2

1. The *Household Book* was published in 1911 and was also used for Helen and Keith Kelsall, *Scottish Lifestyle 300 Years Ago – New Light on Edinburgh and Border Families* (Edinburgh, 1986).
2. cc8/6/17.

McCLELLAN VS FULTON – PISTOLS AT MIDNIGHT

Catherine McClellan and John Fulton of Grangehill were married in 1804 and had two children, John and Isobel. At the time of the marriage he was the proprietor of the estates of Grangehill and Auchlodment, while she, the daughter of the parish minister of Beith, possessed only a small farm. The marriage contract was drawn up not by his own man of business but by one chosen by her uncle in Greenock. The terms agreed seemed reasonable, and he signed it on the day of the marriage, without actually *reading* it. Their marriage was not a happy one. He claimed that this was due to her relatives detaching her affections from him. She said that he had impregnated a servant and was supporting her and the child in Glasgow. (There was a good deal of debate over whether this allegation was relevant to an action for separation rather than divorce.)

In any case, Fulton decided to get away for awhile and obtained a captain's commission in the Ayrshire militia, joining the regiment in England in February 1808. Before he went he purchased the lands of Hill of Beith at £1,500, having borrowed money for this, and for improving his estates. He was not long in England before his agent 'intimated to him, that not only must the improvements stop for want of money, as no person could be found to lend; but that his Creditors had become clamorous on account of some clause in his Marriage Contract which had been put into view.' He was forced to obtain leave of absence, and when he returned to Scotland he discovered that 'by the terms of the Contract he had limited himself to a bare liferent of all his property', all else having been settled on his wife and children.

He believed himself to have been 'duped, deceived and imposed upon' by his wife's relatives, and 'he naturally felt something very different from affection towards them'. It was 'probable that he may have expressed his feelings' to his wife as well. He asked her 'to concur with him in the necessary measures for getting the better of the restrictions in the Contract; but she had been tutored by her relations, and declined to acquiesce in any steps of this kind.' His creditors then made demands and he was forced to convey his property to trustees, retaining only an annuity of £200 a year. (Catherine's procurator made no attempt to deny the allegation of sharp dealing, though there was no need to, as Fulton had voluntarily signed the marriage contract.)

During this difficult period William Dunn, a Beith lawyer, dined at Grangehill, and deponed that 'after dinner a good deal was said respecting the Contract of Marriage between the parties by the Defender, who introduced the subject – and in the course of his remarks he complained loudly against the Pursuer and Mr Fullarton her Uncle, as having tricked him or some expression to that purpose, in the arrangement of that Contract – and also used several severe expressions directed against Mr Fullarton such as the Deponent thought must be injurious to the feelings of Mrs Fulton'. Dunn 'therefore interfered and requested that the subject might be dropt – and it was dropt accordingly'. Before that occasion 'from what the Deponent had previously seen of their conduct to each other, he had supposed them among the happiest couples in the parish.'

Fulton was a very bitter man, and admitted that he was 'deranged' in his mind when all this came to light. His behaviour became so outrageous that Catherine finally left him, taking the children, and brought an action for aliment against him before the Court of Session; he retaliated by bringing an action of adherence before the Commissary Court, but as she had been absent for less than a year the commissaries absolved her. She then brought this case for separation, and witnesses described his bizarre behaviour in the weeks after he had discovered that he had been cheated.

He would often leave the house at night and sleep in outhouses. The servants would try to persuade him to come inside, but he would refuse. One morning 'he was found lying in the Pighouse', and after the servants saw him there he 'still refused to come into the house but left the Pighouse and went into the Barn.' 'Clothes were brought out to him by Mrs Fultons desire' (according to Margaret Love, the chambermaid), 'but he refused to take them; and desired that his victuals should be brought out to him "like a dog" – which was his expression – and that he would never return to the house'. Another servant, Margaret Morrison, once saw him 'with a naked sword going to the dining room in an angry sort of manner', causing everyone to flee the house. His behaviour was so odd, erratic and unpredictable that no one knew what to make of it, and they all went about in fear. Margaret Love said that once he 'ordered the servant boy to get him the keys immediately, otherways "he would blow up the whole house" or the "Holy house", the deponent is not sure which.'

One afternoon Margaret Love 'saw Mrs Fulton move quickly from the dining room with a child in her arms, apparently frightened . . . and she immediately went out of the house, and the deponent and the other servants went with her, being also frightened, but without knowing what had happened.' They remained in the outhouses for some time, and when Fulton's servant boy came out, they asked him what his master was doing, and he 'told them that he was making a din in the dining room and breaking the things, and that the two servant men were standing at the dining room door, and could not get in'. Sarah Boyd, another servant, said that when the boy told them that, Mrs Fulton 'put her hands to her head as if to tear her hair in distress, and cried "what shall I do" – and the deponent had to hold her – and she (Mrs Fulton) was crying'.

Finally, at about midnight one night Fulton discharged a pistol in the dining room, 'which frightened the deponent [Sarah Boyd] and Margaret Love very much'. The servant boy then came and told them that Fulton 'had been enquiring "if these Buggars were in bed" – and on learning that the servants had gone to bed, had desired him to set fire to the bed and blow them up – which information frightened them still more – and the boy seemed to be much disturbed'. Soon after that 'they heard the report of another pistol in the dining room, and afterwards a third'. Fulton then emerged from the dining room with two other men and another pistol was fired. Sarah was 'by all this . . . so much frightened that she was determined on no account to remain longer in the house that night but by the persuasion of her companion Margaret Love she at length agreed to remain till the morning, when she resolved to leave the house'.

When she and Margaret told Catherine this in the morning Catherine said 'that she could not blame them'. Fulton then ordered his wife to leave the house, telling her to 'take the Buggars with her', meaning the female servants, but to leave the children. While his wife was leaving Margaret Love heard Fulton say that 'he "would give three cheers on her going away as he had done before the French, and that if she needed a Drummer he would either be one himself or get one"'. He 'then waved his hat, and gave three huzzas'.

Fulton may have terrorised his household, but there was no physical abuse, and he claimed that after matters were cleared up (because of a technical hitch in the marriage contract he was, in fact, able to reclaim his property rights) his temporary derangement of mind was over and he was back to normal. But if the commissaries needed any persuading, the next incident did it.

When Catherine left him, Fulton warned her that 'if she took away the children to Woodside, he would have them back again that night "if there was a Heaven above or if sword and pistol stood"'. Woodside was her mother's house, and she did not go there on the first night, but a few days later, when they had settled there, a servant of Fulton's turned up and seemed to Isobel Miller, a servant of Catherine's mother, 'to have some design upon the children'. The man 'having asked where Mrs Fulton was, and being told that she was at Breakfast in the dining room, went to the door without his hat, and waved with his hand, and made a signal with his voice' – whereupon Fulton accompanied by two servants 'came into the kitchen where the deponent sat with the Child Isabella in her arms and the boy John beside her'. Isobel, the servant, screamed. Fulton's male servants grabbed the children and were about to go away with them 'when the Company came from the dining room'. Fulton then 'pulled out a pistol which he placed across the Deponents breast, and snapped it – whereupon Mrs Fulton came forward and laid hold of the defender by the breast saying "in the name of God what do you mean",' and Fulton 'put up the pistol'. The servants kept hold of the children, while Isobel and the other female servants tried to tear them away. Some 'Bleachers came from the field to assist the family', and Fulton's servants were forced to relinquish the children. 'During this transaction', said Isobel, 'the children were excessively terrified – and the deponent thought John would never have done with screaming, even after he was taken up stairs – so that the deponent became apprehensive that he was going to take fits'. Isabella, she said, 'also was the worse of what had happened, and for some days was not like the same child'.

There were many witnesses, and the case was vigorously contested, but at the end of it – in 1811 – the commissaries granted the separation, with a lengthy decreet explaining their reasons. They found that before Catherine left her husband's house 'he had repeatedly expressed his orders or desire that she should depart'. Furthermore, he had 'upon many occasions and particularly during the preceding night behaved in so violent and outrageous a manner as to produce well founded apprehensions for their safety and fully to justify this measure'. They found that 'these apprehensions were but too strongly confirmed by the violence with armed force for the purpose of carrying off his children from the house of James Thomson' that he 'soon afterwards actually attempted'. Toward his wife he was proven 'to have used on several occasions before her departure the most brutal and shocking expressions', and though there was 'no direct evidence of personal violence', there was 'abundant reason to conclude . . . that the Defender did at least intend and threaten or attempt personal violence upon different occasions and that there is just ground to conclude that his wife was in danger of violence and was exposed to constant alarm insult and disturbance of such a kind as could not fail to prove utterly destructive of her peace while she remained in his power'. They further found that 'the habits of the Defender had for a long course of time before his wife the Pursuer left his house been disorderly and irregular in the extreme and such as could not fail naturally to produce the greatest domestic misery to the parties'.

After the separation was granted Fulton petitioned for custody of the children, but the commissaries decided that they had no jurisdiction over this question. (This seems strange, as they certainly did pronounce on the question in other cases, but clearly they did not want to get involved in this one.) Although at the time no one suggested that Fulton was mad, he exhibited many of the symptoms of schizophrenia. Did he, perhaps, show some signs of instability even before the marriage, and was the marriage contract in fact well-intentioned? After all, it would have been expected that he would read it before signing his name to it.

As far as lawyers were concerned, this case set a precedent for a wife to sue for separation without requiring proof that physical abuse had taken place. However, the circumstances were so very unusual that it is difficult to imagine many other situations like it.

cc8/6/105. (His unsuccessful adherence case is in cc8/6/88.) The case is cited as a legal precedent in James Fergusson, *Treatise on the Present State of the Consistorial Law in Scotland* (Edinburgh 1829), 185–7 and Maurice Lothian, *The Law, Practice and Style Peculiar to the Consistorial Actions Transferred to the Court of Session* (Edinburgh 1830), 195 (where the pursuer's name is wrongly given as McLeod).

CHAPTER 15

SEPARATION – PART 2: SURVIVING VIOLENCE

As a prelude to the individual sections of this chapter, it is worth remembering that there are two kinds of cases of violently abusive husbands which do not end up in the Commissary Court. If a husband who promised to reform actually *did* reform (having, perhaps given up alcohol), then the couple could be reconciled, and we would never read of them. Conversely, if a violent husband actually killed his wife, such a case would also not appear before the Commissary Court.

WHY DID THEY STAY?

Most wives in the eighteenth and early nineteenth centuries were financially dependent on their husbands and had had little choice but to endure whatever abuse was inflicted on them. However, there were women who could have afforded the financial costs of separation but nevertheless put up with their abusive husbands for a long time. In the upper reaches of society particularly, fear of exposing themselves to the gossip, scandal and pity that would have been consequent on their leaving their husbands and suing for a separation must have deterred many wives from action. In the case of Barbara Cockburn, Lady Saintmairtines, against James Dallas of Saintmairtines, which came before the Privy Council in 1704 (briefly mentioned at the beginning of the last chapter), her lawyer argued:

> It was impossible to think that a Woman who by the whole tenor of her lyfe had given verie good prooff of her Innocence, modesty, and good Nature, could expose herselfe to be pointed out as ane unfortunate Creature, and to be the subject of common discourse to the World, by leaving of her Husband (especially when she runn the hazard of her lyfe in doing so) unless she had been therto constrained by ane usage that was unsupportable.[1]

Margaret Drummond, daughter of William Drummond of Grange, also tried hard to conceal the abuse she suffered from her husband, Lieutenant John Home, in a case of 1736.[2] In her libel she stated that he was guilty of cursing and swearing at her, beating and striking her, sometimes Violently tossing and throwing her out of naked bed and dragging her by the hair of the head thro' the room, and keeping his grip of her hair knocking her head severall times against the wall of the Room, sometimes threatening and swearing that he would kill and murder her and immediately after such threats sometimes takeing hold of charged pistolls and laying them by her bedside when he was abed Sometimes drawing Swords and keeping the Swords naked by her when she was in bed.

Margaret explained to the court that she had married Home 'without consent of her father or other relations', and having chosen to marry him without that consent she 'had thrown herself out of their favour and took her chance in being happie in his conjugall affection without the countenance of her father and other relations to whom she had been undutifull in the greatest degree'. Shocked by his treatment of her she nevertheless submitted to it 'without resenting or publishing as far as it was possible to conceall it for the space of many months . . . not knowing that there lay a remedy at law against such Insults in a husband and believing that the Virtue of suffering suppose even death itself was all that was left her and at the same time apprehending That Discovery made to her friends whom she had offended would have no other effect but irritate her husband and to expose her to more certain and sudden ruine from his hands'. A servant testified that she had often advised her mistress 'to acquaint her father with her maletreatment', but she refused, saying that 'she did not encline to expose her self and him.' But finally an aunt came to stay, and Margaret showed her the bruises, saying that 'she could not answer to herself for concealling her usage from her any longer for she was apprehensive of the consequences', since her husband had 'threatned her life by saying I'll first kill you and then my self'. She asked her aunt to tell her father that, 'which she accordingly did'.

One must also accept that women can love brutes. When Margaret Morrison brought her separation action against Charles Black, carpenter in Inverkeithing, in November 1808, she was living with her father. Her husband had begun beating and abusing her immediately after their marriage in February 1807 and in July 1808 threatened to kill her if she did not leave his house. Mary Brodie, a neighbour, testified that after Margaret had left and was living in her father's house she told the witness that her husband had struck and kicked her, 'and that one night she was affraid he was going to kill her with a knife and that after he went to his bed she was so much affraid of this that she went and sought for the knife that she had seen him have and hid it'. On hearing this Mary had 'observed she must hate' her husband 'now as much as ever she liked him To which she answered No I like him yet, I never can hate him'.[3]

Women may also endure abuse because they believe it is better for the children if their parents stay together. After about five years of marriage, and bearing two children to her husband, Andrew Taylor, custom house officer at Rothesay, Mary Stuart began to suffer extreme physical abuse from him. On one occasion he beat her so violently that she 'was obliged to leave his house and enter into service in order to support herself'. After five months of this Taylor 'solicited her to return to live with him which on his solemn promises of treating her better she did', and about a year later she bore him another daughter. He starting maltreating her again, but 'she endeavoured to bear with him in the hopes of getting her children brought up and Educated so as to be able to do some thing for themselves', and for that reason 'continued to live with him for about eleven or twelve years during which period she experienced all the cruelties from her husband that could be devised'. Mary obtained her separation in July 1785.[4]

However, that case was virtually the only one in which a wife said that she had remained with her husband for the sake of the children. Nancy Cott, looking at divorce actions in eighteenth-century Massachusetts, commented that 'references to offspring in the petitions, when present at all, suggested that parents did not consider their children's well-being of overriding importance.'[5] The same impression is conveyed by Commissary Court records, in both divorce and separation cases. It is possible that wives who were worried about the effects on their children – or about losing them entirely – simply did not raise such actions. The rule of law, unless there were unusual circumstances, gave a husband custody of the children, because as the head of the family he was responsible for their upbringing and education; the idea of mother love being a stronger bond was not yet prevalent in this period. Of course, the extreme brutality of some husbands in separation actions meant that a wife in such circumstances who asked for custody of the children – at any rate while they were very young – would normally have it granted.[6] But in the above case of Margaret Morrison against Charles Black, although she looked after, and supported, their child after leaving him, when he demanded in the course of the legal action that the child be put under his charge she did not fight this but handed the child over.

We saw in the case of Mary Stewart and Andrew Taylor above that a wife who endured years of abuse did not necessarily do so uninterruptedly. Although five months was an unusually long time to live separately before being prevailed on by a husband to return, the pattern of escapes and returns was a very common one.

'CONTRITE' HUSBANDS

The 1749 case of Mary Kerr against John Rutherford of Knowsouth in Roxburgh-shire is in some ways a classic one of serial return-and-relapse, though it is also unusual as the husband was mentally ill. When he started abusing her he at the same time accused her of poisoning his food and that she 'used arts and wrought Charms' against him. This was not just an excuse to maltreat her, for he

hanged or caused hang a Water Dog which used to follow the pursuer and her sister Mrs Elliot, alledging that when the Dog shaked himself in the Room that the pursuer and her sister put powders which were thereby dispersed and infected the defender and frequently in the times above mentioned the defender fell down as in a fright and terror crying out he was sick and that the Complainer with the Charms, Inchantments and Devilry was the occasion of it.[7]

The first time he accused her in this way – in December 1742 – he 'squeezed and pinced her arms and breasts to such a degree that they were all blew and coloured'. One night the following year he 'turned her out of bed and next morning Thrust her out of the house and obliged her to depart the same without allowing time to Change her night dress'. She fled to her aunt's in Jedburgh, and the very same day he sent his servant begging her to return, which she did, only to find him 'in the same Peevish discontented humour'.

One night, when she was four months pregnant, he beat her savagely 'with his hands and feet upon the breast face and other parts of her body, untill she fainted away, and when in that condition he repeated his blows'. He then feared for her life and sent to Jedburgh for a surgeon, a relation of his, who found Mary 'in great disorder, her sides much swelled, her face and other parts of her Body much Bruised'. The next morning, while the surgeon was still in the house, Rutherford attacked her again 'and barbarously beat her with his fist and a piece of hard soap which was in his hand upon the Face to the great Effusion of her Blood'. It took four of his servants, called on by the surgeon, to rescue her and save her life. She stayed away for about ten days, during which time her husband visited her several times, 'affecting extraordinary regrett and sorrow for his conduct . . . and promised to use her in a different manner and as a husband ought to his Wife' if she would return to him. She did so, but two months later he 'relapsed into his former ill behaviour' and used her 'with so much severity that she was obliged to leave him'. Once again he promised to behave better; she returned, and once again he relapsed.

Eventually a meeting was held of friends and relations on both sides, when he admitted his bad behaviour and promised to behave better in future, so she again returned to him; in November 1745 he once more treated her abominably; she left again, was persuaded to return, was badly treated, and so it went on. She left him yet again in November 1747 and stayed with her brother, when Rutherford solemnly promised that he would give her 'a proper obligation for a separate aliment upon her Return to take Effect if he should ever afterwards Maltreat her', but when she returned he relapsed into his old ways. Again she left him; again he promised to be good; again she returned, but 'she found herself worse than before, he closely confined her in a Room and allowed none to come near her but himself, and when she offered to come out of the Room he beat her'. When she asked him 'to fulfil his promise with regard to the aliment in a separate state He answered That Ingagements were not to be keept with such a Wretch and abandoned person'. It was summer 1749 before she finally left him for good and raised the successful separation action against him.

In an 1810 case Christian Comb just once believed the promises of her husband, William Keith, spirit dealer in Newhaven. They had been married in 1797, and according to Christian it was only in 1808 that he had 'got into habits of extravagance and dissipation' and began cursing and threatening her life, once with a gun, once with a spade, and once with a candle when he threatened to set the bed on fire, and she was forced to run out into the street 'without any cloaths upon her except the shift'. She had the sense to leave him then, and lived separately for about six weeks. He then 'caused write and subscribed a letter' to her, 'wherein he acknowledged the impropriety of his conduct, expressed his sorrow therefor and promised in future to conduct himself as became a faithful and prudent husband in all respects'. She therefore went back, but within ten days he was behaving as badly as ever, and she did not repeat the experiment.[8]

About four years before Isobel Dick raised her action against John Carr in the Cowgate of Edinburgh in 1822 she was treated so badly that she left him, taking her year-old infant with her, and lived apart for about a month, 'until she was induced to return to his house upon his promising to keep from liquor, and never to maltreat her again.'[9] For a short time he treated her 'with some degree of civility and discretion', but this did not last, and on one occasion he 'gave her such a severe blow with his fist between the eyes that she was almost deprived of her sight for a considerable time, and her face was much swelled and discoloured'. During that period she would often spend one or two nights elsewhere to escape from him, 'after which she was generally induced to return by his promises of better behaviour, which however he seldom kept long.'

By the time she raised the action Isobel had three children, and the final incident involved her husband striking their two-and-a-half year old daughter with a stick. When Isobel tried to defend her he 'seized a poker or pair of Tongs' and gave her 'such a severe blow or stroke upon the head as to render her quite insensible for some time, and a deep wound was inflicted upon her head from which a great deal of blood issued'. Isobel told the court that there was not much point in asking for an aliment because her husband was drunk so much of the time she did not believe he could pay her one, though if he sobered up he could probably afford £10 or £12 a year. All she wanted now was a decreet as a 'means of preventing him from troubling and molesting her, and putting it in her power to force him to live separate from her'. But the commissaries ordered him to pay her £10 a year.[10]

Jean Hewart, who brought her 1822 action against Alexander Comb, slater in Edinburgh, under benefit of the poor's roll, went so far as to take out 'Letters of Lawburrows', a legal action akin to binding him over to keep the peace, after he struck her 'with a candlestick upon the the head to the great effusion of her blood', when she was 'unable longer to bear such treatment'. After being served with this document he 'engaged his relations to interfere . . . on his behalf', and because of his 'seeming regret and repentance' she 'was prevailed on to renew her cohabitation with him, and he paid the expence occasioned by the Lawburrows'. But though 'this renewed cohabitation took place in consequence of the most solemn assurances . . . that he had repented of his former harsh conduct', yet he was soon treating her as badly as ever, and she left him for good.[11]

In an 1825 case Mary Buchanan (who also brought her action under benefit of the poor's roll) actually went to the magistrates of Edinburgh, who employed her husband, Charles Pantar, and called him before them. She had been forced by his treatment of her to leave him, and in the presence of the magistrates he 'acknowledged his fault . . . and made a solemn promise that upon her returning home he would never more ill use her'. In spite of all this, shortly after she went back to him he relapsed into his former behaviour until one day she 'was compelled to leave the House, and go into that of a neighbour for protection'. Pantar followed her there 'and tearing her Child from her arms threw it upon a Bed and brutally struck and kicked' her, 'and threatened to murder her and thus he continued till forced to desist by his own dog which attacked him and drove him from the house'.[12]

Mary was saved by a dog. How did other wives manage to survive the brutal attacks made on them by their husbands?

POLICE AND DOCTORS

In the 1815 case of Rachel Gardiner against John Colquhoun, chain maker in Edinburgh, their landlady stated that Colquhoun was often drunk and would then strike his wife. The witness added that 'she has often gone ben to try and keep peace betwixt him and his wife and when he would not give over abusing her the Deponent has called the police'. In the 1818 case of Isobel Hislop against James Pirie, painter in Edinburgh, Isobel declared that she had 'long endeavoured to conceal' her husband's 'bad conduct and maltreatment of her from her acquaintances and neighbours; but his outrages having for a considerable time past become so frequent by his cursing and swearing, beating and bruising of her, that the neighbourhood being alarmed they upon different occasions have got him taken into custody by the Police'. Recently he had 'again beat her severely, made a riot and uproar, and having been carried before the Police, and not being able to find bail for his good behaviour he has been confined by order of one of the Police Judges in the Lock up House'.[13] And in the 1822 case that we looked at above, of Isobel Dick against John Carr, she first left him after he called her

> a damned bitch, damned whore, damned liar and many other abusive names, tore most of her clothes off her body by personal violence, seized a table knife, threatened that he would run her through, and cut her throat, making at same time a great noise, and disturbance, until some persons in the neighbourhood alarmed for her safety, sent for two police officers, who, having entered the house, took the knife out of his hands, and thereby rescued the Complainer from the danger she was in at the time of being murdered.

Those three examples come from the nineteenth century, when a police force existed, though in earlier times a city guard could be called out in like circumstances. In all three cases there was considerable noise and disturbance to the neighbourhood, which seems to have been the main factor prompting police to come, and to arrest the abuser. This offered short-term alleviation by removing a brutal husband from the scene but usually resulted in, at most, a few days incarceration, and a husband might well have returned home more belligerent than before.

There are frequent references in the records to wives having been treated by doctors for their injuries but few to a doctor becoming in any way involved. An exception was John Carstairs who was sent for several times by Margaret Agnew 'when she had received blows and bruises' from her husband, Peter Hendry (a 1784 case discussed in the last chapter). On the last occasion she 'was much hurt about the Breast and throat and particularly about the Mouth, and the deponent particularly expresst his disapprobation of the Jarrings and differences betwixt the pursuer and defender as he had done formerly and told them that they would bring one or other of them to the Gallows'.[14] There is no suggestion that he thought the husband's use of physical force against his wife was any more blameable than her displays of bad temper.

A doctor who took a more personal interest in a patient without obvious injuries was James Latt in the 1791 case of Dorothea Proudfoot against Charles Calder. We saw them twice in the last chapter, as she and her sister supported the family by running their public house, and the doctor had examined her when her husband claimed that she had venereal disease, finding that it was simply thrush. Dorothea 'seemed to be unwilling at first to make any complaint against her husband', said Latt. When he first knew her 'she was a plump healthy looking girl but when he saw her some short time after her being delivered of her first child he observed her looking emaciated and lean'. His first thought was that 'this might be owing to a consumption but upon feeling her pulse and asking if she had any breast complaints he found no symptoms of any such disease'. He then conjectured that 'it must be owing to the damp in which she lived and advised her to go to the Country and she accordingly went to the Queensferry', and after her return he 'observed her recovered and looking well'. But 'some considerable time after this the deponent observed her again looking ill and saw her low spirited and frequently crying and as she had removed to a house in the Covenant Closs he thought this could not be imputed to the dampness and upon inquiry into the cause he found it to be owing to the bad usage she had received from the defender'.[15] At least he did enquire.

That was a case where mental and emotional distress, rather than the physical effects of an abusive relationship, was being observed. The doctor did not even suspect the abuse she was suffering, but many of those who could clearly see the physical effects did nothing about the situation that caused them. In the 1811 case of Mary Craik against James Windrim, the doctor declared that he had found Mary 'in great agitation and distress', and severely bruised, and that in his opinion the bruises 'had been occasioned by external violence'. From what he saw, 'and from what was admitted by the Defender to the Deponent . . . the Deponent was of opinion that if the Parties continued to live together in this state of domestic warfare the Pursuer could not get better'.[16] Not exactly a constructive comment.

Police might be called where there was a public disturbance, and doctors might be consulted after the event, but the likeliest people to intervene at the time were, of course, those who were on the spot.

SERVANTS, NEIGHBOURS AND VISITORS

It was usual for households of even very humble means to have at least one general servant, so it is not surprising to find servants frequently appearing as witnesses in separation cases, and in some cases actively intervening to protect their mistresses. For a female servant, direct action during the course of violence could be dangerous, but there were other ways of intervening. For example, in the 1733 case of Anne Muir against Walter Nisbet of Craigentinnie, their servant, Katherine Anderson, saw Nisbet show his wife a pistol one night. Katherine slept in the adjacent room, and later that night she heard him shouting at his wife 'as if he had been in a passion cursing and swearing', and heard Anne 'cry that she was a poor weak defenceless woman' and begging of her husband 'mercy for Christs sake'. Katherine went into their room and removed the pistol which she found on a chair at Nisbet's side of the bed. On other occasions, fearing that he 'might make ill use of some weapons he had in his bed chamber she at one time carried three naked swords out of the Room which usually hung upon the chimney piece without their scabbards and another time the Deponent carried three penknives out of his room'. Whether such intervention would have prevented murder may be doubtful, but as a witness her testimony supported the claim that Anne's life was in real danger.[17]

Some female servants did intervene physically. In the 1741 case of Margaret Crawfurd against Samuel Forbes of Knapernie (discussed in the last chapter),[18] a servant, Jean Greig (aged twenty-two) described the final incident which led Margaret to leave: 'he threw the pursuer down with all his force on the edge of a Chest of Drawers, and then got above her with his knees and feet and drove her head forwards and backwards upon the Drawers, and then knocked her Belly and legs so long and so often with his knees, that the Deponent thought he should have murdered her'. When Mary tried to get up 'he threw her down a second time, when she fell on the edge of a Trunk with her Back, and then Beat her so long with his hands and feet and drove her head sometimes against the trunk and sometimes against the floor, that she the Deponent thought every Blow would have ended her.'

Jean, the witness, had one of their infants in her arms, but at this stage she handed it to another maid, 'and came to the pursuers relief'. When Forbes saw her coming he pulled his wife 'up from the ground by her cloak and threw her down again with all his force, when her head fell upon the hearth and so near the fire that it was like to be burnt still continuing to beat the pursuer with hands and feet'. When Jean got hold of her 'to pull her from him,' he got hold of one arm, while Jean pulled her by the other, until finally he

> happened to take hold of a part of the Deponents gown, pulling it hard, the part he held of rent off from the rest and he fell down, by which accident both the pursuer and Deponent made their escape, the Deponent carrying her into the next Room whereof the pursuer bolted the Door, and the Deponent ran down stairs which so enraged the Defender that he chased the Deponent first to the Kitchen, and then to the Ministers house cursing and Damning himself that he would be revenged upon the Deponent.

Not all of their servants were so willing to help. Margaret Downie, the wetnurse, declared that she never observed Forbes maltreat his wife; admittedly she had seen Margaret 'oft times melancholy and weeping . . . but what was the occasion of it she did not know, for at all times when she suspected there was any ill humour amongst them, she industriously shifted the hearing of it'.

It was easier for male servants to intervene physically. In the 1803 case of Flora McLeod against William McLeod, tenant on a farm in the Isle of Skye, a servant intervened when he saw McLeod 'beat and bruise his said wife by boxing her and knocking her down to the ground taking her up frequently and knocking her down again'; the servant received 'a severe blow on the head' for his efforts. On another occasion when he found McLeod 'beating her and his hand fixed in her hair and giving her the most abusive language such as Bitch and whore etc . . . it was with the greatest difficulty the deponent disengaged his hand from the hold he had of her hair, and enabled her to make her escape'.[19]

There are, however, many more examples of female servants interposing themselves between their masters and mistresses. In the 1811 case of Janet Kettle against Andrew Weir, candlemaker in Edinburgh, both servants, Betty Robertson and Isabel Sawers, declared that Weir was in the habit of coming home very drunk, and they had 'frequently prevented the defender from striking his wife when she was lying in bed and he came home in these outrageous fits'. Betty said that 'Mr Weir's outrage was so great that the deponent would have thought herself entitled to go away and would have left their service the first time she saw his violence in his family but for regard to Mrs Weir with whom she could have continued with satisfaction but she could not possibly have engaged to serve another term on account of his behaviour'. Isabel described an occasion when Janet fled into the servants' bed with her infant, and Weir followed and 'attempted to set fire with a lighted Candle to the Curtains of the bed . . . and would have done so if the deponent and her fellow servant had not stopped his arm and taken the candle out of his hand'.[20]

Servants were the chief, and sometimes only, witnesses to domestic violence in rural areas and in aristocratic and upper gentry households, but even there – and much more so in cities – neighbours and visitors might be aware of what was going on and be in a position to intervene. In a frightening case of 1750, William Carlyle of Brydekirk (near Annan) came after his wife, Agnes Irving, with a drawn sword, and she ran 'to a neighbouring Cottage where she hid herself in a bed'. He 'came in a fury to the cottage' which he had seen her enter

> And not finding her there she being hid as said is He went and searched some other of the cottages in the Neighbourhood and the people of the house where she was hidden apprehensive of her security in the bed got her put into an old Chest which they had scarcely got done when he returned from searching the other Cottages and in a fury began to make a more narrow search in the Cottage where she was hidden and being asked what he wanted he answered his Wife that he might make a sacrifice of her but not finding her he went off.

She then 'fled to one of his Tenents houses where she remained some days'.[21]

In the 1785 case of Mary Stuart against Andrew Taylor, in Greenock, a key witness was Barbara Fisher, who rented a room and shop from him. On one occasion 'the deponent hearing a wrangle from the defenders end of the house was thereby induced to go in and see what the matter was but having been rather rudely treated by the defender she retired and laid down a resolution not to be so officious on any after occasion'. Some time after that she heard another 'disturbance', and one of her 'own children having proposed that she should go in with a view to mediate between them, the deponent thereupon observed that her reception had formerly been such that she would not go into their house at that time'. However, one of Mary's children coming in then, 'crying out that her father would murder her mother made the deponent alter her resolution, and she went into their house accordingly'. She found Mary 'prostrate upon her back on the floor' with Taylor's 'two hands grasped about her neck her eyes appearing as if they would start from their sockets'.[22]

Neighbours often gave shelter to fleeing wives, but, as we have seen, there was an understandable reluctance to actively intervene. In the unresolved case of Isobel Henderson against John Anderson in 1800, various neighbours told the court of his violence. Katharine Jaffrey, one of them, while in bed one night heard Isobel 'crying out "would no body save her"'. Katharine 'wished to go in and see what was the Matter but her husband would not allow her and locked the door to prevent her'. Similarly, in the 1826 case of Janet Brown against George Bremmer, shoemaker in Edinburgh, Elizabeth Binnie once saw Bremmer 'pull her out from the door and strike and kick her, and throw her upon the stair head, using awful oaths'. She had often heard Janet 'calling out murder in the house before that and would have gone into the house if my husband had not stopped me'.[23]

In the 1803 Skye case of McLeod against McLeod above (where we saw a male servant twice intervene to save his mistress) a 60-year-old lieutenant who lived in the neighbourhood once entered their house and found Lieutenant McLeod trying to strike his wife with some crockery he had in his hand. When this failed he followed her into the kitchen and then he 'laid hold of the spit'. The neighbour had stopped McLeod striking her, and 'after seeing him take up such a dangerous weapon as the spit laid hold of the Room brush, with which he threatened him until he laid by the spit'. McLeod 'instantly pulled out his knife, opened it and threatned to stabb the deponent for defending Mrs McLeod having a second time threatned him with the brush he put up his knife but in spite of the deponents exertions he got an opportunity to give her a blow below the eye the marks of which remained for a considerable time after'.[24]

In the 1818 case of Marion Frost against John Mather, originally from Sheffield but now a music teacher in Edinburgh, Marion could have sued for divorce as it was her refusal to recognise his mistress, a Mrs Steele, that was the main cause of his violence against her. About a month before she left him Marion asked the help of a friend, Lieutenant William Douglas; she had seen her husband walking with Mrs Steele and was afraid to go home. He accompanied her and when they got in Mather 'immediately addressed his wife in a great passion asking her why she did not come up and speak to Mrs Steele when she saw her walking with him that evening.' Marion 'answered that she could not do so and spoke to him very calmly'. Mather 'then got up putting himself in an attitude as if he meant to strike his wife and the Deponent rushed between them and prevented him from doing so altho he made repeated Attempts'. Mather then left the room and Douglas followed him, remonstrated with him 'on the impropriety of his conduct and pressed him to return to his wife and be reconciled to her'. Mather answered, 'all I want is to be shot of her'. (Douglas told the court that 'shot in the Yorkshire dialect means free or quit'.)

After they separated they both came to Douglas's house in the hopes of a reconciliation, but Mather 'no sooner came into the room and saw his wife than he broke into violent abuse before them all and applied to his wife epithets so shocking that the Deponent must have turned him out of his house if he had not been restrained by respect for the Pursuer.'[25]

Anything short of a judicial separation granted by the Commissary Court provided no guarantee of the end to a wife's misery, as we shall see below.

PERSECUTION AFTER SEPARATION

The case which more clearly than any other shows a legal separation as granted by the commissaries a necessity even if a couple had already separated was that of Margaret Pringle against Peter White in Edinburgh, raised in December 1779.[26] The couple were married in 1752; she bore a son and two daughters, all of whom died young. From 1768 onwards he treated her very badly. By the year 1776 she had decided to take legal action, but White pre-empted this by proposing a formal separation, agreeing to assign her the rents of certain properties for her aliment. Matters were adjusted by mutual friends, and in May of that year a formal disposition was executed and registered in the burgh court books of Edinburgh. But this was far from the end of Margaret's troubles, for he persecuted her relentlessly.

When they first separated she decided to live in one of the houses for which she had been assigned the rents, and to let a furnished room. She took a young woman as a lodger, a Miss Prophet. But one day in autumn 1777 White 'came into the house with all the fury of a madman, and after Beating and abusing both the Memorialist and Mrs Pringle a sister of Miss Prophets who then happened to be in the Room . . . he drove the young Lady herself out of the house, vowing revenge against her, if he could only lay his hands upon her'. Miss Prophet stayed, and White was refused admittance to the house, but one night he came and broke the windows 'with stones so large a size as, that if they had struck the Inhabitants, must certainly have proved their quietus.'

Margaret gave up trying to live in that house and 'went to reside in the house of Deacon William Thomson weaver in Edinburgh a man of irreproachable character'. But when White learned this he wrote 'Several Threatning Letters' to the deacon, making it impossible for her to go on living there either. Finally, in February 1779 he again tracked down her whereabouts, and started lurking outside the house, hoping either to waylay her on her way to church or to find her in the house alone. 'Being disappointed in these expectations by his being discovered on the street he took an opportunity one evening when Mr Chapman was abroad, of calling at his house and boldly demanding access'. When he got in he 'without any cause or provocation Beat her with a Cane over the head and Shoulders' and 'in a furious and outrageous manner repeatedly threatned with oaths and imprecations that he would destroy both the person and effects of the Complainer, and that he would never allow her to have peace for the future'. There was enough noise at the time to bring neighbours to her assistance, but he followed up the assault by an anonymous letter which 'breathed threats and future maltreatment of the Complainer'.

White raised an adherence action against his wife and managed to drag out the litigation until April 1782, but at least she would then have had immediate legal recourse if he had recommenced his persecutions; and he had to pay her a yearly aliment as well.

In another case of late-onset violence Violet Robertson and George Winton, mason in Edinburgh, were married in April 1808, with his abuse of both alcohol and his wife starting in 1822. At the end of that year she left him, but 'through intercession of their friends and relations, and in consequence of the most solemn promises of amendment made by the said George Winton' she was persuaded to return to him. A contract was drawn up which stated that if it became impossible for her to live with him the arbiters as trustees would pay her an agreed aliment. He relapsed into his old ways, and in December 1824 she left him and went to live in Portobello. She advised the trustees that she had done this, and they found that she had had good cause to leave, and agreed that she should be paid her aliment. That should have been the end of the story, but Winton started coming to her house 'generally very much intoxicated and conducted himself like a deranged person.' The visits became more frequent, and he 'conducted himself in so cruel and unmerciful a manner as to render it unsafe for the Complainer to reside any longer at her residence in Portobello. His temper has been most furious and he has frequently threatened to take away the Complainers life, so that she has been living in a state of continual terror and apprehension and so alarmed has she been, that she has latterly been under the necessity of leaving her house at Portobello, and concealing herself in Edinburgh.' The case was not contested, and she was granted her separation in January 1827.[27]

NOTES

All CC references are in the Scottish Record Office.

1. SRO.PC.2/28/ff.328–337. I am grateful to the late Peter Vasey for this reference.
2. CC8/8/5/4. Home denied anything more than 'a little rough Treatment used by the husband to his wife in pulling her through the Room'.
3. CC8/6/103. Margaret dropped the action because 'she and her Friends being so poor in their circumstances they found themselves unable to go through with it'. Four years later, toward the end of 1812, Black tried to raise an action of adherence to get her back, and the commissaries encouraged her to awaken her separation case against him, and, as she was a menial servant in Leith, admitted her to the poor's roll. By this time she certainly felt no affection for him for she said that 'having got into service she prefers living in that menial situation with what little comfort she has to the name of having a House of her own in which she may say she never spent a comfortable hour and was every day and every hour of the day liable to the attacks and insults of a furiated man.' She was granted a separation in September 1813, though the arguments over the aliment he should pay her went on for a further two years.
4. CC8/5/18.
5. Nancy F. Cott, 'Eighteenth-Century Family and Social Life Revealed in Massachusetts Divorce Records', *Journal of Social History* 10 (1976), 28.
6. An example is the case of Ann Muir against Walter Nisbet of Craigentinnie in 1733, when the commissaries found 'the mother is Intitled to the Custody of the Children during their Infancy'. CC8/5/4.
7. CC8/5/9. It was not only his wife he suspected for one day when the parish minister, William Turnbull, visited, Rutherford told him that he 'had the smell of poison about him'. The minister went upstairs and returned with one of the children and then 'broke a cherry stone which the Child had in his hand and the defender thereupon cried out, That was the poison and told the deponent That his Breast was burning all the time he the deponent was in the house and desired him to go away'. It seems extraordinary that his mental state did not play a more crucial role in the proceedings. Some years later (1762) he was confined in Bedlam and was alleged to be the most violent of the inmates. SRO.SC39/36/6. I am grateful to R. A. Houston for this reference. It appears that there was a family connection between John Rutherford of Knowsouth and John Rutherford Ainslie whose madness was described in Case Study 6.
8. CC8/5/31.
9. CC8/6/134.
10. In her libel Isobel also asked for custody of the children, but there was no mention of this in the decreet.

11. cc8/6/140. This is one of those curious cases where the pursuer alleged that her husband was guilty of adultery but chose to sue for separation only, based on cruelty.
12. cc8/6/145. The neighbour explained to the court that Pantar's watchdog 'was chained at his own door but the chain was of such a length as to admit him into my house, and he flew upon the Defender, which forced him to let go of the hold he had of the Pursuer'. (By 'house' of course is meant 'flat'.)
13. cc8/6/103; cc8/6/116.
14. cc8/6/44. The case did not proceed any further.
15. cc8/5/20.
16. cc8/6/88.
17. cc8/5/4.
18. cc8/5/7.
19. cc8/5/28.
20. cc8/5/32.
21. cc8/5/6.
22. cc8/5/18. This has the appearance of attempted murder, but Barbara added that Mary had her hands fastened in her husband's 'hair or about some other part of his head', and that when she entered and told them that 'their behaviour was very unseemly they quitted their grips of one another and both of them rose', which makes it sound as though Mary was holding her own. Barbara also said that she did 'not know what gave occasion to this Squabble or with whom it originated', which again makes it appear much less than a life-or-death situation.
23. cc8/6/67; cc8/6/152.
24. cc8/5/28.
25. cc8/5/36.
26. cc8/6/40.
27. cc8/6/153.

CATHCART VS HOUSTON – THE SUBMISSIVE WIFE

'But a few years agoe', according to Dame Elenora Cathcart's petition in 1749, she had 'as reasonable a prospect in the eyes of the world, of being comfortably settled, as any Young Lady in this Country. She was Daughter of the late Lord Cathcart, who was universally beloved and esteemed, had been educated in a manner every way suitable to her Rank; had a portion of Five thousand five hundred pounds sterling'. In 1743 Sir John Houston 'made his Addresses to the petitioner in proposals of marriage, founded upon the strongest protestations of esteem and regard', and during his courtship, 'which continued for upwards of eleven moneths, he conducted himself with so much address, as to impress the petitioner with so favourable an opinion of his understanding good nature and honour, that she consented to accept of him for a Husband, although he had then no independent fortune of his own, and that the settlements offered by his mother were extremely moderate, and scarcely suitable to the fortune which the Lady brought along with her.'

But, once married, his behaviour toward her changed entirely. Initially there was no physical abuse, but endless petty fault finding and insults. Sir John, convinced that he was 'sickly', demanded that they go to the Continent, and they set off by coach to Falmouth five days after the wedding, accompanied by Elenora's younger sister, and by her 'gentlewoman', Mistress Herries. Both testified that Sir John treated his bride with 'Coldness and Indifference'. At Falmouth he was 'peevish and Fretfull' and was so nasty to Elenora that their landlady said to Mistress Herries that she thought the best thing that could happen to his wife was Sir John's death. On board ship to Lisbon his behaviour was no better, and Miss Cathcart described her sister frequently ending up in tears and begging her husband's forgiveness – whether justly or unjustly – for her faults. When they left Lisbon, according to Miss Cathcart, his behaviour 'was the same as formerly consisting of Reproaches to the Lady, and Reflections against her Relations, with a number of harsh expressions and taunts', and Mistress Herries said that 'the harshness of Sir John's behaviour towards the Lady was so observable, that the Captain of the Ship who was a Swede, made the Deponent understand that he thought Sir John used the Lady ill.'

Elenora's strategy was described thus: 'as she was at all times exceedingly carefull to conceal, even from him, how much she was shocked with his behaviour, so she used her utmost endeavour to make the World believe, that his conduct toward her was altogether unexceptionable; and that where differences could not be concealed, she and not he, was to blame, which she then considered as the only chance she had of reclaiming, or bringing him to a Right way of thinking.'

Until they reached Pisa Sir John's abuse of his wife appears to have been entirely verbal, but once there the young Miss Cathcart twice saw him strike her sister. The second time she ended up on the ground, blood was 'flowing in great quantities from the wound', and Miss Cathcart 'was so much struck, with what she saw, that it bereft her of the power of stirring from the place where she first had been', but then she cried out, ' "Good God, Sir John you have killed my sister" . . . Sir John Replied, if it was so it was her own fault'.

He also had a more bizarre way of tormenting his wife: 'Sir John kept a variety of Petts, viz. a serpent, vipers, and also a monkey, Tortoise, Rabbits, and a parrot, and as the Lady was affraid of almost all these Creatures, he had generally one or more of them in the Room'. One morning, 'having assembled the Monkey, Parrot Tortoises, and the ass, which he had pulled up stairs to the Dining Room, they were all making hideous and different sorts of noises, that the Lady entering the Room, and starting back in a great fright, Sir John cried, Nay, Madam, you may come in, For these Tortoises very much resemble you, they being equally stupid, slow and useless, only I must own that they are peaceable, and do no mischief whereas you are wicked and malicious'. Miss Herries said that 'while at Calci [ten miles from Pisa], Sir John was still worse humoured than before, that the Lady was so affected with his bad treatment of her, that many times she could neither eat nor sleep, so that the Deponent was affraid it would have turned her head, and been her death'.

At this point Sir John determined to get his hands on more of her money and demanded that she write letters to her relatives, asking for £2,000 of her portion in credit. He produced some of those letters as evidence, for in them she accused herself of behaving badly, but she was able to produce a letter to a relative that she had written and sent without his knowledge, and in it her she explained her strategy: 'Imagine my condition, I love Sir John better than my life, and am upon so bad terms with him, that I have scarce any hopes left. The letters my G. Mamma writes are very great misfortunes to me, tell her, if she has a mind to save me, she must never in the most distant insinuation imagine that Sir John can err to me, She must write an answer to my letter, and put me entirely in the wrong, and write one to Sir John in the fondest way to him, and without Justifieing or asking any thing for me . . . Above all let his Credite be sent with Diligence. If he is in any shape chagrined, I am ruined. I would write this to G. Mamma, but I choose to have it to say I never writ her any thing in secret; I don't get a line that is not seen. Please write me such a letter as Sir John may see, and be so kind as to write and tell him, that it is not at all known in Scotland, that there ever was misunderstanding between us; if it has been heard there, for the Love of God, use all your arts to prevent any one from letting him know it . . . the only chance I have to be Reconciled to Sir John is his believing that no one does, or can Justifie me; So that the greatest favour my friends can do me, is quite to give up my cause. Let them show fondness for him and sorrow for me, and time, if no one is too eager to help me, may yet be my Friend.'

So we see a wife who apparently still loved her brute of a husband and who honestly believed that if she continued to do everything he asked of her he would eventually come to appreciate her worth and love her too. But if there was still love on her part, there was also fear, for according to her sister, 'the Doctrine which Sir John used to inculcate in presence of the Lady was, that tho' a husband was not by Law entitled to beat his wife with a stick of a certain size, he might safely do so with a switch or with his hand, and that he had also the power of locking her up, if he chose it. That though he mortally abhored lifting his hand to a woman, and had never even beat a whore; yet so much did he abhore the Lady, that he could beat her every day, and be happy in doing it.'

In March 1745 Elenora went to England to execute some commissions for her husband, 'to which she agreed the more readily, as she was in hopes that absence for a short time, and cool Reflexion, might work some change upon his mind'. He, meanwhile, went to Naples with Miss Cathcart. When she returned (in January 1746), accompanied by Mistress Ann Stevenson who had been sent over to bring Miss Cathcart home, Miss Cathcart testified that Sir John refused to go to the door to meet his wife and treated her coldly and unpleasantly. Miss Stevenson stayed with them for about three months and testified that 'during all the time the Defender treated the pursuer so harshly that the Deponent was never witness to the like between man and wife'. On one occasion when Sir John was shouting at his wife he called in Mistress Stevenson and said that his wife had confessed 'that she had a design to provoke him, so as to expose him before the Deponent . . . and thereupon the Lady acknowledged, that she had intended to expose him to the Deponent, by provoking him'. But – Miss Stevenson told the court – 'During the forsaid time the Deponent never observed the pursuer Do any thing to provoke the Defender in the Deponents presence; on the contrary, she behaved always most submissively towards the Defender, which made the Deponent have less Regard to what the pursuer had confessed, or was accused of by the Defender, and to believe that she was obliged to say any thing that would please the Defender'. By the time Miss Stevenson left 'Things at length came to that height, that Sir John discharged the Lady so much as to speak to him, but if she had any thing to say to send it in writing, or employ some other person to deliver it.'

After Miss Cathcart and Miss Stevenson went home, a Miss Jolly arrived as Elenora's 'gentlewoman'. Sir John took a house at Montauban, where 'the Lady was almost every day in tears, And Sir John continually giving her hard words'. By this time she was thoroughly terrorised: 'Sir John strictly charged the Lady to take care of his three Dogs, that she was obliged frequently to carry them down to the Court in order to air them, and to wait upon them, and bring them up again, and that she had frequently done, even when she was sick, and in a bad state of health . . . the Lady's whole business thro' the day was to run after and take care of the Dogs, who were now and then attempting to make their escape.' One night a dog did escape, and they went out looking for it: 'the Lady was in such a Fright, thinking the Dog might be lost, that she said to the Deponent she would not go back to the house if the Dog was not found, but would rather go into the Town and beg her bread'.

Sir John then forced his wife to sign an agreement that if she wanted a separation he would have to pay her only £15 a year aliment, and after that he 'used to beat the Lady almost daily'. One evening Mistress Jolly 'saw the Lady come out of Sir John's Room into her own Room, with her face swelled, high coloured, and her Ear-rings broke in pieces in her hand, that having asked the Lady, how her Ear-rings came to be broke, she answered, that Sir John had first given her Blow upon one side of the head, and then upon the other, by which he drove the Ear-rings from her Ears.' Next morning Miss Jolly 'observed the Ladys forehead swelled, with several Bumps, and indeed her forehead was seldom without Bumps.' And 'one morning hearing some high words betwixt Sir John and the Lady, and suspecting Sir John might be beating the Lady, she made an Errand into the Room, where she saw the Lady holding a Handkerchief with her two hands to her face, and her nose running down with blood'.

Breaking point was an incident when the couple disagreed over 'whether that or the other particular servant should have the honour of emptying Sir John's close box, the Ladys mistake in employing the one that was at hand, when the other was absent, was an unpardonable offence'. When Sir John swore that he would break all the bones in her body Elenora had had enough and prepared to flee. Even then, she once more *begged her husband's forgiveness*; when he refused it she ran out to the courtyard. Sir John followed her, 'and griped her by the arm, upon which she fell down to the ground', and he pulled her along the ground'. He then 'called out to two porters to carry her up stairs saying she was mad, which both of them refused to do, saying they knew the matter very well, and that she was not mad.' After that he told Miss Jolly to carry her in, but he still refused to say he forgave his wife, and she 'went off with the Deponent to Montauban without her shoes, having lost them in the struggle abovementioned in the Court . . . being barefoot, she cut her feet upon some sharp stones by the way.' When they arrived at Montauban, 'being afraid of the Defender she applied to the Intendant for security, who put her and the Deponent into a Convent'.

Sir John strongly contested the case – after all, he was able to produce letters in which she confessed her bad behaviour and her love for him. (In one of them she wrote 'You shall find me wax when you return fit to take any impression you please. I form no will or wish, but that of obeying you my dearest Love.'). But his principal witness, Elenora's young sister, provided an enormous amount of evidence of his cruelty, and though he subsequently tried to discredit her the commissaries had heard more than enough to find Elenora entitled to a separation and aliment. They awarded her £150 a year from March 1748 until Martinmas last, and in future £200 per annum ('In respect of the succession devolved upon Sir John by the death of Lady Houston his Mother'). Apart from bygone and future aliment, Sir John also had to pay £250 expenses and a further £183. 15s. to have the decreet, which ran to about 2,000 pages, extracted.

We have seen various survival tactics employed by abused wives, but rarely any so misguided as to think that acquiescing in every form of abuse would ultimately lead a husband to stop the abuse and become a loving spouse.

cc8/5/10. The case takes up two full volumes, but Volume 1 is missing. Fortunately, the 250-page petition which forms the basis for this case study reviews all of the evidence at length. (Sir John's answers to that petition run to over 570 pages.) There are 158 items in the process papers (cc8/6/17), but many are missing, including the summons and libel, and the decreet.

CHAPTER 16

SEPARATION – PART 3: DEFENCE AND DENIAL

DENIAL

A high proportion of separation cases were contested, and the husband's defences were generally these: that he did not abuse her, that the incidents complained of were exaggerated or were part of the normal rough-and-smooth of married life; and besides no witnesses saw it.

In an early case, raised in January 1718, Mr James Campbell (alias Dochartie), late minister of the gospel at Lidgertwood, could not altogether deny some harsh treatment of his wife, Elizabeth Scott, but his lawyer claimed that all the incidents in the libel were clearly 'the effects of a sudden emotion and passion than of any evil designe or purpose'. He added that 'it was not every rough or offensive word or action that could afford proces of separation betwixt man and wife . . . if every Light injury would give cause for separation of man and wife, the married state would be very precarious'. After the evidence had been heard he argued that 'upon the greatest part of the other articles there was no concurrence of two witnesses but only single testimonies', and that 'most of the depositions were not by occular witnesses in the matters of the real injuries, but only ex post facto and ex auditie'.[1]

Elizabeth's procurator countered that 'this frequent falling in a passion was the very ground of separation betwixt man and wife, especially as in this case where that passion so far exceeds all bounds, that the effects of it were a man's unmercifull beating his wife and abusing her after the most scandalous manner'. As for there being few eyewitnesses 'it was very natural to think that a husband who is in use to maltreat his wife, will readily lay hold on an occasion to exercise his barbarity, when he thinks he may safely doe it out of the eye of the world . . . and yet at the same time he may behave with all seeming respect and kindness in presence of strangers the better to conceal his cruel and merciless temper when in private'. This was a very important point, because the defender here was trying to debar his wife's relations as witnesses, while her lawyer was arguing that 'there ought to be a greater liberty allowed in the probation here than in many other cases And if it were otherwise how many married people would live in a most miserable condition, and yet seldom or never be able to obtain a separation for want of strict prooff'. The commissaries always followed this line, allowing even the nearest relatives of an abused wife to appear as a witness unless there was a particular reason why they should not be admitted. Elizabeth was granted her separation in January 1719.[2]

When denying their actions husbands sometimes had to explain away awkward facts. For example, in 1809 Mary Craik alleged that her husband, James Windrim 'while they were both in bed together, struck her in a barbarous and cruel manner upon the breasts and other parts of the body, and afterwards pulled her out of the bed, and dragged her from the one end of the room to the other, whereby one of her fingers was broken'. Windrim denied that any of this had happened, but said that one night when his wife was cursing him he 'rose from his chair with a view to go to the Door, but he was prevented by his wife who laid hold of him, and while attempting to extricate himself from her grasp she fell first upon a Table which was standing in the Room, and afterwards fell on the floor and hurt her little finger.' In an 1812 case Ann Drysdale stated that her husband, James Pittullo, in presence of her brother, 'struck her on the head and face drove her head against the Chimney piece in the dining room by which one of her ear-rings was broke and her nose bled'. Pittullo's version was that his wife was shouting at him when he 'who had always hitherto refrained from lifting his hand or even laying hold of her now highly irritated took her by the arm to put her out when in the struggle his hand touched her about the nose.' His wife, he said, was 'a woman of a very full habit of body and the least agitation or exertion causes her nose to blood. This accordingly took place when she instantly roared out murder.' In 1822 Jean Hewart stated that her husband, Alexander Comb, 'struck her upon one occasion with a candlestick upon the the head to the great effusion of her blood'. Comb claimed that this was an accident; during an argument he 'while saying to her in despair "Woman you will drive me mad" unfortunately accompanied the ejaculation with a motion of his hand which caught a Candlestick standing on the table which in falling scratched the face of the Pursuer who was at the time stooping near the foot of the table.' Such 'explanations' were laughed out of court.[3]

WITHOUT HER CONSENT

Most separation cases were brought by wives who had left home; many were living under the protection of relatives and refused to see their husbands. Some husbands therefore claimed that the legal action had been raised by those relatives without the consent, and possibly even the knowledge, of their wives. Even before the first cases in the Commissary Court, James Dallas of Saintmairtines, defending himself against the action of his wife, Barbara Cockburn, before the Privy Council in 1704, made this claim. The libel raised in her name 'he did not impute to her but to her father, and mother, for ane seperat end of their own'.[4]

In 1764, after Mary Gibson raised an action against her husband, James Hastie of Kameshill, he said that he 'had reason to believe that this proces was carried on without his wifes knowledge or consent and contrary to her inclination', and that the instigators were her father and mother, 'who upon many occasions had discovered an ill will at the Defender and Even an inclination to ruin him'. The commissaries asked for her oath of calumny, in which she swore that she had heard the libel of separation read out in her presence, 'and that she gave her doers or procurator the necessary Informations and Instructions for Drawing said Libell and that the said action of separation had been brought by her of her own free will and choice and no way by the Instigation of her parents or Friends'. After the witnesses provided proof of his maltreatment the commissaries granted her a separation.[5]

In 1770 Kenneth McAndrew, lint presser and shopkeeper in Edinburgh, appeared very reasonable when defending himself against his wife, Susanna Rhind.[6] He was willing to admit that there had been disputes between them, 'and he shall also admitt That there may have been faults on both sides, which is commonly the Case when matters come this Length between Husband and Wife, But he does not blame his Wife entirely for many gross falsehoods which are sett furth in the Lybell because he is sensible, that these are owing to Evil disposed persons who from an Inveterate malice and ill will against him have prompted his wife to take these measures.' He asked the commissaries to 'order the personal appearance of the Parties before them when he will have an opportunity (which he has so much wished for in vain) of reasoning the matter with the Pursuer', for he was sure that 'such an Interview will have the Effect to bring about an amicable compromise, and prevent further Trouble to the Court and Expence to the Parties.'

Susanna responded bitterly: her husband knew that she would 'be able to prove very gross maltreatment, and such as no human creature could put up with, at the same time she is not able to prove the half or rather the tenth part of what she suffered, having no Servant or other person in the house with her'. If she was ordered to attend the examination of the witnesses she would do so, but she thought that 'any other meeting with the Defender (who hopes to gain upon her too easy temper) is altogether unnecessary, as she has already two different times told the Defender since raising the proces, she never would live with him.' The court did not ask her to appear, and after witnesses testified (one said that Susanna 'showed her blae marks upon her legs and arms', and that she 'was in such condition that she could not lift her right arm to her head so as to eat her victuals with that right arm by carrying it to her head'), the separation was granted.

When Ann Tomlin raised her action against William Bowness of Springvale in 1818 the couple had been married for over thirty years and had brought up a large family.[7] Bowness claimed that his wife 'is of a weak and facile Disposition and easily imposed upon, and some evil disposed persons have most improperly interfered with her and induced her to bring the present action with a view to desire some benefit from a separate aliment by getting her to live with them'. He insisted that 'she has frequently expressed her willingness to return, but the undue influence of others of her advisers has been successfully exerted hitherto to prevent her.'

Her procurator replied that a year earlier when Alexander Blair, writer to the signet, was in Dumfries-shire, Ann approached him, 'representing the cruel and barbarous usage of the Defender, the injury which her health thereby sustained and the impossibility of her longer living with him':

> Mr Blair was by no means desirous of being concerned in such a disagreeable business and therefore advised her bearing with her husband as far and as long as possible. On Mr Blair's being afterwards in that part of the Country the Pursuer however having again repeatedly applied to him and stated the continuation of the Defender's bad usage, he took down from her own mouth sundry particulars thereof and afterwards laid a statement before Counsel, who was of opinion that upon the Pursuer's establishing even a small part of the facts condescended upon the Pursuer would be found entitled to a separate aliment – and from the various meetings which Mr Blair had with the Pursuer, he is of opinion that so far from the Pursuer being of the weak and facile disposition represented by the Defender she is as sensible and possessed of as much information as most women he had met with in her situation of life – and certainly her perseverance in the business is rather symptomatic of steadiness and strength of mind than of facility or weakness as alleged.

Bowness managed to drag out the litigation for a long time by making promises of an extrajudicial settlement and then failing to sign the requisite documents, but in 1822 the separation was granted.

Some men whose wives had tolerated an enormous amount of abuse must have truly deceived themselves into thinking that those wives could not possibly be the prime movers in the legal action. However, it was sometimes merely a ploy, as is particularly well illustrated in the 1825 case of Jean Macmillan against James Dawson, brass founder in Glasgow.[8] In his defences Dawson insisted that he did not believe that his wife 'can ever have sanctioned such a statement as that contained in the Summons', and he therefore petitioned the commissaries to order her to appear in court to swear an oath of calumny. He was, in effect, attempting to use the legal process as a further means of abuse.

Jean personally signed the answers which her lawyers drew up, 'to satisfy Your Lordships that the charges contained in the Summons come directly and deliberately from herself . . . and it is trusted that this will have the intended effect':

> For the fact is, that besides delay, the Defender counts much upon the present state of the pursuers health (which has been most seriously affected, by the long continued ill treatment she has experienced from him, and by the weak state of her nerves arising from it) and supposed that she will not be able to support the trying act of appearing and giving her oath. Accordingly, he has been endeavouring to work upon her fears, by causing his emissaries to wait on

her, and lay before her a most appalling account of the ceremony, of taking the oath in this Court, in hopes that this shall deter her from doing herself justice and obeying Your Lordships appointment, in case you should appoint her to give the oath de Calumnia.

The commissaries refused his petition, did not demand any oath from her, and granted the separation after hearing her evidence.

PROVOCATION

A husband had the legal right to argue that he was provoked to treat his wife harshly by her own behaviour, and many husbands, while at the same time denying seriously maltreating their wives, put forward this claim. In the 1729 case of Mary Duncan against John Harrower, shipmaster in Perth (whose sexual jealousy of his wife we saw in Chapter 14), he said that Mary provoked him by her vicious temper, 'and would not only scould him and give him Intolerable names and Language, But also would beat the defender and therefore there could be no ground for a process of separation where the Treatment Complained was but a moderat Castigation which the husband might Lawfully do, where his wifes Insolencies did swell to too high a stream tyde'. But he failed to bring any proof of provocation, while Mary brought plenty of proof of his brutal treatment of her, so she was granted her separation.[9]

Some wives were so conditioned to believe that they must be submissive that they could feel they were behaving badly if they retaliated in any way, even in the most extreme circumstances, as in the 1748 case of Elisabeth McGauchan against James Johnston, writer (lawyer) in Edinburgh. James Smith, another lawyer, married to a relative of Elisabeth's, had often told Johnston off for his treatment of his wife. Interrogated on Johnston's behalf, he told the court that Johnston had also complained to him of his wife's 'having given him provoking Language and injurious treatment'. Smith had spoken of this to Elisabeth 'who said that she cou'd bear with the defenders passion when it was confined to words yet it was not so easy to bear with it when it broke out into blows, and that she did not doubt but upon these Occasions she might have given bad language to the defender for which she was sorry'.[10] (We will see more of this couple later in the chapter.)

A typical statement of defence appeared in the 1785 case of Mary Stuart against Andrew Taylor (in which we saw a neighbour intervening in Chapter 15). He insisted that he

never gave his wife any improper or bad usage altho he has had frequently the most gross provocation from her for she is haughty proud and ill natured in the highest degree, expensive in her dress in so much that the defender found it impossible to support her extravagance without utter ruin to himself and family but what is worse than all she is addicted to idleness and tippling and of such a wandering disposition that she was seldom at home attending to the affairs of her family.

He was unable to prove any of this, and the commissaries 'Found it proven that the defender had maltreated the pursuer by beating and bruising her in a most cruel and barbarous manner as also by turning her out of doors and excluding her his house' and granted the separation.[11]

Defences in such cases were almost formulaic, but a more complex situation can be seen in the 1788 case of Marion Campbell against John Grahame in Renfrewshire.[12] Grahame spent most of his life in Jamaica, and was in his fifties when he returned home in 1781 with a small fortune of £2,000. He stayed at first with his brother, who was married to a sister of Marion's, 'and by the happiness which he saw prevail in his brothers family, he was induced to pay his addresses to the present pursuer who was then a widow much about his own time of life and who had several children by a former husband'. She readily agreed to marry him, but afterwards 'in place of that affectionate attention' which he 'had every reason to expect from her and which was his sole object in the marriage he soon found that he and his interests were very indifferent to her, and that her views were entirely confined to the interests of her children of her first husband, as she was no longer of an age to have any by her present.' He admitted that he was 'of a warm and choleric temper which was considerably increased by the disappointment he had met with in his marriage', and claimed that she took advantage of this in hopes of eventually gaining a separate aliment for herself and children. 'It is very difficult to prove the provocations arising from the indifference of a wife or from the crossings or obstinacy of her temper', he stated, 'The provocation is given in private and if the party provoked is of a passionate heart, there will be plenty of witnesses in his own family, to prove against him the violence and imperiousness of his Disposition'.

She had called him a brute and an adulterer, 'and there can be no doubt that she must have given him much more provocation for the purpose of inflaming and irritating his temper'. Poor man! But the court was unlikely to warm to the cause of a man who raped his servants. One of them had told a witness 'of the attempts he had made upon her virtue', and another recalled a servant leaving because Grahame 'one day when there was no person in the house robbed her of her chastity by compulsion.'

Moreover, he threw his wife out of the house one snowy night, saying 'Damn you, I'll be quit of you and will have no more to do with you', and bolting the door. It was too bad a night to travel, and eventually the servants got her 'into the stable where she fainted there being no fire nor candle till Neil Mcfie brought out a little fire to the stable'. At about midnight Mcfie (a servant) went back to the house and knocked on the door, telling Grahame that his wife 'was fainting and like to die', which Grahame answered 'Let her die there Damn her before I'll take her in'. One of the female servants then persuaded her to share their bed, where she 'was very cold and shivering and that neither the pursuer nor the deponent nor the other Girl slept any that night'. In the morning Grahame allowed her to pack some things and leave; all but one of the servants refused to stay in the house any longer and accompanied her to Greenock. Flora McDugald, one of the servants who told this story, said that her mistress had eaten nothing since dinner the day before, but about two miles from the house they realised that none of them had any money to buy food, 'except the deponent who had two pence with which she bought four biscuits one of which she gave to the pursuer and one to each of the servants and one to herself'. There was no way that Grahame could justify his behaviour, no matter how bitterly he might regret his marriage.

By the end of the eighteenth century cases were being brought by wives who did not necessarily enact the dutiful roles expected of them. In the only conjoined separation case in our period, that of John McLeod, surgeons' instrument maker in Edinburgh against Dorothea Primrose Lyon, and hers against him, in 1825, both parties accused the other of violence.[13] McLeod declared that one night his wife pursued him to the bedroom into which he had shut himself, 'threw Missiles of different kinds through the windows above the door of said Bedroom and at last succeeded in getting the door open by breaking one of the Pannels with a Common Ball used for breaking Coals.' She then attacked him 'and seizing him by the neckcloth threw him down and unless assistance had been procured the said John McLeod would have been strangled.' Both before and since the action was raised she 'attacked and struck the Pursuer in his shop broke and destroyed surgical and other Instruments and the shop furniture which forced the Pursuer on numerous occasions to procure the assistance of officers of Police', and finally she was bound over to keep the peace. Witnesses bore out his story – one had had to drag Dorothea off her husband when she was trying to strangle him.

It was obvious that McLeod would get his separation decreet, but Dorothea had equally convincing proof of his behaviour. Mary Marr, their servant, declared: 'I have seen him ill-use her many a time – I have seen him take hold of her wrists and twist them, and kick her with his foot; and I once saw him twist her wrists so that she was unable to put a cap on her head for many a day'. Mary was asked 'If Mrs McLeod gave any provocation to her husband at any of these times?', and answered, 'When Mr McLeod kept regular hours there was nothing of the kind, but when he did not do so I must say that Mrs McLeod did speak to him, which might provoke him'. The commissaries then asked 'if Mrs McLeod made use of any improper expressions on these occasions to her husband, and if she recollects what they were?' Mary recollected 'some of them – When he was out late and as she thought in improper company she might call him a whore-master, and often a son of a bitch, that was a word she often used.' The commissaries, with entire impartiality, found it proved that 'the Parties have respectively been guilty of grossly maltreating and abusing each other', granted the separation to both, and found her entitled to an aliment.

RECONCILIATION

In Chapters 4 and 5 we saw that the defence of reconciliation or *remissio injuriae* was often used in divorce cases, though rarely successfully. The defence was frequently employed in separation cases as well throughout the period but was never successful. The legal reasoning was as follows: if a wife forgave her husband's adultery and returned to live with him, then that adultery was 'wiped from the slate', but if a woman who had been treated cruelly agreed to return to her husband after he promised to behave better, then she was behaving just as she ought to do; if he then abused her again she was fully entitled to charge him with all the earlier episodes.

For instance, in 1818 James Pirie, painter in Edinburgh, argued it against Isobel Hislop. Her lawyer responded that it 'forms rather a singular plea upon the part of the Defender, that the Respondents long patience, and forbearance with him, should bar her for bringing these, or prior acts before Your Lordship, as a ground of separation, seeing that in place of her submission and patience having the effect of touching him with remorse and being the means of his repentance and reformation, that on the contrary he has become more hardened'.[14]

In 1748 James Johnston claimed that he had been reconciled with Elisabeth McGauchan, whom we heard apologising for her defiance when being abused by her husband.[15] They had agreed on a separation – because of his treatment of her, she said; 'to Gratifie her fancies and caprice', he said – but he would not then leave her alone. The agreement allowed him to visit her, and he became increasingly troublesome, so that she 'was Obliged upon sundry occasions to have recourse to the Landlady and the people in the house to turn him out of Doors'. To escape his attentions she took another room, above that of her landlady, Mrs Mckinnon, who was to tell Johnston that his wife had 'flitted and she did know know whither'. He pestered the poor woman until he found out, and he started visiting Elisabeth again, so 'she ordered the Servant to bolt the door and deny him access, on which occasions he woud have lay'n in the stair or stayed in a Neighbours house watching till the door opened'. Twice he tricked his way into the house; the second time she sent for help, and Baillie Mansfield came, but he still refused to leave. 'Baillie Mansfield told him he had often heard of his bad Usage towards his wife but that this was a proof of it when he refused to go away, altho' he saw her all in tears, But afterwards a friend of her own sent for the Guard and carried him off.'

To found a defence of reconciliation on such behaviour seems extraordinary, but after the commissaries repelled it a first time, he continued to plead it, on the grounds that he had many times bedded with his wife, offering to prove this by her oath. The commissaries questioned her, and she said that 'her husband did many different times come and ly all night in the same bed with her, but that it generally was with the utmost Reluctancy on the part of the deponent, who likeways acquainted her Landlady with the aversion to this kind of Correspondence'. When he found her after she had flitted he again 'lay some nights with her, but the deponent allways expressed the greatest aversion at allowing him to ly all night with her'. At first she would sit up half the night rather than go to bed with him, but her health would not permit her to go on doing this. She added that 'during all the time of Mr Johnston's Visiting and lying all night with her as above he frequently maltreated and used her Ill, and that any Cohabitation that she had with him was never with any intention of any reconciliation on her part'. The commissaries knew that a wife had to obey her husband and found that her testimony under oath 'did not prove a Reconciliation relevant to exclude the Action of Separation and Aliment at her Instance'.[16]

In 1818 David Veitch, in Newbigging, put forward two grounds for his defence of reconciliation with his wife, Amelia Wight.[17] In the first place, she had previously raised an action for separation in 1808, but subsequently returned to him, which proved that they had been reconciled, and secondly, even since raising this action she was still living in the same house as him, which again proved that they were reconciled. Together they ran 'a house or Assylum in Inveresk for the Accommodation of Deranged persons'. Veitch insisted that he 'had a gentle disposition', while she 'in a homely Scotch phrase wears the breeches'. She 'kept possession of the money received for the Boarding and retained possession of all the keys of the house and of all the liquors'.

She responded: it was her mother who had left her the house and grounds, and 'so far from being any assistance', her husband 'from his habits of almost constant intoxication was the very reverse. He used to bring people to the house at night and they remained drinking and rioting with him till morning during which he often abused the Pursuer'. Her earlier action had been dropped because she had paid her husband's debts out of money of her own in exchange for his promise of better conduct in future. There was no need to refer to events prior to that period, for she had plenty of proof of his 'Outrageous and brutal Conduct since that process was dropt, nay within these few months and even since the present process was raised'. As for continuing to live with him, although 'she was kept in continual terror and even danger of her life' she could not leave him 'because she would then not only be leaving the house and furniture which was her own private property but she would also be giving up the Charge of the boarders, and would then lose the business of which she took the sole management – and which form her and her familys chief support'.

The commissaries made her restrict her proof to events after 1808 but did not accept the defence of reconciliation. Witnesses testified to his drunken violence and also helped to paint the necessary picture of the dutiful wife. One, a constable, was asked by the court 'If he ever saw or heard Mrs Veitch use Mr Veitch ill and if she is a high tempered woman', and answered, 'No She may be a high tempered woman as she has great concerns to manage but I never heard her use him any way opprobriously'. When granted her separation Amelia did not bother asking for either aliment or expenses from her husband.

SOME UNSUCCESSFUL CASES

In fourteen cases the commissaries either dismissed the action or absolved the husband. In two of those the marriage was not proven, three were for miscellanous reasons, and nine were because the wife had not proven her charges.

The 1748 case of Ann Montgomery against George Moir of Leckie is one of the oddest of all in our period.[18] Her libel referred to his 'terrible fitts of passion of Cursing and Damning and stamping with his Feet And Lifting and shaking his Fist at her', but not to any actual acts of violence. When the commissaries asked for specific incidents, she declared that once they were forced to get out of a coach because the water was so high and walk some distance on a dangerous road, 'and During all that time the Defender never offered to give the least Assistance to the pursuer tho it was a most Violent Storm'. His lawyer responded that such an charge was 'of such a nature as rather to excite Laughter when such a fact is proposed as an Article in a proces of Separation'.

It took a long time to get to the gist of the problem. William Govan younger of Boquhaple testified that Moir had told him that on their second night in bed together Ann had taken him 'by the privy member and complained that he had only one stone'; Leckie 'told her that he had two tho one of them was larger than the other', whereupon Ann 'complained That he was a Cheat'. On hearing this Govan asked Leckie 'what he had performed the first night' with his wife, and Leckie answered that 'he had done it twice or thrice'. Leckie also told Govan that 'he had gone soon thereafter to Doctor Mcfarlane and laid himself open to him and that the Doctor had given his opinion That he was able to get children tho' not to satisfy some women's immoderate appetites'.

Leckie also 'unbosom'd himself' to his old tutor, George Home of Argatly. On the second night, he told Home, his wife 'had put down her hand and handled his privy member and cry'd That he was a cheat to marry any woman of her fortune for that he was not able to get her with child'. Home immediately asked Leckie 'if he had done nothing to her the first night', to which he answered that 'he had given her three Bobs'. But, he said that his wife 'told him of one Mrs Bogle who said to her That her husband had done her over Ten times in one night'. Leckie also told Home of the doctor's opinion that he 'was able to get Children'. The question of children appears to have been the crucial one, for according to Leckie, her belief was that 'he was uncapable to gett her with Child, thereby to gain that part of her Uncle's Fortune, which was secured to the Issue of the Marriage'.

Another witness, William Graham of Gartur, declared that he had visited Leckie a few months after the marriage when Leckie 'burst into Tears and call'd himself the most miserable man in the world for that he had married a wife who was not pleased with any thing he could say or do' – 'so miserable and overwhelm'd with grief' was he that 'when he went to bed he frequently wish'd he might never awake or rise again'.

At about that time his wife was apparently contemplating an action against him on the grounds of impotence, claiming that he 'was burnt up in a hot Country and had given dry bobbs to her'.

By the time she raised the action Ann had long since gone to live with her uncle, and as she could not have raised an action for annulment or divorce she was simply trying to get an aliment out of him. Witnesses had seen her in tears and heard them quarrelling, but no abuse, and the case appears to have been abandoned.[19]

Earlier in this chapter we noted that a wife's provocation was almost never considered to justify a husband's brutality. The exception is the case of Isobel Moore against Robert Cuming, late shipmaster in Leith, now residing in Edinburgh, in 1764.[20] She alleged acts of violence on his part; he alleged similar acts on hers. Witnesses saw him beat and kick her, saw her throw things at him and hit him with a stick, and heard them both call each other bad names. In spite of the bad treatment she received, Isobel appears to have been the dominant one in the relationship, for one of their servants several times heard Cuming ask his wife 'to allow him to bed with him as they at that time lay separately', and he did this 'with his Hatt off as a favour', but Isobel 'answered she would never yield her Body to him and that she would see him damned sooner'. A neighbour once advised Isobel to 'flatter' her husband 'or behave in a more discreet manner to him To which she said she neither would nor could do so'. But in her answers to his defences she defied him 'to prove any thing in her conduct ever since she was his wife that would in the least Justify the barbarous and inhuman treatment she had met with from him'.

He did so. His wife had caused him to be taken by a press gang; he was away for four years and underwent great hardship. Witnesses bore this out. Isobel had said 'she would do all she could to get the defender pressed or put to the Sea Service and that her father would get it done as she could live much happier if the defender were away from her', and when he was pressed she 'looked over the window when the Sailors were Carrying off the Defender, and the Deponent Observed her smiling upon that Occasion'. Another witness had been told by a neighbour that 'she had been desired by this Pursuer to bring the press Gang . . . and that she accordingly had brought the said Gang to carry off the Defender'. The witness had heard Isobel 'herself acknowledge that she was the occasion of pressing the defender into the Sea Service and the reason she gave for this was that the defender was turned so bad a husband and was ruining any substance that she and her children had'. In spite of proof of beatings and bruises, the commissaries 'Found no Sufficient foundation for the separation and aliment Lybelled' and absolved Cuming.

In 1811 Agnes Johnston, a widow in Lochmaben, claimed that her husband, Walter Dinwoodie of Auchingath (for whom it was also a second marriage), treated her very badly, 'abusing her upon all occasions and subjecting her to hard labour incompatible with her years and strength', and finally throwing her down and attempting to murder her.[21] His story was that she had been advised that her legal claims on him 'in case of his death would exceed her provisions by the marriage contract' and had been making his life a misery by pestering him to destroy the marriage contract. Finally she had left him, in hopes of forcing him to comply with her wishes.

The commissaries demanded specific details of ill treatment from her, and she said that he forced her 'to work like a menial servant and in particular during harvest obliged her to make ready the victuals of a Band of Shearers and even after she had sprained her arm by lifting a large Pot from the fire to such a degree that she could make no use of it, he obliged her to continue that work and carry to the field the shearers victuals upon her head'. Dinwoodie responded that neither of them were 'in a high rank of life'. His wife was 'the daughter of a Herd', who at one time had been a servant of his father, a small tenant of the Earl of Hopeton. Afterwards she married 'John Smith a Weaver in Lochmaben who by his industry acquired a small house and byre in that village and about an acre of moss ground'. Her 'advanced years is 56.' His own farm of Auchingath 'after taxes draws about £36 a year, and the two farms in possession of his sons are rented at £78 a year.' The significance of all this was 'the *station* of the parties . . . for the behaviour that in the higher ranks of life might be esteemed severe, indicates in those of a lower station no more than what is their bounden duty it being consistent with the established manners of the Class of Society to which they belong.' According to Dinwoodie, the strain to her arm did not come about 'by lifting a large pot from the fire, she received it by a fall in the byre occasioned by her feet sliding on some Cow's dung'. And the '*great* band of shearers', he said,

> was never above *nine persons*, as all he had in crop that year was eight acres of oats and this *great band* (for whom it was cruelty and oppression for the pursuer to make their victuals) took their victuals in the House, the field where the oats was growing being close to it and none of their victuals was carried to the field.

Furthermore, she could have called on the assistance of her servant maid 'if making victuals for nine shearers for a day or two was so great oppression to her'. He did not believe that this was 'such an act of *Cruelty* and *oppression* to the wife of a Tenant of a small farm as to justify her in leaving her husbands house', and repeated that the only reason she had done so was because he refused to destroy the marriage contract. She was unable to produce any evidence of his alleged attempt on her life, and the commissaries absolved him.

ALIMENT

We will finish the chapter, and the section of the book on separation, to look briefly at the amounts awarded by the commissaries. This was something they did not have to calculate in divorce cases, where the innocent party was entitled to whatever he or she would have got on the spouse's death, and any disagreement was handled elsewhere. But in separation cases it was up to the commissaries to determine the amount of the aliment, based on an account of the husband's circumstances produced by the wife, and an alternative version produced by the husband if he disagreed with it. As we shall see, their calculations appear to have been made on an entirely arbitrary and ad hoc basis, though in at least one case they took future eventualities into account. In the 1741 decreet of Margaret Crawford against Samuel Forbes of Knapernie, they awarded her £40 a year while his mother was alive; when she died there would be 'a considerable increase' to his estate 'by the falling of her Jointure', so after that he would have to pay her a higher amount. He also had to pay her an additional £20, the expense 'of her inlying of the child of which she was pregnant at the commencement of the proces', plus, of course, the expenses of the process.[22]

In 1798 Janet Miller had an annuity of £30 a year from her first husband, plus a house which paid £4 a year rent, all of which went to her husband, David Hume. The commissaries, when awarding her a separation, found her entitled to that amount and 'prohibited the said David Hume Defender from intermeddling with the said annuity and the rent of the said House'.[23]

In many contested cases the husband provided a totally different version of his financial state than the wife, and the wrangles could go on for a long time. But in at least two uncontested cases the wives appealed against the commissaries' awards. Janet Coke had suffered such a deep wound from being struck on the head with a poker by her husband, John Kirk, blacksmith in Leith, that neighbours had had to cut off part of her hair' and it caused her to be 'long ill after this and at one time was deranged . . . from the loss of blood.'[24] The commissaries awarded her a separation in October 1808, and she stated that her husband earned a guinea a week, and owned property in St Andrews with a yearly rental of about £37, making an income of £92. He did not contest this, but the commissaries awarded her only £7 a year aliment commencing the following January.

Janet appealed against this decision: she had been forced to take their child and leave him in 1803, and had been living separately from him since then, 'and by the greatest exertions of industry, not unfrequently attended with pain to herself in consequence of the irretrievable shake which her constitution had received from her husband's usage, she was enabled to earn a scanty subsistence to herself and her Child to a certain extent for in point of fact notwithstanding of these exertions she is in debt.' She had asked for £25 a year from Martinmas 1803, and for an additional £10 yearly for educating, clothing and maintaining the child. The £7 awarded, she submitted, was only a fourteenth part of her husband's aggregate income. 'Even in the case of an illegitimate child, and where the male parent is in the lowest rank of life the aliment is never below six pounds', so to award her, who was not in the lowest rank and who had been a dutiful wife, such a pitiful amount seemed highly unfair. The commissaries altered their decreet: they back-dated the payment to begin as of Whitsunday 1804 and raised the amount to £12 a year plus £10 for supporting the child as long as it lived with her. This was still only about half of what she had asked for, but wives often asked for much more than they expected to get, so she may have been satisfied after all.

Another disputed aliment was that granted to Janet or Jessie Kettle in 1811.[25] Her husband, Andrew Weir, had gone off to London and she learned that he was earning a salary of £100; as she had two young children to support she asked for at least £40 a year. The commissaries awarded her £15 for herself and £5 for each of the children as long as they remained with her. She appealed: fixing a separate aliment for the children implied that he had power to remove them from her, and while she knew that the general rule of law was that a father was entitled to the custody of his lawful children, there were exceptions, and this was one of them. Furthermore, she had never asked for a separate aliment for her children. The £15 was inadequate, and so was £25, for that was the amount of the rent of the house he got by marrying her, 'consequently the defender is not found bound to contribute one shilling of his own earnings for the maintenance of his injured wife and infant family.' The commissaries altered their interlocutor and awarded her £20 but withdrew the aliment for the children. Her procurator appealed against this to the Court of Session which found her entitled to £35, to be reduced to £25 'when the defender shall relieve her of supporting their children', a finding that emphasises both the arbitrary nature of the commissaries' awards, and also the difficult legal position of a mother at a time when a father's claim to custody of his children took precedence.

A final question is how a husband's liability for aliment could be enforced. As everyone at the time knew the answer to this, there was no need to state it in the records, but fortunately in one relatively early decreet the commissaries did so. In the 1748 case which has illustrated various points in this chapter − that of Elisabeth McGauchan against James Johnston − they ordained him to pay her £15 a year plus £15 for the expenses of the process. If he did not do so within 15 days the officers of the court were to 'attour fence and arrest' his 'readiest moveable goods gear debts sums of money and others whatsomever pertaining and belonging to him wherever the same may or can be apprehended within the Jurisdiction of the Commissariot of Edinburgh'.[26]

NOTES

All cc references are in the Scottish Record Office.
1. cc8/5/2.
2. Other lawyers also made the point about the difficulty in proving domestic violence. In the 1825 case of Macmillan vs Dawson, her lawyer said that the charges were 'not one half of what might have been detailed in the summons. The situation of parties, connected as husband and wife, affords to a cruel husband numberless opportunities of venting his rage, and inflicting ill treatment upon his helpless wife, which escape all notice, and are quite beyond the reach of observation and of evidence.' cc8/6/145.

3. cc8/6/88; cc8/5/32; cc8/6/140.
4. SRO.PC.2/28/ff.328–337. I am grateful to the late Peter Vasey for this reference.
5. cc8/5/11.
6. cc8/6/28.
7. cc8/6/123.
8. cc8/6/145.
9. cc8/5/3.
10. cc8/5/9. Smith also once heard Elisabeth say to her husband that 'she wou'd bear any thing' from her husband 'if he would keep down his hands but that her body was not able to endure such treatment'.
11. cc8/5/18.
12. cc8/5/19.
13. cc8/6/149.
14. cc8/6/116.
15. cc8/5/9.
16. Johnston appealed against the decision: his wife had expressly deponed 'to her frequently bedding with him both in the room she first hired, and in the house she called her own . . . had it not been agreeable to herself she easily coud have fallen upon a method of getting free of him . . . And in case the word bedding may not be thought to go no further than the actuall lying in bed as she speaks of Reluctancy she may if thought necessary be Interrogate upon her receiving the proper douceurs of a marriage bed, and whether by her they were not returned by equal warmth . . . there was no evidence of there being any force on the part of the husband, on the contrary a direct proof of her going to bed voluntarily and willingly, and if she at last conceived such an aversion at it as to exclude her husband from this piece of happiness; he heartily regretts it, but had nothing to blame himself for; Having done all in his power to please her during their so cohabiting'. The commissaries were having none of it and refused his petition.
17. cc8/5/37.
18. cc8/6/17.
19. The commissaries held the case as concluded on 15 November 1749, but there is no interlocutor after that. The inventory – which lists this as the last of 70 items – notes that on 16 Nov. the pursuer's agent borrowed all of the writs. Apparently two more items were borrowed in June 1750, followed by a bill of advocation for Leckie 'with Remit thereon' which in turn was borrowed (and apparently not returned). On the front of the inventory is a note that the account of expenses was borrowed on 30 April 1751; that too is not amongst the papers. It is possible, therefore, that the commissaries did award Ann an aliment, but without a surviving decreet it cannot be counted amongst the successful cases.
20. cc8/5/11.
21. cc8/5/32.
22. cc8/5/7.
23. cc8/5/24. Janet asked the commissaries for an additional aliment on top of that, but they ignored this request.
24. cc8/5/30.
25. cc8/5/32.
26. cc8/5/9.

CHAPTER 17

THE OVERALL PICTURE
ASSESSED

Having examined aspects of divorce, annulment and separation in the period 1684 to 1830, we return now to the three questions posed at the end of Chapter 1. Why was there such a sharp rise in numbers of divorce cases in the 1770s? Why did separation cases not follow the same pattern? And, once the numbers of divorce suits began to shoot up, why did they not climb much higher than they did, to something approaching twentieth-century figures?[1]

WHY DID SO MANY MORE PEOPLE SUE FOR DIVORCE?

The rise in divorce suits toward the end of the eighteenth century – from a total of 118 cases between 1684 and 1770 to 786 cases between 1771 and 1830 – was not unique to Scotland. Nancy Cott found that in Massachusetts 'more than half of the petitions and decrees between 1692 and 1786 occurred after 1764, and more than a third of them after 1774', while Sheldon S. Cohen discovered that in Connecticut the number doubled between 1785 and 1797. In neither of these states was there any change in legislation during this period. The European principality of Neuchâtel underwent a similarly dramatic rise: of the 426 requests for divorce in the eighteenth century, 78 were heard in the first fifty years and 348 from 1757 to 1806. Even in England there was a resurgence of separation cases on the grounds of adultery or cruelty, all of which led Lawrence Stone to conclude that 'there was some deep shift of mood and morals in Protestant areas in the late eighteenth century which made legal separation and divorce much more acceptable solutions to marital disharmony than they had been earlier'. Or, as Cott put it in trying to explain the convergence of the rise in divorce cases with the War of Independence, 'a certain personal outlook – one that implied self-assertion and regard for the future, one that we might label more "modern" than "traditional" – may have led a person to seek divorce and also to support American independence'.[2]

Merrill Smith argues for late eighteenth-century Pennsylvania that increasingly marital breakdown was caused by a clash between the new ideal of companionate marriage, expected by the wife, and the old patriarchal pattern, anticipated by the husband.[3] This is too simplistic; the ideal of companionate marriage dates back to at least the seventeenth century, while the patriarchal model is still with us. But that there was a new intellectual climate in the eighteenth century, particularly in countries, like Scotland, where the Enlightenment flourished – is undeniable. New ideas about personal freedom help to explain why from the 1760s onward the structure of Scottish church discipline, which had operated so successfully as an agent of social control for two centuries, began to fall apart.

This was also a period of immense social and economic change, when traditional community structures were being shattered, and when men and women were flocking into the cities. There was also a rise in living standards during the same period in Scotland which, as noted earlier, has been attributed less to the expansion of wage rates and employment opportunities for males than for their expansion for women and children.[4]

We saw in Chapter 14 that a wife's financial independence might have been an element in her husband's violence against her, but that such a woman was at least in a position to bring a legal action against her husband. There is certainly evidence of some of the women bringing divorce actions being in a similar position. When, in 1783, Rebeccah Gibson petitioned for money for aliment and expenses for her case against her husband, Giuseppe Puppo, musician in Edinburgh, he responded:

> Mrs Puppo is in much better circumstances than the defender she herself following the same profession with him and being as often engaged by the managers to perform in the Concert hall as the defender himself and her emoluments thence arising are little inferior to his – Besides she is also very much employed in private teaching which is a Branch of the profession the defender seldom or never practices and which is productive of very considerable profits.[5]

Rebeccah could have afforded a divorce action even without the aliment, and the same was true of Charlotte Franklin who brought her action in 1814. She declared that she had continued to live in the marital home because she and her sister used it 'as a boarding school for young Ladies which they had been enabled to do from the kindness of their husbands' Creditors who on seeing a state of their affairs were so much pleased with the conduct of the Pursuer and her Sister who had not contracted one house debt or any debt on their own account'.[6]

Apart from a new intellectual climate, and the possibility of economic independence for an increasing number of women, another possible explanation for the rise in cases of divorce for adultery is that there was more adultery. Britain was at war between 1776 and 1782 and then, in common with the rest of Europe, almost continuously from 1794 to 1815. Roderick Phillips noted that 'military conflicts separated husbands and wives for prolonged periods and provided opportunities for adultery', a fact strikingly borne out in the Scottish divorce records; by 1815 there was scarcely a man of any social class, whether pursuer or defender, who did not have a military or naval designation. The proportion of divorced wives who bore bastard children doubled from 12 per cent in Period 1 to 24 per cent in Period 2. The social dislocation of the war years continued to have repercussions in its immediate aftermath: twenty-two divorce petitions, the highest of any decade, were presented in 1816. The downturn in numbers in the 1820s may reflect a return to more stable conditions, or the economic depression which followed the war. However, it was only temporary, for between November 1836 and November 1841 an average of nineteen divorces were granted per year, a figure as high as for the war years.[7]

WHY WAS THE SEPARATION STORY DIFFERENT?

The question of why separation cases did not rise at the same time and at the same level is much more difficult to answer. It certainly had nothing to do with the attitude of the commissaries. On the contrary, while they were putting up barriers to an easy divorce toward the end of our period by demanding that pursuer and witnesses, unless they were paupers, appear personally in court, rather than appointing local commissioners – and, even more crucially, were refusing wives who did not know the whereabouts of their husbands the right to sue for adherence and then divorce for desertion – they were at the same time expressing their strongly negative feelings about men who maltreated their wives, and beginning to consider cases where there was no physical violence.

Of course, an abused wife was likely to look to other avenues of escape before going the length of a suit for judicial separation before the Commissary Court. Bringing a suit before the court was only necessary if the husband refused to allow his wife to live separately, or refused to adhere to a separation agreement, or continued to persecute her after she had left him. Nor was a separation decreet particularly satisfactory for either party. A husband would have to support his wife in a separate establishment for the rest of his life without being allowed to remarry, while a separated wife was, as Roderick Phillips put it, 'neither in a functioning marriage nor able to form a new marriage, yet expected to live the socially and sexually restricted life of a married woman'.[8]

And if the court was sympathetic to abused wives, that does not mean that the culture as such was sympathetic. The idea that the wife was somehow at fault was pervasive and has continued up to the present day. The fact that a husband's intercourse with another woman entitled a wife to a quick and easy divorce, while his beating and abusing her allowed her, at best, only the limited redress of judicial separation, speaks volumes about how seriously the latter behaviour was taken in comparison with the former.

We saw in Chapter 15 that many women did try and leave their husbands but were persuaded by friends, relatives and/or promises of better behaviour to return. Two cases came to an end when the husbands informed the court that their wives had returned to them and they were 'reconciled'.[9] This must have happened in a number of abandoned cases. Elizabeth Liddle was married to George Nimmo in August 1756 and began to experience violence from him a few months later. In July 1760 she raised an action for separation against him, but her relatives persuaded her not to go on but to see if 'her husband would afterwards treat her as he ought to do and in that view has lived ever since in a house [flat] near by her husband's'. She did not cohabit with him as his wife nor did she receive any financial support from him, yet he felt free to come into her room at any time and abuse her. She endured this for *twelve years* before reviving court proceedings and obtaining a judicial separation.[10] The pressures on abused wives must have been enormous.

WHY DID DIVORCE FIGURES NOT RISE MORE?

In comparison with separation cases, and with divorce actions at the beginning of our period, the figures for divorce are very high at the end of it, but a figure of twenty-two divorce petitions in a year is still incredibly low by modern standards, even allowing for the fact that the population roughly doubled in our period.[11] Why, in a country where divorce was so readily available to both sexes, did so few avail themselves of this option? Amongst the reasons for not divorcing, Phillips suggests popular distrust of the law, its institutions and personnel. He also suggests that most couples were locked into a family economy which was very difficult to get free of.[12] This helps to explain further why divorce rose at the end of the eighteenth century when that economy was breaking down, but adds to the puzzle of why it did not rise much more than it did. Economic constraints were undoubtedly a key factor, for though divorce may have been *relatively* cheap in Scotland, it was unlikely to cost less than the equivalent of four to eight months' salary for a working man, and proportionally more for a woman, so the motivation would have had to be high.

Phillips makes a useful distinction between marriage breakdown and divorce. There were various stages along the route: there might be marriage breakdown without the couple parting, the couple might informally agree to separate and live independently, or there might be a formal agreement in a local court, none of which would show up in evidence of marriage breakdown at national level.[13] With the financial and other constraints in operation during our period only a small fraction of failed marriages would culminate in divorce. So the question of why the number of divorces remained so low can be approached from the angle of what drove that tiny minority to the extremity of divorce.

In contrast to the abused wives who sued for separation when they could have gone for a divorce, a number of wives suing for divorce alleged that their husbands were guilty of cruelty as well as adultery, although this was totally irrelevant in a divorce action. Some may have simply been trying to blacken their husbands' character in the eyes of the commissaries, but the details in others are convincing enough to make the reader feel that the discovery of an adulterous connection, enabling a divorce action, came not as a dreadful shock but as a great relief.

In some instances, the guilty party had become an embarrassment. This was particularly true of wives who had become prostitutes. Finding them in the records was unexpected since the economic forces that might drive a single woman into prostitution are less likely to have prevailed with a married woman. The most usual explanation was alcohol. In a society where alcohol was cheap and vast quantities were drunk, we saw in Chapter 9 that some women would pillage the house of furniture and goods to pay for their drink habit, and ultimately sell their bodies for the purpose. It is not surprising that a husband married to such a woman should have wanted to rid himself of the legal tie. Nor is it surprising that a wife infected with venereal disease should have investigated where it came from and used the evidence to rid herself of such a husband. But those motives would apply in only a minority of cases.

A strong sense of betrayal was certainly one reason and accounts for most of the cases brought to the court within a short time after the discovery of the adultery. In one of the earliest cases (1691) John Ker, merchant burgess of Edinburgh, discovered that not only had his wife, Cecill Scott, been five months and three weeks gone with child to another man at the time she married him, she had continued to meet her lover about three times a week after the marriage.[14] But this motive cannot account for the cases where the couple had been living apart for years, the guilty party cohabiting with someone else who was then named as paramour in the case.

For England, Sybil Wolfram thought that in many of the cases where the divorce suit was brought long after the separation, this was because the separation had occurred for other reasons, but divorce was not possible except for adultery (or in the case of women, adultery compounded by other offences), which occurred later.[15] This may occasionally have been true for Scotland as well, but much less often since divorce was available for desertion. And in such cases the divorce action would have been raised immediately the adultery was discovered, not years later.

The likeliest reason for the majority of divorce suits is simply the desire to remarry. The only time this was suggested was in contested cases where the guilty party claimed that the sole reason for the pursuer bringing the divorce action was in order to marry someone else, a claim never denied by the pursuer. But as it was irrelevant to the case there was no particular reason to mention it. In cases of desertion, particularly, there is no convincing motive for spending so much money divorcing unless there was someone else on the scene. Since men were likelier to desert than women, the fact that as much as a quarter of desertion actions were brought by men can only be explained by their having taken up with a woman who demanded a legal marriage.

But how many people felt strongly enough to demand a legal marriage? The majority of cases in the Scottish records involve spouses who were already living separately, one of them with a new partner. We have seen various instances of bigamy, but most couples did not risk a criminal prosecution; they simply cohabited without a marriage ceremony. Nor were such relationships confined to the lower classes. For example, William Penson, professor of music in Edinburgh, had been living 'in open and notour adultery with Jane Penson Daughter of the late Thomas Penson Architect' for some years before his wife brought a divorce suit in 1828.[16]

While acknowledging that a low divorce rate was not synonymous with a low marriage breakdown rate, Roderick Phillips nevertheless believes that 'emotional incompatibility or indifference were in themselves seldom a reason for marriage breakdown before the nineteenth century.' He also thinks that 'the de facto dissolution of marriage (desertion or mutual agreement to separate) was unthinkable – simply inconceivable for most men and women in traditional European society.'[17] Neither conclusion can stand for Scotland at the end of the eighteenth and beginning of the nineteenth century.

In uncontested adherence cases witnesses were often asked if the deserting spouse had given a reason for the desertion. The impression gained from the bulk of these is *precisely* that of simple incompatibility. Thomas Nugent, farmer, deserted Ann Grant of Park about ten days after their marriage in 1793. When she brought an adherence case against him in 1806 a witness declared that he saw Nugent the day he left the country, 'when he told him that the pursuer Ann Grant had so many oddities that he resolved to live no longer with her'.[18] In the 1823 case of Frances Piper against James Hathorn, writer (lawyer) in Edinburgh, a fellow lawyer was told at the time by Hathorn why he left her:

he was highly displeased with many parts of the conduct of the pursuer his wife among others that she used to drink ale with the Landlady of the house that she had taken some small sum of money from him and many such little circumstances which he said it rendered it impossible for him to live in her society and accordingly he expressed his determination to the deponent that he would never again live with her or speak to her.

The witness added that Hathorn 'often stated to him that he would afford his wife sufficient cause for divorcing him with a view of getting separated from her'.[19]

Those examples were of men, but similar ones can be found for women. In the 1820 case of John Buchannan, baker in Edinburgh, against Johan Kelly, a witness 'understood he had got into difficulties about money matters and she the Defender had money of her own and she would not give any of it up to relieve him, and she went away and took all her own with her'.[20]

Letters provide added depth to the 1820 case of Thomas Fyffe against Elizabeth Morrison. Six or seven weeks after their marriage in June 1816 she left their home in Glasgow and returned to Edinburgh. Elizabeth's sister was told by Elizabeth at the time that 'he spoke harshly to her and staid from home at night and did not attend to their house and subsistance She said he did not strike her but that she could not live with him.' Fyffe wrote to his wife in September 1816; he had learned from his father that Elizabeth was pregnant and thought it his duty to ask her to return. He considered her reasons for leaving him 'altogether of such a frivolous nature to cause a woman of your years and understanding act such an imprudent part.' While he admitted that there might be 'blame attachable on both sides', he thought he had done his best for her and believed that 'by this time you will have thought more on the duties of a wife than ever and that we may still be happy in each other through time and at last meet in a happy eternity'. Elizabeth replied that she had indeed been pregnant but had miscarried two weeks earlier and thought that 'the Lord has been kind to me'. As for coming back to his house, she was 'just in the same mind [as] that day I left Glasgow and that is I never will set my foot in it more . . . I never will make you unhappy and myself also so as to come home to you that is the thing I never will do so you need never write me more on that subject'. She had found employment as a servant and considered that preferable to an unsatisfactory marriage.[21]

In adultery cases pursuer after pursuer described the second household set up by their spouse after deserting or mutually agreeing to separate, and one gets a very different picture from the traditional one of marriage until death. The individuals encountered in these records might be atypical, but only in going to the length of a divorce action, not in the situations they described. The hundreds bringing divorce cases may represent thousands who saw no need to, being settled in new partnerships unblessed by wedlock, or even preferring life as a domestic servant or back in the parental home to a miserable marriage. Most cases were uncontested, so this was hardly a world in which marriage was clung to at all costs; alternative futures were thinkable and realisable.

Such a scenario has also been suggested for early nineteenth-century England by John Gillis, who believes there were 'vast numbers of people living together, enjoying flexible relationships'. According to a commentator on London in the 1790s, 'in one Westminster neighbourhood, where only two-sevenths of the couple were believed to be legally wed, the reasons were not so much ideological as social: "we don't see any need of such a thing; we have agreed between ourselves and that is enough."' In a more recent book R. B. Outhwaite disagrees with Gillis, commenting sarcastically, 'It is perhaps convenient for such arguments that there is "no way that the actual extent of common law marriage can be measured".'[22] However, the evidence for Scotland strongly supports the Gillis stance.

In view of all this, the question of why there were so few divorces should surely be turned round to ask why there were as many as there were. By the early nineteenth century this was a society which tolerated stable unions without enquiring too closely into their legal base (as long as they were not harming anyone), and no longer persecuted women who chose to live apart from their husbands, so there would have had to be a strong motive to cause anyone to go to court and spend such a large proportion of their income to acquire a formal divorce.

NOTES

All cc references are in the Scottish Record Office.

1. Some of the material in this chapter previously appeared in my article, ' "Disregarding the Matrimonial Vows" – Divorce in Eighteenth and Early Nineteenth-Century Scotland', *Journal of Social History*, vol.30, no.2 (Winter 1996), 465–82.

2. Nancy F. Cott, 'Divorce and the Changing Status of Women in Eighteenth-Century Massachusetts', *William and Mary Quarterly*, 33 (1976), 592–3; S. S. Cohen, ' "To Parts of the World Unknown": The Circumstances of Divorce in Connecticut, 1750–1797', *Canadian Review of American Studies*, 11 (1980), 287. Jeffrey R. Watt, *The Making of Modern Marriage – Matrimonial Control and the Rise of Sentiment in Neuchftel, 1550–1800* (Ithaca and London 1992), 219; Lawrence Stone, *Road to Divorce – England 1530–1987* (Oxford 1992), 40–1.

3. Merrill D. Smith, *Breaking the Bonds – Marital Discord in Pennsylvania 1730–1830* (New York and London, 1991), 6, 21.

4. Rosalind Mitchison and Leah Leneman, *Sexuality and Social Control – Scotland 1660–1780* (Oxford, 1989), and the revised version, *Girls in Trouble – Sexuality and Social Control in Rural Scotland 1660–1780* (Edinburgh, forthcoming), c.2; Leah Leneman and Rosalind Mitchison, *Sin in the City – Sexuality and Social Control in Urban Scotland 1660–1780* (Edinburgh, forthcoming), c.1; A. J. S. Gibson and T. C. Smout, *Prices, Food and Wages in Scotland 1550–1780* (Cambridge 1995), 338–9, 353.

5. cc8/5/17.

6. cc8/5/33.

7. Roderick Phillips, *Putting Asunder: A History of Divorce in Western Society* (Cambridge 1988), 235, 418. (The figures for wives bearing bastards are 9 out of 73 and 96 out of 391.)

8. Ibid., 162–3. In France during the Revolution the Legislative Assembly that passed a remarkably liberal divorce law abolished legal separation, describing it as 'gothic' and 'barbarous'.

9. Reid vs Cumming, 1789, cc8/6/51; Carse vs Lawrie, 1812, cc8/6/96.

10. cc8/5/13. He had to pay her aliment from then on as well.

11. Michael Flinn, ed., *Scottish Population History* (Cambridge 1977), 241, 271, 302.

12. Phillips, *Putting Asunder*, 373.

13. Ibid., 317.

14. cc8/5/1.

15. Sybil Wolfram, 'Divorce in England 1700–1857', *Oxford Journal of Legal Studies* (vol.5, no.2), 176.

16. cc8/6/153.

17. Phillips, *Putting Asunder*, 359, 362.

18. cc8/5/29/3. The witness added that Nugent also said that 'he would leave her as an honest man for though he had seen in her Drawers a bill due by Provost Lennox of Kirkcudbright for a considerable sum and had also seen some silver yet he had touched none of them.'

19. cc8/5/41. Frances was a servant and, as we have seen in earlier chapters, class disparities could lead to unhappy marriages. But another lawyer was told by Hathorn that her 'bad temper' was the chief reason he left her.

20. cc8/5/38.

21. cc8/5/39.

22. John R. Gillis, *For Better, For Worse – British Marriages 1600 to the Present* (Oxford 1985), 186; R. B. Outhwaite, *Clandestine Marriage in England 1500–1800* (London and Rio Grande 1995), 139.

BIBLIOGRAPHY

The main sources for this book were Commissary Court registers of extracted decreets and process papers – respectively found under the references cc8/5 and cc8/6 at the Scottish Record Office, Edinburgh. Other works consulted include:

Barker-Benfield, G. J., *The Culture of Sensibility: Sex and Society in Eighteenth-Century Britain* (Chicago, 1992)

Adam, Sir Charles Elphinstone (ed.), *View of the Political State of Scotland in the Last Century* (Edinburgh, 1887)

Anglesey, Marquis of, *One-Leg – The Life and Letters of Henry William Paget 1768–1854* (London, 1961)

Burke's Landed Gentry

Bynum, W. F., 'Treating the Wages of Sin: Venereal Disease and Specialism in Eighteenth-Century Britain', in W. F. Bynum and R. Porter (eds), *Medical Fringe and Medical Orthodoxy, 1750–1850* (London, 1987), pp.5–28

Cairns, John W., 'A Note on *The Bride of Lammermoor*: Why Scott Did Not Mention the Dalrymple Legend until 1830', *Scottish Literary Journal*, 20 No.1 (May 1993), pp.19–36

Checkland, Sydney, *The Elgins, 1766–1917 – A Tale of Aristocrats, Proconsuls and Their Wives* (Aberdeen, 1988)

Clive, Eric M., *The Law of Husband and Wife in Scotland* (3rd ed., Edinburgh, 1992)

Cohen, S. S., ' "To Parts Unknown": The Circumstances of Divorce in Connecticut, 1750–1797', *Canadian Review of American Studies*, 11 (1980), pp.275–93

Complete Baronetage 1665–1707 (Exeter, 1904)

Cott, Nancy F., 'Divorce and the Changing Status of Women in Eighteenth-Century Massachusetts', *William and Mary Quarterly*, 33 (1976), pp.586–614

Cott, Nancy F., 'Eighteenth-Century Family and Social Life Revealed in Massachusetts Divorce Records', *Journal of Social History* 10 (1976), pp.20–43

Fergusson, James, *Reports on Some Recent Decisions by the Consistory Court of Scotland in Actions of Divorce* (Edinburgh, 1817)

Fergusson, James, *Treatise on the Present State of the Consistorial Law in Scotland* (Edinburgh, 1829)

Forte, A. D. M., 'Some Aspects of the Law of Marriage in Scotland: 1500–1700' in Elizabeth Craik, ed., *Marriage and Property – Women and Marital Customs in History* (Aberdeen, 1984), pp.104–118

Fraser, Patrick, *Treatise on the Law of Scotland as applicable to The Personal and Domestic Relations* (Edinburgh, 1846), vol.1

Fry, Michael, *The Dundas Despotism* (Edinburgh, 1992)

Gibson, Colin S., *Dissolving Wedlock* (London, 1994)

Gillis, John R., *For Better, For Worse – British Marriages 1600 to the Present* (Oxford, 1985)

Gourvish, T. R., 'The cost of living in Glasgow in the early nineteenth century', *Economic History Review*, 2nd series, vol.25 (1972), pp.65–80

Grant, Francis J. (ed.), *The Commissariot of Edinburgh: Consistorial Processes and Decreets, 1658–1800* (Edinburgh, 1909)

Guthrie, Charles J., 'The History of Divorce in Scotland', *Scottish Historical Review* 9 (1911), pp.39–52

Hardy, J. R., 'The Attitudes of Church and State in Scotland to Sex and Marriage, 1500–1707' (unpublished M.Phil. thesis, University of Edinburgh, 1978)

Hilton, Boyd, *The Age of Atonement; the Influence of Evangelicalism on Social and Economic Thought, 1750–1865* (Oxford, 1988)

Horstman, Allen, *Victorian Divorce* (London and Sydney 1985)

Houston, R. A. and Manon van der Heijden, 'Hands Across the Water: The Making and Breaking of Marriage Between Dutch and Scots in the Mid Eighteenth Century', *Law and History Review*, vol.15, no.2 (Fall 1997)

Jaeger, Muriel, *Before Victoria* (London, 1956)

Kelsall, H. and K. Kelsall, *Scottish Lifestyles 200 Years Ago* (Edinburgh, 1986)

Leneman, Leah and Rosalind Mitchison, *Sin in the City – Sexuality and Social Control in Urban Scotland 1660–1780* (Edinburgh, forthcoming)

Lochhead, Marion, *The Scots Household in the 18th Century* (Edinburgh, 1948)

Lothian, Maurice, *The Law, Practice and Style Peculiar to the Consistorial Actions Transferred to the Court of Session* (Edinburgh, 1830)

Marshall, Rosalind K., *Virgins and Viragoes – A History of Women in Scotland from 1080 to 1908* (London, 1983)

Mathieson, Cyril, *The Life of Henry Dundas First Viscount Melville 1742–1801* (London, 1933)

Mitchison, Rosalind and Leah Leneman, *Sexuality and Social Control – Scotland 1660–1780* (Oxford, 1989) and new edition: *Girls in Trouble – Sexuality and Social Control in Rural Scotland 1660–1780* (Edinburgh, forthcoming)

Monro, Alexander, Essay on Female Conduct in the form of letters to his daughter, c.1738, National Library of Scotland MS.6658. Copy by his daughter, Margaret 1739, MS.6659

Outhwaite, R. B., *Clandestine Marriage in England 1500–1800* (London and Rio Grande, 1995)

Phillips, Roderick, 'Women and family breakdown in eighteenth-century France: Rouen 1780–1800', *Social History* 2 (1976), pp.197–218

Phillips, Roderick, *Putting Asunder: A History of Divorce in Western Society* (Cambridge, 1988)

Porter, Roy and Lesley Hall, *The Facts of Life – The Creation of Sexual Knowledge in Britain, 1650–1950* (New Haven and London, 1995)

Ranger's Impartial List of the Ladies of Pleasure in Edinburgh (privately printed Edinburgh 1775; reprinted Edinburgh 1978)

Report of the Royal Commission on Divorce and Matrimonial Causes, 1853 (*Parliamentary Papers*, 1852–3, vol.40)

Report of the Royal Commission on Divorce and Matrimonial Causes, 1912 (*Parliamentary Papers*, 1912–13, vol.18)

The Scots Peerage

Sellar, W. D. H., 'Marriage, divorce and the forbidden degrees: Canon law and Scots law', in W. N. Osborough (ed.) *Explorations in Law and History – Irish Legal History Society Discourses, 1988–1994* (Dublin, 1995), pp.59–82

Smith, David Baird, 'The Reformers and Divorce: A Study in Consistorial Jurisdiction', *Scottish Historical Review* 10 (1912), pp.10–36

Smith, Merrill D., *Breaking the Bonds – Marital Discord in Pennsylvania 1730–1830* (New York and London, 1991)

Smith, Norah, 'Sexual Mores in the Eighteenth Century: Robert Wallace's "Of Venery"', *Journal of the History of Ideas*, 39 (1978), pp.419–33

Stone, Lawrence, *Uncertain Unions – Marriage in England 1660–1753* (Oxford, 1992)

Stone, Lawrence, *Road to Divorce – England 1530–1987* (Oxford, 1992)

Stone, Lawrence, *Broken Lives – Separation and Divorce in England 1660–1857* (Oxford, 1993)

Thomas, Keith, 'The Double Standard', *Journal of the History of Ideas*, 20 (1959), pp.195–216

The Trial of R. Fergusson, Esq for Crim. Con. with the Rt. Hon. Lady Elgin (London, 1807)

Walton, F. P. (ed.), *Lord Hermand's Consistorial Decisions, 1684–1777* (Edinburgh, Stair Society, VI, 1940)

Watt, Jeffrey R., 'Divorce in Early Modern Neuchâtel, 1547–1806', *Journal of Family History*, 14 (1989), pp.137–55

Watt, Jeffrey R., *The Making of Modern Marriage – Matrimonial Control and the Rise of Sentiment in Neuchâtel, 1550–1800* (Ithaca and London, 1992)

Wolfram, Sybil, 'Divorce in England 1700–1857', *Oxford Journal of Legal Studies* (vol.5, no.2), pp.155–86

SUBJECT INDEX

References are to page numbers and also endnotes where applicable: such a reference appears as '28n'.

NAME INDEX

Both pursuers and defenders are listed alphabetically by surname and first name. The arrangement ignores any prefixed titles.